GUIDE TO
REAL
CIDER

TED BRUNING

GW00702438

BOOKS

Author: Ted Bruning

Design: Rob Howells
Typeset by T&O Graphics, Broome, Bungay, Suffolk
Printed in Great Britain by Ashford Colour Press

Published by CAMRA Books, Campaign for Real Ale,
230 Hatfield Road, St Albans AL1 4LW
Tel: 01727 867201 Fax: 01727 867670
Managing Editor: Mark Webb

ISBN 1-85249-121-3

© CAMRA Books 1996

To David Kitton, the Pioneer

Acknowledgements: The editor's heartfelt thanks are due to
Jo Bates, Roger Protz, Roy Bailey, George Thomas, David Hughes
and Chris Cryne, but the greatest gratitude must be reserved for the
dozens of CAMRA members who scoured the length and breadth
of Britain, seeking out obscure cidermakers and the pubs and shops
where their produce could be found.

This publication has been assisted by a donation from the 1995
Stockport Beer and Cider Festival organised by Stockport and South
Manchester CAMRA.

CONTENTS

FOREWORD
by the Most Honourable the Marquess of Bath

Cidermaking has a special importance to those of us who were born in the West Country. Wherever one might travel, one can find local fruit or berries from which the juice can be extracted and then fermented to produce a particular intoxicating beverage. This invariably acquires an importance within the local culture in that it comes to be regarded as responsible for that festival spirit which lightens the hum-drum routine of daily life. In Wessex, and in the region immediately to the north of us that might be described as West Mercia, we rejoice in the tradition of making cider from apples, and perry from pears. This is indeed an ancient tradition. It became firmly established in this part of the world in Celtic times, when the Glastonbury area was known as the Isle of Apples, with Rhiannon as its apple-goddess.

Even in Saxon times, there was still a reverence for the practice of harvesting apples which has continued right down to the present day in the Wassailing ceremonies around Yuletide, when quantities of cider are consumed while toasting the prospects of a bumper crop next season. The great pity is that the market has been so flooded with the mass-produced and over-processed "ciders" churned out by a handful of major industrial firms that our discernment has been diminished. But there are farms and cideries where the ancient craft as practised down the centuries has never died out. It is the purpose of this book to reveal where they may be found.

CIDER SEASONS

Unnoticed in the orchard's chilly calm,
The pink-white blossom shoulders through the leaves.
The reborn world uncurls in field and farm;
The birds are building underneath the eaves.
The morning bustles on: the valley floor
Lifts from the mist that drifts away like smoke,
And there, in crumbling barn or lofty store,
The winter liquor ripens in the oak.

Late warmth enfolds the tavern's cob and thatch,
The blazing summer day sinks into haze.
The drinkers come; the door is off the latch,
The benches sag with gossip, elbows raise.
Then darkness gathers by the narrow panes,
The clock winds on, and cider talk drops low,
Till hand in hand along the dusky lanes,
Slowly, the apple-tasting lovers go.

The sun falls swiftly; evenings end in flames.
The branch grows brittle in the sudden cold.
The apples, with their many-coloured names,
Bow to the ground, or lie where they have rolled.
By cart and lorry then, to press and mill,
And vessels in their ranks beneath the rafter,
Where cidermakers work with patient skill
The miracle that changes juice to laughter.

Loud voices, rattling sticks, and stamping feet –
The orchard ground is bare, and hard, and white.
The bonfire cracks and sizzles, fierce with heat,
But breath still steams against the frozen night.
The singing starts, and all heads turn to where
The wassail queen comes glimmering through the field,
Sharp stars reflected in her midnight hair,
To pour a blessing on the New Year's yield.
    – Sam Wood

INTRODUCTION

LET'S start with the rats: it's all true. Farm cidermakers in olden days really did drop dead rats into the vats from time to time.

They didn't do it to add "body" to the final product, though: in the days when all cider was fermented by natural yeast, it was the traditional remedy when a vat was slow to start working to throw in a piece of meat – an old chop, say, a lump of bacon, perhaps even a nice freshly-caught rat.

And although they didn't know it, what the cidermakers of yore were actually adding was a primitive yeast nutrient in the form of the nitrogen and vitamins given off by the decomposing meat – the rustic equivalent of buying a little bottle of powder from the home-brew shop to get a stubborn batch of damson wine working properly.

Cider has come a long way since those days of wild yeasts and dead rats: in fact, it has been the drinks industry's biggest success story of the last 30 years.

Sales soared from 18 million gallons in 1963 to 92 million in 1994, and are still rising. Bulmer's predicts a market of well over 100 million gallons by the year 2000, and it seems that Britain has really got the taste for this most natural of alcoholic drinks.

But has it? Some would say not. For the vast bulk of the cider we drink so much of is an industrial product so far removed from the pure, natural drink of olden days that most people don't know what real cider is or even that it exists.

At its simplest, cider is apple-juice fermented by naturally-occurring yeast and left to mature. This is cider as it was known to the ancients of pre-Roman Britain, and as it is still made by a handful of producers today.

Defining traditional cider, though, is not as simple as defining real ale.

In the case of ale, either it undergoes its secondary fermentation in its cask and is real, or it doesn't and isn't, and there's little room for argument.

But cidermaking departs from its purest form by insidious degrees, and many of the makers who use extra sugar, a modicum of concentrate, and cultured yeast, many who fine, filter or even pasteurise claim the distinction of being bona fide traditional craftspeople.

It comes down to common sense. There's a world of difference between the carbonated and characterless national brands and the still (not flat!) and flavoursome output of companies like Biddenden, Perry's, James White, Heck's, Franklin's and a host of others medium-sized, small, and tiny. The test is in the taste: once you've had the real thing, you'll know; and you'll never go back to the fizz. The present marked revival in the fortunes of traditional cider owes a great deal to irony.

Pasteurised, carbonated national brands began to emerge in the 1960s from Bulmer's, Taunton, and Showering's, who exploited cider's tax-exempt status and the cost-efficiencies of mass production and distribution to formulate commercial, nationally-branded keg ciders exactly as the brewers were doing with beer.

Sales boomed until 1976, when Denis Healey made cider of less than 8.5 per cent alcohol dutiable for the first time in two centuries. Cider's advance faltered, but the tax was, and still is, lower than the duty on beer, and by the end of the seventies cider had regained its impetus.

But by the mid-eighties the leading brands had become tired, so the major cidermakers started bombarding every niche in the market with heavily-promoted, mass-produced brands such as K, Max, Copperhead, and the hugely-successful Diamond White.

One of the niches the big cidermakers sought to exploit was the "traditional" market. In 1986 Showering's launched a national cask cider brand, Addlestone's. It was a problem child almost from birth, so volatile that it proved uncontainable. Soon pub cellars were awash with foaming cider undergoing violent secondary fermentation, so Showering's started serving Addlestone's under controlled CO_2 pressure – using a very visible but dummy handpump.

Then Bulmer's swallowed up neighbouring cidermaker Symonds and adapted its Scrumpy Jack brand to keg, serving it with a fake handpump and promoting it nationally with mock-rural imagery. Taunton followed with Cidermaster, and soon the three real-looking ciders with their fake handpumps started to appear in pubs all over the country.

Before long, pubgoers far beyond the traditional cider areas had got the idea that there was such a thing as real cider, even though all the national brands were actually keg. The result was that combined sales of real and real-looking cider rose from 720,000 gallons, two per cent of pub cider sales, in 1987 to 3.5 million gallons and 8.4 per cent in 1992. A market, unwittingly, had been made.

At the same time, independent pub chains such as Wetherspoon and Tap & Spile had begun stocking real ciders to enhance their "authentic" image. They reasoned that customers who demanded only real ales would feel the same about their cider – and they were right.

In this, the free trade chains have led the brewers by a mile. For years, brewers large and small bought in their ciders more or less as commodities, caring more about the availability of bulk discounts than to quality. The so-called "premium" end of the market was taken up with super-strength artificial brands such as Diamond White and K. Real cider was an embarrassing survival, saddled with a terrible image of bucolic brawling and with no place in discerning pubs.

Even traditional family brewers shared this mentality: it was impossible to convince them that long-established artisanal cidermakers had the same authenticity, heritage, and values that they did themselves, and deserved the respect that they always insisted upon for themselves.

Gradually this attitude has changed as brewers, notably Whitbread, have begun to realise that if they want to compete with the Wetherspoons of this world they have to offer the same range of products. The idea that customers might actually want real cider is also dawning on some of the regional brewers, who are beginning to list traditional products alongside the old keg brands.

This advance in the availability of real cider seemed to have reached critical mass in 1995 when both Bulmer's and Taunton launched national real cider brands.

Both already sold perfectly adequate real ciders in their home patches, but decided that neither would be suitable for mass distribution. For a while we saw Taunton's Somerset Leveller and Bulmer's Old Hazy competing nationally. It was something of a false dawn in that Somerset Leveller failed to survive Taunton's acquisition by the Gaymer Group; but the increased market activity provided a useful opportunity for Division II cidermakers such as Weston's, Biddenden, and Thatchers to increase their presence in both the pub and supermarket trades.

Not only are the bigger independent cidermakers beginning to stir, but much smaller makers are also finding a new dynamism, even as the micro-brewers did 20 years ago. In the last five years, a handful of old-established makers have gone out of business – only to be replaced by more than two dozen enthusiastic newcomers exploiting the 7,000-litre duty-exempt annual allowance bequeathed by Denis Healey.

Much of the credit for all this must go to CAMRA, partly for creating the real ale culture in which real cider could also flourish, and partly for the cider bars which have become an integral part of almost every local ale festival and of the Great British Beer Festival itself.

CAMRA relaunched its cider campaigning group, APPLE, two years ago, and at the same started a quarterly periodical, The Cider Press. This year's CAMRA annual general meeting triumphantly confirmed our commitment to re-establishing real cider as a part of the cultural mainstream.

CAMRA's crusade is not inspired by political correctness, reactionary fogeyness, green radicalism, anti-corporate socialism, or digger-and-leveller anarchism, although you will find all these strands of opinion in its ranks and more.

No, it's inspired by pleasure, pure and simple. Real cider is good. By and large, it's made by people who care, people who don't cut corners, people who love what they make and delight in the subtleties of making it.

They make cider as well as they can for their own fulfilment as much as for the public's pleasure. And that's the real reason why real cider is gaining in popularity: it's great stuff.

More and more people are realising that cider and Woodpecker are not synonymous; that traditional cider is delicious; and that there is a terrific variety of different brands, strengths and regional styles of real cider – that there's a whole cider sub-culture, in fact, ready and waiting to burst into the mainstream.

Harley Gum, Huffcap, Merrylegs and Tumper
Perry in the 21st Century

by Kevin Minchew, cyder and perry maker

PERRY is in decline. Once produced on most farms in Gloucestershire, Herefordshire and Worcestershire, it now owes its existence to a dwindling number of small-scale producers.

But it was not always so: indeed, perry was once widely popular and even enjoyed royal favour. Queen Elizabeth I was served perry on her visit to Elmley Castle in 1575, and it was no mere coincidence that later that same year she directed that the City of Worcester's coat of arms should carry three pears sable.

Perry's decline has been gradual but inevitable, entwined as it has been with the fortunes of the rural landscape.

Changes in agricultural methods, the economics of farming, and government policies have affected all traditional crafts and skills, including perry production. Small makers have had to survive unaided in a highly competitive market where the odds are stacked against them. Perry, once the joy of monarch and labourer alike, has found no niche in the modern market which does it proper credit.

So why do people doggedly persist in its manufacture? Why do enthusiasts pursue it and continue to proclaim its virtues? One explanation might lie in the unique qualities of different perry pear varieties.

A significant difference between perry and cyder is that perry cannot be successfully standardised. Perry pear varieties do not readily blend, and there is no short-cut to homogenised blandness. Each perry pear variety is distinctive and there is a myriad of varieties. Hundreds once existed, multiplied through grafting and propagation; and although reduced in number today, they still exist in profusion.

But it is not only pear variety which makes perry unattractive to the big industrial producer: variations in season and soil also play their part.

There is no guarantee of consistency from year to year, and the inexact nature of perry making is indicated by the adage: "Mill your pears one year, press them the next, and drink it the year after" – in other words, just as the taste cannot be duplicated year to year, so the methods of production must change.

But even though perry is not readily susceptible of industrial production, the perry maker is no magician. Expertise comes from experience – trial and error as well as an intimate knowledge of the raw materials. Some pears are best picked and then stored; others don't like storage. Some pears fall; others, like the Nailer, have to be shaken from the tree if they are not to remain on the branch into the New Year.

The problem is that there are no heirs to a complex area of knowledge which was once widely shared. Certainly the consumers of old knew a bit about perry: a farm's reputation for perry might secure it the best labourers at the annual hiring fair, while until recently one Worcestershire hotel reserved its best perry for its favourite customers; lesser mortals had to make do with champagne.

When perry making was commonplace, competition was fierce, and as perry pear varieties varied from one parish to the next, they were often a source of great local pride. In times of war – especially war with France – perry became a drink of national significance as well, taking the place of imported wines and spirits and sometimes going to sea with the navy as an alternative, and surely a better alternative, to lime juice in fighting off scurvy.

But it is not only this narrowing of the base of knowledge which threatens perry today.

Orchard strongholds are encroached upon by urban expansion, road-building, and changes in land use, and replanting is scarcely economic since a perry pear tree can take 50 years to bear – although it can continue cropping for more than 300 years. Perry production is labour intensive and time consuming too, and the results are not always certain.

But there are grants for replanting, and set-aside land can be used, so there is room for a regeneration – preferably, for the sake of continuity, concentrated on the small areas where perry pears are still grown.

But the regeneration should not be founded on nostalgia, which would do a disservice to perry's distinctive quality. Perry's continuation must be on the strength of its unique qualities, not on abstract notions of tradition or regional pride.

And if following generations are to have perry to enjoy, it is our responsibility to examine our present situation and start the processes of education and investment. If perry and cyder are to remain as intrinsic parts of the cultural identity of the countryside these problems must be addressed, for their loss is at the expense of the wider community.

It is not enough that perry should be preserved as a relic, effectively consigned to antiquity. It is a dynamic drink whose quality must not be compromised in its revival, lost to the demands of a mass market. Perry should be seen as the equal in quality of the finest wines, but still the domain of all social classes.

SPLENDOUR IN THE GLASS

CAMRA has always been somewhat suspicious of bottled ciders for the simple reason that in order to make anything but completely dry cider stable enough to bottle without risk of explosion, you generally have to muck about with it. That usually means pasteurising it, which can create a nasty sickly burnt-sugar aftertaste, or filtering it, which can strip out much of the flavour along with the unwanted yeast, or fermenting it to dryness and then resweetening it with saccharine. None of these options really measures up to the standard of natural purity which can be achieved with draught cider, so CAMRA regards cider in bottle as second best. There is an important role for traditional bottled cider, however, second-best though it might be.

Many, perhaps most, publicans who stock traditional cider only do so from Easter to around October. In winter, they say, demand falls off, and any draught traditional cider they order goes off before they can sell it. Perhaps it's time to try persuading them to lay in a few bottles for those of their clientele who still fancy a glass of cider even though the weather's cold.

Even if they retort that single bottles are too much trouble, all is not lost. Many ciders now come in the Weston's-style three-pint jar: not just the Weston's range itself, but Burrow Hill and Sheppy's as well; James White, Countryman, Cornish, Norbury, Stancombe, Franklin's, and Hindlip are among the many traditional ciders available in containers of two to five litres; and bag-in-box is also becoming more common. The argument that the cider will spoil before it sells no longer stands up. There is another role for bottled cider, and that is at table. Many Kentish ciders already promote themselves as an alternative to table wine; many English vineyards produce cider of a very high quality as a sideline; and there is a growing market for traditional ciders refermented in bottle by the Méthode Champenoise. Bollhayes, Gospel Green, Burrow Hill and others are actively involved in it.

These ciders may be more Fortnum & Mason than Frog & Nightgown, but the notion of cider by the wine glass rather than the pint does overcome the rather rough image that cider conjures up in many people's minds; and many ciders are easily delicate and subtle enough to justify being sipped rather than swigged.

Finally, another point in bottled cider's favour is that most of the population doesn't live within reach of a pub which sells the draught traditional version. But many of us do live within reach of a Waitrose, an Oddbins, a Majestic or other multiple where bottled traditional ciders are available. And better a bottled second-best than none at all.

DOING IT YOURSELF

by equipment dealer and cider maker Alex Hill

In recent years there has been a strong revival of small-scale cidermaking, encouraged both by the general increase in interest in cider and also by reason of the potential profitability to the producer.

Under current legislation it is possible to make up to 7,000 litres or around 1,500 gallons a year for sale free of duty. This is a historic concession made to traditional cidermakers when excise was first charged on cider in the 1970s. It offers good opportunities for profitable production of relatively small quantities and has provided many larger commercial cidermakers with an easy entry into the market.

Cider production is relatively easy. All that is required is efficient equipment, a supply of apples, and space for production and storage.

Modern cider mills and presses are compact, give efficient yields, and are considerably faster than some of the older equipment still in use on some farms today. Equipment to mill and press around 120 gallons of cider a day costs less than £1,000, and equipment to produce 600 gallons a day for the same labour costs about £4,000.

A supply of apples for cidermaking is not usually difficult to find. In most areas of the country, apple growers are keen to sell their substandard culinary fruit. Producers wishing to introduce a West Country flavour to their cider can purchase bittersweet fruit from producers from Hereford to Devon. Cider apples and culinary apples have in recent years cost around £100 a ton delivered, but are often available for much less if the buyer is prepared to gather them. Juice yields vary with the season and apple variety, but around 130-150 gallons or 600-700 litres a ton can be expected.

Those considering commercial cider production will need premises which meet Environmental Health standards. These are not usually difficult to meet: there should be a solid floor which can be washed, a supply of water to wash equipment, and a clean area for storage. In practice a building the size of a double garage – say twenty square metres – with an outside hardstanding should suffice.

To maximise profit, it is important to produce a quality product which can be sold to the drinker with as short a distribution chain as possible. Those with farm shops and public houses are in a strong position, as they can sell directly to the public at full retail price. As far as publicans are concerned, cider has advantages and disadvantages. On the plus side, cider keeps very well

– two years or more in bulk or in bottle – and can be very profitable. On the minus side, it can only be made in the apple season, and space is required for bulk storage throughout the rest of the year. (Cider can be sold in quantities of over twenty litres without a licence; for retail sales of less than twenty litres an off-licence is required).

Given the ease of entry into the business, the relative lack of red tape, and the potential for quite good profits, it is surprising that there are not more small-scale commercial cidermakers.

Some may be put off by the mystique surrounding cider, but any misgivings in this area can be easily overcome by attendance at one of the excellent courses run by the Worcestershire College of Agriculture.

Perhaps the easiest and most pleasant way to start one's cidermaking career is to acquire some modest equipment and start making for your own consumption. Most cidermakers started this way.

More information and a catalogue of equipment are available from Vigo Vineyard Supplies, telephone 01 823 680 230.

Avon

BATH

BEEHIVE (P)
3 Belvedere, Lansdown Road.
☎ 01 225 420 274.
🍎 **Bulmers Traditional,
Taunton Traditional,
Thatcher's Cheddar Valley**
Sturdy stone pub built on
hillside, well worth the climb.

Belvoir Castle (P)
33 Belvoir Bldgs, Twerton.
☎ *01 225 425 725.*
🍎 *Bulmers Traditional*

Britannia Inn (P)
London Rd, Piccadilly.
☎ *01 225 429 023.*
🍎 *Bulmers Traditional*

Dark Horse Inn (P)
Northampton Street.
☎ *01 225 425 994.*
🍎 *Taunton Traditional*

Hadley Arms (P)
North Rd, Combe Down.
☎ *01 225 837 177.*
🍎 *Taunton Traditional*

KING'S HEAD (P)
14 High Street, Weston.
☎ 01 225 310 443.
Open 11-11
🍎 **Taunton Traditional**
Friendly two-bar village local.
Basic snacks only.

ROSE & CROWN (P)
6 Brougham Place, Larkhall.
☎ 01 225 425 700.
Open 11-11
🍎 **Thatcher's, Taunton
Traditional**
Friendly old-fashioned
suburban local. Family room;
bar food; separate restaurant.

Rummer (P)
New Market Row.
☎ *01 225 460 332.*
🍎 *Taunton Traditional*

BRISTOL

ANCHOR (P)
60 Ham Green, Pill.
☎ 01 275 372 253.
🍎 Bulmers Traditional

Anchor Made For Ever (P)
Kingswood.
☎ *0117 949 6691.*
🍎 *Taunton Traditional*

APPLE TREE (P)
Phillip Street, Bedminster.
☎ 0117 966 7097.
Open 10.30-11 Mon-Sat,
12-5 Sun
🍎 **Taunton Traditional**
Basic cider house – probably
smallest pub in the city. No real
ale.

Assize Courts (P)
15 Small Street.
☎ *0117 929 1085.*
🍎 *Bulmers Traditional*

Avon Packet (P)
Southville.
☎ *0117 953 5477.*
🍎 *Taunton Traditional*

Avonmouth Tavern (P)
Portview Rd.
☎ *0117 982 7726.*
🍎 *Taunton Traditional*

Bear & Ragged Staff (P)
*Southmead Rd, Westbury-on-
Trym.*
☎ *0117 950 0435.*
🍎 *Bulmers Traditional*

Bear Hotel (P)
261 Hotwell Rd, Hotwells.
☎ *0117 926 8385.*
🍎 *Bulmers Traditional*

BEAUFORT (P)
23 High Street, Clifton
☎ 0117 973 5906
Open 12-2.30, 5.30-11
☙ **Bulmers Traditional**
Comfortable one-bar pub. Bar
food lunchtime and evening;
no smoking area.

BERKELEY (P)
15-17 Queens Road, Clifton
Open all permitted hours
☙ **Weston's Bounds Brand**
Big pub with mixed clientele
biased towards younger
generation at weekends.

Blaise Inn (P)
Henbury Rd, Henbury.
☎ *0117 950 5396.*
☙ *Taunton Traditional*

BRIDGE (P)
Main Road, Shortwood.
☎ 0117 937 2328
Open all permitted hours
☙ **Taunton Traditional**
Large two-bar cider house on
Avon cycleway. Hot bar snacks.
Pool, crib, boules.

Brewers Droop Home Brew
(OL)
36 Gloucester Road, Bishopston.
☎ *0117 942 7923.*
☙ *Rich's Farmhouse*

BRISTOL BREWHOUSE (P)
117-119 Stokes Croft, Bristol
☎ 0117 942 0306
Open 11-11
☙ **Rich's Farmhouse**
Large brewpub selling Ross's
beers. Loud music. Bar food
lunchtime.

CADBURY HOUSE (P)
68 Richmond Rd, Montpelier
☎ 0117 924 7874
Open 11-11 Mon-Sat, 7-10.30
Sun (closed Sun lunch)
☙ **Bulmers Traditional**
Busy town pub with terrace
and beer garden. Bar food
lunchtime and evening.

Cheers (P)
7 St Nicholas Street.
☎ *0117 983 1303.*
☙ *Bulmers Traditional*

CORONATION TAP (P)
8 Sion Place, Clifton Village
☎ 0117 973 9617
Open 12-3, 5.30-11; 12-4,
7-10.30 Sun
☙ **Taunton Traditional,**
Bulmers West Country, Inch's
Famous cider pub. Pine-
panelled single bar, shove-
ha'penny but no juke-box or
fruit machine. Bar meals
lunchtimes.

COTHAM PORTER STORES (P)
15 Cotham Road South, Bristol
☎ 0117 924 9198
Open 11.30-11 Mon-Sat, 12-3, 7-
10.30 Sun
☙ **Thatchers, Taunton**
Traditional, Bulmer's West
Country & No 7
Traditional one-bar pub,
popular with locals and
students. Dominoes, crib,
backgammon.

Eagle Tavern (P)
49 West Street, St Phillips.
☎ *0117 955 8622.*
☙ *Bulmers Traditional*

Eastfield Inn (P)
219 Henleaze Rd.
☎ *0117 962 4191.*
☙ *Bulmers Traditional*

Eldon House (P)
6 Lower Clifton Hill, Clifton.
☎ *0117 926 4964.*
☙ *Bulmers Traditional*

English Rose (P)
Broadlands Drive, Shirehampton.
☎ *0117 982 3322.*
☙ *Bulmers Traditional, Taunton*
Traditional

ESSEX ARMS (P)
237 Two Mile Hill, Kingswood
☎ 0117 967 4161.
☙ **Taunton Traditional**
Noted cider house with
garden.

Forgemans Arms (P)
87 Barrow Rd, Barton Hill.
☎ 0117 941 3502.
🍎 *Bulmers Traditional*

Gatcombe House (P)
Gatcombe Rd.
☎ 0117 949 3352.
🍎 *Taunton Traditional*

George Inn (P)
*104 Kingsland Rd,
St Philips.*
☎ 0117 955 4679.
🍎 *Bulmers Traditional*

George & Dragon (P)
Winterbourne.
☎ 01 454 775 313.
🍎 *Taunton Traditional*

Grosvenor Inn (P)
Bedminster.
☎ 0117 966 3325.
🍎 *Taunton Traditional*

Harriers (P)
Bishport Place, Hartcliffe.
☎ 0117 978 4124.
🍎 *Bulmers Traditional*

Hartcliffe Inn (P)
Brock Rd.
☎ 0117 935 9092.
🍎 *Taunton Traditional*

Horse & Jockey (P)
Church Rd.
☎ 0117 967 1327.
🍎 *Taunton Traditional*

HOWLIN' WOLF (P)
155 St Michael's Hill
☎ 0117 973 5960
Open all permitted hours
🍎 **Bulmers Old Hazy**
One-room pub famous for live
blues and blues memorabilia.

Lamb & Lark (P)
*158 Burchells Green Rd,
Kingswood.*
☎ 0117 949 7741.
🍎 *Bulmers Traditional*

Lansdowne (P)
Clifton Rd, Clifton.
☎ 0117 973 4949.
🍎 *Taunton Traditional, Bulmers
Traditional*

Long Cross Inn (P)
Lawrence Weston.
☎ 0117 982 3381.
🍎 *Taunton Traditional*

Longs Bar (P)
Market Street, Old Market.
☎ 0117 927 6785.
🍎 *Taunton Traditional*

Midland Inn (P)
14 Midland Rd, St Philips.
☎ 0117 929 0122.
🍎 *Bulmers Traditional*

Mouse (P)
Waters Lane, Westbury-on-Trym.
☎ 0117 962 2144.
🍎 *Bulmers Traditional*

New Hobgoblin (P)
69 Gloucester Rd.
☎ 0117 940 1575.
🍎 *Bulmers Traditional*

Old Pie & Pint (P)
51 Stokes Croft.
☎ 0117 942 4470.
🍎 *Bulmers Traditional*

Omnibus Club (C)
Lawrence Hill.
☎ 0117 954 1608.
🍎 *Taunton Traditional*

ORCHARD (P)
12 Hanover Place, Cumberland
Road
☎ 0117 926 2678
Open 11-3, 5-11
🍎 **Taunton Traditional,
Thatcher's**
Friendly single-bar pub near SS
Great Britain.

Pied Horse (P)
St George.
☎ 0117 955 1266.
🍎 *Taunton Traditional*

Pit Pony (P)
153 Easton Rd, Easton.
☎ 0117 955 6510.
🍎 *Bulmers Old Hazy*

Porcupine (P)
30 St Nicholas Street.
☎ 0117 949 7763.
🍎 *Bulmers Old Hazy*

Queens Head (P)
22 Queen's Rd, Bishopsworth.
☎ 0117 964 1955.
🍎 *Bulmers Traditional*

Red Lion (P)
Wells Rd, Knowle.
☎ 0117 972 1898.
🍎 *Taunton Traditional*

Rising Sun (P)
Alfred Rd, Windmill Hill.
☎ 0117 949 3009.
🍎 *Bulmers Traditional*

Rising Sun (P)
Ashton Rd.
☎ 0117 966 4900.
🍎 *Taunton Traditional*

Rising Sun (P)
Bishopsworth.
☎ 0117 978 3775.
🍎 *Taunton Traditional*

Rising Sun (P)
29 Pembroke Rd, Shirehampton.
☎ 0117 982 6229.
🍎 *Bulmers Traditional*

Seven Stars (P)
Thomas Lane, Redcliffe.
☎ 0117 987 2275.
🍎 *Bulmers Traditional*

Ship & Castle (P)
Ashton Gate.
☎ 0117 966 0548.
🍎 *Taunton Traditional*

Shirehampton WMC (C)
High Street, Shirehampton.
☎ 0117 982 6513.
🍎 *Taunton Traditional*

Stapleton Road Tavern (P)
Stapleton Rd.
☎ 0117 955 6350.
🍎 *Taunton Traditional*

Star Inn (P)
Castle Rd, Pucklechurch.
☎ 0117 937 2391.
🍎 *Taunton Traditional*

Swan (P)
Bath Rd, Swinford.
☎ 0117 932 3101.
🍎 *Taunton Traditional*

Talbot Hotel (P)
304 Wells Rd, Knowle.
☎ 0117 977 7177.
🍎 *Bulmers Traditional*

Three Tuns (P)
St George's Rd, Hotwells.
☎ 0117 926 8434.
🍎 *Bulmers Traditional*

Treble Chance (P)
Greystoke Ave, Southmead.
☎ 0117 950 0360.
🍎 *Bulmers Traditional*

Trout Tavern (P)
Temple Street, Keynsham.
☎ 0117 986 2275.
🍎 *Taunton Traditional*

Wedlocks (P)
1 Bower Ashton Terrace, Ashton Gate.
☎ 0117 966 5544.
🍎 *Bulmers Traditional*

White Hart (P)
181 Whitehall Rd, Whitehall.
☎ 0117 951 7295.
🍎 *Bulmers Traditional*

WHITE SWAN (P)
North Street, Downend
☎ 0117 956 0261
Open 11-11, 12-4; 7-10.30 Sun
🍎 **Taunton Traditional,
Bulmers Old Hazy &
Traditional, Inch's**
Popular traditional cider house with fine garden. Bar food lunchtime and evening; separate restaurant. Usher's ales.

BURRINGTON

Plume of Feathers (P)
Rickford.
☎ 01 761 462 682.
🍎 Bulmers Traditional

BUTCOMBE

Mill Inn (P)
Butcombe Village.
☎ 01 761 462 406.
🍎 Taunton Traditional

CHEW MAGNA

PONY & TRAP (P)
Knowle Hill
☎ 01 275 332 627
🍎 **Bulmers Traditional**
Traditional half-timbered local
with children's room and
garden.

CHEW STOKE

Stoke Inn (P).
☎ 01 275 332 120.
🍎 Taunton Traditional

CHURCHILL

Churchill Inn (P).
☎ 01 934 852 251.
🍎 Bulmers Old Hazy

CLAPTON IN GORDANO

BLACK HORSE (P)
Clevedon Lane
☎ 01 275 842 105
🍎 Taunton Traditional
Unspoilt country pub of Queen
Anne vintage with original
stone floor. Children's room
and garden.

CLEVEDON

Drum & Monkey (P)
Kenn Rd.
☎ 01 275 873 433.
🍎 Bulmers Traditional

Royal Oak (P)
35 Copse Rd.
☎ 01 275 873 075.
🍎 Bulmers Traditional

COLEFORD

Kings Head (P).
☎ 01 373 812 346.
🍎 Bulmers Traditional

COMPTON DANDO

Compton Inn (P).
☎ 01 761 490 321.
🍎 Taunton Traditional

CONGRESBURY

Spotted Horse (P).
☎ 01 934 832 092.
🍎 Taunton Traditional

FAILAND

Failand Inn (P)
Clevedon Rd.
☎ 01 275 392 220.
🍎 Taunton Traditional

FELTON

Airport Tavern (P)
Bridgewater Rd, Lulsgate.
☎ 01 275 472 217.
🍎 Bulmers Traditional

HAWKESBURY UPTON

BEAUFORT ARMS (P)
High Street
☎ 01 454 238 217
Open 12-3, 5.30-11 Sun-Fri, 12-
11 Sat.
🍎 **Wilkin's**
18th-century two-bar local, also
popular with Cotswold Way
walkers. Dining room in
converted stable.

HIGH LITTLETON

Star (P)
High Street.
☎ 01 861 470 433.
🍎 Bulmers Traditional

HUISH

Palmers End (P)
West Rd.
☎ 01 934 832 245.
🍎 Bulmers Old Hazy

LONG ASHTON

Miners Rest (P).
☎ *01 275 393 449.*
🍎 *Taunton Traditional*

MIDSOMER NORTON

Crossways Tavern (P)
Redfield Rd.
☎ *01 761 412 245.*
🍎 *Bulmers Traditional*

WHITE HART (P)
The Island
☎ 01 761 418 270
Open 11.30-3, 5.30-11
🍎 **Taunton Traditional**
Multi-room Victorian gem. No
food Sun. Children's room;
disabled access.

NAILSEA

BLUE FLAME (P)
West End
☎ 01 275 856 910
Open 12-3, 6-11
🍎 **Bulmers Traditional**
Cottage-style real ale pub with
facilities for disabled.

OLD DOWN

FOX (P)
Inner Down
☎ 01 454 412 507
Open 12-3, 6-11
🍎 **Taunton Traditional**
Local stone, exposed oak
beams, real fire, hanging
baskets, garden – in short, the
works.

PAULTON

SOMERSET INN (P)
Bath Road
☎ 01 761 412 828
🍎 **Bulmers Traditional**
Traditional country pub with
superb views.

Winterfield Inn (P)
Salisbury Rd.
☎ *01 761 412 022.*
🍎 *Bulmers Traditional*

PENSFORD

RISING SUN (P)
Church Street
☎ 01 761 490 402
Open 11.30-2.30, 7-11
🍎 **Bulmers Traditional**
Fifteenth-century stone pub
with garden leading to River
Chew (unfenced!) Good food,
but no evening meals Mon-Sun
and must book Sun lunch.

Travellers Rest (P)
Pensford Hill.
☎ *01 761 490 374.*
🍎 *Bulmers Traditional*

RADSTOCK

Fir Tree (P)
Frome Rd, Writhlington.
☎ *01 761 433 139.*
🍎 *Bulmers Traditional*

Westhill Gardens Sports &
Social (C).
☎ *01 761 418 270.*
🍎 *Taunton Traditional*

SALTFORD

BIRD IN HAND (P)
High Street
☎ 01 225 873 335
Open 12-2.30, 6.30-11.
🍎 **Taunton Traditional**
Large food pub on Bath-Bristol
cycleway.

SANDFORD

Railway Hotel (P)
Station Rd.
☎ *01 934 822 362.*
🍎 *Bulmers Traditional*

SHOSCOMBE

APPLE TREE (P)
☎ 01 761 432 263
Open 7-11 Mon-Fri, 12-3, 7-11
Sat/Sun
🍎 **Thatcher's**
Friendly village alehouse in
hidden valley. Local ales.

STAPLE HILL

HUMPERS (OL)
26 Soundwell Road
☎ 0117 956 5525
Open late, but closed 2-4.30
weekday afternoons.
🍎 **Richards**
Keenly-priced real ale and
cider off-licence. Polypins
available.

STAPLETON

MASON'S ARMS (P)
124 Park Road
☎ 0117 939 3919
Open 11-3, 7-11
🍎 **Taunton Traditional**
Cosy two-bar pub, good range
of real ales.

SWINEFORD

Swan (P)
Bath Rd, Bitton.
☎ *0117 932 3101.*
🍎 *Bulmers Traditional*

TEMPLE CLOUD

Temple Inn (P)
Main Rd.
☎ *01 761 452 244.*
🍎 *Bulmers Traditional*

THORNBURY

Ship Inn (P)
Camp Rd.
☎ *01 454 423 257.*
🍎 *Bulmers Traditional*

Wheatsheaf (P)
Chapel Street.
☎ *01 454 412 356.*
🍎 *Bulmers Traditional*

TIMSBURY

Guss & Crook (P)
South Rd.
☎ *01 761 470 373.*
🍎 *Bulmers Traditional*

WELLOW

FOX & BADGER (P)

Railway Lane
☎ 01 225 832 293
Open 11-3, 6-11 Sun-Thurs,
11-11 Fri/Sat
🍎 **Thatcher's**
Two bar village pub. Real fire
and flagstones, local ales.
Parking tricky.

WESTON-SUPER-MARE

Ancaster Hotel (P)
1 Drove Rd.
☎ *01 934 628 838.*
🍎 *Bulmers Traditional*

Heron (P)
Locking Rd.
☎ *01 934 413 020.*
🍎 *Taunton Traditional*

Weston Working Men's Club
(C)
8 Orchard Street.
☎ *01 934 418 202.*
🍎 *Bulmers Traditional*

WHITEWAY

Whiteway & District
Community Centre (C)
Kelsyon View.
☎ *01 451 830 424.*
🍎 *Bulmers Traditional*

WICK

Carpenters (P)
10 Church Rd.
☎ *01 179 372 993.*
🍎 *Bulmers Traditional*

WIDCOMBE

White Hart Inn (P).
☎ *01 225 427 955.*
🍎 *Bulmers Traditional*

WINTERBOURNE DOWN

CROSS HANDS (P)
Down Road
☎ 01 454 850 060
Open 12-11
🍎 **Taunton Traditional**
Five regular ales and guests in
carefully extended village local.

YATE

CODRINGTON ARMS (P)
North Road
☎ 01 934 833 377
❧ **Bulmers Traditional**
Traditional locals' pub with garden.

Sandbridge (P)
Kennedy Way.
☎ *01 454 327 995.*
❧ *Bulmers Traditional*

YATTON

Market Inn (P)
North End Rd.
☎ *01 934 832 209.*
❧ *Bulmers Traditional*

Bedfordshire

ASTWICK

TUDOR OAKS (P)
Taylors Road, Astwick
☎ 01 462 834 133
Open 11-11 Mon-Fri, 11-3, 6-11 Sat, 12-3, 7-10.30 Sun
❧ **Theobolds medium plus guests**
Big pub/motel on A1 south of Biggleswade. Seven real ales, excellent food.

BEDFORD

Eastend Club (C)
Mile Rd.
☎ *01 234 354 789.*
❧ *Bulmers Old Hazy*

HOGSHEAD (P)
45 High Street
☎ 01 234 353 749
Open all permitted hours.
❧ **Bulmer's Old Hazy**
Whitbread alehouse. 10 real ales, occasional festivals. Disabled access.

New Inn (P)
117 Tavistock Rd.
☎ *01 234 261 799.*
❧ *Bulmers Old Hazy*

Saracens Head (P)
13 St Pauls Square.
☎ *01 234 266 519.*
❧ *Bulmers Old Hazy*

DUNSTABLE

Norman King (P)
Church Street.
☎ *01 582 661 603.*
❧ *Bulmers Old Hazy*

Swan (P)
Northall.
☎ *01 525 220 444.*
❧ *Bulmers Old Hazy*

Old Sugar Loaf (P)
High Street, North Dunstable.
☎ *01 582 601 326.*
❧ *Taunton Traditional*

LEIGHTON BUZZARD

Clay Pipe (P)
Clipstone Brook.
☎ *01 525 384 387.*
❧ *Bulmers Traditional*

LUTON

WHEELWRIGHTS ARMS (P)
34 Guildford Street
☎ 01 582 20023
Open 10.30-11; 12-10.30 Sun.
❧ **Bulmer's Traditional**
Lively town-centre freehouse, near Arndale Centre. Changing range of real ales. Pet's corner in garden. Accommodation. No food Sunday.

STOTFOLD

FOX & DUCK (P)
Arlesey Road
☎ 01 462 732 434
Open 11-3, 6-11
❧ **Inch's**
Mainly food pub with up to five real ales including two from Charles Wells. Bar food lunchtime and evening; no smoking area.

STAG (P)
47 Brook Street
☎ 01 462 730 261

Open 5-11 Mon-Wed, all permitted hours Thurs-Sun.
Biddenden, Lyme Bay Jack Ratt
Brewpub with guest ales. Popular local.

WINGFIELD

PLOUGH (P)
Tebworth Road
☎ 01 525 873 077
Open 12-3, 6-11 (7-10.30 Sun)
Biddenden cider
Attractive and friendly thatched pub, family room, local real ales.

WOOTTON

Black Horse (P)
Potters Cross.
☎ *01 234 767 936.*
**Bulmers Old Hazy*

Berkshire

BRACKNELL

OLD MANOR (P)
Church Road
☎ 01 344 304 990
Open all permitted hours
Weston's Old Rosie
Rare surviving attractive old building amid the concrete. A multi-bar JD Wetherspoon pub complete with bric-a-brac and real ales.

Tut'n'Shive (P)
Crown Wood.
☎ *01 344 489 976.*
**Bulmers Old Hazy*

COOKHAM

Gate (P)
The Pound.
☎ *01 628 521 701.*
**Taunton Traditional*

ETON

HOGSHEAD (P)

77 High Street
☎ 01 753 861 797
Open all permitted hours
Bulmers Old Hazy
Typical Hogshead in the middle of the tourist area at the end of the Windsor-Eton pedestrian bridge. Regular jazz evenings. Bar food lunchtime and evening.

FRILFORD HEATH

Merry Miller (P)
Cothill.
☎ *01 865 390 390.*
**Bulmers Old Hazy*

HAWTHORN HILL

Royal Foresters (P)
Drift Rd.
☎ *01 628 770 564.*
**Bulmers Traditional*

MAIDENHEAD

Tut'n'Shive (P)
81 Queen Street.
☎ *01 628 20870.*
**Bulmers Old Hazy*

NEWBURY

Captains Cabin (P)
Northbrook Street.
☎ *01 635 523 249.*
**Taunton Traditional*

READING

College Arms (P)
128 Wokingham Rd.
☎ *01 734 351 504.*
**Bulmers Traditional*

HOBGOBLIN (P)
Broad Street
☎ 01 734 508 119
Open 11-11 Mon-Sat, 12-3, 7-10.30 Sun
Inch's Stonehouse, Bulmers Traditional, and at least one guest
Local Mecca for real ale and cider. Knowledgeable staff. Occasional live music.

HOP INN (OL)
48 Erleigh Road
☎ 01 734 667 265
Open 10-10 Mon-Sat, 12-10 Sun
🍎 **Weston's Old Rosie**
Off-licence near University &
hospital. Handpumped ale and
cider to take away.

Greyhound (P)
Mount Pleasant.
01 734 863 023.
🍎 *Taunton Traditional*

Malthouse (P)
Greyfriars Rd.
☎ 01 734 574 276.
🍎 *Bulmers Old Hazy*

MONKS RETREAT (P)
Friar Street
☎ 01 734 507 592
Open all permitted hours
🍎 **Weston's Old Rosie**
JD Wetherspoon pub created
from old electrical store.

Pineapple (P)
Brimpton Common.
☎ 01 734 814 376.
🍎 *Bulmers Traditional*

Rising Sun (P)
18 Forbury Rd.
☎ 01 734 572 974.
🍎 *Bulmers Old Hazy*

THREE GUINEAS (P)
Station Approach
☎ 01 734 572 743
Open all permitted hours
🍎 **Weston's Vintage**
Genuine free house on station
concourse

SLOUGH

MOON & SPOON (P)
86 High Street
☎ 01 753 531 650
Open all permitted hours
🍎 **Weston's**
Typical Wetherspoon in
converted bank, much needed
oasis in town whose older pubs
are uniformly grim. Bar food
lunchtime and evening; no-
smoking area.

SONNING

Reading Cricket & Hockey
Club (C)
Sonning Lane.
☎ 01 734 699 049.
🍎 *Bulmers Traditional*

STRATFIELD SAYE

New Inn (P)
☎ 01 734 332 255.
🍎 *Bulmers Traditional*

WARGRAVE

Vintage Roots (P)
Sheeplands Farm.
🍎 *Dunkerton's range*

WHITE WALTHAM

BEEHIVE (P)
Waltham Road
☎ 01 628 822 877
Open 11-3, 5.30-11
🍎 **Cider range varies**
Two-bar village inn facing
cricket pitch. Good range of
Whitbread ales. Petanque. No
smoking area. Week-long cider
festival to celebrate Apple Day
every October.

WINDSOR

FORT & FIRKIN (P)
Barry Ave
☎ 01 753 869 897
Open all permitted hours
🍎 **Weston's inc perry**
Formerly the Old Trout, now
the Queen's local brewery. Bar
food lunchtime and evening;
no-smoking area.

WOKINGHAM

Redan (P)
24 Peach Street.
☎ 01 734 786 817.
🍎 *Bulmers Old Hazy*

Buckinghamshire

CHESHAM

Kings Arms (P)
Germain Street.
☎ *01 494 783 626.*
🍎 *Taunton Traditional*

FARNHAM COMMON

Stag Inn (P)
Hawthorne Lane.
☎ *01 753 642 226.*
🍎 *Bulmers Old Hazy*

HADDENHAM

RISING SUN (P)
9 Thame Road
☎ 01 844 291 744
Open 11-3, 6-11 Sun-Thurs;
11-11 Fri/Sat
🍎 **Rich's**
One-bar free house with guest
ales. No food Sunday
lunchtime.

HANSLOPE

GLOBE INN (P)
Hartwell Road
☎ 01 908 510 336
Open 12-2, 6-11 Mon-Fri, 11-11
Sat, 12-10.30 Sun
🍎 **Bulmer's Traditional**
Pleasant pub with good ale and
excellent restaurant (book at
weekends). Garden includes
children's play area.

HEDGERLEY

WHITE HORSE (P)
Village Lane
☎ 01 753 643 225
Open 11.30-3, 5.30-11; 12-3,
7.30-10.30 Sun
🍎 **Cider range varies**
Wonderful two-bar stone-
floored country pub. Food
lunchtime only; guest ales.

HIGH WYCOMBE

WYCOMBE WINES (OL)
20 Crendon Street
☎ 01 494 437 228
🍎 **Weston's Scrumpy**
Off-licence near station also
sells draught ales.

LACEY GREEN

BLACK HORSE (P)
Main Road
☎ 01 844 345 195
Open 11.30-3, 5.30-11 Mon-Fri,
11-3, 5.30-11 Sat, 12-3, 7-10.30
Sun
🍎 **Westons Old Rosie**
Traditional and friendly local,
Children's play area in garden.

LITTLE MISSENDEN

CROWN (P)
☎ 01 494 862 571
Open 11-2.30, 6-11 Mon-Sat, 12-
2.30, 7-10.30 Sun
🍎 **Cider range varies**
Real old village pub with
warm atmosphere. No food
Sunday. Off A413.

LITTLEWORTH COMMON

BLACKWOOD ARMS (P)
Common Lane
☎ 01 753 642 169
Open 11-2.30, 5.30-11 Sun-
Thurs, 11-11 Fri/Sat and Bank
Holidays
🍎 **Cider range varies**
Real ale heaven in idyllic
woodland. Over 1,000 beers
sold last year. Bar food
lunchtime and evening.

MILTON KEYNES

Countryman Arms (P)
Bradwell Common Boulevard.
☎ *01 908 676 346.*
🍎 *Bulmers Traditional*

Park Beefeater (P)
4 Chandos Place, Bletchley.
☎ *01 908 648 069.*
🍎 *Bulmers Old Hazy*

PRESTWOOD
King's Head (P)
High Street
☎ 01 494 862 392
Open 11-11 Mon-Sat, 12-3, 7-10.30 Sun
🍎 **Bulmer's Traditional, Inch's**
Very traditional pub. No machines, no music, no meals – and no draught lager. Shove ha'penny played.

TERRICK

CHILTERN BREWERY (OL)
Nash Lee Road
☎ 01 296 613 647
Open 9-5 Mon-Sat
🍎 **Weston's Old Rosie, Dunkerton's**
Shop and visitors centre attached to independent brewer.

THORNBOROUGH

LONE TREE (P)
Buckingham Road
☎ 01 280 812 334
Open 11.30-2.30, 5-11 Mon-Fri, 11.30-2.30, 6.30-11 sat, 12-3, 7-10.30 Sun.
🍎 **Inch's Stonehouse, Weston's Old Rosie, Bulmers Old Hazy**
Good range of real ales and country wines. Booking advised for meals.

WENDOVER

KING & QUEEN (P)
17 Soull Street
☎ 01 296 623 272
Open 12-3, 6-11; 12-11 Sat; 12-10.30 Sun
🍎 **Rich's**
Sixteenth-century two-bar pub where traditional cider is brought up from cellar and not advertised, so ask. Bar food lunchtime and evening till 8pm.

Cambridgeshire

BRANDON CREEK

SHIP (P)
☎ 01 353 676 228
Open 11-3, 6.30-11; all day Sat
🍎 **Kingfisher**
Welcome find on long dry stretch of A10 offering excellent food and good range of ales. Riverside pub excellent for walkers and sailors. Bar food lunchtime and evening.

CAMBRIDGE

Bath Hotel (P)
Benet Street.
☎ *01 223 350 969.*
🍎 *Bulmers Old Hazy*

CAMBRIDGE BLUE (P)
85 Gwydir Street
☎ 01 223 613 82
Open 12-2.30, 6-11.
🍎 **Theobolds**
Free house owned by Nethergate Brewery. No smoking room. Model railway in garden.

Dobblers Inn (P)
184 Sturton Street.
☎ *01 223 356 092.*
🍎 *Bulmers Old Hazy*

Dog & Pheasant (P)
169 High Street, Chesterton.
☎ *01 223 566 333.*
🍎 *Bulmers Old Hazy*

EMPRESS (P)
72 Thoday Street
☎ 01 223 247 236
Open 11-2.30, 6.30-11
🍎 **Crone's, Old Hazy**
Busy open-plan local with several separate drinking areas.

Fountain (P)
12 Regent Street.
☎ *01 223 66540.*
🍎 *Bulmers Traditional*

JUG & FIRKIN (OL)
90 Mill Road
☎ 01 223 315 034
Open 10.30-1.30, 3-10 Mon-Fri,
10-10.30 Sat, 12-2.30, 7-9.30 Sun
Amazing off-licence with 300
bottled beers, wide range of
ciders, and real ales including a
house beer brewed by Tolly
Cobbold.

Lion & Lamb (P)
High Street, Milton.
☎ *01 223 860 202.*
🍎 *Bulmers Old Hazy*

Salisbury Arms (P)
Tenison Rd.
☎ *01 223 576 363.*
🍎 *Bulmers Old Hazy*

TAP & SPILE (P)
14 Mill Lane
☎ 01 223 357 026
Open all permitted hours
🍎 **Weston's Old Rosie, Crone's
Organic, Bulmers Old Hazy**
Riverside alehouse with
waterfront garden. Nine real
ales, home-cooked food at
lunchtime.

WRESTLERS (P)
337 Newmarket Road
☎ 01 223 566 554
Open 12-11
🍎 **Bulmers Old Hazy**
Bustling alehouse with six
beers, Thai food, live music.

EATON SOCON

Mill Tavern (P)
Church Lane.
☎ *01 480 219 612.*
🍎 *Bulmers Old Hazy*

HELPSTON

BLUEBELL (P)
10 Woodgate
☎ 01 733 252 394
Open 11-2.30, 6-11
🍎 **Bulmers Traditional**
Traditional stone-built
seventeenth-century village
tavern with wood-panelled
and genuine accretion (rather
than purpose-bought
assembly) of bits and bobs.
Rare example of dying breed of
food-free pubs.

LITTLEPORT

GEORGE & DRAGON (P)
Station Road
☎ 01 353 862 639
Open all permitted hours
🍎 **Crone's, Bulmers Old Hazy**
Relaxed and comfortable pub
which is much older than it
looks.

MILTON

WAGGON & HORSES (P)
High Street
☎ 01 223 860 313
Open 12-2.30, 5-11 Sun-Fri, 12-
11 Sat
🍎 **Weston's Old Rosie,
Reedcutter**
Unassuming pub offering two
regular real ales and two
guests. Friday night is curry
night; roast lunch Sun. No food
Sat lunch or Sun eve.

NEEDINGWORTH

QUEEN'S HEAD (P)
High Street
☎ 01 480 463 946
Open all permitted hours
🍎 **Inch's Stonehouse**
Friendly two-bar local which is
a great patron of small
independent brewers. Curries a
speciality.

NEWTON

QUEENS HEAD (P)
High Street
☎ 01 223 870 436
Open 11.30-2.30, 6-11 Mon-Sat,
12-2, 7-10.30 Sun.
🍎 **Crone's**
Pub has appeared in every
edition of Good Beer Guide.
Idyllic village pub with
excellent food. Be there on Guy
Fawkes's Night when a year-
old firkin of Adnams Tally Ho
is broached.

PAPWORTH EVERARD

Kisby's Hut (P).
☎ 01 480 831 257.
🍎 *Bulmers Old Hazy*

PETERBOROUGH

BOGART'S (P)
17 North Street
☎ 01 733 349 995
Open 11-11 Mon-Sat, closed
Sun.
🍎 **Weston's Old Rosie plus guests**
Bar & grill with guest ales. No
food evenings.

HAND & HEART (P)
12 Highbury Street
☎ 01 733 69463
Open 10.30-2.30, 6-11.
🍎 **Changing range of ciders and perries**
Quiet two-bar pub. Beers
include John Smith's Magnet,
hard to find so far south. Hard
to find: 300 yards from old
A15.

Tut'n'Shive (P)
Westgate.
☎ 01 733 348 945.
🍎 *Bulmers Traditional*

ST IVES

White Hart (P)
Market Place.
☎ 01 480 463 275.
🍎 *Bulmers Old Hazy*

SAWSTON

Greyhound (P)
High Street.
☎ 01 223 832 260.
🍎 *Bulmers Old Hazy*

SOHAM

Red Lion (P)
17 High Street.
☎ 01 353 720 843.
🍎 *Bulmers Old Hazy*

STOW CUM QUY

PRINCE ALBERT (P)
Newmarket Road
☎ 01 223 811 294
Open 11.30-3, 5-11 Sun-Fri,
11.30-11 Sat
🍎 **Bulmers Old Hazy**
First authenticated 1,000-ale
pub in the country. Evening
meals have to be booked.
Disabled access.

SUTTON

ANCHOR INN (P)
Sutton Gault
☎ 01 353 778 537
Open 12-2.30, 6.30-11
🍎 **James White**
350-year-old riverside inn, gas-
lit, crammed with antiques.
Good food, all beers on gravity.
No smoking area. Hard to find:
signposted off B1381 in Sutton
village 6 miles E of Ely.

UPPER BENEFIELD

Wheatsheaf (P)
☎ 01 832 205 254.
Whittlesey
🍎 *Bulmers Old Hazy*

George (P)
Market Square.
☎ 01 733 202 516.
🍎 *Bulmers Old Hazy*

Cheshire

APPLETON THORN

VILLAGE HALL (C)
Stretton Road
☎ 01 925 261 187
Closed Mon-Wed. Open 8.30-11
Thurs-Sun
🍎 **Cider range varies**
Victorian village school
converted into club. Now hub
of the community and CAMRA
Club of the Year 1995. Children
welcome.

ASTON

BHURTPORE INN (P)
Wrenbury Road
☎ 01 270 780 917
Open 12-2.30, 6.30-11 Mon-Fri,
12-3, 6.30-11 Sat, 12-3, 7-10.30
Sun
**⚫ Biddenden, Broadoak,
Bulmer's Traditional, Inch's,
Rich's, Sheppy's, Thatcher's,
Weston on rotating basis**
Former smallholding, now
very popular two-bar local
with six real ales, extensive
range of bottled beers. Good
food lunchtime and evening;
separate restaurant.

BARTHOMLEY

WHITE LION (P)
Audley Road
☎ 01 270 882 242
Open 11.30-11
⚫ Bulmers Traditional
Black and white thatched
village pub dated 1614. Scene
of a Civil War massacre.
Families welcome,
accommodation.

BURLEYDAM

COMBERMERE ARMS (P)
☎ 01 948 871 223
Open all permitted hours
⚫ Cider range varies
Haunted sixteenth-century free
house. Families welcome.
Disabled facilities. On A525
three miles from Audlem.

CHESTER

UNION VAULTS (P)
44 Egerton Street
☎ 01 244 322 170
Open all permitted hours from
noon
⚫ Cider range varies
Multi-room Boddington Ale
Houses pub with disabled
access. Food lunchtime and
evening.

WETHERSPOONS (P)
88 Foregate Street
☎ 01 244 312 281
Open all permitted hours
⚫ Weston's, guests
Big new open-plan
Wetherspoon pub. Food 12-10.
Disabled access/WC, no
smoking area for diners.

CONGLETON

Town Hall (C).
☎ 01 260 270 350.
⚫ Bulmers Old Hazy

CREWE

ALBION (P)
1 Pedley Street
☎ 01 270 256 234
Open 4-11 Mon; 7-11 Tue-
Thurs; 1-11 Fri; 12-11 Sat; 12-3,
7-10.30 Sun
⚫ Bulmers Traditional, guests
Traditional two-room corner
local with guest ales from small
independent brewers. Beer
garden.

FRODSHAM

ROWLAND'S BAR & BISTRO
(P)
31 Church Street
☎ 01 928 733 361
Bar open all permitted hours.
Restaurant open 12-2, 6.30-10
Tues-Fri, 6.30-10 Sat
⚫ Cider range varies
Friendly and popular single-
room pub with ever-changing
guest ales and separate
restaurant.

HYDE

Clarendon Hotel (P)
81 Market Street.
☎ 0161 368 5172.
⚫ Bulmers Old Hazy

NANTWICH

WILBRAHAM ARMS (P)
58 Welsh Row
☎ 01 270 626 419

Open all permitted hours
♦ **Cider range varies**
Two-room Georgian hotel near canal. Letting rooms; real ales from independent brewers; bar food lunchtime and evening. Stages annual cider festival during town folk festival every Sept.

ORFORD

K&J CONVENIENCE STORE (OL)
56 Bowness Ave
Open 10-10 Mon-Sun
♦ **Callestock and Weston ciders**
Housing estate mini-market, near Jolly Tanners pub.

WHEELOCK

COMMERCIAL HOTEL (P)
Game Street
☎ 01 270 760 122
Open 8-11 Mon-Sat, 12-2, 8-11 Sun
♦ **Cider range varies**
Victorian canalside pub with three regular real ales plus guest. Live music Thurs. Full-size snooker table and bar skittles. No smoking area.

Cleveland

GUISBOROUGH

TAP & SPILE (P)
Westgate
☎ 01 287 632 983
Open 11-3, 5-11 Sun-Wed, 11-11 Thurs-Sat
♦ **Crone's, Bulmers Old Hazy**
Old town-centre pub refurbished as part of ale house chain. No-smoking area.

HARTLEPOOL

Raby Arms (P)
Front Street.
☎ *01 429 274 058.*
♦ *Bulmers Traditional*

MIDDLESBROUGH

TAP'N'BARREL (P)
86 Newport Road
☎ 01 642 219 995
Open 11-11; 11-4.30, 7-11 Sat
♦ **Scatterbrain**
Cosy, gas-lit, Victorian-style conversion of old shop. Family room, disabled access.

Cornwall & Channel Islands

BODMIN

George & Dragon (P)
3 St Nicholas Street.
☎ *01 208 72514.*
♦ *Bulmers Old Hazy*

Mace Stores (OL)
Higher Bere Street.
☎ *01 208 72174.*
♦ *Veryan range*

ROYAL OAK (P)
Blisland
☎ 01 208 850 739
♦ **Bulmers Old Hazy**
Overlooking Cornwall's only village green. Disabled access.

BOLVENTOR

JAMAICA INN (P)
☎ 01 566 86250
♦ **Bulmers Old Hazy**
Setting for one of the silliest and most famous of all costume melodramas, now a thoroughly touristified roadhouse.

BOTUS FLEMING

RISING SUN (P)
☎ 01 752 842 792
Open 12-3, 6-11.
♦ **Inch's**
Unspoilt pub in quiet village on outskirts of Saltash. Owned by same family for three generations. Off A388.

BUDE

JERSEY COW (OL)
5 Belle Vue
☎ 01 288 55130
🍎 **Gray's**
Farm shop with cafe

Widemouth Manor Hotel (P).
☎ 01 288 361 263.
🍎 *Taunton Traditional*

CALLINGTON

Manor House (P)
Rilla Hill.
☎ 01 579 62354.
🍎 *Bulmers Traditional*

CHURCHTOWN

St Agnes Hotel (P)
Vicarage Rd, St Agnes.
☎ 01 872 552 307.
🍎 *Bulmers Old Hazy*

CRANTOCK

Crantock Bay Hotel (P)
☎ 01 637 830 229.
🍎 *Veryan range*

OLD ALBION INN (P)
Langurroc Road
☎ 01 637 830 243
Open 12-11
🍎 **Weston's Old Rosie and guests**
Traditional thatched two-bar village inn with family room. Bar food lunchtime and evening. Sunday speciality is oak-roasted beef.

DULOE

Old Plough House (P).
☎ 01 503 262 050.
🍎 *Bulmers Traditional*

Trefanny Inn (P)
Trefanny Hill.
☎ 01 503 220 376.
🍎 *Bulmers Traditional*

FALMOUTH

Meudon Hotel (R)
Mannan Smith.
☎ 01 326 250 541.
🍎 *Veryan range*

QUAYSIDE INN (P)
Arwenack Street
☎ 01 326 312 113
Open all permitted hours
🍎 **Bulmers Old Hazy**
Large quayside pub with over 200 whiskies in upstairs bar.

FIVE LANES

KINGS HEAD (P)
☎ 01 566 86241
Open all permitted hours
🍎 **Inch's**
Ancient coaching inn with stone-floored public bar, separate restaurant, good accommodation. Now bypassed but worth turning off for: off A30 west of Launceston.

FOWEY

King of Prussia (P)
Town Quay.
☎ 01 726 832 450.
🍎 *Bulmers Old Hazy*

Sam's Deli (OL)
Fore Street.
☎ 01 726 832 652.
🍎 *Veryan range*

FRADDON

Queen & Railway (P)
St Columb Rd.
☎ 01 726 860 343.
🍎 *Bulmers Traditional*

HELSTON

BLUE ANCHOR (P)
Coinagehall Street
☎ 01 326 562 821
Open 10.30-3, 6-11 (all day if busy)
🍎 **Porthallow Vineyard**
Ancient and famous pub brewery producing renowned

Spingo beers from old brewhouse at the back. Unspoilt fifteenth-century rambling granite building with thatched roof. Two bars. Families welcome. Bar food lunchtime and evening.

LAUNCESTON

Grimaldi's Deli (OL)
White Hart Arcade.
☎ 01 566 774 743.
🍎 *Veryan range*

WHITE HORSE (P)
14 Newport Square
☎ 01 156 772 084
🍎 **Bulmers Traditional**
Eighteenth-century coaching inn with letting rooms, children's room, disabled access.

LISKEARD

Spar Stores (OL)
161 Dean Street.
☎ 01 579 342 108.
🍎 *Veryan range*

LOOE

Talland Bay Hotel (P)
Talland Bay.
☎ 01 503 72667.
🍎 *Veryan range*

LOSTWITHIEL

Royal Talbot Hotel (P).
☎ 01 208 872 498.
🍎 *Bulmers Old Hazy*

MAWGAN PORTH

Travellers Rest (P)
Trevarrian Rd.
☎ 01 637 860 245.
🍎 *Bulmers Old Hazy*

NANCENOY

TRENGILLY WARTHA (P)
☎ 01 326 340 332
Open 11-3, 6-11
🍎 **Porthallow**
One of Cornwall's most

famous real ale pubs with ever-changing guest ales and menu. Great walking country. Families welcome. Accommodation. Off B3291, OS 731 282.

NEWQUAY

Sunny Side Caravan Park (C)
Quintrell Downs.
☎ 01 637 873 338.
🍎 *Bulmers Old Hazy*

PADSTOW

Harbour Inn (P).
Strand Street.
☎ 01 841 533 148.
🍎 *Bulmers Old Hazy*

T Henwood & Sons (OL)
6 The Strand.
☎ 01 841 532 325.
🍎 *Veryan range*

Spar Stores (OL)
2 Middle Street.
☎ 01 841 533 400.
🍎 *Veryan range*

PAR

Par Inn (P)
2 Harbour Rd.
☎ 01 726 813 961.
🍎 *Bulmers Old Hazy*

Welcome Home Inn (P)
39 Par Green.
☎ 01 726 813 319.
🍎 *Bulmers Old Hazy*

Youngers Foodstores (OL)
107 Par Green.
☎ 01 726 812 740.
🍎 *Veryan range*

PERRANPORTH

Green Parrot (P)
St George's Hill.
☎ 01 872 573 284.
🍎 *Bulmers Traditional*

PHILLACK

Bucket of Blood (P)
Hayle.
☎ *01 736 752 378.*
🍎 *Bulmers Old Hazy*

PHILLEIGH

ROSELAND INN (P)
King Harry Ferry Road
☎ 01 872 580 254
Open 11.30-3, 6.30-11
🍎 **Bulmers West Country**
Seventeenth-century country
pub with slate floors and oak
beams. Two bars, separate
restaurant with good home-
cooked food.

POLPERRO

BLUE PETER (P)
The Quay
☎ 01 503 272 743
Open all permitted hours
🍎 **Haye Farm**
Polperro's smallest pub,
reached by flight of steps from
harbour. Good food.

PORT ISAAC

Port Isaac Stores (OL)
44 Fore Street.
☎ *01 208 880 202.*
🍎 *Veryan range*

Porthtown
Nelsons Bar (P)
Beach Rd.
☎ *01 209 891 447.*
🍎 *Bulmers Traditional*

PORTSCATHO

Today Foodstore (OL).
☎ *01 872 580 702.*
🍎 *Veryan range*

REDRUTH

Spice of Life (P)
West End, Little Vauxhall.
☎ *01 209 215 455.*
🍎 *Bulmers Old Hazy*

ST AUSTELL

Queenie's General Stores (OL)
London Apprentice
☎ *01 726 72974.*
🍎 *Veryan range*

Queen's Head (P)
1 The Square, St Stephen.
☎ *01 208 862 371.*
🍎 *Bulmers Old Hazy*

**Trevereek Holiday Park Site
Shop** (OL)
Hewaswater.
☎ *01 726 882 540.*
🍎 *Veryan range*

Trewiddle Country Club (C)
Pentewan Rd.
☎ *01 726 67013.*
🍎 *Bulmers Old Hazy*

ST IVES

Mermaid Bistro (R)
21 Fish Street.
☎ *01 736 796 816.*
🍎 *Veryan range*

Tate Gallery (R)
Porthmear Beach.
☎ *01 736 797 297.*
🍎 *Veryan medium still*

ST MAWES

Anna's Deli (OL)
☎ *01 326 270 045.*
🍎 *Veryan range*

Spar Stores (OL).
☎ *01 326 270 703.*
🍎 *Veryan range*

SALTASH

Union Inn (P)
The Beach.
☎ *01 752 844 770.*
🍎 *Bulmers Old Hazy*

SEATON

OLDE SMUGGLERS INN (P)
Tregunnick Lane
☎ 01 503 250 646
Open 12-3, 6.30-11 (11-11
summer)

♦ Inch's
Seventeenth-century pub on coastal path two minutes from beach. Families welcome.

STRATTON
KINGS ARMS (P)
Howells Road
☎ 01 288 352 396
Open 12-3, 6.30-11
♦ Clawford Vintage
Delightful seventeenth-century two-bar pub with slate floors. Families welcome. Accommodation.

TREGONY
Londis (OL)
Fore Street.
☎ 01 872 530 633.
♦ Veryan range

TRURO
Carley's Wholefood (OL)
36 St Austell Street.
☎ 01 872 77686.
♦ Veryan range

Chacewater Stores (OL)
33 Fore Street, Chacewater.
☎ 01 872 560 305.
♦ Veryan range

The Cheeseboard (OL)
Pannier Market, Lemon Quay.
☎ 01 872 70813.
♦ Veryan range

CITY INN (P)
Pydar Street
☎ 01 872 72623
Open all permitted hours
♦ Taunton Traditional
Lively town pub with separate bars and a large garden. Local CAMRA favourite with many guest beers and good value food.

Dairyland Country Life Museum Shop (OL)
Tresillian Barton, Summercourt.
☎ 01 872 510 246.
♦ Veryan range

Dolphin Inn (P)
Grampound.
☎ 01 726 882 435.
♦ Bulmers Old Hazy

Liskey Caravan Park Shop (OL)
Greenbottom.
☎ 01 872 560 274.
♦ Veryan range

LUGGER HOTEL (P)
Portloe
☎ 01 872 501 322
♦ Veryan range
Harbourside hotel bar with separate restaurant

Mount's Bay Wines (OL)
22 New Bridge Street.
☎ 01 872 222 466.
♦ Veryan range

Spar Stores (OL)
Probus.
☎ 01 726 882 419.
♦ Veryan range

Tregain (R)
Portloe.
☎ 01 872 501 252.
♦ Veryan range

TYWARDREATH
NEW INN (P)
Fore Street
☎ 01 726 813 901
Open 11-2.30, 6-11
♦ Bulmers Traditional
Popular village local near Par Sands, with large garden.

VERYAN
Roseland Stores (OL)
☎ 01 872 501 204.
♦ Veryan range

Tretheak Caravan Park Shop (OL)
☎ 01 872 501 658.
♦ Veryan range

ZELAH
HAWKINS ARMS (P)
High Road

☎ 01 872 540 339
Open 11-3, 6-11
🍎 **Inch's**
Homely village pub with
accommodation, good food,
no-smoking area. Families
welcome.

Scilly Isles

ST MARY'S

Lock Stock & Barrel (P)
Old Town.
☎ *01 720 22300.*
🍎 *Bulmers Old Hazy*

Jersey

ST HELIER

LAMPLIGHTER (P)
Mulcaster Street
☎ 01 534 23119
Open 9.30-11; 11-1, 4.30-11 Sun
🍎 **Bulmers Traditional**
Quiet gas-lit single bar town
pub.

The Organic Shop (OL)
Stopford Rd.
🍎 *Dunkerton's*

TOWN HOUSE (P)
New Street
☎ 01 534 615 000
Open 9.30-11; 11-1, 4.30-11 Sun
🍎 **Bulmers Traditional**
Enormous two-room pub with
good food lunchtimes, live
music. Home of Tipsy Toad
brewery. Families welcome.

ST PETER

STAR & TIPSY TOAD (P)
Grande Route
☎ 01 534 485 556
Open 10-11; 11-1, 4.30-11 Sun.
🍎 **Bulmers Traditional**
Tipsy Toad's second pub. Live
music; play area for children;
food lunchtime and evening;
disabled access.

Cumbria

CARTMEL FELL

MASON'S ARMS (P)
Strawberry Bank
☎ 01 539 568 486
Open all permitted hours
🍎 **Knickerbockerbreaker plus
guests**
Truly extraordinary pub. Brews
its own beer but stocks dozens
of others too, has a wide range
of food, family room, self-
catering flats – and makes its
own cider as well! Hard to
find: up the hill from Bowland
Bridge.

GRASMERE

Travellers Rest (P).
☎ *01 539 435 604.*
🍎 *Bulmers Old Hazy*

GREAT LANGDALE

OLD DUNGEON GHYLL (P)
☎ 01 539 437 272
Open all permitted hours
🍎 **Weston's Old Rosie**
Multi-room real ale pub in
superb setting under Langdale
Fells. Climbers' Bar is basic and
informal with live music. Also
has a more sedate bar, a
lounge, and a dining room.
Accommodation, bar food
lunchtime and evening.

INGS

WATERMILL INN (P)
☎ 01 539 821 309
Open 12-2, 6-11
🍎 **Taunton Traditional**
Local CAMRA favourite with
widest choice of real ales for
miles around, in beautiful
surroundings. Good value
meals, accommodation,
disabled access.

KENDAL

Beers In Particular (OL)
151 Highgate.
☎ *01 539 735 714.*
🍎 *Weston's Old Rosie*

Booth's (OL)
45 Highgate.
☎ *01 539 723 731.*
🍎 *Weston's Old Rosie*

Burgundy's Wine Bar (P)
☎ *Lowther Street.*
01 539 733 803.
🍎 *Bulmers Old Hazy, Weston's Old Rosie*

Cask House (P)
All Hallows Lane.
☎ *01 539 733 803.*
🍎 *Bulmers Old Hazy, Biddenden*

Oddbins (OL)
31 Stricklandgate.
☎ *01 539 730 016.*
🍎 *Weston's range*

PENRITH

Castle Hotel (P)
2 Norfolk Rd.
☎ *01 768 863 086.*
🍎 *Bulmers Old Hazy*

Derbyshire

APPLEBY MAGNA

Black Horse (P)
2 Top Street.
☎ *01 530 270 588.*
🍎 *Bulmers Old Hazy*

BELPER

Grapes Inn (P)
High Street.
☎ *01 773 826 928.*
🍎 *Bulmers Old Hazy*

LORD NELSON (P)
Bridge Street
☎ 01 773 824 465
Open 2.30-11, 11-11 Fri/Sat
🍎 **Range varies**

Two-room town tavern busy at weekends but relaxed during the week.

Sports Centre (P)
Kilburn Rd.
☎ *01 773 825 285.*
🍎 *Bulmers Old Hazy*

BUXWORTH

NAVIGATION INN (P)
Canal Basin
☎ 01 663 732 072
Open all permitted hours
🍎 **Range varies**
Multi-room stone pub with restaurant at interchange of canal and tramway just off B6062. Food all day, families welcome, disabled access.

CASTLE DONINGTON

Cross Keys (P)
Bondgate.
☎ *01 332 812 214.*
🍎 *Bulmers Traditional*

CHESTERFIELD

ROYAL OAK (P)
43 Chatsworth Road
☎ 01 246 277 854
Open 11.30-11
🍎 **Lyme Bay Jack Ratt**
Traditional cider is just part of the mix in pub which sells seven real ales, seven bottle-conditioned beers, and 80 whiskies.

DERBY

ALEXANDRA HOTEL (P)
Siddals Road
☎ 01 332 293 993
Open 11-2.30, 4.30-11
🍎 **Cider range varies**
Two-room bare-board alehouse much beloved by local CAMRA. Six guest beers.

BRUNSWICK INN (P)
Railway Terrace
☎ 01 332 290 677
Open all permitted hours
🍎 **Weston's Old Rosie**

Pub which not only brews own beer but has guest ales from all over the country. Railway connection evident in many-room inn with stone floors, family room, no smoking area, disabled access.

Master Locksmith (P)
Meteor Centre, Mansfield Rd.
☎ 01 332 295 868.
🍏 *Bulmers Old Hazy*

GLOSSOP

STAR INN (P)
2 Howard Street
☎ 01 457 853 072
Open 12-11
🍏 **Cider range varies**
Typical two-bar market pub. Low ceilings, cosy atmosphere, no food.

HASLAND

Rutland Hotel (P)
16 Stephenson Place.
☎ 01 246 205 857.
🍏 *Bulmers Old Hazy*

ILKESTON

DEWDROP INN (P)
Station Street
☎ 0115 932 9684
Open 1.30-3, 7-11
🍏 **Perry's**
Victorian pub originally the Middleton Hotel. Lounge, bar, snug. Families welcome. Food lunchtime. Accommodation.

MAKENEY

HOLLY BUSH (P)
Holly Bush Lane
☎ 01 332 841 729
Open 12-3, 6-11; 12-11 Sat.
🍏 **Weston's Old Rosie**
Grade II-listed character pub – beer still brought up from cellar in jugs. Families welcome. Food lunchtime.

SHARDLOW

Hoskins Wharf (P)
196 London Rd.
☎ 01 332 792 844.
🍏 *Bulmers Traditional*

Devon

ASHBURTON

Lantern (P)
Knowle Hill.
☎ 01 364 652 697.
🍏 *Bulmers Old Hazy*

LONDON INN (P)
11 West Street
☎ 01 364 652 478
Open 11-2.30, 5.30-11
🍏 **Luscombe**
Revered fifteenth-century coaching inn. Home of Thompson's Brewery. Large separate restaurant, families welcome, accommodation.

Silent Whistle (P)
Lawrence Rd.
☎ 01 364 652 382.
🍏 *Bulmers Traditional*

ASHILL

ASHILL INN (P)
☎ 01 884 840 506
Open 12-2.30 (not Mon), 5.30-11; 12-11 Sat; 12-2.30, 7-10.30 Sun
🍏 **Taunton Traditional**
Early nineteenth-century local. Family room; bar food lunchtime and evening.

AXMINSTER

Andrewhayes Caravan Park Shop (OL)
Andrewhayes Farm, Dalwood.
🍏 *Lyme Bay Jack Ratt*

AXMINSTER INN (P)
Silver Street
☎ 01 297 34947
Open all permitted hours
🍏 **Taunton Traditional**
Palmer's beers in basic town pub. Family room.

George Hotel (P)
George Street.
☎ 01 297 32209.
🍎 Taunton Traditional

Raymond Hill Post Office (OL)
Charmouth Rd.
☎ 01 297 32281.
🍎 Lyme Bay Jack Ratt

AVETON GIFFORD

Taverners (P)
Fore Street.
☎ 01 548 550 316.
🍎 Bulmers Traditional

BAMPTON

EXETER INN (P)
Tiverton Road
☎ 01 398 331 345
Open 11-2.30, 331 345
🍎 Taunton Traditional
Friendly local with family
room, disabled access.

BARNSTAPLE

ROLLE QUAY (P)
Rolle's Quay
☎ 01 271 45182
Open all permitted hours
🍎 Inch's
Welcoming town pub known
for its extensive range of real
ales and well-priced food.
Family room, disabled access.

Stags Head (P)
☎ Forches Street.
01 271 42036.
🍎 Bulmers Traditional

Union Inn (P)
Princess Street.
☎ 01 271 42863.
🍎 Taunton Traditional

BEER

ANCHOR INN (P)
Fore Street
☎ 01 297 203 386
Open all permitted hours
🍎 Lyme Bay Jack Ratt &
Lymelight
Two-bar seaside pub with good
food and real ales. Separate
restaurant, eight letting rooms.

BARREL OF BEER (P)
Fore Street
☎ 01 297 20099
Open 11.30-2.30, 5-11; 11.30-11
sat; 12-10.30 Sun; all day in
summer
🍎 **Bulmers Old Hazy & West
Country**
Excellent local in picturesque
seaside village. Bar food
lunchtime and evening.

Beer Albion FC (C)
Stovar Long Lane.
☎ 01 297 24324.
🍎 Lyme Bay Jack Ratt &
Lymelight

BEER SOCIAL CLUB (C)
Berry Hill
☎ 01 297 20217
Open 11-11
🍎 **Lyme Bay Jack Ratt,
Taunton Traditional**
Lively social club with snooker
and pool. Visitors welcome.
Two bars, family room. Bar
food at lunchtime, children
welcome.

Beerhead Caravan Park (OL)
Beerhead.
☎ 01 297 24128.
🍎 Lyme Bay Jack Ratt

DOLPHIN HOTEL (P)
Fore Street
☎ 01 297 20068
🍎 **Lyme Bay Jack Ratt**
Olde-worlde pub with separate
restaurant and letting rooms.

Garland Hotel (P)
Stovar Lane.
☎ 01 297 20958.
🍎 Lyme Bay Jack Ratt &
Lymelight

Rock Villa Off-Licence (OL)
Fore Street
☎ 01 297 21491
Open 10-10
🍎 Lyme Bay Jack Ratt &
Traditional

Smugglers Haunt (R)
Fore Street.
☎ 01 297 20682.
🍎 Lyme Bay Jack Ratt

BIDEFORD

THE BIG SHEEP (OL)
Abbotsham
🍎 **Gray's**
Hyperactive, and probably the country's only sheep-themed, countryside and crafts centre. Attractions include sheep-racing.

First In Last Out (P)
Clovelly Rd.
☎ *01 237 474 863.*
🍎 *Taunton Traditional*

Patch 'n' Parrot (P)
Cooper Street.
☎ *01 237 473 648.*
🍎 *Taunton Traditional*

BIDEFORD EAST-THE-WATER

Blacksmiths Arms (P).
01 237 476 392.
🍎 *Taunton Traditional*

SHIP ON LAUNCH (P)
14 Barnstaple Street
☎ 01 237 472 426
Open all permitted hours
🍎 **Taunton Traditional**
Seafaring inn with genuine ships' timbers. Haunt of local cider-drinkers, also handy for walkers and cyclists using Tarka Trail. Family room, disabled access.

BITTAFORD

Horse & Groom (P).
☎ *01 752 892 358.*
🍎 *Bulmers Traditional*

BOVEY TRACEY

Bell Inn (P)
Town Hall Place.
☎ *01 626 83349.*
🍎 *Taunton Traditional*

King of Prussia (P).
☎ *01 626 83224.*
🍎 *Taunton Traditional*

OLD THATCH INN (P)
Station Road
☎ 01 626 833 421
Open 11.30-3, 6-11
🍎 **Green Valley**
Low-ceilinged open-plan pub near Gateway to the Moor. Bar food lunchtime and evening.

BRANSCOMBE

FOUNTAIN HEAD (P)
☎ 01 297 680 359
Open 11-2.30, 6.30-11
🍎 **Green Valley**
Fourteenth-century two-bar pub with huge log fires, wood-panelled walls, stone-flagged floor. Main outlet for Branscombe Vale ales. Lounge was once the village forge. Good wholesome food lunchtime and evening, self-catering accommodation.

MASONS ARMS (P)
☎ 01 297 680 300
Open 11-3, 6-11; 12-4, 7-10.30 Sun; all day in summer
🍎 **Inch's**
Old thatched pub with up to five real ales. Letting rooms; children's certificate; bar food lunchtime and evening; separate restaurant; disabled access.

SEA SHANTY (R)
The Beach
☎ 01 297 680 226
🍎 **Lyme Bay Jack Ratt**
Seafront restaurant on National Trust-owned beach. Ring for opening times, reservations.

BRIXHAM

Bullers Arms (P)
The Strand.
☎ *01 803 853 329.*
🍎 *Bulmers Traditional*

Burton Hotel (P)
Burton Rd.
☎ *01 803 852 805.*
🍎 *Bulmers Traditional*

Globe (P)
61 Fore Street.
☎ *01 803 852 154.*
🍎 *Bulmers Traditional*

Queens Arms (P)
31 Station Hill.
☎ *01 803 852 074.*
🍎 *Bulmers Traditional*

BROADHEMBURY

DREWE ARMS (P)
☎ *01 404 841 267*
Open 11-2.30, 6-11 Mon-Sat, 12-2.30, 7-10.30 Sun
🍎 **Bulmers Traditional, Bollhayes**
Picturesque exterior amid thatched whitewashed cottages, old-fashioned interior with separate public bar. Otter ales. Bar food lunchtime and evening.

BUCKFASTLEIGH

Buckfastleigh Wines (OL)
4 Fore Street
☎ *01 364 43790*
Open 10.30-9 (early closing Wed); 12-2, 7-9 Sun
🍎 *Churchward, Inch's, Luscombe*

Globe (P)
Chapel Street.
☎ *01 364 42223.*
🍎 *Luscombe*

WATERMAN'S ARMS (P)
Market Street
☎ *01 364 43200*
🍎 **Luscombe**
Thirteenth-century coaching inn. Bar food.

WHITE HART (P)
3 Plymouth Road
☎ *01 364 42336*
Open 11-3, 6-11
🍎 **Inch's**
Town-centre pub with family room, bar food, letting rooms.

BUCKLAND MONACHORUM

DRAKE MANOR INN (P)
☎ *01 822 853 892*
Open 11.30-2.10, 6.30-11
🍎 **Bulmers Traditional**
Sixteenth-century inn in picturesque village. Usher's ales. bar food lunchtime and evening.

BUDLEIGH SALTERTON

King William Hotel (P).
☎ *01 395 442 075.*
🍎 *Taunton Traditional*

Knowle Hill Farm Shop (OL)
Knowle.
🍎 *Gray's*

South Farm Shop (OL).
☎ *01 395 443 329.*
🍎 *Lyme Bay Jack Ratt*

ROLLE ARMS (P)
East Budleigh
☎ *01 395 442 017*
Open all permitted hours
🍎 **Lyme Bat Jack Ratt**
Two-bar pub with bar food lunchtime and evenings.

CHAGFORD

GLOBE (P)
High Street
☎ *01 647 433 485*
Open 11-3, 7-11
🍎 **Addlestone's on genuine handpump**
Two-bar sixteenth-century coaching inn in centre of pleasant country town.

CHITTLEHAMHOLT

EXETER INN (P)
☎ *01 769 540 281*
Open 11.30-3, 6-11
🍎 **Bulmers Traditional**
Atmospheric sixteenth-century thatched village pub on the edge of Exmoor.

CHITTLEHAMPTON

Bell Inn (P)
☎ 01 769 540 368.
🍎 *Bulmers Old Hazy*

CHRISTOW

Canonteign Falls Visitors Centre (OL/R)
🍎 *Gray's*

CHUDLEIGH KNIGHTON

Anchor Inn (P)
Fore Street.
☎ 01 626 853 123.
🍎 *Bulmers Traditional*

White Hart (P)
Fore Street.
☎ 01 626 852 139.
🍎 *Bulmers Traditional*

CLAYHIDON

HALF MOON INN (P)
☎ 01 823 680 291
Open 12-2.30, 7-11
🍎 **Bollhayes**
Popular village pub offering good vale home-made food and good range of real ales in the shadow of the Blackdown Hills. Family room, disabled access.

CLYST ST GEORGE

Richfresh Farm Shop (OL)
Marsh Barton Farm.
🍎 *Grays*

COCKINGTON

DRUM INN (P)
☎ 01 803 605 143
Open 11-2.30, 7-11; 11-11 school summer holidays.
🍎 **Range varies**
Large family pub with big garden in picturesque village. Skittles. Dartmoor ales. Family room, disabled access.

COLYTON

Gerrard Arms (P)
Rosemary Lane.
☎ 01 297 552 588.
🍎 *Lyme Bay Jack Ratt*

Spar (OL)
The Square.
☎ 01 297 552 215.
🍎 *Lyme Bay Jack Ratt*

WHITE HART (P)
Swan Hill Rd, Colyford
☎ 01 297 552 358
Open all permitted hours
🍎 **Lyme Bay Jack Ratt**
Good food and family room in pub on Seaton Electric Tramway route.

COMBE MARTIN

Royal Marine (P)
Seaside Rd.
☎ 01 271 882 470.
🍎 *Bulmers Old Hazy*

COPPLESTONE

CROSS HOTEL (P)
01 363 84273
Open 11-3.30, 5.30-11; 12-3, 7-10.30 Sun
🍎 **Inch's**
Village local in same ownership for nearly 60 years. No food.

CORNWOOD

MOUNTAIN INN (P)
Lutton
☎ 01 752 837 247
Open 11-3, 6-11 Mon-Sat, 12-3, 6-10.30 Sun.
🍎 **Luscombe**
Traditional Devon cob construction. Famous for its hot beef rolls. Family room.

CREDITON

DARTMOOR RAILWAY INN (P)
Station Road
☎ 01 363 772 489
Open 12-3, 5 (7 Sun)-11; 11-11 Fri/Sat

🍎 **Inch's**
Large two-room pub near station. Bar food lunchtime and evening; separate restaurant.

KINGS ARMS (P)
Park Street
☎ 01 363 774 298
Open 11-11
🍎 **Taunton Traditional**
Popular local pub. Family room; bar food lunchtime.

Lees Wine Stores (OL)
21 High Street.
🍎 *Gray's*

MITRE (P)
9 High Street
☎ 01 363 772 508
Open 11-2.30(not Tues), 6-11; 12-3, 7-10.30 Sun
🍎 **Taunton Traditional**
Basic local. Bar food lunchtime.

THREE LITTLE PIGS (P)
1 Parliament Street
☎ 01 363 774 587
Open all permitted hours
🍎 **Taunton Traditional**
Former market inn. Family room; bar food lunchtime and evening.

White Hart (P)
Exeter Rd.
☎ *01 363 82240.*
🍎 *Bulmers Traditional*

CROYDE

Manor House Inn (P)
St Marys Rd.
☎ *01 271 890 241.*
🍎 *Taunton Traditional*

CROCKERNWELL

CROWS NEST (P)
☎ 01 647 281 267
Open all permitted hours
🍎 **Taunton Traditional**
Splendid views over Dartmoor. Food all day. On old A30.

CULLOMPTON

Market House Inn (P)
Higher Bullring.
☎ *01 672 861 663.*
🍎 *Bulmers Old Hazy*

Pony & Trap (P)
10 Exeter Hill.
☎ *01 884 33254.*
🍎 *Bulmers Traditional*

DARTINGTON

FARM FOOD SHOP (OL)
Cider Press Centre, Shinners Bridge
☎ 01 803 864 171
Open 9.30-5.30 seven days. Closed Sunday in winter
🍎 **Ciders from up to eight West Country producers**
Shop one of nine on four-acre site belonging to Dartington Trading Co. Also cafe and restaurant.

DARTMOUTH

Ferry Boat Inn (P)
Manor Rd, Dittisham.
☎ *01 803 722 368.*
🍎 *Bulmers Traditional*

DAWLISH

Exeter Inn (P)
Beech Street.
☎ *01 626 865 677.*
🍎 *Taunton Traditional*

LANSDOWNE HOTEL (P)
8 Park Road
☎ 01 626 862 069
Open all permitted hours
🍎 **Taunton Traditional, Bulmers Traditional**
Basic two-bar town pub with no real ale. Family room; bar food lunchtime and evening.

PRINCE OF WALES (P)
Old Town
☎ 01 626 862 145
Open all permitted hours
🍎 **Inch's**

Two-bar town pub with excellent beer. Bar food lunchtime and evening.

SWAN INN (P)
Old Town
☎ 01 626 863 677
Open 11-3, 5-11; 11-11 Sat; 12-4, 7-10.30 Sun
🍎 **Reddaways, Bulmers Traditional**
Pleasant two-bar seventeenth-century pub. Bar food lunchtime.

DEVONPORT

Kerr St Social Club (C)
☎ *01 752 56278.*
🍎 *Taunton Traditional*

DODDISCOMBELEIGH

NOBODY INN (P)
☎ 01 647 252 394
Open 12-2.30, 7-11
🍎 **Gray's**
Sixteenth-century inn with many original features. Famous for its food (especially cheeses), 200 whiskies, and 700 wines. No smoking area lunchtime.

DREWSTEIGNTON

DREWE ARMS (P)
The Square
☎ 01 647 21224
Open 11-3, 6-11 Sun-Fri, 11-11 Sat
🍎 **Gray's**
Amazing survival of early twentieth-century village pub, maintained unaltered by landlady "Aunt Mabel" Mudge until her retirement aged ninety-nine in 1995. (She celebrated her hundredth shortly after). Grade II listed, and jealously defended by locals.

DUNSFORD

ROYAL OAK (P)
☎ 01 647 252 256
Open 12-2.30, 6.30-11

🍎 **Gray's, Brimblecombe**
Popular local which hosts beer festivals in summer. Letting rooms; bar food lunchtime and evening; separate non-smoking restaurant; family room. Excellent base for Dartmoor walks.

STEPS BRIDGE INN (P)
☎ 01 624 52330
🍎 **Gray's**
Restaurant and bar on River Teign near Exeter. In National Park – good base for walks long or short. Food includes cream teas.

EXETER

Birks Hall (C)
Exeter University,
New North Rd.
☎ *01 392 263 395.*
🍎 *Bulmers Traditional*

Admiral Vernon (P)
High Street, Alphington.
☎ *01 392 76990.*
🍎 *Taunton Traditional*

Clifton Inn (P)
Clifton Rd, Newtown.
☎ *01 392 73527.*
🍎 *Taunton Traditional*

Devon Arms (P)
Kenton.
☎ *01 626 890 213.*
🍎 *Bulmers Traditional*

DOUBLE LOCKS (P)
Canal Banks, Marsh Barton
☎ 01 392 56947
Open all permitted hours
🍎 **Gray's**
Recently bought by Smile's brewery, but maintains wide ale range. Good menu, live music, disabled access. Hard to find: follow lane next to incinerator over canal.

GATE (P)
60 New North Road
☎ 01 392 423 761
Open all permitted hours
🍎 **Bulmers Old Hazy, Inch's, guests**

True traditional cider house.
No food.

Green Gables Inn *(P)*
Buddle Lane.
☎ *01 392 58404.*
🍎 *Bulmers Traditional*

LOCOMOTIVE INN (P)
36 New North Road
☎ 01 392 75840
Open 11-11
🍎 **Taunton Traditional**
City-centre cider pub, but
range has contracted sharply of
late. Bar food.

Pack Horse Inn *(P)*
58 St David's Hill.
☎ *01 392 54757.*
🍎 *Bulmers Traditional*

Poachers Inn *(P)*
Ide.
☎ *01 392 73847.*
🍎 *Bulmers Traditional*

RED COW INN (P)
St Davids
☎ 01 392 72318
🍎 **Taunton Traditional,
Bulmers Old Hazy & West
Country**
Plain two-bar boozer popular
with students. Big menu.
various snakebite recipes a
speciality – lack of disabled
facilities therefore surprising.

ROYAL OAK INN (P)
Okehampton Street, St Thomas
☎ 01 392 55665
Open 11-2.30, 5-11; 12-3, 7-10.30
Sun
🍎 **Taunton Traditional**
Basic local with skittle alley. No
food.

Ship Inn *(P)*
St Martins Lane.
☎ *01 392 72040.*
🍎 *Taunton Traditional*

Twisted Oak *(P)*
Ide.
☎ *01 392 73666.*
🍎 *Taunton Traditional*

EXMOUTH

ALBION (P)
38 Albion Street
☎ 01 395 272 960
Open all permitted hours
🍎 **Taunton Traditional,
Bulmers Traditional**
Basic back-street boozer: no
real ale; no food.

BICTON INN (P)
5 Bicton Street
☎ 01 395 272 589
Open all permitted hours
🍎 **Taunton Traditional**
Basic but friendly back-street
popular with students. Bar
food lunchtime and evening.

COUNTRY HOUSE INN (P)
176 Withycombe Village
☎ 01 395 263 444
Open 10.30-2.30, 5-11.
🍎 **Taunton Traditional**
Village local, once a forge, now
boasts aviary in garden and
barbecues by stream. Book for
food.

DEER LEAP (P)
Esplanade
☎ 01 395 265 030
Open all permitted hours
🍎 **Bulmers Old Hazy**
Busy beach-side pub aimed
mainly at tourists. Food
lunchtime and evening;
disabled access.

First & Last *(P)*
10 Church Street.
☎ *01 395 263 275.*

BULMERS TRADITIONAL.
Pilot Inn (P)
Chapel Hill
☎ 01 395 26338
Open all permitted hours
🍎 **Taunton Traditional**
Ex-Whitbread pub, now a free
house and much the better for
it. Basic boozer: no food.

REILLY'S (P)
8 Victoria Road
☎ 01 395 225 440
Open all permitted hours

❛ Thatchers
Wine bar-style outlet; no food
or real ale.

Working Mens Club *(C)*
Victoria Road
☎ *01 395 273 618.*
❛ *Taunton Traditional*

YORK INN (P)
Imperial Road
☎ 01 395 22248
Open all permitted hours
**❛ Bulmers Old Hazy, Taunton
Traditional**
Popular local with family
room. No food.

FENNY BRIDGES

FENNY BRIDGES INN (P)
☎ 01 404 850 218
Open 11-3, 6-11; 12-3, 7-10.30
Sun
**❛ Weston's Old Rosie and
perry**
Plush but friendly two-bar
roadhouse with family room.
Bar food lunchtime and
evening.

GEORGEHAM

KING'S ARMS (P)
Chapel Street
☎ 01 271 890 240
Open 12-3.30, 6-11
❛ Thatcher's
Friendly village pub with
occasional live music. Bar food
lunchtime and evening;
accommodation.

ROCK (P)
Rock Hill
☎ 01 271 890 322
Open 11-2.30, 6-11 Sun-Fri,
11-11 Sat
❛ Hancock's
Sixteenth-century gem: local
CAMRA Pub of the Year twice
running. Eight beers, children
welcome, accommodation,
disabled access.

HARBERTON

CHURCH HOUSE INN (P)
☎ 01 803 863 707
Open 12-3, 6-11
❛ Churchward's
Very ancient one-room village
pub, with small family room
hidden behind medieval oak
screen. Guest beers.

HEAVITREE

Windsor Castle *(P)*
North Street.
☎ *01 392 213 693.*
❛ *Taunton Traditional*

HOLBETON

DARTMOOR UNION (P)
Fore Street
☎ 01 752 830 288
Open 11.30-3, 6-11 Mon-Sat, 12-
3, 7-10.30 Sun.
❛ Symons
Ancient cider press, once the
local workhouse, now pub
with banqueting room, family
room, beer garden. Disabled
access.

MILDMAY COLOURS (P)
☎ 01 752 830 248
Open 11-3, 6-11
❛ Symons, Luscombe
Picturesque old manor house,
now pub with own brewery.

HOLCOMBE ROGUS

PRINCE OF WALES (P)
☎ 01 823 672 070
Open 11.3-3 (not Tues), 6.30-11
❛ Ciders vary
Pleasant country pub with
excellent selection of ales and
separate restaurant. Family
room, disabled access.

HOLNE

CHURCH HOUSE INN (P)
☎ 01 364 631 208
Open 12-2.30, 7-10.30 Sun-
Thurs (longer hours summer),
11-11 Fri/Sat.

♣ Gray's
Traditional village inn on edge
of Dartmoor. Good food, but
book for restaurant. Family
room, accommodation.

HONITON

KING'S ARMS (P)
Stockland
☎ 01 404 881 361
Open 12-3, 6-11; 12-3, 7-10.30
Sun
♣ Lyme Bay Jack Ratt
Beautiful old two-room village
pub with family room,
restaurant and bar food
lunchtime and evening.

White Lion (P)
High Street.
☎ *01 404 42066.*
♣ *Bulmers Traditional*

Wine World (OL)
83 High Street.
☎ *01 404 43767.*
♣ *Lyme Bay Jack Ratt*

HONITON CLYST

YOUNG HAYES FARM SHOP
(OL)
☎ 01 404 822 201
♣ Gray's
Whole hog Devon farm shop –
clotted cream, jam, chutney,
cheese, home-made sausages,
and, of course, local cider.

HORNDON

ELEPHANTS NEST (P)
☎ 01 822 810 273
Open 11-2.30, 6.30-11.
♣ Taunton Traditional
Sixteenth-century moorland
pub popular with walkers and
riders. Big menu lunchtime
and evening, great selection of
ales. Disabled access.

ILFRACOMBE

Sandpiper Inn (P)
The Quay.
☎ *01 271 865 260.*
♣ *Bulmers Traditional*

ILSINGTON

CARPENTERS ARMS (P)
☎ 01 364 661 215
Open 11-2.30, 6-11.
♣ Churchward's
Farmers' and villagers' local on
edge of Dartmoor.

IVYBRIDGE

IMPERIAL (P)
28 Western Road
☎ 01 752 892 269
Open all permitted hours
♣ Range varies
Old-fashioned homely pub
with good food, especially
formidable mixed grill. Family
room, disabled access.

KENN

Ley Arms (P)
Kennford.
☎ *01 392 832 341.*
♣ *Bulmers Traditional*

KENTON

DEVON ARMS (P)
Fore Street
☎ 01 626 890 213
Open 11-3, 5-11; 12-3, 7-10.30
Sun
♣ Bulmers West Country
Pleasant seventeenth-century
two-bar village inn catering for
locals and visitors alike. Up to
four real ales. Six letting rooms;
bar food lunchtime and
evening.

KINGSKERSWELL

Park Inn (P).
☎ *01 803 872 216.*
♣ *Taunton Traditional*
Kingsbridge

Hermitage Inn (P)
Mill Street.
☎ *01 548 853 234.*
🍎 *Taunton Traditional*

King of Prussia (P)
Church Street.
☎ *01 548 852 099.*
🍎 *Bulmers Traditional*

Royal Oak (P)
Malborough.
☎ *01 548 561 481.*
🍎 *Bulmers Traditional*

KINGS NYMPTON

Grove Inn (P).
☎ *01 769 580 406.*
🍎 *Bulmers Traditional*

KINGSTAMERTON

Fellowship (P)
☎ *01 752 36243.*
🍎 *Taunton Traditional*

LAPFORD

OLD MALT SHOVEL (P)
☎ 01 363 83330
Open 11.30-3, 6-11; 12-4, 7-10.30
Sun; all day in summer
🍎 **Inch's and guests**
Stone-floored village inn with
inglenook fireplace. Family
room; bar food lunchtime and
evening. Skittle alley.

YEO VALE HOTEL (P)
☎ 01 363 83844
Open 11.30-3, 6-11; 11-11 sat;
12-4, 7-10.30 Sun
🍎 **Inch's**
Pleasant main road pub
recently reopened after being
closed for several years. Family
room; bar food lunchtime and
evening; skittle alley. Near
station.

LIFTON

Fox & Grapes Hotel (P)
Tinhay.
☎ *01 566 784 217.*
🍎 *Taunton Traditional*

LOWER ASHTON

MANOR INN (P)
☎ 01 647 252 304
Open 12-2.30, 7-11; 12-2.30, 7-
10.30 Sun; closed Mon.
🍎 **Green Valley**
Local pub of the year 1993 with
good range of ales. Small two-
bar pub in picturesque Teign
Valley. Hard to find: just off
B3193, over bridge.

LUPPITT

LUPPITT INN (P)
☎ 01 404 819 613
Opening times vary
🍎 **Ciders vary**
Unaltered farmhouse pub -
beer served through a hatch
from the kitchen. No food, but
locally-brewed Otter ales. Not
to be missed.

LYDFORD

MUCKY DUCK (P)
Lydford Gorge
☎ 01 822 820 208
Open 12-11, closed Mon
🍎 **Inch's**
Slate-floored, stone-walled
two-bar local. Family room,
accommodation.

LYMPSTONE

Globe Inn (P).
☎ *01 395 263 166.*
🍎 *Taunton Traditional*

REDWING INN (P)
Church Road
☎ 01 395 22215
Open 11.30-3, 6-11; 11-11 sat;
12-4, 7-10.30 Sun
🍎 **Taunton Traditional,
Bulmers Traditional**
Popular, unpretentious two-bar
village free house. Bar food
lunchtime and evening.

SWAN INN (P)
Strand
☎ 01 395 27228
Open 11-3, 5-11; 11-11 Sat; all

day in summer
Taunton Traditional
Popular, friendly L-shaped
pub; bar food lunchtime and
evening; separate restaurant.

LYNTON

Queens Hotel (P)
Queen Street.
☎ *01 598 52625.*
**Bulmers Traditional*

MORCHARD

STURT ARMS (P)
☎ 01 363 85102
Open 11-3, 5.30-11; 12-3, 7-10.30
Sun
Inch's, Taunton Traditional
Pleasant roadhouse, formerly
the Devonshire Dumpling.
Family room; good bar food
lunchtime and evening.

MORETONHAMPSTEAD

Lynch Stores (OL)
12 Court Street.
**Gray's*

White Hart (P).
☎ *01 647 440 406.*
**Bulmers Traditional*

MILTON COMBE

WHO'D HAVE THOUGHT IT
(P)
☎ 01 822 853 313
Open 11.30-3, 6.30-11 Mon-Sat,
12-3, 7-10.30 Sun
**Bulmers Traditional, Inch's
sweet**
Three-room sixteenth-century
inn in steep wooded valley
near Lopwell Dam. Bar meals
lunchtime and evening, no
smoking area for diners.

MUSBURY

GOLDEN LION (P)
The Street
☎ 01 297 552 413
Open 11-3, 6-11; 12-3, 7-10.30
Sun
Taunton Traditional

Pleasant two-bar village pub
with fine collection of pub bric-
a-brac, eg horse brasses, jugs
etc. Bar food lunchtime and
evening

NEWTON ABBOT

DARTMOUTH INN (P)
63 East Street
☎ 01 626 53451
Open all permitted hours
Inch's
Oldest pub in town,
specialising in guest ales (Over
1,200 so far). Pub of the Year
three times. Family room; bar
food lunchtime and evening.

Heavitree Arms (P).
☎ *01 626 53116.*
**Taunton Traditional*

Office (P)
Queen Street.
☎ *01 626 54238.*
**Bulmers Traditional*

Ponsworthy Stores (OL)
Ponsworthy.
**Gray's*

Railway Hotel (P)
Queen Street.
☎ *01 626 54166.*
**Bulmers Traditional*

Saracens Head (P)
2 Fairfield Terrace.
☎ *01 626 65430.*
**Bulmers Traditional*

*Stover International Caravan
Park Shop* (OL)
Lower Staple Hill.
**Gray's*

Swan Inn (P)
Highweek Street.
☎ *01 626 65056.*
**Taunton Traditional*

Union Inn (P)
Denbury.
☎ *01 803 812 595.*
**Bulmers Traditional*

YE OLDE CIDER BAR (P)
99 East Street
☎ 01 626 54221
Open 11-11
🍎 **Inch's, Richards' (inc perry), Hunt's plus guests**
No beer, no carpets, no cushions, no music – but loads of customers. Pies, pasties and rolls always available. Family room.

NEWTON POPPLEFORD

CANNON INN (P)
High Street
☎ 01 395 568 266
Open 11-3, 6-11
🍎 **Taunton Traditional**
Two-bar country local with bar food lunchtime and evening; children's certificate; accommodation.

EXETER INN (P)
High Street
☎ 01 395 568 295
Open 11-3, 6-11; 11-11 sat; 12-3, 7-10.30
🍎 **Taunton Traditional**
Small one-bar village pub. Bar food lunchtime and evening.

NORTH BOVEY

RING OF BELLS (P)
☎ 01 647 40375
11-3, 6-11. 11-11 summer.
🍎 **Gray's**
Rambling, low-beamed, thatched, thirteenth-century Dartmoor village pub. Good food, local ales, family room, accommodation.

OFFWELL

Elliott's Nursery (OL)
Hill Close.
☎ *01 404 831 549.*
🍎 *Lyme Bay Jack Ratt*

OTTERTON

Kings Arms (P)
Fore Street.
☎ *01 395 68416.*
🍎 *Bulmers Traditional*

OTTERY ST MARY

KINGS ARMS (P)
Gold Street
☎ 01 404 812 486
Open 10.30-2.30, 5.30-11; 10.30-11 Sat.
🍎 **Taunton Traditional**
Busy town local. Evening meals at weekends. Family room, disabled access, separate public bar, no smoking area.

PAIGNTON

Oldenburg (P)
48 Winner Street.
☎ *01 803 555 596.*
🍎 *Bulmers Old Hazy*

Old Well House (P)
5 Torquay Street.
☎ *01 803 551 292.*
🍎 *Bulmers Old Hazy*

Torbay Inn (P)
34 Fisher Street.
☎ *01 803 551 484.*
🍎 *Bulmers Traditional. Peter Tavy*

PETER TAVY INN (P)
☎ 01 822 810 348
Open 11-30-3, 6.30-11 Mon-Sat, 12-3, 7-10.30 Sun.
🍎 **Inch's Scrumpy & Sweet**
Ancient moorland pub with low ceiling and flagstone floors. Family room. Bar food evening and lunchtime.

PLYMOUTH

BORINGDON ARMS (P)
Boringdon Terrace, Turnchapel
☎ 01 752 402 053
Open all permitted hours
🍎 **Countryman**
Much-loved free house with frequent beer festivals and good food. Six letting rooms, family room, no juke box.

BREWERY TAP (P)
Edgcumbe Street, Stonehouse.
☎ 01 752 262 536
Open all permitted hours
🍎 **Countryman, Sheppy's,
Taunton Traditional**
Large L-shaped street-corner
local. Bar food at lunchtime.

Crown Hotel (P)
43 Chapel Street.
☎ 01 752 606 991.
🍎 *Bulmers Traditional*

KING'S HEAD (P)
21 Bretonside
☎ 01 752 665 619
Open all permitted hours
🍎 **Haye Farm, Countryman**
Big one-bar pub, reputed to be
Plymouth's oldest - and still
gas-lit. Now brewing its own
beer. Bar food at lunchtime.
Next to Bretonside bus station.

Lord High Admiral (P)
33 Stonehouse Street.
☎ 01 752 221 508.
🍎 *Bulmers Traditional*

New Inn (P)
Turnchapel.
☎ 01 752 402 765.
🍎 *Bulmers Traditional*

STAR OF THE WEST (P)
7 Brownlow Street, Stonehouse
☎ 01 752 221 125
Open all permitted hours
🍎 **Taunton Traditional,
Sheppy's**
Basic one-bar pub 10 minutes'
walk from city centre. No food.

WREN POTTERY (OL)
47 Southside Street, Barbican
☎ 01 752 220 655
Open 9-5.30, plus 7-9.30 in
summer.
🍎 **Cripple Cock, Really Fowl,
Gasping Goose**
Tourist gift shop.

POUNDSGATE

TAVISTOCK INN (P)
☎ 01 364 631 251
Open 11-2.30, 6-11

🍎 **Bulmers West Country**
Very old, unspoilt Dartmoor
village inn. Extremely popular
in summer. Family room,
separate public bar.

PRINCETOWN

PLUME OF FEATHERS (P)
Two Bridges Road
☎ 01 822 890 240
Open all permitted hours
🍎 **Range varies**
Oldest building in village. Slate
floors, exposed beams, stone
walls. Accommodation and
camping for walkers. Family
room, disabled access.

RINGMORE

JOURNEY'S END (P)
Ringmore Village
☎ 01 752 810 205
🍎 **Cider range varies**
Olde-worlde two bar pub with
family room. Bar food
lunchtime and evening, no-
smoking area for diners. B&B.

SALCOMBE

WS Ellis & Co (OL)
Fore Street
☎ 01 548 842 806
Open 9am-8pm
🍎 *Bromell's*

SANDFORD

ROSE & CROWN (P)
Rose & Crown Hill
☎ 01 363 772 056
Open 7-11 Mon-Thurs; 12-3, 7-
11 Fri/Sat; 12-3, 7-10.30 Sun
🍎 **Inch's**
Popular friendly one-bar local;
bar food lunchtime and
evening Fri, Sat, Sun only.

SCORRITON

TRADESMANS ARMS (P)
☎ 01 364 631 206
Open 12-2, 7-11
🍎 **Luscombe**
300-year-old moorland pub

with family room,
accommodation and camping.
No-smoking area. Hard to find:
OS 704 685.

SEATON

KING'S ARMS (P)
Fore Street
☎ 01 297 23431
Open 11.30-2.30, 6.30-11; 12-3,
7-10.30 Sun
🍺 Inch's
Small local with family room.
Bar food lunchtime and
evening.

New Look News (OL)
Harbour Rd.
☎ *01 297 21713.*
🍺 *Lyme Bay Jack Ratt*

Rossini's (R)
Harbour Rd.
☎ *01 297 625 272.*
🍺 *Lyme Bay Jack Ratt &*
Lymelight

Seaton Cricket Club (C)
Court Lane.
☎ *01 297 22030.*
🍺 *Lyme Bay Jack Ratt*

Tower Service Station (OL)
Seaton Down Hill.
☎ *01 297 22026.*
🍺 *Lyme Bay Jack Ratt*

SHALDON

CLIFFORD ARMS (P)
34 Fore Street
☎ 01 626 872 311
Open 11-2.30, 5-11; 11-11 Sat
🍺 Churchwards
Large popular pub with good
food. Family room.

SLAPTON

TOWER INN (P)
Slapton Village
☎ 01 548 580 216
🍺 Cider range varies
Olde Worlde two-bar pub with
family room. Bar food
lunchtime and evening, no-
smoking area for diners. B&B.

QUEEN'S ARMS (P)
☎ 01 548 580 800
Open 11.30-3, 6-11.
🍺 Cider range varies
Fourteenth-century village
centre pub. Good food. In same
ownership as Tower Inn.

SIDMOUTH

Balfour Arms (P)
26 Woolbrook Rd.
☎ *01 395 512 993.*
🍺 *Bulmers Traditional*

Dove Inn (P)
Fore Street.
☎ *01 395 513 445.*
🍺 *Taunton Traditional*

Marine Bar (P)
Esplanade.
☎ *01 395 513 145.*
🍺 *Taunton Traditional*

Oak Down Caravan Park Shop
(OL)
Weston.
🍺 *Lyme Bay Jack Ratt*

Royal York Hotel (P)
Tappers Bar.
☎ *01 396 513 043.*
🍺 *Taunton Traditional*

Sidbury Social Club (C)
Sidbury.
☎ *01 395 597 453.*
🍺 *Taunton Traditional*

Salty Monk (R)
Church Street, Sidford.
☎ *01 395 513 174.*
🍺 *Lyme Bay Jack Ratt &*
Lymelight

Trumps (OL)
8 Fore Street.
☎ *01 395 512 446.*
🍺 *Lyme Bay Jack Ratt & Vintage*

The Wineseller (OL)
High Street.
☎ *01 395 515 122.*
🍺 *Lyme Bay Jack Ratt, Vintage*

STARCROSS

Anchor Inn (P)
Cockwood.
☎ 01 626 890 203.
🍺 *Bulmers Traditional*

Ship Inn (P)
Church Rd, Cockwood.
☎ 01 626 890 373.
🍺 *Bulmers Traditional*

STAVERTON

SEA TROUT INN (P)
☎ 01 803 762 274
Open 11-3, 6-11
🍺 **Luscombe**
Three sixteenth-century
cottages knocked into one.
Disabled access.

STOCKLAND

KINGS ARMS (P)
☎ 01 404 881 361
Open 12-3, 6.30-11
🍺 **Reed's**
Seventeenth-century coaching
inn with everything: beer from
local brewer, family facilities,
food lunchtime and evening,
letting rooms, disabled access –
even (in summer) a rail service!

STOKE GABRIEL

Church House Inn (P).
☎ 01 803 782 384.
🍺 *Taunton Traditional*

STOKENHAM

TRADESMANS ARMS (P)
☎ 01 548 580 313
Open 12-2.30, 6-11. (Closed
Mon-Thurs evenings in winter)
🍺 **Luscombe**
Elegant fifteenth-century free
house in South Hams village.
Interesting menu and selection
of whiskies.

TAVISTOCK

Brentnor Inn (P)
Brentnor.
☎ 01 822 81240.
🍺 *Bulmers Traditional*

Cornish Arms (P)
West Street.
☎ 01 822 612 145.
🍺 *Taunton Traditional*

Duke of York (P)
Ford Street.
☎ 01 822 614 928.
🍺 *Bulmers Traditional*

TEIGNMOUTH

BLUE ANCHOR (P)
Teign Street
☎ 01 626 772 741
Open all permitted hours
🍺 **Thatcher's**
One-bar quayside pub with
pool table and juke-box. Seven
real ales.

Endeavour (P)
Northumberland Place.
☎ 01 626 773 722.
🍺 *Bulmers Traditional*

GOLDEN LION (P)
85 Bitton Park Road
☎ 01 626 776 442
Open 12-4, 6-11
🍺 **Inch's**
Two-bar local with changing
range of ales.

Kangaroo (P)
Teign Street.
☎ 01 626 74661.
🍺 *Thatcher's*

King's Arms (P)
French Street.
☎ 01 626 775 268.
🍺 *Bulmers Traditional*

Queensberry Arms (P)
Northumberland Place.
☎ 01 626 778 648.
🍺 *Taunton Traditional*

Teign Wines (OL)
Clarendon House, Orchard Gardens.
☎ *01 626 775 651.*
🍎 *Wide range of bottled ciders*

THORVERTON

EXETER INN (P)
☎ 01 392 860 206
Open 11.30-3, 6-11; 12-3, 7-10.30 Sun
🍎 **Inch's**
Old coaching inn with collection of antique farm implements, own well, and skittle alley. Family room; bar food lunchtime and evening.

TIVERTON

BARLEY MOW (P)
97 Barrington Street
☎ 01 884 252 028
Open 11-3, 6-11; 11-11 Fri/Sat; 12-10.30 Sun
🍎 **Taunton Traditional**
Small two-bar local in old narrow terraced street. No food.

COUNTRY CUPBOARD (OL)
24 Bampton Street
☎ 01 884 257 220
🍎 **Engelfield, Kingston Vale, Sheppy, Torre**
Exceptional off-licence which has always stocked a wide range of ciders.

Cross Keys (P)
Gold Street.
☎ *01 884 252 129.*
🍎 *Taunton Traditional*

HARE & HOUNDS (P)
138 Chapel Street
☎ 01 884 252013
Open all permitted hours
🍎 **Taunton Traditional**
Large two-bar estate pub. No food.

PRINCE REGENT (P)
Lowman Green
☎ 01 884 252 882
Open 11-11 (4-11 Tues); 12-10.30 Sun

🍎 **Lane's**
Popular local near river. Bar food lunchtime and evening

RACEHORSE (P)
Wellbrook Street
☎ 01 884 252 606
Open all permitted hours
🍎 **Taunton Traditional**
Popular local with skittle alley, children's garden with pets, and barbecues in summer. Family room, disabled access.

Twyford Inn (P)
Bampton Street.
☎ *01 884 252019*
🍎 *Bulmers Old Hazy*

TOPSHAM

Highfield Harvest Organic Farm Shop (OL),
Clyst Rd.
🍎 *Gray's*

TORQUAY

Fortune of War (P)
St Marychurch Rd.
☎ *01 803 32627.*
🍎 *Taunton Traditional*

Kents Tavern (P)
Wellswood Village.
☎ *01 803 292 522.*
🍎 *Taunton Traditional*

Printers Elbow (P)
Union Street.
☎ *01 803 214 785.*
🍎 *Bulmers Traditional*

Railway (P)
31 East Street.
☎ *01 803 297 468.*
🍎 *Bulmers Traditional*

Royal Standard Inn (P)
68-70 Hele Rd.
☎ *01 803 328 149.*
🍎 *Bulmers Traditional*

South Devon College of Arts (C)
Ebdon Bldgs.
☎ *01 803 291 212.*
🍎 *Bulmers Traditional*

Stumble Inn (P)
Meadfoot Lane.
☎ *01 803 299 996.*
🍎 *Taunton Traditional*

White Hart Inn (P)
Temperance Street.
☎ *01 803 293 190.*
🍎 *Bulmers Traditional*

TOTNES

Globe Inn (P)
Castle Hill.
☎ *01 803 862 145.*
🍎 *Bulmers Traditional*

KINGSBRIDGE INN (P)
9 Leechwell Street.
☎ 01 803 863 324
Open 11-2.30, 5.30-11.
🍎 **Luscombe**
Friendly low-ceilinged pub
with family room.

WALKHAMPTON

WALKHAMPTON INN (P)
☎ 01 822 855 556
Open all permitted hours in
summer, closed 3-6 in winter.
🍎 **Inch's**
Traditional village pub on edge
of Dartmoor. Family room, bar
food lunchtime and evening.

WELCOMBE

Old Smithy (P)
☎ *01 237 24745.*
🍎 *Bulmers Old Hazy*

WESTON

OTTER INN (P)
☎ 01 404 42594
Open 11-3, 6-11; 12-3,
7-10.30 Sun
🍎 **Inch's**
Sixteenth-century riverside
former cider house. Family
room; bar food lunchtime and
evening; spit-roasts, for some
reason, on Thursdays.

WESTWARD HO!

Westward Ho! Golf Club (C)
Golf Links Rd.
☎ *01 237 477 233.*
🍎 *Bulmers Traditional*

WHIMPLE

NEW FOUNTAIN INN (P)
Church Road
☎ 01 404 822 350
Open 11-3, 6-11
🍎 **Inch's**
Popular village local serving
good home-made food.
Children welcome.

WHIPTON

Whipton Inn (P).
☎ *01 392 67615.*
🍎 *Taunton Traditional*

WIDECOMBE-IN-THE-MOOR

RUGGLESTONE INN (P)
☎ 01 364 621 327
Open 11.30-2.30, 7-11.
Longer hours in summer.
🍎 **Lower Whiddon Cider**
Unspoilt Dartmoor pub
popular with walkers. Was
furthest-flung outpost of
Charrington IPA until the beer
was axed and replaced by the
(much better) local Cotleigh
Tawny Owl. Disabled access.
Hard to find: half-mile south of
village, OS 721 766.

WOODBURY

MALTSTERS ARMS (P)
Green Way
☎ 01 395 232 218
Open 11-3, 6-11; 12-3, 7-10.30
Sun
🍎 **Various traditional ciders in
summer**
Single bar village pub with
skittle alley. Noted bar food
lunchtime and evening.

YARCOMBE

Belfry Country Hotel (H)
☎ 01 404 861 234.
🍎 Lyme Bay Lymelight

YELVERTON

East Dart Hotel (P)
Postbridge.
🍎 Gray's

Royal Oak (P)
Meavy.
☎ 01 822 852 944.
🍎 Taunton Traditional

Dorset

ASHLEY HEATH

STRUAN HOTEL (P)
Horton Road
☎ 01 425 473 553
Open 11-3, 6-11
🍎 Inch's
Principally a food pub. Bar
food lunchtime and evening;
separate restaurant; letting
rooms.

BEAMINSTER

Beaminster Fine Wines (OL)
21 The Square.
☎ 01 308 862 350.
🍎 Lyme Bay Jack Ratt

Beaminster Social Club (C)
Fleet Street.
☎ 01 308 862 246.
🍎 Taunton Traditional

KNAPP INN (P)
23 Clay Lane
☎ 01 308 862 408
Open all permitted hours
🍎 **Lyme Bay Jack Ratt**
Bar Food lunchtime and
evening.

New Inn (P)
Stoke Abbott.
☎ 01 308 868 333.
🍎 Taunton Traditional

RED LION (P)
The Square
☎ 01 308 862 364
🍎 **Taunton Traditional**
One-bar eighteenth-century
coaching inn. Palmer's ales.
Food lunchtime.

Royal Oak (P)
Hogshill Street.
☎ 01 308 862 418.
🍎 Taunton Traditional

BLANDFORD FORUM

HALF MOON INN (P)
Salisbury Road
☎ 01 747 852 456
Open 11-3, 5-11
🍎 Inch's
Two-bar town pub. Bar food
evening and lunchtime; family
room.

BOURNEMOUTH

Cricketers Arms (P)
4 Wyndham Rd.
☎ 01 202 551 589.
🍎 Bulmers Traditional

FIREFLY & FIRKIN (P)
Holdenhurst Road
☎ 01 202 293 569
Open 10-11
🍎 Weston's
Busy and cavernous Firkin pub
on site of old fire station.
Frequent live bands. Bar food
lunchtime and evening.

HIGH MEAD FARM SHOP (OL)
The Market Gardens, Ham
Lane, Longham
☎ 01 202 574 252
Open Mon-Sat 8.30-5,
Sun 9.30-4
🍎 Gray's
Hard to find: off B3073
between A31 and A347, near
Haskin's Garden Centre.

HOP & KILDERKIN (P)
303 Wimborne Rd, Winton
☎ 01 202 520 277
Open 11-11
🍎 **Bulmers Traditional & Old
Hazy**

Newly-opened Hogshead alehouse in residential area. Promises to start stocking guest ciders from small independent makers. Food to 8pm.

Jug of Ale *(P)*
Old Christchurch Rd.
☎ *01 202 780 260.*
🍎 *Bulmers Traditional*

Manor *(P)*
287 Christchurch Rd.
☎ *01 202 571 087.*
🍎 *Bulmers Traditional*

MOON IN THE SQUARE (P)
4-8 Exeter Road
☎ 01 202 314 940
Open 10.30-11
🍎 **Weston's**
Comfortable Wetherspoon pub on two levels, smoke-free upstairs. Half-a-mile from beach. Bar food lunchtime and evening.

STUDLAND DENE HOTEL (P)
Studland Road
☎ 01 202 765 445
Open 11-2.30, 7-11; all day in summer
🍎 **Thatcher's Farmhouse Dry**
Smart hotel overlooking the sea; restaurant popular with tourists; attractive cliff-top gardens.

BRADFORD ABBAS

ROSE & CROWN (P)
Church Road
☎ 01 935 74506
🍎 **Taunton Traditional**
Quiet one bar fourteenth-century pub. Traditional games include Nine Men's Morris and Shut The Box. Accommodation; bar food lunchtime and evening.

BRIDPORT

CROWN INN (P)
West Bay Road
☎ 01 308 422 037
🍎 **Taunton Traditional**
Prominent pub halfway between town and coast.

The Dairymaid *(OL)*
14A West Street.
☎ *01 308 456 850.*
🍎 *Lyme Bay range*

GREYHOUND (P)
East Street
☎ 01 308 422 944
Open all permitted hours
🍎 **Taunton Traditional**
Large busy town pub popular with younger set

Lord Nelson Hotel *(P)*
East Street.
☎ *01 308 897 302.*
🍎 *Taunton Traditional*

ODDFELLOWS ARMS (P)
North Allington
☎ 01 308 22665
Open 11-2.30, 6.30-11 (11-11 summer)
🍎 **Taunton Traditional**
Small welcoming boozer with no food.

BROADWINDSOR

Broadwinsor Stores *(OL)*
The Square.
☎ *01 308 68200.*
🍎 *Lyme Bay Jack Ratt*

BURTON BRADSTOCK

ANCHOR (P)
High Street
☎ 01 308 897 228
🍎 **Inch's**
Sixteenth-century village inn. Families welcome. Bar food lunchtime and evening.

Bridge Cottage Stores *(OL)*
☎ *01 308 897 222.*
🍎 *Lyme Bay range*

DOVE INN (P)
Southover
☎ 01 308 897 897
Open 11-2.30, 7-11
🍎 **Thatcher's range, Taunton Traditional, Sheppy's**
Attractive three-bar smugglers' inn near the sea. Up to four real ciders and five ales available. Families welcome. Food lunchtime and evening.

CHARMOUTH

Wood Farm Caravan Park Shop (OL)
☎ *01 297 560 431.*
🍎 *Lyme Bay Jack Ratt*

CHETNOLE

CHETNOLE INN (P)
☎ 01 935 872 337
Open 11-2.30, 6.30-11
🍎 **Perry's medium**
Popular village pub opposite church in unspoilt countryside. Excellent range of real ales, good food lunchtime and evening. Disabled access.

CHRISTCHURCH

Ship Inn (P)
48 High Street.
☎ *01 202 484 308.*
🍎 *Bulmers Old Hazy*

CORSCOMBE

FOX INN (P)
☎ 01 935 891 330
Open 12-2.30, 7-11
🍎 **Bridge Farm**
Sixteenth-century thatched stone two-bar village pub. One of a handful of pubs to win an Egon Ronay star for its food. Family room.

CRANBORNE

FLEUR DE LYS (P)
Wimbourne Street
☎ 01 725 517 282
Open 11-3, 6-11
🍎 **Inch's**

Smart two-bar pub with pleasant garden and patio. Bar food evening and lunchtime.

SHEAF OF ARROWS (P)
The Square
☎ 01 725 517 456
Open 11.30-3, 6-11; 11.30-11 Thurs-Sat
🍎 **Old Rascal**
Thriving two-bar local with skittle alley. Beers from small independent brewers. Food lunchtime and evening, accommodation.

DEWLISH

Royal Oak (P)
☎ *01 258 837 352.*
Donhead St Mary
🍎 *Bulmers Traditional*

Donhead Sports Club (C)
☎ *01 747 828 130.*
🍎 *Taunton Traditional*

DORCHESTER

Exhibition Hotel (P)
London Rd.
☎ *01 305 262 360.*
🍎 *Taunton Traditional*

EAST CHALDON

SAILORS RETURN (P)
☎ 01 305 853 847
Open 11(12 Sun)-2.30, 6-11
🍎 **Broadoak**
Quiet pub with separate public bar. Bar food lunchtime and evening.

HAZELBURY BRYAN

ANTELOPE (P)
Pidney
☎ 01 258 817 295
Open 11-3, 5.30-11, 11-11 Sat.
🍎 **Inch's**
Remote, unspoilt, one-bar country pub with real character. Accommodation, disabled access. Hard to find: OS 745 091, off B3134.

IBBERTON

CROWN INN (P)
Church Lane
☎ 01 258 817 448
Open 11-3, 7(5.30 summer)-11
🍎 **Burrow Hill**
Idyllic country pub with
flagstone floor and large
inglenook. Families welcome,
food lunchtime and evening,
disabled access. Hard to find:
nestles under Bulbarrow Hill
four miles SW of A357 from
Shillingstone, OS 788 077.

LANGTON MATRAVERS

KINGS ARMS (P)
High Street
☎ 01 929 422 979
Open 11.30-3 (not Mon), 6.30-11
🍎 **Bulmers Traditional**
Stone-floored pub divided into
several separate areas. Bar food
lunchtime and evenings in
summer.

LAYMORE

SQUIRREL INN (P)
☎ 01 460 30298
Open 11.30-2.30, 6-11.
🍎 **Vickery**
Red-brick pub in the middle of
nowhere with great selection of
ales, accommodation, food
lunchtime and evening,
disabled access. 800 yards off
B3165, OS 387 048.

LITTON CHENEY

WHITE HORSE INN (P)
☎ 01 308 482 539
🍎 **Taunton Traditional**
Village local next to Youth
Hostel. Families welcome; bar
food lunchtime and evening.
Longham Ferndown

HIGH MEAD FARM SHOP (OL)
Ham Lane
🍎 **Gray's**
Produce shop on farm near
Bournemouth noted as a
blueberry producer.

LOWER BURTON

SUN INN (P)
☎ 01 305 250 445
Open 11-2.30, 6.30-11
🍎 **Bulmers Old Hazy**
Bar food lunchtime and
evening; disabled access.

LYME REGIS

Antonio Trattoria (R)
7 Church Street.
☎ *01 297 442 352.*
🍎 *Lyme Bay Jack Ratt*

Buddles (OL)
1 Coombe Street.
☎ *01 297 443 164.*
🍎 *Lyme Bay range*

Cobb Arms (P)
The Cobb.
☎ *01 297 443 242.*
🍎 *Taunton Traditional*

HARBOUR INN (P)
The Cobb
☎ 01 297 442 299
Open all permitted hours
🍎 **Lyme Bay Jack Ratt**
Waterfront pub in renowned
harbour, bar food lunchtime
and evening.

Querns (R)
1 Mill Lane.
☎ *01 297 442 988.*
🍎 *Lyme Bay Jack Ratt &*
Lymelight

Royal Standard (P)
☎ *01 297 89262.*
🍎 *Taunton Traditional*

The Slipway (OL)
The Cobb.
☎ *01 297 442 552.*
🍎 *Lyme Bay range*

Ye Olde Tobacco Shop (OL)
50 Broad Street.
☎ *01 297 445 655.*
🍎 *Lyme Bay range*

MAIDEN NEWTON

Castle Inn (P)
☎ 01 300 320 481.
🍎 *Taunton Traditional*

MILBORNE PORT

QUEEN'S HEAD (P)
High Street
☎ 01 963 250 314
Open 11-3, 5.30-11 Mon-Sat, 12-3, 7-10.30 Sun
🍎 **Taunton Tradition, Bridge Farm, plus guest**
Traditional two-bar village free house with seven real ales including a porter in winter. Old-style pub games, family room, bar food 12-2, 7-9.30. Letting rooms.

NETTLECOMBE

MARQUIS OF LORNE (P)
☎ 01 308 485 236
Open 11-2.30, 6-11.
🍎 **Taunton Traditional**
Jewel in crown of brewer Palmer's of Bridport, sixteenth-century stone inn in shadow of Eggardon Hill (OS 956 517). Excellent food lunchtime and evening, children's play area, accommodation, no-smoking area. It's just a pity that Palmer's will only allow its tenants to stock Taunton products: to complain about this short-sighted policy, and to push the case that traditional craft brewers should support traditional craft cidermakers, write to John Palmer, Chairman, JC & RH Palmer, The Old Brewery, West Bay Road, Bridport, Dorset DT6 4JA.

OKEFORD FITZPAINE

ROYAL OAK (P)
Lower Street
☎ 01 258 860 308
Open 12-2.30, 5.30-11; 11-2.30-6.30-11 sat
🍎 **Taunton Traditional**

Lively stone-floored two-bar pub with skittle alley. Bar food lunchtime and evening.

OSMINGTON MILLS

SMUGGLERS INN (P)
☎ 01 305 833 125
Open 11-2.30, 6.30-11; 11-11 summer
🍎 **Mill House**
Beamed pub on cliff-top near coastal path. Good restaurant, accommodation, disabled access.

PAMPHILL

VINE INN (P)
☎ 01 202 882 259
Open 11-2.30, 7-11
🍎 **Bulmers Traditional, Inch's**
Tiny two-bar country pub off B3082 near National Trust's Kingston Lacy house and estate. Good base for rambles.

PIDDLEHINTON

THIMBLE (P)
☎ 01 300 348 270
Open 12-2.30, 7-11.
🍎 **Thatchers**
Part of the bar of this extended country pub straddles the River Piddle. Beers from many Dorset brewers. Food lunchtime and evening, disabled access.
Poole

HARBOURSIDE BEERS (OL)
The Quay
☎ 01 202 661 515
🍎 **New Forest, Dunkerton's, Cripple Cock, Thatcher's, Broadoak, Really Fowl, many others**
Specialist off-licence in Harbourside Trading craft centre. 70+ British beers, 60 Belgian beers, country wines. Run by CAMRA member.

NEW LONDON TAVERN (P)
63 Langland Street
☎ 01 202 674 760

DORSET

Open 11-4, 6-11 (11-11 summer)
🍺 **Taunton Traditional**
Two-bar local boozer near quayside. Eldridge Pope ales; no food.

Nightcaps (OL)
38 Norrish Rd, Upper Parkstone.
🍺 *Thatchers*

SWEET HOME INN (P)
25 Ringwood Rd, Parkstone
☎ 01 202 676 297
Open 11-2.30, 6-11
🍺 **Inch's**
Two-bar Victorian town pub. Large garden with children's play area. Bar food lunchtime.

Wine Lodge (OL)
84 High Street
☎ *01 202 686 937*
Open 10-5.30, 7-9 sat; 12-2 sun
🍺 *Thatcher's, Countryman*

PORTLAND

CORNER HOUSE (P)
49 Straits, Easton
☎ 01 305 822 526
Open 11-3 6-11
🍺 **Taunton Traditional**
Basic local with awards for cellar skills.

POWERSTOCK

Three Horseshoes (P)
☎ *01 308 85328.*
🍺 *Taunton Traditional*

PULHAM

Halsey Arms (P)
☎ *01 258 817 344.*
🍺 *Taunton Traditional*

PUNCKNOWLE

CROWN INN (P)
Church Street
☎ 01 308 897 711
Open 11-2.30, 7-11
🍺 **Taunton Traditional**
Attractive thatched two-bar inn with extensive menu lunchtime and evening. Families welcome, accommodation, disabled access.

RIMPTON

WHITE POST INN (P)
☎ 01 935 850 717
Open 12-3, 6.30-11
🍺 **Bridge Farm**
Free house on Somerset border commanding fine views. Good value food lunchtime and evening.

ROUSDON

Westhayes Caravan Park Shop (OL)
☎ *01 297 23456.*
🍺 *Lyme Bay range*

SANDFORD ORCAS

MITRE INN (P)
☎ 01 963 220 271
Open 11.30-2.30, 7-11.
🍺 **Bridge Farm**
Flagstone-floored eighteenth-century country local with good food lunchtime and evening (not Mon evening). Accommodation, disabled access.

SHAFTESBURY

FARMER BAILEY'S CHEESE CENTRE (OL)
High Street
☎ 01 747 851 288
Open 9-5 Mon-sat
🍺 **Rosie's**
Main deli in breathtaking hilltop town.

FOUNTAIN INN (P)
Breach Lane, Enmore Green.
☎ 01 747 52062
Open 11-2, 6.30-11; 11-11 Sat
🍺 **Taunton Traditional**
Comfortable pub with younger clientele and skittle alley.

KINGS ARMS (P)
Bleke Street
☎ 01 747 852 746
Open all permitted hours
🍺 **Inch's**

One-bar pub with coffee-shop in summer. Bar food lunchtime and evening.

SHIP INN (P)
Bleke Street
☎ 01 747 853 219
Open 11-3, 5-11 Mon-Wed; 11-11 Thurs-sat
🍎 **Taunton Traditional**
Ancient three-roomed wood-panelled pub. Bar food lunchtime and evening; children welcome.

SHERBORNE

DIGBY TAP (P)
Cooks Lane
☎ 01 935 813 148
Open 11-2.30, 5.30-11
🍎 **Taunton Traditional**
Basic beerhouse in former hotel tap-room. Stone floors and wood panelled walls. Big ale range. Food Mon-Sat lunchtimes. Families welcome.

Greyhound (P)
Cheap Street.
☎ *01 935 812 785.*
🍎 *Inch's*

SOUTHBOURNE

Grange Hotel (P)
Overcliffe Drive.
☎ *01 202 433 093.*
🍎 *Bulmers Traditional*

SOUTH PERROTT

Coach & Horses (P)
☎ *01 935 89270.*
🍎 *Taunton Traditional*

SWANAGE

Bankes Arms Hotel (P)
Beach Rd, Studland.
☎ *01 929 44225.*
🍎 *Bulmers Old Hazy*

RED LION (P)
High Street
☎ 01 929 423 533
Open 11-11
🍎 **Bulmers Traditional**

Down-to-earth two-bar pub, where all beers and cider are dispensed by gravity. Food lunchtime and Fr-Sat evening. Children's room.

SYMONDSBURY

ILCHESTER ARMS (P)
☎ 01 308 422 600
Open 11-3, 7-11.
🍎 **Taunton Traditional**
Stone-flagged village pub with skittle alley, accommodation, food lunchtime and evening, disabled access.

WAREHAM

Antelope Inn (P)
13 West Street.
☎ *01 929 552 827.*
🍎 *Bulmers Old Hazy*

QUAY INN (P)
The Quay
☎ 01 929 552 735
Open 11-3, 7-11; longer in summer
🍎 **Bulmers Old Hazy**
Pleasant two-bar food-oriented pub in picturesque setting. Bar food lunchtime and evening; letting rooms.

WEST STAFFORD

Wise Man (P)
☎ *01 305 263 694.*
🍎 *Taunton Traditional*

WEYMOUTH

Alexandra Inn (P)
Charlestown.
☎ *01 305 783 250.*
🍎 *Taunton Traditional*

Boot (P)
High St West, North Quay.
☎ *01 305 786 793.*
🍎 *Taunton Traditional*

DORSET BREWERS (P)
33 Hope Street
☎ 01 305 786 940
Open 11-11
🍎 **Taunton Traditional**

Basic old pub opposite former Devenish brewery. Food lunchtime.

Duke of Albany *(P)*
Park Street.
☎ *01 305 786 328.*
🍎 *Taunton Traditional*

Duke of Cornwall *(P)*
St Edmunds Street.
☎ *01 305 786 593.*
🍎 *Taunton Traditional*

King's Arms *(P)*
Trinity Rd.
☎ *01 305 770 055.*
🍎 *Taunton Traditional*

New Bridge Hotel *(P)*
14 Westham Rd.
☎ *01 305 782 323.*
🍎 *Bulmers Traditional*

Rock Hotel *(P)*
41 Abbotsbury Rd.
☎ *01 305 784 563.*
🍎 *Taunton Traditional*

WHITCHURCH CANONICORUM

FIVE BELLS (P)
☎ 01 297 489 262
Open 12-3, 6-11
🍎 **Taunton Traditional**
Food lunchtime and evening. Disabled access.

WIMBORNE MINSTER

Albion *(P)*
High Street.
☎ *01 202 882 492.*
🍎 *Taunton Traditional*

WORTH MATRAVERS

SQUARE & COMPASSES (P)
☎ 01 929 439 229
Open 11-3, 6-11; 11-11 Sat.
🍎 **Bulmers Traditional, Inch's, Thatcher's**
Stone sculptures, fossils, and beach finds decorate fine pub with sea views. In same family since 1904. No smoking area. Ring ahead for campsite.

UPLYME

UPLYME BUTCHERS (OL)
Lyme Road
☎ 01 297 443 236
🍎 **Lyme Bay range**
An off-licence that is also a butcher's shop – stocks Real Meat Co products as well as real cider!

YETMINSTER

Railway Inn *(P)*
Station Approach.
☎ *01 935 872 622.*
🍎 *Taunton Traditional*

Co Durham

BISHOP AUCKLAND

TAP & SPILE (P)
13 Cockton Hill Road
☎ 01 388 602 550
Open 11-3, 6-11; 11-11 Fri/Sat
🍎 **Crone's**
Big on games: shove-ha'penny, table skittles etc. Quieter lounge. Changing range of ales. Disabled access.

CHESTER-LE-STREET

Railway Hotel *(P)*
Durham Rd.
☎ *0191 410 3561.*
🍎 *Bulmers Traditional*

DARLINGTON

TAP & SPILE (P)
99 Bondgate
☎ 01 325 381 679
Open all permitted hours
🍎 **Weston's Old Rosie, Bulmers Old Hazy**
Alehouse-style pub with no-smoking family room, bar food Mon-Sat lunchtime.

Pennyweight *(P)*
Bakehouse Hill.
☎ *01 325 464 244.*
🍎 *Bulmers Old Hazy*

DURHAM

Big Jug (OL)
88 Claypath.
☎ *0191 384 8354.*
🍺 *Bulmers Traditional*

BREWER & FIRKIN (P)
58 Saddler Street
☎ 0191 386 4134
Open 12-11.
🍺 **Weston's Old Rosie**
Popular young people's
alehouse with live music and
discounted drinks for CAMRA
members.

Garden House (P)
North Rd.
☎ *0191 384 0273.*
🍺 *Bulmers Old Hazy*

Market Tavern (P)
Market Place.
☎ *0191 386 2069.*
🍺 *Bulmers Traditional*

FRAMWELLGATE MOOR

TAP & SPILE (P)
27 Front Street
☎ 0191 386 5451
Open 11.30-3, 6-11
🍺 **Westons Old Rosie**
A Tap & Spile since 1988, three-
room pub with family room
and no smoking area.

NEWTON AYCLIFFE

Leisure Centre (C)
Beveridge Arcade, Dalton Way.
☎ *01 325 300 800.*
🍺 *Bulmers Old Hazy*

NO PLACE

BEAMISH MARY INN (P)
☎ 0191 370 0237
Open 12-3, 6-11; 12-11 Fri/Sat
🍺 **Cider range varies**
Former national Pub of the
Year named after long-gone
local colliery. Live music in
converted stables, guest ales,
and house beer brewed by Big
Lamp. Disabled access.

Essex

BRENTWOOD

FOUNTAIN HEAD (P)
155 Ingrave Road
☎ 01 277 212 151
Open all permitted hours
🍺 **Thatcher's Medium,
Cheddar Valley, Weston's
perry**
Local with trade from nearby
golf course, with traditional
pub games including table
skittles. Six real ales include
two from Crouch Vale.
Food 12-3.

Swan (P)
123 High Street.
☎ *01 277 211 848.*
🍺 *Bulmers Old Hazy*

BRIGHTLINGSEA

RAILWAY TAVERN (P)
58 Station Road
☎ 01 206 302 581
Open 5-11; 12-11 Fri/Sat
🍺 **Theobolds**
Popular two-bar local with
railway mementos. Families
welcome, disabled access.

BUCKHURST HILL

Queens (P)
Queens Rd.
☎ *0181 504 4796.*
🍺 *Taunton Traditional*

COLCHESTER

HOGSHEAD (KINGS ARMS)
(P)
63 Crouch Street
☎ 01 206 572 886
Open 11-11
🍺 **Bulmers Old Hazy**
Spacious single-bar local, food
lunchtime and evening.
Disabled access.

ODD ONE OUT (P)
28 Mersea Road

☎ 01 206 578 140
Open 4.30-11; 11-11 Fri-Sat
🍎 **Crone's, Old Cove**
Friendly two-bar real ale pub
with no-smoking area.

Seige House (P)
75 East Street.
☎ *01 206 867 121.*
🍎 *Bulmers Traditional*

TAP & SPILE (P)
125 Crouch Street
☎ 01 206 573 572
Open 11-2.30, 5.30-11; 11-11 Sat
🍎 **Crone's**
Pleasant one-bar pub just
outside centre. Four regular
real ales, five guests. Food
lunchtime.

DAGENHAM

Beacon & Tree (P)
715 Green Lane.
🍎 *Bulmers Traditional*

Davisons (OL)
Long Bridge Rd.
🍎 *Bulmers Traditional*

EPPING

FOREST GATE (P)
Bell Common
☎ 01 999 572 312
Open 10-2.30, 5.30-11; 12-3, 7-
10.30 Sun
🍎 **Bulmers Traditional**
Traditional small bar on the
very edge of Epping Forest.
Food lunchtime and evening.

HALSTEAD

PHEASANT (P)
Audley End, Gestingthorpe
☎ 01 787 61196
🍎 **Castlings Heath Cottage
Cider**
Traditional two-bar pub with a
range of real ales and bar food
lunchtime and evening.
Families welcome.

HATFIELD HEATH

WHITE HORSE INN (P)
The Heath
☎ 01 279 730 351
Open 11-3, 5-11
🍎 **Matching**
Three-bar pub overlooking
village green where cricket is
still played. Bar food lunchtime
and evening (not Sun).

LAYER DE LA HAYE

Kingsford Park Hotel (P)
☎ *01 206 34301.*
🍎 *Bulmers Old Hazy*

LEIGH-ON-SEA

ELMS (P)
London Road
Open all permitted hours
🍎 **Weston's Old Rosie**
Large comfortable
Wetherspoon pub.

LOUGHTON

LAST POST (P)
227 High Road
☎ 0181 532 0751
Open all permitted hours
🍎 **Weston's Old Rosie**
Wetherspoon pub in former
main post office. Food all day.

NAVESTOCK HEATH

PLOUGH INN (P)
Sabines Road
☎ 01 277 372 296
Open 11-3.30, 6-11.
🍎 **Bulmers Old Hazy**
Great real ale pub with 11
handpumps. Local pub of the
year 1992-5. Families welcome.
Bar food lunchtime and
evening. Disabled access. Hard
to find: OS 538 970.

PLESHEY

WHITE HORSE (P)
The Street
☎ 01 245 237 281
Open 11-3, 7-11

Matching

Pleasant rambling old pub in picturesque village. Families welcome. Bar food lunchtime and evening.

RAYLEIGH

Crown (P)
84 High Street.
☎ *01 268 742 340.*
Bulmers Traditional

ROCHFORD

GOLDEN LION (P)
35 North Street
☎ 01 702 545 487
Open all permitted hours
Rich's
Frequent local pub of the year award-winner. A 300-year-old former tailor's shop, bar food lunchtime, separate restaurant lunchtime. Families welcome.

RUNCTON

Runcton Farm Shop (OL)
Lagnes Rd.
☎ *01 243 787 847.*
Bulmers Traditional

SOUTHEND

BAKER'S BAR (P)
15-17 Alexandra Street
☎ 01 702 390 403
Open 12-12 Mon-Thurs, noon-1am Fri/Sat
Thatchers Medium, Chiddingstone Dry
Former bakery in basement, now a very popular town-centre venue.

CORK & CHEESE (P)
10 Talza Way, Victoria Circus
☎ 01 702 616 914
Open 11-11 Mon-Sat
Cheddar Valley and Weston's Old Rosie are regulars; guests include Biddenden, Ben Crossman, Topp's, Bulmers Traditional
Local pub of the year 1995 and 1996. Busy town centre pub,

food lunchtime. Near BR and bus stations.

Guildford (P)
Sutton Rd.
Biddenden

LAST POST (P)
Weston Road
Open 10-11
Weston's range
Another old post office-turned Wetherspoon. Food lunchtime, disabled access.

Leo's Superstore (OL)
55 Sutton Road
☎ *01 702 613 264*
Open 8-8
Weston's

LIBERTY BELLE (P)
10-12 Marine Parade
☎ 01 702 466 936
Open 10-11.
Cider range varies
Right on the seafront, a maverick with loads of real ales including many from independent brewers. Accommodation. Families welcome.

SUNROOMS (P)
20 Market Place
☎ 01 702 436 661
11am-midnight
Old Hazy on handpump, also cidre Breton in litre bottles
Lively young people's pub with loos worth a visit in themselves. Bar food lunchtime and evening.

SUTTON ARMS (P)
Southchurch Road
☎ 01 702 611 023
Open all permitted hours
Bulmers Traditional
Lively town pub, bar food lunchtime.

SOUTH FAMBRIDGE

ANCHOR HOTEL (P)
Fambridge Road
☎ 01 702 203 535

Open 11-3, 6-11; 11-11 Sat.
🍎 **Addlestone's**
Traditional free house with
good range of ales. Food till 9.

SOUTHMINSTER

STATION ARMS (P)
39 Station Road
☎ 01 621 772 225
12-3, 5.30-11 Mon-Fri, 11-11 Sat.
🍎 **Biddenden**
Weatherboarded High St
pub/restaurant. Good food
and ale. Restaurant open
evenings only, closed
Wed/Sun.

STOCK

HOOP (P)
21 High Street
☎ 01 227 841 137
Open 10-11
🍎 **Rich's**
Very popular small pub with
good food lunchtime and
evening.

STOW MARIES

PRINCE OF WALES (P)
Woodham Road
☎ 01 621 828 971
Open 11-11
🍎 **Theobolds**
Beautifully restored rural gem
run by living legend Rob
Walster who also runs well-
known real ale wholesale
company. Excellent food
lunchtime and evening.
Children welcome.

TILLINGHAM

CAP & FEATHERS (P)
8 South Street
☎ 01 621 779 212
Open 11.20-3, 6-11
🍎 **Thatcher's**
Unspoilt fifteenth-century inn
owned by Crouch Vale
brewery. Own smoke-house for
fish and meat. Bar food
evening and lunchtime. Former
national pub of the year. Bar

skittles, shove ha'penny, bar
billiards. Family room, no-
smoking area. Three letting
rooms.

WITHAM

White Hart Hotel *(P)*
Newland Rd.
☎ *01 376 512 245.*
🍎 *Bulmers Traditional*

WOODFORD GREEN

GALE'S WINE MERCHANT
(OL)
204 High Road
☎ 0181 504 9347
Open 10-10 Mon-Sat, 11-3, 6-10
Sun
🍎 **Weston's perry, Rich's,
Biddenden, James White**
Very old-fashioned off-licence,
also sells real ale.

Gloucestershire

ALDERTON

Hob Nails Inn *(P)*
Little Washbourne.
☎ *01 242 620 237.*
🍎 *Bulmers Traditional*

ARLINGHAM

RED LION (P)
The Cross
☎ 01 452 740 269
Open 12-3, 7-11; 11-11 Sat
🍎 **Bulmers Traditional**
Large two-bar village pub,
partly sixteenth-century. Food
lunchtime and evening.

ASHCHURCH

Dowty Sports Club *(C)*
☎ *01 684 852 047.*
🍎 *Bulmers Traditional*

ASHLEWORTH

BOAT INN (P)
The Quay
☎ 01 452 700 272

Open 11-3, 6-11 summer, 11-2.30, 7-11 winter
🍎 **Weston's range**
Fifteenth-century riverside pub near medieval tithe barn. Bar food lunchtime.

AYLEBURTON

Cross Inn (P)
☎ *01 594 842 823.*
🍎 *Bulmers Traditional*

BERKELEY

Pier View Hotel (P)
34 Old Minster Rd.
☎ *01 453 811 255.*
🍎 *Bulmers Traditional*

BISHOPS CLEEVE

SWALLOW (P)
Bishops Drive
☎ 01 242 674 861
Open all permitted hours
🍎 **Minchew's range inc perry**
1950s local, food lunchtime and evening (but booking advisable).

BLAISDON

RED HART (P)
Longhope
☎ 01 452 830 477
Open 12-3 6-11; 12-3, 7-10.30 Sun
🍎 **Bulmers Traditional, Weston's range plus guests**
Local and regional pub of the year with constantly changing range of real ales. Food lunchtime and evenings except Sun. Separate restaurant. Disabled access. Children's certificate. Camping site. Traditional pub games.

BLAKENEY

Kings Head (P)
High Street.
☎ *01 594 510 336.*
🍎 *Bulmers Traditional*

BLEDINGTON

KING'S HEAD (P)
☎ 01 608 658 365
Open 11-2.30, 6-11; 12-2.30, 7-10.30 Sun
🍎 **Inch's**
Delightful sixteenth-century stone-built pub overlooking village green. Reputation for food: book at weekends. Families welcome.

BOURTON-ON-THE-WATER

Bourton Rovers FC (C)
Rissington Rd.
☎ *01 451 821 977.*
🍎 *Bulmers Traditional*

British Legion Club (C)
The Naight.
☎ *01 451 820 478.*
🍎 *Bulmers Traditional*

Duke of Wellington (P)
Sherbourne Street.
☎ *01 451 820 539.*
🍎 *Bulmers Traditional*

BREDON

Fox & Hounds (P)
Church Street.
☎ *01 684 72377.*
🍎 *Bulmers Traditional*

Royal Oak (P)
Main Rd.
☎ *01 684 72393.*
🍎 *Bulmers Traditional*

BRINCOMBE

Kings Arms (P)
Bourne Lane.
☎ *01 453 882 552.*
🍎 *Bulmers Traditional*

BROAD CAMPDEN

BAKERS ARMS (P)
☎ 01 386 840 515
Open 11.30-3, 5.30-11
🍎 **Bulmers Traditional**
Fine old Cotswold country pub, stone-built and oak-

beamed, specialising in locally-brewed ales. Food lunchtime and evening.

BROADWELL

Rising Sun (P)
4 Poolway Rd.
☎ *01 594 833 428.*
🍎 *Bulmers Traditional*

BROCKWEIR

BROCKWEIR COUNTRY INN (P)
☎ 01 291 689 548
Open 12-2.30, 6-11.
🍎 **Bulmers Traditional**
Unspoilt pub on banks of River Wye, with oak beams from a locally-built ship. Families welcome, accommodation, food lunchtime and evening.

CHALFORD

NEW RED LION (P)
High Street
☎ 01 453 882 384
Open all permitted hours Mon-Sat, 12-4, 7-10.30 Sun
🍎 **Weston's range**
Cotswold stone pub circa 1700 in wooded valley. On Thames/Severn Canal walk. Home-cooked food lunch and evening, real ales, no smoking area.

CHELTENHAM

BAYSHILL INN (P)
St George's Place
☎ 01 242 524 388
Open 11-3, 5-11; 11-11 Sat
🍎 **Bulmers Traditional**
Popular no-frills town pub near bus station. Changing guest ales, food lunchtime.

BEEHIVE (P)
Montpelier Villas
☎ 01 242 579 443

Open 12-11; 12-3, 7-10.30 Sun.
🍎 **Minchews ciders and perry**
Old-style local, no jukebox or fruit machines. Bar food 12-2, 6-9.

Beaufort Arms (P)
184 London Rd.
☎ *01 242 526 038.*
🍎 *Bulmers Traditional*

Cassidy's (P)
40 Swindon Rd.
☎ *01 242 523 645.*
🍎 *Bulmers Traditional*

CLUNY'S WINE SHOP (OL)
1 Whaddon Road
☎ 01 242 238 058
Open 4-10 weekdays, 12-10 Sat, 12-2, 7-9 Sun
🍎 **Weston's, Inch's. Draught to order**
Privately-owned lock-up – Peter Emery's promise: "If I haven't got it, I'll get it."

Dawn Run (P)
14 Albion Street.
☎ *01 242 521 054.*
🍎 *Bulmers Traditional*

Kings Arms (P)
140 Gloucester Rd.
☎ *01 242 511 198.*
🍎 *Bulmers Traditional*

Prince of Wales (P)
11 Portland Street.
☎ *01 242 234 044.*
🍎 *Bulmers Traditional*

Shakespeare Inn (P)
386 High Street.
☎ *01 242 513 685.*
🍎 *Bulmers Traditional*

SUFFOLK ARMS (P)
Suffolk Road
☎ 01 242 524 713
Open 11.30-11
🍎 **Thatchers**
Friendly one-bar local on outer ring road. Food lunchtime and evening.

Tut 'n Shive (P)
2 Rotunda Terrace.
☎ 01 242 583 205.
🍎 Bulmers Old Hazy

WHOLE HOG (P)
Montpelier Walk
☎ 01 242 523 431
Open 11-11
🍎 **Bulmers Old Hazy &
Traditional**
Bareboard alehouse with
serious real ale range. Food
lunchtime and all day Sat/Sun.

CHIPPING CAMPDEN

British Legion Club (C)
High Street.
☎ 01 386 840 676.
🍎 Bulmers Traditional

Ebrington Arms (P)
Ebrington.
☎ 01 386 593 223.
🍎 Bulmers Traditional

Red Lion (P)
High Street.
☎ 01 386 840 760.
🍎 Bulmers Traditional

VOLUNTEER (P)
Lower High Street
☎ 01 386 840 688
Open 11.30-3, 7-11
🍎 **Bulmers Old Hazy**
Early eighteenth-century stone
pub near centre of archetypal
Cotswold town. Superb range
of ales. Accommodation, food
lunchtime and evening,
disabled access.

CINDERFORD

Belfry (P)
Littledean.
☎ 01 594 827 858.
🍎 Taunton Traditional

Mount Pleasant Inn (P)
St Whites Rd.
☎ 01 594 826 927.
🍎 Bulmers Traditional

Nags Head (P)
Church Rd.
☎ 01 594 822 315.
🍎 Bulmers Traditional

Railway Hotel (P)
Station Street.
☎ 01 594 822 064.
🍎 Bulmers Traditional

Royal Forresters Inn (P)
Littledean Hill.
☎ 01 594 822 034.
🍎 Bulmers Traditional

Upper Bilson Inn (P)
30 Valley Rd.
☎ 01 594 826 522.
🍎 Bulmers Traditional

CIRENCESTER

Brewers Arms (P)
70 Cricklade Street.
☎ 01 285 653 763.
🍎 Bulmers Traditional

Waggon & Horses (P)
London Rd.
☎ 01 285 652 022.
🍎 Taunton Traditional

CLEARWELL

LAMB (P)
The Cross, High Street
☎ 01 594 835 441
Open 12-3, 7-11.
🍎 **Bulmers Traditional plus
occasional guests**
Splendid range of ales in 200-
year-old two-bar pub built to
serve local ironminers. Food
lunchtime and evening.

COLEFORD

Feathers (P)
Market Place.
☎ 01 453 758 931.
🍎 Bulmers Traditional

Millwall District Social Club
(C)
Millwall.
☎ 01 594 33253.
🍎 Bulmers Traditional

OSTRICH INN (P)
Newland
☎ 01 594 833 260
Open 12-2.30, 6.30-11; 12-3,
6.30-10,30 Sun
🍎 **Weston's range**
Traditional thirteenth-century
village inn specialising in cask
ales and ciders and home-
cooked food. Two letting
rooms.

Pike House (P)
Berry Hill.
☎ *01 594 833 010.*
🍎 *Bulmers Traditional*

Rising Sun (P)
Five Acres.
☎ *01 594 832 283.*
🍎 *Bulmers Old Hazy*

CONDERTON

YEW TREE (P)
☎ 01 386 725 363
Open 12-3, 6-11; all permitted
hours Sun
🍎 **Minchew's cider and perry,
Weston's range**
Sixteenth-century beamed pub
with open fire, flagstone floor.
Good real ale range. Games
include table skittles, shove
ha'penny.

DRYBROOK

Hearts of Oak (P)
The Cross.
☎ *01 594 544 001.*
🍎 *Bulmers Traditional*

Swan Inn (P)
Brierley.
☎ *01 594 860 460.*
🍎 *Bulmers Traditional*

DURSLEY

Carpenters Arms (P)
Uley Rd.
01 453 542 023.
🍎 *Bulmers Traditional*

Royal British Legion (C)
May Lane.
☎ *01 453 542 530.*
🍎 *Taunton Traditional*

FRAMPTON-ON-SEVERN

THREE HORSESHOES (P)
The Green
☎ 01 452 740 463
Open all permitted hours
🍎 **Weston's range, plus bottled
ciders**
Real old village pub with open
fires, cask ales, traditional
games, food lunchtime and
evenings.

FORTHAMPTON

LOWER LODE HOTEL (P)
☎ 01 684 293 224
Open 12-3, 6-11; all permitted
hours Sat/Sun
🍎 **Weston's Scrumpy Supreme**
Fifteenth-century riverside pub
with five real ales. Bar food
lunchtime. Four letting rooms.
Caravan/campsite.

GLOUCESTER

Bristol Hotel (P)
Bristol Rd.
☎ *01 452 528 232.*
🍎 *Bulmers Old Hazy*

County Arms (P)
Millbrook Street.
☎ *01 452 522 505.*
🍎 *Bulmers Traditional*

Duke of Wellington (P)
72 Tredworth Rd.
☎ *01 452 520 503.*
🍎 *Bulmers Traditional*

Queens Head (P)
68 Kingsholm Rd.
☎ *01 452 413 344.*
🍎 *Bulmers Traditional*

GUITING POWER

Farmers Arms (P)
☎ *01 451 850 358.*
🍎 *Bulmers Traditional*

HAYDENS ELM

HOUSE IN THE TREE (P)
☎ 01 242 680 241
Open all permitted hours
🍎 **Own-label ciders plus
Bulmers Traditional, Inch's,
and occasionally Minchew's**
Locals' two-bar pub which sells
more cider than beer. Food
lunchtime and evening.

LEONARD STANLEY

White Hart (P)
The Street.
☎ *01 453 822 702.*
🍎 *Bulmers Traditional*

LOWER SWELL

GOLDEN BALL (P)
☎ 01 451 830 247
Open 11-3, 6-11; 12-3,
7-10.30 Sun
🍎 **Weston's GWR, Bounds
Brand, perry**
Seventeenth-century Cotswold
delight, even has ale from local
Donnington brewery. Home-
cooked food lunchtime and
evening, watch out for the
ham! No-smoking area. Three
letting rooms. Traditional
games include Aunt Sally.

LYDBROOK

Jovial Collier (P)
Upper Lydbrook.
☎ *01 594 860 068.*
🍎 *Bulmers Traditional*

LYDNEY

Highland Inn (P)
Tutnall Street.
☎ *01 594 842 662.*
🍎 *Bulmers Traditional*

Miners Arms (P)
Whitecroft.
☎ *01 594 562 483.*
🍎 *Bulmers Traditional*

VINEY

**St Swithin's Sports & Social
Club** (C)
St Swithin's Rd, Viney.
☎ *01 594 510 658.*
🍎 *Bulmers Traditional*

Woodman (P)
Parkend.
☎ *01 594 563 273.*
🍎 *Bulmers Traditional*

MICHELDEAN

White Horse (P)
High Street.
☎ *01 594 542 375.*
🍎 *Bulmers Traditional*

MICKLETON

Butchers Arms (P)
Chapel Lane.
☎ *01 386 438 285.*
🍎 *Bulmers Old Hazy*

Kings Arms (P)
High Street.
☎ *01 386 438 257.*
🍎 *Bulmers Traditional*

MORETON-IN-MARSH

Royal British Legion (C)
Station Approach.
☎ *01 608 50580.*
🍎 *Bulmers Traditional*

Wellington (P)
London Rd.
☎ *01 608 650 836.*
🍎 *Bulmers Traditional*

NAILSWORTH

Crown Inn (P)
☎ *01 453 832 498.*
🍎 *Bulmers Traditional*

NEWNHAM-ON-SEVERN

BIRD'S (OL)
9 High Street.
☎ 01 594 516 211
Open 9-30 8 Mon-Thurs, 9.30-
8.30 Fri/Sat, closed Sun
🍎 **Weston's inc perry,**

Thatchers, Dunkerton's, Inch's, Biddenden range
Wow! Wine merchants in seventeenth-century timber-framed delight with deli snacks and cider list to die for. Also as wide a collection of bottled UK beers as anywhere.

Newnham Club (C)
High Street.
☎ *01 594 516 379.*
🍏 *Bulmers Traditional*

RAILWAY (P)
Station Road
☎ 01 594 516 317
Open 5-11; 11-11 Sat
🍏 **Inch's**
Friendly pub with food in the evening. Closed lunchtime Mon-Fri.

NORTH NIBLEY

Black Horse Inn (P)
Barrs Lane.
☎ *01 453 546 841.*
🍏 *Bulmers Traditional*

OVERBURY

OVERBURY FAYRE (OL)
☎ 01 386 725 340
Open 10-9; 9-9 Sun
🍏 **Minchew's and others**
Traditional store with tea-room and deli in stone and black-and-white village.

PAINSWICK

Falcon Inn (P)
New Street.
☎ *01 452 812 189.*
🍏 *Bulmers Traditional*

POPE'S HILL

GREYHOUND (P)
☎ 01 452 760 344
Open 11-3.30, 5.30-11
🍏 **Bulmers Traditional or Inch's**
Olde-worlde pub with good real ale range, food lunchtime and evening, disabled access. Families welcome. On A4151.

PRESTBURY

Beehive Inn (P)
33 Bouncers Lane.
☎ *01 242 224 741.*
🍏 *Bulmers Traditional*

PUCKLECHURCH

STAR (P)
37 Castle Road
Open all permitted hours
🍏 **Taunton Traditional plus guests**
One of the area's best-known cider houses. Jellied eels a speciality.

RUSPIDGE

NEW INN (P)
☎ 01 594 824 508
Open 7-11; 11-11 Sat
🍏 **Bulmers Traditional**
Basic village pub with good selection of traditional games. Beers from small independent brewers. Closed daytime in the week.

ST BRIAVELS

Crown Inn (P)
Pystol Lane.
☎ *01 594 530 205.*
🍏 *Bulmers Traditional*

SAPPERTON

BELL INN (P)
☎ 01 285 760 298
Open 11-2.30, 6.30-11
🍏 **Weston's Old Rosie**
Large two-bar village free house. Food lunch and evening.

DANEWAY INN (P)
Daneway
☎ 01 285 760 297
Open 11-2.30, 6.30-11
🍏 **Taunton Traditional**
Superb old inn set at western end of disused but legendary Sapperton canal tunnel. Magnificent fireplace in lounge. No-smoking family

room, large garden. Food lunchtime and evening. Hard to find: OS 939 034.

SHURDINGTON

Bell Inn (P)
Main Rd.
☎ 01 242 862 245.
🍎 *Bulmers Traditional*

SHORTSTANDING

New Inn (P)
☎ 01 594 810 311.
🍎 *Bulmers Traditional*

SLAD

WOOLPACK INN (P)
Butterow
☎ 01 452 813 429
Open 12-3, 6-11.
🍎 **Bulmers Traditional, Weston's Old Rosie, bottled ciders**
Three-bar pub built 1640 and still comparatively unmodernised. Five real ales, food lunch and evening. No juke box; games in cellar. Every literate cider-lover should drink Old Rosie in Laurie Lee's home village.

SLING

MINER'S ARMS (P)
☎ 01 594 836 632
Open 11-11
🍎 **Freeminer own-label ciders, Bulmers Traditional**
Village pub belonging to local Freeminer brewery which has its own cider made for it, and plans to make its own. Also boasts large selection of whiskies and foreign bottled beers. Huge sandwiches, food lunchtime and evening. Disabled access.

Montague Inn (P)
Clements End Rd.
☎ 01 594 833 830.
🍎 *Bulmers Traditional*

Orepool Inn (P)
☎ 01 594 833 277.
🍎 *Taunton Traditional, Bulmers Traditional*

STAVERTON

Pheasant Inn (P)
Cheltenham Rd.
☎ 01 452 713 246.
🍎 *Bulmers Old Hazy*

STINCHCOMBE

Yew Tree (P)
The Quarry.
☎ 01 453 542 612.
🍎 *Bulmers Traditional*

STONEHOUSE

Globe (P)
High Street.
☎ 01 453 822 567.
🍎 *Bulmers Traditional*

Kings Head (P)
Eastington.
☎ 01 453 822 934.
🍎 *Bulmers Traditional*

Royal Arms (P)
38 Bath Rd.
☎ 01 453 822 718.
🍎 *Bulmers Traditional*

Ship Inn (P)
Bristol Rd.
☎ 01 453 823 829.
🍎 *Bulmers Traditional*

SPA INN (P)
Oldends Lane
☎ 01 453 822 327
Open 12-3, 7-11
🍎 **Bulmers Traditional**
Cosy local, busy at lunchtime with custom from adjoining industrial estate. Food lunchtime and evening. Quoits and outdoor skittles played.

STOW-ON-THE-WOLD

Bell Inn (P)
Park Street.
☎ 01 451 30663.
🍎 *Bulmers Traditional*

British Legion (C)
Union Street.
☎ *01 451 830 242.*
🍎 *Bulmers Traditional*

QUEEN'S HEAD (P)
Off main square
☎ *01 451 830 563*
Open 11-2.30, 6-11
🍎 **Weston's**
Popular inn in beautiful
Cotswold town. Donnington
ales. Food lunchtime and some
evenings.

White Hart (P)
The Square.
☎ *01 451 830 674.*
🍎 *Taunton Traditional*

STROUD

Butchers Arms (P)
Sheepscombe.
☎ *01 452 812 113.*
🍎 *Bulmers Traditional*

Cross Hands (P)
Summer Street.
☎ *01 453 763 147.*
🍎 *Bulmers Traditional*

Horse & Groom (P)
Parliament Street,
Upper Leazes.
☎ *01 453 757 082.*
🍎 *Bulmers Traditional*

Old Neighbourhood (P)
Chalford Hill.
☎ *01 453 883 385.*
🍎 *Bulmers Traditional*

PELICAN (P)
Union Street
☎ *01 453 763 817*
Open 11.30-11
🍎 **Bulmers Traditional**
Popular pub close to covered
market. Big range of real ales;
own 50-seat theatre; live music
twice a week. Food lunchtime.

Queen Victoria (P)
Gloucester Street.
☎ *01 453 756 827.*
🍎 *Bulmers Old Hazy*

TETBURY

Crown Inn (P)
12 Gumstool Hill.
☎ *01 666 502 496.*
🍎 *Bulmers Old Hazy*

Greyhound (P)
3 Hampton Street.
☎ *01 666 502 611.*
🍎 *Bulmers Old Hazy*

United Services Club (C)
Chipping Street.
☎ *01 666 502 647.*
🍎 *Taunton Traditional*

TEWKESBURY

Crown Inn (P)
High Street.
☎ *01 386 725 293.*
🍎 *Bulmers Traditional*

HEN & CHICKS (R)
73 Church Street
☎ *01 684 292 703*
Open 10-5 Tues-Thurs, Sun; 7-
10.30 Fri/Sat
🍎 **Minchew's**
Half-timbered fifteenth-century
restaurant opposite famous
Norman abbey. Cider and
perry much used in cooking.
Disabled access.

Kings Head (P)
Barton Street.
☎ *01 684 293 267.*
🍎 *Bulmers Traditional*

WHITE BEAR (P)
Bredon Road
☎ *01 684 296 614*
Open 11-3, 6.30-11; 11-11 Sat
🍎 **Bulmers Traditional**
Basic one bar pub with Wye
Valley ales from Hereford.
Disabled access.

Town Crest Club (C)
East Street.
☎ *01 684 292 086.*
🍎 *Bulmers Traditional*

TREDWORTH

Plough Inn (P)
Upton.
☎ *01 452 382 540.*
🍎 *Taunton Traditional*

Victory (P)
167 High Street.
☎ *01 452 528 221.*
🍎 *Bulmers Traditional*

TWYNING

FLEET INN (P)
☎ 01 684 274 310
Open all permitted hours
🍎 **Weston's range**
Idyllic fifteenth-century
riverside pub with six real ales,
food all day. Separate public
bar, three dining rooms. No
smoking areas, disabled access.
2 miles Tewkesbury, 3 miles
from M50 J3.

WATERLEY BOTTOM

NEW INN (P)
☎ 01 453 543 659
Open 12-2.30, 7-11
🍎 **Inch's**
Cotleigh and other real ales in
beautiful setting. Regional pub
of the year 1993. Food
lunchtime and evening;
accommodation.

WINCHCOMBE

BELL INN (P)
Gretton Street
☎ 01 242 602 205
Open 11-11
🍎 **Bulmers Traditional**
Superb range of real ales in
friendly local. Accommodation;
food at lunchtime.

OLDE CORNER CUPBOARD (P)
Gloucester Street
☎ 01 242 602 303
Open 11-2.30, 5.30-11
🍎 **Weston's range, Bulmers
Traditional**
Sixteenth-century inn in classic
Cotswold town. Bar food lunch

and evening. Self catering flat
to let.

WOOTTON-UNDER-EDGE

Plough (P)
Charfield.
☎ *01 453 843 321.*
🍎 *Taunton Traditional*

YORKLEY

Bailey Inn (P)
Bailey Hill.
☎ *01 594 562 670.*
🍎 *Bulmers Traditional*

Nags Head (P)
☎ *01 594 562 592.*
🍎 *Bulmers Traditional*

Hampshire

ALRESFORD

**ALRESFORD ALE & CIDER
HOUSE** (P)
9 East Street
☎ 01 962 732 140
Open 11-11
🍎 **Own-label ciders from
Thatchers**
Welcoming local near
Watercress Line. Food
lunchtime and evening.

Bush (P)
Ovington.
☎ *01 962 732 764.*
🍎 *Bulmers Traditional*

ANDOVER

Hare & Hounds (P)
Charlton Down, Hatherden.
☎ *01 264 735 503.*
🍎 *Bulmers Traditional*

Railway Tavern (P)
71 Weyhill Rd.
☎ *01 264 362 474.*
🍎 *Bulmers Old Hazy*

Station Hotel (P)
63 Bridge Street.
☎ *01 264 336 585.*
🍎 *Bulmers Old Hazy*

BISHOPSTOKE
Foresters Arms (P)
1 Stoke Common Row
☎ 01 703 620 287
Open 11-3, 7-11
🍎 **Inch's**
Popular two-room sporting
local. Reputedly haunted.

BURSLEDON

Manor House (P)
Portsmouth Rd.
☎ *01 703 402 786.*
🍎 *Bulmers Old Hazy*

CHARTER ALLEY

WHITE HART (P)
White Hart Lane
☎ 01 256 850 048
Open 12-2.30, 7-11
🍎 **Inch's, Thatcher's**
Friendly village local with
dining room and no-smoking
lounge. Fine range of real ales.
Skittle alley.

COWPLAIN

Rainbows (P)
214 Milton Rd.
☎ *01 705 252 782.*
🍎 *Bulmers Traditional*

EASTLEIGH

CRICKETERS (P)
Chestnut Avenue
☎ 01 703 642 851
Open all permitted hours
🍎 **Bulmers Traditional and
Old Hazy**
Typical Hogshead alehouse
with bar food lunchtime and
evening and separate
restaurant.

EASTNEY

Cellars at Eastney (P)
56 Cromwell Rd.
☎ *01 705 826 249.*
🍎 *Bulmers Traditional*

SIR LOIN OF BEEF (P)
152 Highland Rd, Eastney
☎ 01 705 820 115
11-11
🍎 **Bulmers Traditional plus
guests**
Eight ales in genuine free
house handy for Royal Marines
Museum and seafront. No-
smoking area.

EMSWORTH

Lord Raglan (P)
35 Queen Street.
☎ *01 243 372 587.*
🍎 *Bulmers Traditional*

EVERTON

CROWN INN (P)
Old Christchurch Road
☎ 01 590 642 655
Open 11-2.30, 6-11.
🍎 **Bulmers Traditional**
Two-bar Victorian village inn
with good food lunchtime and
evening. Whitbread beers and
guests. Disabled access.

FAREHAM

Cheese & Ale House (P)
54 Trinity Street.
☎ *01 329 288 722.*
🍎 *Bulmers Traditional*

Cob & Pen (P)
Wallington Shore Rd.
☎ *01 329 221 624.*
🍎 *Bulmers Old Hazy*

FARNBOROUGH

RAILWAY ENTHUSIASTS CLUB
(P)
103 Hawley Lane
☎ 01 252 542 574
Open Tuesday evening and
some other nights
🍎 **Weston's Old Rosie and Oak
Conditioned**

Railway enthusiasts' social club with pub licence. Base for many club activities. Signposted off Hawley Lane.

GOSPORT

Hogshead (P)
156 Priory Rd.
☎ *01 705 582 584.*
♦ *Bulmers Traditional*

QUEEN'S HOTEL (P)
143 Queen's Road
☎ 01 705 582 645
Open 11.30-2.30, 7-11; 11-11 Sat
♦ Inch's
Backstreet haven for ale-lovers.

HARDLEY

Hogshead in the Forest (P)
Long Lane.
☎ *01 703 842 270.*
♦ *Bulmers Old Hazy*

HYTHE

Drummond Arms (P)
Prospect Place.
☎ *01 703 843 728.*
♦ *Bulmers Traditional*

Lord Nelson (P)
High Street.
☎ *01 703 862 665.*
♦ *Bulmers Traditional*

Travellers Rest (P)
Frost Lane.
☎ *01 703 842 356.*
♦ *Bulmers Old Hazy*

LANGSTONE

Royal Oak (P)
19 High Street.
☎ *01 705 483 125.*
♦ *Bulmers Traditional*

LASHAM

ROYAL OAK (P)
☎ 01 256 381 213
Open 11-2.30, 6-11
♦ Thatcher's
Cosy two-bar country pub with fine garden. Guest ales. good

value food lunchtime and evening.

LIPHOOK

Rising Sun (P)
Milland.
☎ *01 428 76347.*
♦ *Bulmers Traditional*

LITTLE LONDON

PLOUGH (P)
Silchester Road
☎ 01 256 850 628
Open 12-3, 6-11
♦ Inch's
Old-fashioned two-bar village local with good ale range. Bar food lunchtime and evening; disabled access.

LYMINGTON

Borough Arms (P)
39 Avenue Rd.
☎ *01 590 672 814.*
♦ *Bulmers Old Hazy*

LYNDHURST

Hunters Wine Bar (P)
24 High Street.
☎ *01 703 282 217.*
♦ *Bulmers Traditional*

MICHELDEVER

DEVER ARMS (P)
Winchester Road
☎ 01 962 774 339
Open 11.30-3, 6-11.
♦ Inch's plus occasional guests
Popular village pub with wooden beams and open fires. High quality food; real ale from small independent brewers. Hard to find: OS 517 389.

NEW MILTON

Woodpecker (P)
Ashley Common Rd.
☎ *01 425 618 276.*
♦ *Bulmers Traditional*

PORTSMOUTH

Air Balloon (P)
598 Mile End Rd.
☎ *01 705 694 464.*
🍎 *Bulmers Traditional*

Brewery Tap (P)
17 London Rd, North End.
☎ *01 705 699 943.*
🍎 *Inch's*

CONNAUGHT ARMS (P)
117 Guildford Rd, Fratton
☎ 01 705 646 455
Open 11.3-2.30, 6-11 Mon-
Thurs; 11.30-11 Fri/Sat.
🍎 **Broadoak**
Pub near shopping centre
specialising in beers from
independent breweries and
pasties.

Content Pig (P)
249 Fratton Rd.
☎ *01 705 463 041.*
🍎 *Bulmers Traditional*

DOLPHIN (P)
41 High Street, Old Portsmouth
☎ 01 705 823 595
Open 11-11
🍎 **Bulmers Old Hazy &
Traditional**
One of city's oldest pubs, in
shadow of Anglican cathedral.
Whitbread's first Hogshead
alehouse with 14 beers, two
ciders, food lunchtime and
evening.

Fort Cumberland (P)
Eastney Rd.
☎ *01 705 864 994.*
🍎 *Taunton Traditional*

Guardsman (P)
129 Fratton Rd.
☎ *01 705 819 931.*
🍎 *Bulmers Old Hazy*

OLD OYSTER HOUSE (P)
291 Locksway Rd, Milton
☎ 01 705 827 456
Open 12-3, 6-11; 12-11 Sat
🍎 **Inch's**
Large one-bar pub with a
nautical theme.

Old Vic (P)
104 St Pauls Rd.
☎ *01 705 297 013.*
🍎 *Bulmers Traditional*

Ship (P)
10 The Hard.
☎ *01 705 824 152.*
🍎 *Bulmers Traditional*

TAP (P)
17 London Rd, North End
☎ 01 705 614 861
Open 10.30-11
🍎 **Ciders vary; occasional
perry**
Pub opened in 1985 as brewery
tap to now-defunct Southsea
Brewery. Today a genuine free
house with a wide range of
ales. Food lunchtime; disabled
access.

Unicorn (P)
158 Fratton Rd.
☎ *01 705 822 769.*
🍎 *Bulmers Traditional*

ROMSEY

Dolphin Hotel (P)
9 The Cornmarket.
☎ *01 794 522 516.*
🍎 *Bulmers Old Hazy*

SHIRLEY

Windsor Castle (P)
High Street.
☎ *01 703 786 051.*
🍎 *Bulmers Old Hazy*

SOUTHAMPTON

**ALEXANDRA CASK ALE
EMPORIUM** (P)
6 Bellevue Road
☎ 01 703 335 071
Open all permitted hours
🍎 **Bulmers Traditional and
Old Hazy**
Hogshead alehouse popular
with students. Bar food
lunchtimes and most evenings.
No-smoking area.

Grapes Inn (P)
41 Oxford Street.
☎ 01 703 333 220.
🍎 Bulmers Old Hazy

HEDGEHOG & HOGSHEAD (P)
161 University Road
☎ 01 703 581 124
Open 11-3, 5.3-11; 12-3,
7-10.30 Sun
🍎 **Weston's Old Rosie**
Busy alehouse with live music
most evenings. Bar food
lunchtime and evening.

HOGSHEAD & ANCHOR (P)
76 East Street
☎ 01 703 228 098
Open all permitted hours
🍎 **Bulmers Old Hazy**
Hogshead pub near East St
shopping centre. Nautical
theme to decor. Bar food to
7pm.

HOGSHEAD & EAGLE (P)
1 Palmerston Road
☎ 01 703 333 825
Open all permitted hours
🍎 **Bulmers Traditional and
Old Hazy**
Hogshead pub opposite park.
Live jazz Tuesdays; bar food
lunchtime and most evenings.
No smoking area lunchtimes.

SOUTH WESTERN ARMS (P)
38 Adelaide Rd, St Denys
☎ 01 703 324 542
Open 11-3, 6-11; 11-11 Thurs-
Sat
🍎 **Bulmers Traditional and
others**
One-bar local. Separate
drinking area upstairs. Bar
food lunchtime and evening,
no smoking area.

SOUTHSEA

Bold Forester (P)
177 Albert Rd.
☎ 01 705 838 743.
🍎 Bulmers Old Hazy &
Traditional

Florence Arms (P)
Florence Rd.
☎ 01 705 875 700.
🍎 Taunton Traditional

Royal Albert (P)
115 Albert Rd.
☎ 01 705 22834.
🍎 Bulmers Traditional

TOTTON

Old Farmhouse (P)
Ringwood Rd.
☎ 01 703 862 399.
🍎 Bulmers Traditional

WHITCHURCH

PRINCE REGENT (P)
104 London Road
☎ 01 256 892 179
Open 11-11
🍎 **Inch's**
Genuine local with fine views
over Test Valley. Ales from
small brewers, food all day.

WINCHESTER

Jolly Farmer (P)
Andover Rd.
☎ 01 962 852 665.
🍎 Bulmers Old Hazy

Porthouse (P)
Upper Brook Street.
☎ 01 962 869 397.
🍎 Bulmers Traditional

WINCHFIELD

WOODY'S (P)
Station Hill
☎ 01 252 842 129
Open 12-2.30, 5.30-11
🍎 **Thatchers**
Unassuming pub with fine
garden. Varying beer range,
food lunchtime and evening.
Disabled access.

Herefordshire

ABBEY DORE

NEVILLE ARMS (P)
☎ 01 981 240 319
🍎 **Gwatkins**
Country local serving perry in summer and cider in winter. Ask for the perry, which is served on electric pump and not advertised.

ALMELEY

SEPTEMBER DAIRY PRODUCTS (OL)
New House Farm
☎ 01 544 327 400
Open usual shop hours
🍎 **Cider range varies**
Farm shop selling usual range – bacon, milk, cream, eggs etc – as well as farm ciders and dairy ice-cream. Hard to find: OS 317 517.

BELBROUGHTON

OLDE HORSESHOE (P)
High Street
☎ 01 562 730 233
Open 11-3, 6-11
🍎 **Thatchers**
Village pub with small lounge. Excellent menu. Disabled access.

BRINGSTY COMMON

LIVE & LET LIVE (P)
☎ 01 886 821 462
Open 12-3, 6-11; 11-11 Sat
🍎 **Bulmers Traditional**
Wye Valley ales in cottage-cum-inn down unmetalled track on common. No frills – and no food! Great view of Malvern Hills.
Hard to find: signed off A44, OS 699 547.

BROMYARD

White Horse (P)
Cruxwell Street.
☎ *01 885 482 279.*
🍎 *Bulmers Traditional*

FAWLEY

British Lion (P)
Kings Caple.
☎ *01 432 840 280.*
🍎 *Bulmers Traditional*

GLASBURY

Maesllwch Arms (P)
☎ *01 497 847 637.*
🍎 *Bulmers Traditional*

GOODRICH

Cross Keys Inn (P)
☎ *01 600 890 203.*
🍎 *Bulmers Traditional*

HEREFORD

BARRELS (P)
69 St Owen Street
☎ 01 432 274 968
Open all permitted hours
🍎 **Westons Scrumpy Supreme; Bulmers Traditional**
Historic traditional town pub with Wye Valley Brewery in yard. Guest ales as well: a true gem.

Booth Hall (P)
East Street.
☎ *01 432 344 487.*
🍎 *Bulmers Old Hazy*

Brewers Arms (P)
97 Eign Rd.
☎ *01 432 273 746.*
🍎 *Bulmers Old Hazy*

Buckingham House Inn (P)
141 Whitecross Rd.
☎ *01 432 276 087.*
🍎 *Bulmers Traditional*

CASTLE POOL HOTEL (P)
Castle Street
☎ 01 432 356 321
Open 12-3, 6-11

🍎 **Weston's Old Rosie**
Hotel in Georgian quarter. Pool is all that remains of castle moat and is home to a variety of ducks, geese, etc. Bar food lunchtime & evening; separate restaurant; letting rooms.

CIDER MUSEUM (OL)
21 Ryelands Street
☎ 01 432 354 207
Open 10-5.30 seven days (summer); 1-5 Mon-Sat Nov-Mar
🍎 **King Offa Cider Brandy; King Offa Pear Brandy; Hereford Cider Liqueur; Hereford Apple Aperitif; King Offa Cider**
This independent museum, established in 1981, tells the story of cider from its primitive beginnings to modern mass-production. It also hosts a wide variety of special events, and is home to the King Offa Distillery, where cider brandy is made on a Calvados still brought back from Normandy some 10 years ago. The liqueur is a 25 per cent abv compound of brandy and cider, and the aperitif is an 18 per cent abv mixture of brandy and fresh apple juice. Cider for distilling comes from Bulmer's; the own-label cider is currently Weston's.

Heart of Oak (P)
Newtown Rd.
☎ *01 432 276 056.*
🍎 *Bulmers Traditional*

Horse & Groom (P)
140 Eign Street.
☎ *01 432 355 026.*
🍎 *Bulmers Traditional*

IMPERIAL RESTAURANT (P)
Widemarsh Street
☎ 01 432 273 646
Open 10-11
🍎 **Westons range, Bulmers Old Hazy**
Restaurant with separate bars and function rooms. Caters to everybody – shoppers, tourists, office workers, retired people, youngsters etc.

LANCASTER (P)
1 St Martins Street
☎ 01 432 275 480
Open 11.30-3, 6-11
🍎 **Bulmers Old Hazy**
Two-bar riverside free house; beers from independent brewers. Food lunchtime and evening.

Nell Gwyn (P)
Monkmoor Street.
☎ *01 432 354 393.*
🍎 *Bulmers Traditional*

Sportsman (P)
Widemarsh Common.
☎ *01 432 272 831.*
🍎 *Bulmers Traditional*

Spread Eagle (P)
King Street.
☎ *01 432 272 205.*
🍎 *Bulmers Old Hazy*

VICTORY (P)
88 St Owen Street
☎ 01 432 274 998
Open 11-11
🍎 **Bulmers Traditional**
Wye Valley ales in pub with clever and well-executed galleon theme. Good value food, live music, disabled access.

Volunteer (P)
21 Harold Street.
☎ *01 432 276 803.*
🍎 *Bulmers Traditional*

LEDBURY

PRINCE OF WALES (P)
Church Lane
☎ 01 531 632 250
Open 11-3, 7-11.
🍎 **Westons GWR, Draught Vintage**

Much-photographed half-timbered pub down cobbled lane in one of Herefordshire's most picturesque towns. Family room; bar food lunchtime; separate restaurant.

ROYAL OAK (P)
The Southend
☎ 01 531 632 110
Open 11-11
🍎 **Weston's range; Hartland's; own make**
Remarkable resurrection of brewery in fifteenth-century pub which made its own ale until 1921 and now does so again. Also making own cider. Bar food lunchtime and evening, separate restaurant, 10 letting rooms.

TALBOT (P)
New Street
☎ 01 531 632 963
Open 11.30-3, 5-11
🍎 **Weston's range**
Half-timbered former coaching inn with much panelling etc. Bar food lunchtime and evenings, separate restaurant, letting rooms.

White Hart (P)
Church Street.
☎ *01 531 632 620.*
🍎 *Bulmers Traditional*

LEOMINSTER

Chequers Inn (P)
Etnam Street.
☎ *01 568 612 473.*
🍎 *Bulmers Traditional*

Hop Pole (P)
Bridge Street.
☎ *01 568 612 779.*
🍎 *Bulmers Traditional*

Radnorshire Arms (P)
Bargates.
☎ *01 568 611 448.*
🍎 *Bulmers Traditional*

Three Horse Shoes (P)
Corn Sq.
☎ *01 568 613 019.*
🍎 *Bulmers Traditional*

LYONSHALL

Royal George (P)
☎ *01 544 340 210.*
🍎 *Bulmers Traditional*

MUCH MARCLE

ROYAL OAK (P)
☎ 01 531 660 300
Open 11-3, 6-11
🍎 **Weston's range**
Family-run country inn in Weston's home village. Garden/patio overlooks cider orchards. Bar food lunchtime and evening, no smoking area, camping/caravanning site.

MUNSTONE

Rose Gardens Inn (P)
☎ *01 432 267 087.*
🍎 *Bulmers Traditional*

NORTON CANON

THREE HORSE SHOES (P)
☎ 01 544 318 395
🍎 **Weston's range**
Two-bar village pub with family room. Quoits and skittles played. Campsite. Pembridge

THE CIDER HOUSE (R)
Hays Head Farm
☎ 01 544 388 161
Open 10-6; also 7.30-11 Fri/Sat
🍎 **Dunkerton's**
Impressive restaurant made out of two dismantled and reerected barns at Dunkerton's cider mills. All Dunkerton's ciders on draught; local real ales; Cordon Bleu cuisine but also Cordon Bleu snacks for those who have come for the cider and perry. No-smoking area; disabled access. All true cider-lovers must make their hajj here at least once.

ROSS-ON-WYE

CROWN & SCEPTRE (P)
Market Place
☎ 01 989 562 765
Open 11-3, 6-11; 11-11 Fri/Sat
in summer
🍎 **Bulmers Traditional**
Centre for real ale in Ross.
Excellent food. Local pub of the
year.

Drop Inn (C)
14 Station Street.
☎ *01 989 563 256.*
🍎 *Bulmers Traditional*

Horse & Jockey (P)
New Street.
☎ *01 989 768 180.*
🍎 *Bulmers Traditional*

King Charles II (P)
13 Broad Street.
☎ *01 989 62039.*
🍎 *Bulmers Old Hazy*

Kings Arms (P)
Gloucester Rd.
☎ *01 989 769 994.*
🍎 *Bulmers Traditional*

Noahs Ark (P)
Tudorville.
☎ *01 989 563 060.*
🍎 *Bulmers Traditional*

Prince of Wales (P)
Walford Rd.
☎ *01 989 562 517.*
🍎 *Bulmers Traditional*

Stag Inn (P)
Henry Street.
☎ *01 989 62893.*
🍎 *Bulmers Traditional*

Vine Tree (P)
Walford Rd.
☎ *01 989 562 882.*
🍎 *Bulmers Traditional*

STRETTON SUGWAS

Travellers Rest (P)
☎ *01 432 760 268.*
🍎 *Bulmers Traditional*

TILLINGTON

BELL INN (P)
Tillington Road
☎ 01 432 760 395
Open 11-3, 6-11; 11-11 sat
🍎 **Bulmers Traditional**
Village pub with separate
restaurant. Lively public bar,
mellow lounge. Food
lunchtime and evening.

WEOBLEY

OLD SALUTATION (P)
Market Pitch
☎ 01 544 318 443
Open 11-3, 7-11.
🍎 **Westons range**
Much-drawn, painted and
photographed half-timbered
gem in premiere market town.
Bar food lunchtime and
evening; no smoking area;
wheelchair ramp to separate
restaurant but no disabled WC.

WHITCHURCH

Crown Hotel (P)
☎ *01 600 890 203.*
🍎 *Bulmers Traditional*

WHITNEY-ON-WYE

RHYDSPENCE INN (P)
☎ 01 497 831 262
Open 11-2.30, 7-11
🍎 **Dunkerton's**
Food pub of national status.
Retains many fourteenth-
century features despite
gentrification. Families
welcome; accommodation. One
mile west of village on A438.
Wigmore

OLDE OAK (P)
☎ 01 568 770 247
Open 12-2, 6.30-11, longer in
summer; 12-3, 7-10.30 Sun
🍎 **Weston's**
Half-timbered two-bar local
with guest ales, bar food
lunchtime and evening,
separate restaurant (smoke-
free), three letting rooms.
Quoits played.

WOOLHOPE

CROWN INN (P)
☎ 01 432 860 468
Open 12-2.30, 6-11; 12-3, 6.30-
10.30 Sun
🍎 **Weston's range**
Quiet one-room local with
three regular real ales and a
guest. Bar food lunchtime and
evening, separate smoke-free
restaurant. Air filters in bar.

YARPOLE

Bell Inn (P)
☎ 01 568 780 359.
🍎 Bulmers Traditional

Hertfordshire

ASHWELL

Bushel & Strike (P)
Mill Street.
☎ 01 462 742 394.
🍎 Bulmers Old Hazy

AYOT ST LAWRENCE

BROCKET ARMS (P)
☎ 01 438 820 250
Open 11-2.30, 7-11.
🍎 **Weston's Old Rosie**
Ancient village pub in quaint
rural setting. Excellent food
and ale. Near George Bernard
Shaw home and memorial.

BALDOCK

OLD WHITE HORSE (P)
1 Station Road
☎ 01 462 893 168
🍎 **Bulmers Old Hazy**
Busy young people's pub just
off town centre. Adventurous
beer stocking policy, occasional
live music.

BARLEY

FOX & HOUNDS (P)
High Street
☎ 01 763 848 459.

Open 12-3, 6-11.
🍎 **Thatcher's, Biddenden**
Ancient pub in pretty village.
Now brewing own beer. Good
food. Unusual carved pub sign
spans street.

BENINGTON

LORDSHIP ARMS (P)
Whempstead Road
☎ 01 438 869 665
Open 11-3, 6-11.
🍎 **Cider range changes**
Country local with excellent
reputation for food and ale. No
keg ciders.

BISHOP'S STORTFORD

TAP & SPILE (P)
31 North Street
☎ 01 279 654 978.
Open 11-3, 5.30-11 Mon-Thurs,
all permitted hours Fri-Sun.
🍎 **Weston's range**
Big ale-house with seven real
ales, food at lunchtime,
function room, live music
occasionally.

Three Horseshoes (P)
Takeley.
☎ 01 279 870 313.
🍎 Taunton Traditional

BRICKET WOOD

GATE (P)
Station Road
☎ 01 923 672 470
Open 12-3 (not Mon), 5.30-11
🍎 **Inch's**
Nine real ales, Belgian fruit
beers and fruit wines as well as
real cider in recently extended
pub.

DATCHWORTH

TILBURY (P)
1 Watton Rd.
☎ 01 438 812 496.
Open 11-3, 5-11 Mon-Thurs, all
permitted hours Fri-Sun.
🍎 **Rich's**
Two-bar village pub with good

reputation for food and big real ale range.

HARPENDEN

Harpenden Wines (OL)
68 High Street.
🍎 *Dunkerton's*

HATFIELD

COCK INN (P)
Broad Oak
☎ 01 279 718 273
Open 12-3, 6-11 Mon-Sat, 12-3, 7-10.30 Sun.
🍎 **Addlestone's**
Coaching inn with above-average food and five real ales. Bar billiards.

HATFIELD HEATH

WHITE HORSE (P)
☎ 01 279 730 351
Opening times vary
🍎 **Matching**
Traditional drinkers' pub with proper saloon, snug, and public bars. Real ale on gravity dispense. Bar food.

HERONSGATE

LAND OF LIBERTY, PEACE & PLENTY (P)
Long Lane
☎ 01 923 282 226
Open all permitted hours
🍎 **Lyme Bay Jack Ratt**
Pub built in 1840s outside tee-total Chartist settlement of O'Connorsville. Four guest ales from micro-brewers and six draught Belgian beers. Hard to find: off J17 of M25, OS 023 949.

HERTFORD

Blackbirds (P)
15 Parliament Square.
☎ *01 992 583 400.*
🍎 *Bulmers Old Hazy*

WHITE HORSE (P)
33 Castle Street
☎ 01 992 501 950

Open 12-2.30, 5.30-11 Mon-Fri, 12-3, 7-11 Sat-Sun.
🍎 **Biddenden**
Timber-framed town pub now brewing own beer. Upper floor is non-smoking area where children are welcome.

HITCHIN

ASSIZES (P)
24 Bancroft
☎ 01 462 455 776
Open 11-2.30, 5.30-11 Mon-Thurs, 11-11 Fri-Sat, 12-4, 7-10.30 Sun
🍎 **Weston's Old Rosie**
Timber-framed town pub with good reputation for food and wine, live music Wednesdays.

Tut'n'Shive (P)
63 Bancroft.
☎ *01 462 451 473.*
🍎 *Bulmers Old Hazy*

HODDESDON

Young's (OL)
33 Chaucer Way.
☎ *01 992 441 937.*
🍎 *Bulmers Traditional*

ICKLEFORD

CRICKETERS (P)
107 Arlesey Road
☎ 01 462 432 629
Open 11-3, 5.30-11 Mon-Fri, all permitted hours Sat-Sun.
🍎 **Ciders vary**
Lively village pub with up to 10 real ales.

LONDON COLNEY

BOWMAN'S FARM SHOP (OL)
Coursers Road
☎ 01 462 424 055
Open 9-5.30 daily.
🍎 **Weston's range inc perry**
Shop is part of open farm with fishing lake, farm trail, and frequent special events.

MARSWORTH

RED LION (P)
90 Vicarage Road
☎ 01 296 668 366
Open 11-3, 6-11 Mon-Sat, 12-3,
7-10.30 Sun.
🍏 **Weston's Old Rosie & First Quality**
Seventeenth-century part-thatched country pub, public bar, snug, saloon, games area, garden. Five real ales, food, games inc shove-ha'penny, crib, bar billiards.

OLD KNEBWORTH

LYTTON ARMS (P)
Park Lane.
☎ 01 438 812 312
Open 11-3, 5-11 Mon-Thurs, 11-11 Fri Sat.
🍏 **Cider range varies. Often includes perry**
Large Lutyens-designed pub on edge of Knebworth Park. 12 beers and annual festivals. Bar food Mon-Sat.

RICKMANSWORTH

Clarendon Arms (P)
Chandlers Cross.
☎ *01 923 262 924.*
🍏 *Bulmers Traditional*

ROYSTON

Jockey (P)
Baldock Street.
☎ *01 763 243 377.*
🍏 *Bulmers Old Hazy*

ST ALBANS

BLACKSMITH'S ARMS (P)
56 St Peters Street
☎ 01 727 855 761
Open all permitted hours but may close weekday afternoons if slack
🍏 **Bulmers Old Hazy**
Busy town centre Hogshead alehouse with four real ales on handpump and up to eight on stillage.

TAP & SPILE (P)
Holywell Hill
☎ 01 727 858 982
Open 12-3, 6-11 Sun-Fri,
12-11 Sat
🍏 **Crone's**
Up to eight real ales in recently converted pub outside city centre. Real fire. Limited parking.

SAWBRIDGEWORTH

GATE (P)
81 London Road
☎ 01 279 722 313
Open 11.30-2.30, 5.30-11 Mon-Sat, 12-3, 7-10.30 Sun.
🍏 **Cider range changes**
Good reputation for real ales. Basic lunch menu.

STEVENAGE

Coach & Horses (P)
High Street.
☎ *01 438 314 195.*
🍏 *Bulmers Old Hazy*

TOWER HILL

BOOT (P)
☎ 01 442 833 155
Open 11.30-11
🍏 **Weston's Old Rosie, Rich's Zum**
Six real ales and good home cooking. Children's play area boasts a tank! Hard to find: on Bovingdon-Chipperfield road.

TRING

Greyhound (P)
Chesham Rd, Wiggington.
☎ *01 442 824 631.*
🍏 *Bulmers Old Hazy*

KINGS ARMS (P)
King Street
☎ 01 442 823 318
Open 11.30-2.30, 7-11.
🍏 **Biddenden, Bulmers Old Hazy**

Unofficial tap for Tring Brewery. Five real ales; no smoking area at lunchtime. Near Natural History Museum.

Valiant Trooper (P)
Trooper Rd.
☎ 01 442 85203.
🍎 *Bulmers Traditional*

WARE

Tut'n'Shive (P)
22 High Street.
☎ 01 920 463 255.
🍎 *Bulmers Old Hazy*

Humberside

BEVERLEY

TAP & SPILE (P)
1 Flemingate
☎ 01 482 881 547
Open all permitted hours
🍎 **Bulmers Old Hazy, Weston's Old Rosie, Crone's**
Sympathetic conversion of medieval timber-framed building opposite Minster. Bar food to 8pm, no-smoking area, table skittles.

BRIDLINGTON

New Crown Hotel (P)
158 Quay Rd.
☎ 01 262 604 370.
🍎 *Bulmers Old Hazy*

CLEETHORPES

Spanish Steps (P)
207 North Promenade.
☎ 01 472 603 037.
🍎 *Bulmers Old Hazy*

GRIMSBY

TAP & SPILE (P)
Garth Lane
☎ 01 472 357 493
Open 11.30-4, 7-11; 11.30-11 Fri/Sat
🍎 **Crone's**
Local pub of the year 1995. Bar food lunchtime; disabled access.

Trawl Inn (P)
Yarborough Rd.
☎ 01 472 343 372.
🍎 *Bulmers Old Hazy*

HULL

Kings Ale House (P)
10 King Street.
☎ 01 482 210 446.
🍎 *Bulmers Old Hazy*

NEW CLARENCE (P)
77 Charles Street
☎ 01 482 443 181
Open 11-11; 12-3, 7-10.30 Sun
🍎 **Weston's**
Big one-bar Tetley Festival Alehouse with changing guest ales. Food lunchtime and evening, disabled access.

OLDE BLACK BOY (P)
150 High Street
☎ 01 482 326 516
Open 12-11
🍎 **Weston's, Crone's, Bulmers Old Hazy**
Tap & Spile, but not branded as such in deference to its 600-year history. Food at lunchtime, no-smoking area.

Old Zoological (P)
Spring Bank.
☎ 01 482 493 998.
🍎 *Bulmers Old Hazy*

Spring Bank (P)
29 Spring Bank.
☎ 01 482 581 879.
🍎 *Bulmers Old Hazy*

TAP & SPILE (P)
169 Spring Bank
☎ 01 482 323 518
Open 12-11
🍎 **Weston's, Crones, Bulmers Old Hazy**
Good conversion of old corner local. Food lunchtime and evening.

GOOLE

Half Moon (P)
Main Street,
Redness.
☎ 01 405 704 484.
🍎 *Bulmers Old Hazy*

North Eastern (P)
70 Boothferry Rd.
☎ 01 405 763 705.
🍎 *Bulmers Old Hazy*

SCUNTHORPE

Crosby Hotel (P)
Normandy Rd.
☎ 01 724 843 830.
🍎 *Bulmers Old Hazy*

Isle of Wight

COWES

ANCHOR INN (P)
1 High Street
☎ 01 983 292 823
Open 11-11
🍎 **Godshill**
Ancient town pub with low
beamed ceilings and stone
floors. Good range of beers, but
not cheap. Family room; food
lunchtime and evening.

TRAVELLERS JOY (P)
Pallance Rd (off A3020)
☎ 01 983 298 024
🍎 **Inch's**
Open 11-3, 6-11
Cask ales from all over the
country in three-times local
pub of the year. Food
lunchtime and evening;
disabled access.

NEWPORT

Castle Inn (P)
91 High Street.
☎ 01 983 522 528.
🍎 *Bulmers Traditional*

PRINCE OF WALES (P)
36 South Street
☎ 01 983 525 026
Open 10.30-11
🍎 **Bulmers Old Hazy**
Town-centre pub specialising
in cooking with beer. Usher's
ales. Food lunchtime and
evening.

NITON

BUDDLE INN (P)
St Catherine's Road
☎ 01 983 730 243
Open 11-11
🍎 **Hamstead Vineyard**
Old stone pub with smuggling
history. Whitbread ales, food
lunchtime and evenings, family
room. Hard to find: follow
signs for St Catherine's Point.

SHOREWELL

Crown Inn (P)
☎ 01 983 740 293.
🍎 *Bulmers Old Hazy*

Kent

ASHFORD

BEAVOR RD OFF-LICENCE
(OL)
36 Beavor Road
☎ 01 233 622 904
Open 11-10.30
🍎 **Usually three draught ciders**
Specialist real ale off-licence
run by CAMRA member.

Honest Miller (P)
Brook.
☎ 01 233 812 303.
🍎 *Bulmers Old Hazy*

BADLESMERE

RED LION (P)
Ashford Road
☎ 01 233 740 320
Open 11.30-2.30 Mon-Thurs;
11.30-11 Fri/Sat; 12-10.30 Sun
🍎 **Theobolds**

Gas-lit sixteenth-century two-bar village pub. Also stocks cask mild. Bar food lunchtime and Thurs-Sat evenings.

BECKENHAM

Bottle & Basket (OL)
255 Beckenham Rd.
☎ *0181 778 7588.*
🍎 *Bulmers Traditional*

BEXLEY

George (P)
74 High Street.
☎ *01 322 523 843.*
🍎 *Bulmers Old Hazy*

BEXLEYHEATH

Bricklayers Arms (P)
58 Mayplace Rd West.
☎ *0181 303 8810.*
🍎 *Bulmers Old Hazy*

BOXLEY

Kings Arms (P)
Boxley Street.
☎ *01 622 755 177.*
🍎 *Bulmers Old Hazy*

BROMLEY

BITTER END (OL)
139 Masons Hill
☎ 0181 466 6083
Open 5-9 Mon; 12-3, 5-10 Tues-Fri; 11-10 Sat; 12-2, 7-9 Sun
🍎 **Weston's range year-round; Gibbon Strangler, Chiddingstone, Chafford, Pippin's, Biddenden seasonally**
Friendly specialist off-licence where staff are happy to give advice.

Palace Tavern (P)
. Napier Rd.
☎ *0181 460 2675.*
🍎 *Bulmers Old Hazy*

Prince Frederick (P)
31 Nichol Lane.
☎ *0181 688 2878.*
🍎 *Bulmers Old Hazy*

BROUGHTON MONCHELSEA

RED HOUSE (P)
Hermitage Lane
☎ 01 622 743 986
Open 12-3, 7-11; 12-11 Sat/Bank Hols
🍎 **Bulmers Old Hazy**
Popular real ale pub with selection of imported speciality beers. Bar food lunchtime and evening; families welcome.

CANTERBURY

Black Griffin (P)
40 St Peters Street.
☎ *01 227 455 563.*
🍎 *Bulmers Old Hazy*

City Arms (P)
7 Butchery Lane.
☎ *01 227 457 900.*
🍎 *Bulmers Old Hazy*

Jolly Sailor (P)
75 Northgate Street.
☎ *01 227 463 828.*
🍎 *Bulmers Traditional*

CHATHAM

Hogshead (P)
Railway Street.
☎ *01 634 842 931.*
🍎 *Bulmers Traditional*

Prince of Wales (P)
3 Railway Street.
☎ *01 634 842 931.*
🍎 *Bulmers Traditional*

CHIDDINGSTONE

Wheatsheaf (P)
Bough Beech.
☎ *01 732 700 254.*
🍎 *Bulmers Old Hazy*

CHISLET

SIX BELLS (P)
Church Lane
☎ 01 227 860 373
Open 12-3, 6.30-11
🍎 **Theobolds or Biddenden**
Big free house with Bat & Trap

in large garden. Bar food lunchtime and evening.

CLAYGATE

WHITE HART (P)
☎ 01 892 730 313
Open 11-3, 6-11
🍎 **Biddenden**
Splendid country pub set among orchards and hop gardens. Letting rooms; bar food lunchtime and evening; separate restaurant; disabled access.

COOLING

HORSESHOE & CASTLE (P)
Main Road
☎ 01 634 221 691
Open 11.30-3, 7-11.
🍎 **Rich's medium**
Village pub with Dickensian connections. Bar food lunchtime and evening; no-smoking restaurant.

DARTFORD

Phoenix (P)
149 Lower Hythe Street.
☎ *01 474 833 210.*
🍎 *Bulmers Old Hazy*

WAT TYLER (P)
80 High Street
☎ 01 322 272 546
Open all permitted hours
🍎 **Biddenden or Thatchers**
Medieval town-centre pub. Bar food lunchtime.

DOVER

THE CABIN (R)
91 High Street
☎ 01 304 206 118
Open 6.30-9.30 (last sitting) Tues-Sat
🍎 **Gibbon Strangler; Biddenden range**
Small traditional English restaurant specialising in game. Book ahead.

Prince Albert (P)
83 Biggin Street.
☎ *01 304 206 877.*
🍎 *Bulmers Old Hazy*

EAST FARLEIGH

Bull (P)
Station Rd.
☎ *01 622 726 282.*
🍎 *Bulmers Old Hazy*

EDENBRIDGE

Old Eden (P)
121 High Street.
☎ *01 732 862 398.*
🍎 *Bulmers Old Hazy*

EGERTON FORSTAL

QUEENS ARMS (P)
☎ 01 233 756 386
Open 11-3, 6-11
🍎 **Biddenden**
Old village local offering beers from small independent brewers and renowned for its all-day breakfast.

EYNSFORD

MALT SHOVEL INN (P)
Station Road
☎ 01 322 862 164
Open 11-3, 7-11
🍎 **Weston's Old Rosie**
Real ale free house run by same couple for 25 years. Good selection of bottled beers. Bar food lunchtime and evening; separate restaurant specialising in seafood.

FAVERSHAM

BROGDALE ORCHARDS (R, OL)
Brogdale Road
☎ 01 795 535 286
Open 9.30-5 seven days
🍎 **Weston's, Biddenden, Theobolds and most local ciders**

Home of National Fruit Collection, holding over 2,000 cider apple varieties. Orchard tours. Disabled access.

ELEPHANT (P)
31 The Mall
☎ 01 795 590 157
Open all permitted hours
🍎 **Crippledick, Pawley Farm**
Renowned real ale free house hosting numerous beer festivals in permanent marquee. Bar food lunchtime and evening; families welcome.

SHIPWRIGHTS ARMS (P)
Hollowshore
☎ 01 795 590 088
Open all permitted hours
🍎 **Pawley Farm**
Seventeenth-century riverside pub with no mains water or electricity. Bar food lunchtime and evening; no-smoking family room.

FOLKESTONE

HARVEY'S WINE BAR (P)
10 Langhorne Gardens
☎ 01 303 253 758
Open 11.30-11
🍎 **Biddenden**
Basement bar under Langhorne Gardens Hotel. Real ales; bar food lunchtime.

Pullman (P)
7 Church Street.
☎ *01 303 252 524.*
🍎 *Bulmers Old Hazy*

FORDCOMBE

Chafford Arms (P)
Spring Hill.
☎ *01 892 74267.*
🍎 *Bulmers Old Hazy*

FORDWICH

Fordwich Arms (P)
King Street.
☎ *01 227 710 444.*
🍎 *Bulmers Old Hazy*

GILLINGHAM

Roseneath (P)
79 Arden Street.
☎ *01 634 852 553.*
🍎 *Bulmers Old Hazy*

GREAT CHART

HOODEN HORSE (P)
The Street
☎ 01 233 625 583
Open 11-2.30, 6-11
🍎 **Biddenden**
Hop-strewn and candelit free house with excellent bar food and wide range of ales.

HYTHE

Bell (P)
Seabrook Rd.
☎ *01 303 267 175.*
🍎 *Bulmers Old Hazy*

KEARSNEY

Pickwicks (P)
120 London Rd.
☎ *01 304 822 016.*
🍎 *Bulmers Old Hazy*

KEMSING

RISING SUN (P)
Cotmans Ash Lane
☎ 01 959 522 683
Open 11-3, 6-11
🍎 **Biddenden, Theobolds, Sepham Farm**
Converted hunting lodge makes excellent country venue for family days out. Family room; bar food lunchtime and evening.

KILNDOWN

GLOBE & RAINBOW (P)
☎ 01 892 890 283
Open 11-2.30, 6-11
🍎 **Biddenden**
Big pub with extensive gardens. Home-cooked food in bar and separate restaurant. Letting rooms. Full-length skittle alley for hire.

KENT

LUDDESDOWN

COCK (P)
Henley Street
☎ 01 474 814 208
Open 12-2.30, 5-11; 12-11
Fri/Sat
🍎 **Gray's, Theobolds**
Popular but isolated two-bar
pub. Bar food at lunchtime and
until 8pm. OS 664 672.

LYMPNE

County Members (P)
Aldington Rd.
☎ *01 303 267 759.*
🍎 *Bulmers Old Hazy*

MAIDSTONE

HOGSHEAD (P)
Earl Street
☎ 01 622 758 516
Open all permitted hours
🍎 **Bulmers Old Hazy**
Busy Whitbread alehouse with
five regular ales and four
changing guests. Bar food
lunchtime Mon-Sat.

Swan (P)
437 Loose Rd.
☎ *01 622 743 590.*
🍎 *Bulmers Old Hazy*

MARGATE

YE OLDE CHARLES (P)
382 Northdown Rd,
Cliftonville
☎ 01 843 221 817
Open 11-11
🍎 **Bulmers Old Hazy**
Spacious Edwardian pub; bar
food lunchtime and evening;
separate restaurant.

OAD STREET

PLOUGH & HARROW (P)
☎ 01 795 843 351
Open all permitted hours
🍎 **Range varies**
Popular free house with six
changing guest ales. Bar food
lunchtime and evening.

PENSHURST

Leicester Arms (P)
High Street.
☎ *01 892 870 551.*
🍎 *Bulmers Old Hazy*

PETTERIDGE

HOPBINE (P)
Petteridge Lane
☎ 01 892 722 561
Open 12-2.30, 6-11
🍎 **Weston's Old Rosie**
Unspoilt one-bar King &
Barnes pub with regular folk
groups. Bar food lunch time
and evenings.

PLAXTOL

GOLDING HOP (P)
Sheet Hill
☎ 01 732 882 150
Open 11-3, 6-11 Mon-Fri; all
permitted hours Sat/Sun
🍎 **Weston's**
Real ale pub with large garden
running down to stream. Bar
food lunchtime and evening

ROCHESTER

MAN OF KENT (P)
6-8 John Street
☎ 01 634 818 771
Open 12-11
🍎 **Theobolds**
Back street real ale pub; bar
food lunchtime and evening.
Traditional Kent dartboard.

ROLVENDEN LAYNE

ANOTHER HOODEN HORSE
(P)
26 Maytham Road
☎ 01 580 241 837
Open 11-2.30, 6-11
🍎 **Biddenden**
Exposed timbers, hops,
brewery memorabilia in one-
bar out-of-the-way pub with
great range of ales.

SANDGATE

SHIP INN (P)
65 High Street
☎ 01 303 248 525
Open 11-3, 6-11
 Biddenden, Bulmer's Old Hazy
Haunted two-bar seaside pub with good food. Beer casks on wooden stillage. Portraits of regulars hang in the bar.

SHEERNESS

QUEENS HEAD (P)
264 High Street
☎ 01 795 662 475
Open all permitted hours
 Occasional real ciders
Real ale free house, but persists in serving keg Scrumpy Jack on fake handpump.

SHOREHAM

ROYAL OAK (P)
High Street
☎ 01 959 522 319
Open 10.30-3, 6-11
 Weston's
Two-bar village inn with cartoons of locals on walls. Ramblers welcome. Bar food lunchtime and evening. Unusual games include Toad in the Hole and Tripletell.

SITTINGBOURNE

KINGS HEAD (P)
London Road
☎ 01 795 423 177
Open 11.30-2.30, 5-11; 11-11 Sat
 Theobolds
Real ale free house with changing guests mainly from independent beers.

PLOUGH (P)
58 East Street
☎ 01 795 472 645
Open 11-11; 12-3, 7-10.30 Sun
 Biddenden
Young people's pub - pool, video games, loud jukebox - which tried out real cider last

summer and found it worked. Bar food lunchtime.

SNARGATE

RED LION (P)
☎ 01 797 344 648
Open 11-2, 7-11
 Biddenden
Country pub on B2080 described as a must by its many fans. Ales include Bateman's.

SOUTHFLEET

Wheatsheaf (P)
8 High Cross Rd.
☎ *01 474 833 210.*
 Bulmers Old Hazy

STAPLEHURST

LORD RAGLAN (P)
Chart Hill Road
☎ 01 622 843 747
Open 12-3, 6-11
 Biddenden
Families welcome at unspoilt rural pub with excellent range of ales and good food lunchtime and evening (not Sun evening). Disabled access.

STOCKBURY

HARROW INN (P)
Hill Green Road
☎ 01 795 842 546
Open 11-2.30, 6-11; 12-3, 7-10.30 Sun.
 Inch's or Weston's
Country free house overlooking village green. Bar food lunchtime and evening.

STONE STREET

PADWELL ARMS (P)
☎ 01 732 761 532
Open 12-3, 6-11
 Biddenden

Prize-winning country pub handy for Ightham Moat. Good range of ales; picturesque setting overlooking orchards. Bar food lunchtime and Thurs/Fri evening.

STROOD

RIVERSIDE TAVERN (P)
8 Canal Road
☎ 01 634 719 949
Open all hours
🍎 **Theobolds**
Large friendly two-bar pub with excellent views of Rochester Castle and Cathedral. Restaurant area. Bar food to 9pm.

TENTERDEN

Eight Bells (P)
43 High Street.
☎ *01 580 62788.*
🍎 *Bulmers Old Hazy*

TONBRIDGE

CARDINALS ERROR (P)
Lodge Oak Lane
☎ 01 732 358 704
Open 11-2.30, 5.30-11 Mon-Fri; 11-11 Sat; 12-4, 7-10.30 Sun
🍎 **Weston's, Chiddingstone**
Sixteenth-century half-timbered country pub, said to be haunted. Bat & Trap played in large garden. Bar food 12-2, 6-9.

PRIORY WINE CELLARS (OL)
64 Priory Street
☎ 01 732 359 784
Open 4-9 Mon; 11-2, 4-9 Tues-Thurs; 11-2, 4.9.30 Fri/Sat; 11.30-1.30, 7-9 Sun.
🍎 **Biddenden bottled and draught; Inch's**
Real ale off-licence with wide range of bottled beers.

TUDELEY

Pig In Hiding (P)
Hart Lake Rd.
☎ *01 732 358 934.*
🍎 *Bulmers Traditional*

TUNBRIDGE WELLS

THE BITTER END (OL)
107 Camden Road
Open 4-9 Mon; 11-2, 4-9 Tue-Fri; 11-10 Sat; 12-2, 7-9 Sun
Second shop belonging to John Rothwell and Nigel Cazaly: see Bitter End, Bromley, for details.

Duke of York (P)
17 The Pantiles.
☎ *01 892 530 482.*
🍎 *Bulmers Old Hazy*

Hogshead & Compasses (P)
45 Little Mount Sion.
☎ *01 892 530 744.*
🍎 *Bulmers Old Hazy*

WEST WICKHAM

Pickhurst Tavern (P)
Pickhurst Lane.
☎ *0181 462 1876.*
🍎 *Bulmers Traditional*

WHITSTABLE

Old Neptune (P)
Marine Terrace.
☎ *01 227 272 262.*
🍎 *Bulmers Old Hazy*

WILLESBOROUGH

HOODEN HORSE ON THE HILL (P)
Silver Hill Road
☎ 01 233 662 226
Open 11-2.30, 6-11.
🍎 **Biddenden**
Stone floors, hop bines and candlelight in pub with fine range of ales and Mexican cuisine. Large garden.

WINGHAM

Anchor *(P)*
High Street.
☎ *01 227 720 229.*
🍎 *Bulmers Old Hazy*

WROTHAM

THREE POST BOYS (P)
The Square
☎ *01 732 780 167*
Open all permitted hours
🍎 **Weston's range**
Quiet one-bar real ale house
with superb garden. Bar food
lunchtime and evening.

WYE

Tickled Trout *(P)*
Bridge Street.
☎ *01 233 812 227.*
🍎 *Bulmers Old Hazy*

Lancashire

ACCRINGTON

GEORGE HOTEL (P)
185 Blackburn Road
☎ *01 254 383 441*
Open 12-11
🍎 **Bulmers Traditional**
Open plan college local with
bistro and conservatory.
Accommodation.

BLACKPOOL

HOGSHEAD (P)
139 Church Street
☎ *01 253 26582*
Open all permitted hours
🍎 **Bulmers Old Hazy**
Popular ale house near Winter
Gardens full of Blackpool FC
memorabilia. Good food
lunchtime and up to 13 real
ales.

Pump & Truncheon *(P)*
13 Bonny Street.
☎ *01 253 751 176.*
🍎 *Bulmers Old Hazy*

BURY

Shoulder of Mutton *(P)*
Lumb Carr Rd, Holcombe.
☎ *01 706 822 001.*
🍎 *Bulmers Old Hazy*

Tap & Spile *(P)*
Old Manchester Rd.
☎ *0161 764 6461.*
🍎 *Bulmers Old Hazy*

CHORLEY

Hare & Hounds *(P)*
Bolton Rd, Abbey Village.
☎ *01 254 830 334.*
🍎 *Bulmers Old Hazy*

TUT 'N' SHIVE (P)
Market Street
☎ *01 257 262 858*
Open all permitted hours
🍎 **Addlestones on genuine
handpump**
Formerly the Royal Oak, the
name of the old Chesters
brewery is still in evidence on
the internal tilework. Quiet bar
for those who can't take the
loud music, bar food at
lunchtime

White Hart *(P)*
Mealhouse Lane.
☎ *01 257 262 016.*
🍎 *Bulmers Old Hazy*

CROSBY

**LEGENDARY LANCASHIRE
HEROES** (OL)
59 College Road
☎ *0151 920 6074*
Open 3-10 Mon-Fri; 11.30-10
Sat; 12-10 Sun
🍎 **Thatchers, Biddenden**
Small but busy off-licence and
shop

DARWEN

PUNCH HOTEL (P)
Chapels
☎ *01 254 702 510*
Open 12-11
🍎 **Thatcher's**
Large friendly multi-room pub

95

stocking Whitbread range including seasonal beers. Letting rooms; food lunchtime and evening; disabled access.

HAMBLETON

Shard Bridge Inn (P)
Old Bridge Lane.
☎ 01 253 700 298.
🍎 *Bulmers Old Hazy*

LANCASTER

PRIORY (P)
36 Cable Street
☎ 01 524 32606
Open all permitted hours
🍎 **Weston's inc perry in summer**
Student pub handy for bus station. Ales by Lancaster brewery Mitchells.

Fibber McGee's (P)
James Street.
☎ 01 524 63720.
🍎 *Bulmers Old Hazy*

LATHOM

SHIP INN (P)
Wheat Lane
☎ 01 704 893 117
Open 12-3, 5.30 (7 Sat)-11
🍎 **Range varies**
Canalside pub with several bars including family room. Bar food lunchtime and evening; separate restaurant; no-smoking area; disabled access. On Leeds-Liverpool canal near Burscough Bridge off A5209.

LEYBURN

Bolton Arms (P)
Redmire.
☎ 01 969 624 336.
🍎 *Bulmers Old Hazy*

LITTLEBOROUGH

Red Lion (P)
6 Halifax Rd.
☎ 01 706 378 195.
🍎 *Bulmers Traditional*

LYTHAM ST ANNES

Taps Hotel (P)
Henry Street.
☎ 01 253 736 226.
🍎 *Bulmers Old Hazy*

MORECAMBE

Dog & Partridge (P)
19 Bare Lane.
☎ 01 524 426 246.
🍎 *Bulmers Old Hazy*

ORMSKIRK

EAGLE & CHILD (P)
Maltkiln Lane, Bispham Green
☎ 01 257 462 297
Open 12-3, 5.30-11; 12-10.30 Sun
🍎 **Bulmers Old Hazy, Weston's, Inch's**
Sixteenth-century country pub with seven real ales. Good food lunchtime and evening. Hard to find: M6 J27, follow signs for Parbold, then Bispham Green.

PRESTON

HOGSHEAD (P)
99 Fylde Road
☎ 01 772 252 870
Open all permitted hours
🍎 **Old Hazy, guests inc Biddenden, Art's**
Former doctor's surgery now dispensing a different medicine. Wide range of real ales, bar food lunchtime and evening, two-pint take-outs. Near university.

Kings Arms (P)
2 Stanley Street.
☎ 01 772 250 866.
🍎 *Bulmers Old Hazy*

Mansion House (P)
Liverpool Rd.
☎ 01 772 613 262.
🍎 *Bulmers Old Hazy*

NEW BRITANNIA (P)
6 Heatley Street
☎ 01 772 253 424

Open 11-3, 6-11; 7-10.30 only
Sun.
♦ Bulmers Traditional
One-bar pub near university,
often crowded at weekends.

OLD BLACK BULL (P)
35 Friargate
☎ 01 772 254 402
Open 10.30-11
**♦ Thatcher's, but varies
occasionally**
Ornate Tudor-style listed
building, large lounge, tiny
vault. Bar food lunchtime.

REAL ALE SHOP (OL)
47 Lovat Road
☎ 01 772 201 591
Open 11-2, 5-10 Mon-Sat, 12-2,
6-10 Sun.
**♦ Thatchers, Dunkerton's,
occasional guests**
Superb off-licence: four-pint
jugs, dozens of foreign bottled
beers, country wines, party
barrels, homebrew supplies –
even fancy dress hire.

STANLEY ARMS (P)
1 Lancaster Road
☎ 01 772 254 004
Open all permitted hours
♦ Bulmers Traditional
Grade II listed town-centre gin-
palace next to Guildhall, with
up to eight real ales and
excellent selection of bottled
beers. Separate restaurant
upstairs open at lunchtime. No
trainers!

TAP & SPILE (P)
185 Fylde Road
☎ 01 772 769 172
Open 11.30-3, 5.30-11 Mon-
Thurs, 11.30-11 Fri-Sat, 12.30-3,
7-10.30 Sun.
**♦ Bulmers Old Hazy, Weston's
cider and perry**
Recently-opened branch with
up to eight ales. Once the Hole
in the Wall, a regular for local
railwaymen. Bar snacks until
7pm.

SOUTHPORT

**LEGENDARY LANCASHIRE
HEROES** (OL)
101 Shakespear Street
☎ 01 704 533 668
Open 12-10.30 seven days
**♦ Thatchers, Biddenden,
Weston's, Inch's, Broadoak**
Small but busy real ale off-
licence

WETHERSPOON'S (P)
93 Lord Street
☎ 01 704 530 217
Open all permitted hours
♦ Weston's
Large open-plan Wetherspoon
pub. Other ciders available
during beer festivals. Food to
10pm (9.30 Sun); no-smoking
area; disabled access.

WARRINGTON

TUT'N'SHIVE (P)
2 Rylands Street
☎ 01 925 411 138
Open all permitted hours
♦ Bulmers Traditional
Single-bar distressed-look
alehouse in town centre. Meals
12-2.30, hot snacks to 7pm.

WHALLEY

Whalley Arms (P)
King Street.
☎ *01 254 822 800.*
♦ Bulmers Old Hazy

WIGAN

Halfway House (P)
149 Ormskirk Rd.
☎ *01 942 205 877.*
♦ Bulmers Old Hazy

Tudor House Hotel (P)
Newmarket Street.
☎ *01 942 700 296.*
♦ Biddenden

Leicestershire

CROXTON KERRIAL

PEACOCK (P)
School Lane
☎ 01 476 870 324
Open 11.30-2.30, 6.30-11.
🍎 **Cider range varies**
Large comfortable seventeenth-century Tynemill Inns pub. Children's certificate. bar food lunchtime and evening; disabled access.

FRISBY-ON-THE-WREAKE

BELL (P/OL)
Main Street
☎ 01 664 434 237
Open 12-2, 6-11 Mon-Sat; 12-2.30, 7-10.30 Sun
🍎 **Weston's Old Rosie (take-home only)**
Popular village pub with a good range of real ales, bar food 12-1.45 and 6.30-9.30, family room.

HEMINGTON

JOLLY SAILOR (P)
Main Street
☎ 01 332 810 448
Open 11-11
🍎 **Biddenden**
Popular village inn near East Midlands Airport. Disabled access.

HINKLEY

Rugby Road Wine Cellars (OL)
83 Rugby Road
☎ *01 455 632 431*
Open 9am-10pm seven days
🍎 *Weston's, Thatcher's*

LEICESTER

BARLEY MOW (P)
93 Granby Street
☎ 0116 254 4663
Open 11-11 Mon-Fri; 11-3, 7-11 Sat; 12-3 Sun

🍎 **Bulmers Old Hazy**
Newly-refurbished Everard's pub with guest ales. Bar food lunchtime and evening.

BOTTLE STORE (OL)
66 London Road
☎ 0116 285 6505
Open 10.30-10; closed Sun.
🍎 **Weston's and Biddenden ranges**
Off-licence with huge selection of bottled beers and occasional draught ciders.

FLYNN'S (OL)
171 Knighton Church Rd, Knighton
☎ 0116 270 6331
Open 9-10 Mon-Sat, 10-10 Sun.
🍎 **Thatchers Scrumpy**
Corner deli and bakery with real ale to take home and good range of bottled beers.

LEICESTER WHOLEFOOD CO-OPERATIVE (OL)
Unit 3, Freehold Street
☎ 0116 251 2525
Open 9.30-6 Mon-Thurs, 9.30-7 Fri, 9.30-5.30 Sat.
🍎 **Dunkerton's, Aspall's and Green Valley organic ciders**
Also organic beers and wines. Own car park.

Nag's Head & Star (P)
72 Oxford Street.
☎ *0116 254 3335.*
🍎 *Bulmers Old Hazy*

OLD HORSE (P)
198 London Road
☎ 0116 254 8384
Open 11-3, 5-11 Mon-Sat; 12-3, 7-10.30 Sun
🍎 **Bulmers Old Hazy**
Everard's alehouse popular with students. Bar food lunchtime and evening. Disabled access.

RAINBOW & DOVE (P)
185 Charles Street
☎ 0116 255 5916

Open 11.30-3, 5.30-11 Mon-Thurs; 11.30-11 Fri; 11-11 Sat; 12-3, 7-10.30 Sun
 Bulmers Old Hazy
Basic Banks's pub with range of guest ales and regular festivals. Food 12-2 Mon-Sat.

THREE CRANES (P)
82 Humberstone Gate
☎ 0116 251 7146
Open all permitted hours
 Bulmers Traditional
City free house specialising in independent breweries' beers. Table skittles played. Bar food lunchtime and evening. Letting rooms.

WILKIES (P)
29 Market Street
☎ 0116 255 6877
Open 12-11; closed Sun.
 Bulmers Old Hazy
Popular continental-style bar with wide range of bottled beers as well as guest ales. Bar food lunchtime and evening; separate restaurant specialising in German and Spanish food.

LEICESTER FOREST EAST

Airmans Rest (P)
Ratby Lane.
☎ *0116 238 6695.*
 Bulmers Old Hazy

LOUGHBOROUGH

Blacksmiths Arms (P)
47 Wardsend.
☎ *01 509 237 540.*
 Bulmers Traditional

SWAN IN THE RUSHES (P)
21 The Rushes
☎ 01 509 217 014
Open 11-2.30, 5-11.
 Cider range varies
Popular two-bar Tynemill Inns alehouse with letting rooms, good bar food lunchtime and evening, and disabled access.

TAP & MALLET (P)
36 Nottingham Road
☎ 01 509 210 028
Open 11.30-2.30, 5-11; 11-11 Sat
 Bulmers Traditional
Popular free house with children's play area in large garden. Bar food lunchtime.

Tap & Spile (P)
Bedford Square.
☎ *01 509 239 120.*
 Bulmers Old Hazy

THREE NUNS (P)
30 Churchgate
☎ 01 509 213 660
Open 11-11
 Bulmers Old Hazy
Alehouse serving breakfast from 9am Thurs-Sat. Braille menu; disabled access.

LUTTERWORTH

The Off-Licence & Beer Room (OL)
35 Station Road
☎ *0116 286 7942*
Open 10-10 Mon-Sat; 12-2, 7-10 Sun.
 Inch's and Weston's

NARBOROUGH

MAC'S SUPERMARKET (OL)
Copt Oak Court
☎ 0116 275 3289
Open 7am-10pm Mon-Sat
 Weston's

OADBY

COW & PLOUGH (P)
Stoughton Farm Park, Gartree Road
☎ 0116 272 0852
Open 5-9
 Weston's range
Regional CAMRA pub of the year with bizarre opening hours owing to Farmworld Leisure Park location. Converted barn with family area and snug; ales from micro brewers; bar food, no smoking area, disabled access.

SWATLAND'S (OL)
38 London Road
☎ 0116 271 9122
Open 10-10 seven days.
🍎 **Weston's range**

ROTHLEY

Royal Oak (P)
14 Cross Green.
☎ *0116 230 2158.*
🍎 *Bulmers Traditional*

SYSTON

Syston Off-Licence (OL)
1329 Melton Rd.
🍎 *Weston's range*

SYSTON WINES (OL)
1110 Melton Road
☎ 0116 260 2093
Open 9am-9.30pm Mon-Sat; 10-2, 5-9 Sun.
🍎 **Weston's range**

Lincolnshire

BOSTON

EAGLE (P)
144 West Street
☎ 01 205 361 116
Open 11-2.30, 6-11 Sun-Fri, 11-11 Sat
🍎 **Biddenden**
Town pub with six real ales. Folk club alternate Mondays.

GAINSBOROUGH

EIGHT JOLLY BREWERS (P)
Ship Court, Silver Street
☎ 01 427 677 128
Open 11-3, 7-11
🍎 **Weston's Old Rosie plus occasional guests**
Real ale heaven with up to eight beers at a time, mainly from small independent brewers. Adjacent car park is pay and display until 6pm.

GRANTHAM

BLUE BULL (P)
64 Westgate
☎ 01 476 70929
Open 11-3, 7-11
🍎 **Weston's plus occasional guests**
Local CAMRA favourite with lively atmosphere and good home-cooked food (not Sun evening). Separate restaurant.

BLUE PIG (P)
9 Vine Street
☎ 01 476 63704
Open all permitted hours
🍎 **Bulmers Traditional**
Rare Tudor survival. Popular drinking house with good-value lunchtime food.

TOLLEMACHE INN (P)
17 St Catherine's Road
☎ 01 476 594 696
Open 11-11
🍎 **Weston's plus guests**
New Wetherspoon pub with five real ales, bar food lunchtime and evening, no smoking area, disabled access.

LINCOLN

GOLDEN EAGLE (P)
21 High Street
☎ 01 522 521 058
Open 11-3, 5.30-11 Sun-Fri, 11-11 Sat
🍎 **Cider range varies**
Friendly local with changing guest ales and ciders. Hosts an annual cider festival.

JOLLY BREWER (P)
26 Broadgate
☎ 01 522 528 583
Open all permitted hours
🍎 **Bulmers Old Hazy**
Popular 1930s city centre pub. Families welcome lunchtime. No food Sun.

PORTLAND ARMS (P)
50 Portland Street
☎ 01 522 513 912
Open all permitted hours

🍎 Cider range varies
Lively tap room and cosy best room in traditional free house with guest beers from near and far.

SMALL BEER (OL)
91 Newland St West
☎ 01 522 528 628
Open 10.30-10.30
Back-street off-licence renowned near and far for its huge range of bottled and draught beers and ciders.

TAP & SPILE (P)
21 Hungate
☎ 01 522 534 015
Open all permitted hours
🍎 Crone's
Formerly the White Horse, now part of real ale pub chain. Real fire. Disabled access.

VICTORIA (P)
6 Union Road
☎ 01 522 536 048
Open all permitted hours
🍎 Weston's
Noted real ale free house.

LOUTH

Louth Wholefoods (OL)
Eastgate.
🍎 Dunkerton's range

ROTHWELL

NICKERSON ARMS (P)
Hillrise
☎ 01 472 371 300
Open 12-2, 7-11
🍎 Addlestone's
Attractions include 10 real ales, Belgian classics, unpasteurised imported lagers, malt whiskies, live jazz, a connoisseur's wine list and excellent food – and all set in unspoilt Wolds village. No smoking area.

SPILSBY

Red Lion (P)
East Kirkby.
☎ 01 790 3406.
🍎 Bulmers Traditional

STAMFORD

Dolphin (P)
60 East Street.
☎ 01 780 55494.
🍎 Bulmers Old Hazy

MARSH HARRIER (P)
7 All Saints' Place
☎ 01 780 62169
🍎 Crone's
Recently rescued from awful themed decor, this ancient three- room pub has reverted to a more traditional feel and as well as real cider sells Nethergate ales and a selection of beers from Belgium.

WADDINGHAM

BRANDY WHARF CIDER CENTRE (P)
Brandy Wharf.
☎ 01 652 678 364
Open 12-3, 7-11. Closed Xmas, New Year.
🍎 Weston's range, up to 16 others draught, 60 bottled
Remarkable centre complete with tavern and museum in four acres beside River Ancholme. Smoking not encouraged. Own orchard. Year-round programme of special events.

London

CENTRAL

Barley Mow (P)
50 Long Lane, EC1.
☎ 0171 606 6591.
🍎 Bulmers Old Hazy

Bull (P)
Devonshire Row, EC2.
☎ 0171 247 6792.
🍎 Bulmers Traditional

Chiswell St Vaults (P)
Chiswell Street, EC1.
☎ 0171 588 2642.
🍎 Bulmers Traditional

Edgar Wallace (P)
40 Essex Street, WC2.
☎ *0171 353 3120.*
🍎 *Bulmers Old Hazy*

Hogshead (P)
23 Wellington Street, WC2.
☎ *0171 836 6930.*
🍎 *Bulmers Old Hazy*

ROUNDHOUSE (P)
1 Garrick St WC2
☎ 0171 836 9838
Open all permitted hours
🍎 **Bulmers Old Hazy & Traditional**
Well-located S&N pub. Bar food lunchtime and evening.

Round Table (P)
26 St Martin's Ct, WC2.
☎ *0171 836 6436.*
🍎 *Bulmers Traditional*

SWAN (P)
Cosmo Place WC1
Open 11-11
🍎 **Bulmers Traditional**
Eighteenth-century pub now a T&J Bernard alehouse. Pavement seating on pedestrian precinct. Bar food lunchtime and evening.

EAST

Bow Bells (P)
Bow Rd, E3.
☎ *0181 519 8772.*
🍎 *Taunton Traditional*

DRUM (P)
557 Lea Bridge Rd, E10
☎ 0181 539 6577
Open all permitted hours
🍎 **Weston's**
One of the first Wetherspoon pubs. Still has a local character. Bar food lunchtime and evening; no smoking area.

FALCON & FIRKIN (P)
360 Victoria Park Rd, E9
☎ 0181 985 0693
Open all permitted hours
🍎 **Weston's Old Rosie**
Large brew pub on edge of park. Families welcome. Bar food lunchtime and evening; disabled access.

GEORGE (P)
High Street, E11
☎ 0181 989 2921
Open all permitted hours
🍎 **Weston's**
Large popular corner local. Bar food lunchtime and evening; no smoking area.

Good Sam's (P)
87 Turner Street, E1.
☎ *0171 247 9146.*
🍎 *Bulmers Traditional*

Lord Cardigan Arms (P)
Anglo Rd, E3.
☎ *0181 980 6329.*
🍎 *Taunton Traditional*

LORD RODNEY'S HEAD (P)
285 Whitechapel Rd, E1.
Open 11-11
🍎 **James White**
Splendid East End ale house on Whitechapel market. B&T ales. No food.

Old Globe (P)
191 Mile End Rd, E1.
☎ *0171 790 3524.*
🍎 *Bulmers Old Hazy*

Royal Standard (P)
1 Black Horse Lane, E17.
☎ *0181 503 2523.*
🍎 *Bulmers Traditional*

Theatre Royal Bar (P)
Gerry Raffles Square, E15.
☎ *0181 534 7374.*
🍎 *Bulmers Traditional*

NORTH

BEER SHOP (OL)
Pitfield Street, N1
☎ 0171 739 3701
Open 11.30-7 Mon-Sat
🍎 **Weston's, Dunkerton's, Biddenden**
Impressive range of bottled beers from around the world in shop which was home to the fabled and sorely-missed Pitfield Brewery.

Bush Hill Park Hotel (P)
141 St Marks Rd, Enfield.
☎ *0181 363 1008.*
🍏 *Bulmers Old Hazy*

FINNOCK & FIRKIN (P)
100 Upper Street, N1
☎ 0171 226 3467
Open all permitted hours
🍏 **Weston's Old Rosie**
Non-brewing recent Firkin
conversion. Bar food lunchtime
and evening; disabled access.

FLOUNDER & FIRKIN (P)
54 Holloway Rd, N7
☎ 0171 609 9574
Open all permitted hours
🍏 **Weston's Old Rosie**
Early Firkin. Bar food 12-3, 6-8;
disabled access.

HALF MOON (P)
749 Green Lanes, N21
☎ 0181 360 5410
Open all permitted hours
🍏 **Weston's Old Rosie**
Comfortable and popular
Wetherspoon shop conversion.
Bar food lunchtime and
evening; no smoking area.

HOGSHEAD (P)
New Arcade, 385 Holloway
Rd, N7
☎ 0171 609 9962
Open 11-11
🍏 **Bulmers Old Hazy**
New Whitbread alehouse
popular with students. bar
food to 7pm; disabled access.

Kings Head (P)
59 Essex Rd, N1.
☎ *0171 226 1825.*
🍏 *Bulmers Old Hazy*

LAMB (P)
54 Church Street, N9
Open 11-11
🍏 **Weston's Old Rosie**
Scottish Courage ales including
Old Peculier. Bar food
lunchtime and evening;
disabled access.

MOON UNDER WATER (P)
148 High Street, Barnet
☎ 0181 441 9476
Open all permitted hours
🍏 **Weston's**
Big Wetherspoon which was
local pub of the year 1995. Bar
food lunchtime and evening;
no smoking area.

PHOENIX BAR (P)
Alexandra Palace, N22.
Open 11-11
🍏 **Thatchers Cheddar Valley**
The finest way to spend a fine
afternoon in London must be
to sit on the patio of the
Phoenix with a glass or several
of fine cider. The bar is actually
within the Alexandra Palace
complex - hence its name, as
Ally Pally was completely
burnt down in 1980 and has
been rebuilt. On even a
moderately clear day you can
see the whole of the City,
Canary Wharf Tower and
Crystal Palace. Impressive beer
range, bar food lunchtime.

ROCHESTER CASTLE (P)
145 High Street, N16
☎ 0171 249 6016
Open all permitted hours
🍏 **Weston's**
Huge single bar with
conservatory attracts varied
clientele. Bar food lunchtime
and evening; no smoking area.

ROSE & CROWN (P)
86 High Street, N6
☎ 0181 340 6712
Open all permitted hours
🍏 **Bulmers Old Hazy**
Whitbread alehouse. Bar food
lunchtime and evening;
disabled access.

STEPTOE'S (P)
102 Church Street, N16
☎ 0171 254 2906.
Open all permitted hours
🍏 **Bulmers Old Hazy**
Chic two-room Charles Wells-
owned alehouse with pleasant
garden. Bar food lunchtime.

TALLY HO (P)
749 High Street, N12
☎ 0181 445 4390
Open all permitted hours
❧ Weston's
Imposing Wetherspoon pub
with upstairs bar. Decorated
with old local photos. Bar food
lunchtime and evening; no-
smoking area.

TAP & SPILE (P)
29 Crouch Hill, N4
☎ 0171 272 7748
Open all permitted hours
❧ Crone's
Early Tap & Spile in small
corner site. Good ale range; bar
food lunchtime; disabled
access.

TAPPIT HEN (P)
295 Holloway Rd, N7.
☎ 0171 607 9207
Open all permitted hours
❧ Weston's range
High street alehouse popular
with students. Bar food
lunchtime and evening. Beware
keg Taunton Cidermaster on
fake handpump.

TOLLGATE (P)
28 Turnpike Lane, N8
☎ 0181 889 9085
Open all permitted hours
❧ Weston's Old Rosie
Large Wetherspoon. Bar food
lunchtime and evening; no
smoking area; disabled access.

Torrington Arms (P)
4 Lodge Lane, N12.
☎ 0181 445 4710.
❧ Bulmers Old Hazy

TUT'N'SHIVE (P)
235 Upper Street, N1
☎ 0171 359 7719
Open 11-11
❧ Bulmers Old Hazy
Large one bar pub with
comedy nights, poetry
readings. Bar food lunchtime;
disabled access.

WENLOCK ARMS (P)
26 Wenlock Rd, N1
☎ 0171 608 3406
Open all permitted hours
❧ Cider range varies
Back-street Mecca for ale, cider
and perry lovers. One-bar pub
in rundown area taken over
and transformed by genuine
enthusiasts. Salt beef
sandwiches to die for.

WETHERSPOON (P)
148 High Street, Barnet.
Open 11-11.
❧ Weston's Old Rosie
Good range of ales in
converted carpet shop with
unusual perspex roof. Bar food
lunchtime and evening.

WHITE LION OF MORTIMER
(P)
125 Stroud Green Rd, N4
☎ 0171 281 4773
Open 11-11
❧ Weston's Old Rosie
Big Wetherspoon. Bar food
lunchtime and evening; no-
smoking area.

WHOLE HOG (P)
430 Green Lanes, N13
Open 11-11
❧ Weston's
Typical Wetherspoon pub with
food all day, no-smoking area,
and full disabled access.

NORTH-WEST

FRIAR & FIRKIN (P)
120 Euston rd, NW1
☎ 0171 387 2419
Open all permitted hours
❧ Weston's Old Rosie
Standard basic Firkin with
brewery in cellar. Bar food
until 7.30; disabled access.

FUSILIER & FIRKIN (P)
7 Chalk Farm Rd, NW1
☎ 0171 485 7858

Open all permitted hours
🍎 **Weston's Old Rosie**
Basic Firkin opposite Camden Lock Market, so busy at weekends. Bar food until 7pm.

HEAD OF STEAM (P)
1 Eversholt Street, NW1
☎ 0171 388 2221
Open 11-11
🍎 **Biddenden medium**
Modern pub on Euston Station forecourt converted into railway theme bar by real ale entrepreneur Tony Brookes.

KING OF BOHEMIA (P)
10 High Street, NW3.
☎ 0171 435 6513.
Bulmers Old Hazy.
Malthouse (P)
7 Stanmore Hill, Stanmore
Open all permitted hours
🍎 **Cider range varies**
Formerly a wine bar, now an alehouse with up to six real ales and frequent festivals. Bar food lunchtime and evening.

Mowbray Stores (OL)
96 Edgware Way, Edgware.
☎ *0181 958 8217.*
🍎 *Bulmers Traditional*

NORTH STAR (P)
104 Finchley Rd, NW3
☎ 0171 435 6287
Open all permitted hours
🍎 **Bulmers Traditional**
London outpost of Scottish & Newcastle's T&J Bernard chain. Bar food to 9pm. Expensive.

Pembroke Castle (P)
Gloucester Ave.
☎ *0171 483 2927.*
🍎 *Bulmers Old Hazy*

SOUTH-EAST

BIRD IN HAND (P)
35 Dartmouth Rd, SE23
☎ 0181 699 7417
Open all permitted hours
🍎 **Weston's**

Small Victorian Wetherspoon; cheap beer lunchtime attracts pensioners. Bar food lunchtime and evening; no smoking area.

BITTER EXPERIENCE (OL)
129 Lee Rd, SE3
☎ 0181 852 8819
11-9.30; 12-3, 7-9 Sun.
🍎 **Biddenden, Weston's Old Rosie, Rich's, Thatcher's on draught; Biddenden, Weston's, Breton in bottle**
Outstanding specialist off-licence.

Crown (P)
49 Tranquil Vale, SE3.
☎ *0181 852 0326.*
🍎 *Bulmers Traditional*

CRYSTAL PALACE TAVERN (P)
105 Tanners Hill, SE8
☎ 0181 692 1536
Open 3pm-midnight Mon-Thurs; 3pm-2am Fri/Sat; 1-10.30 Sun
🍎 **Range varies**
One-bar 1930s pub specialising in live music and real ales. At least one traditional cider or perry always available, with festival every July. Families welcome. Large garden. Food Sat-Sun only.

Davison's (OL)
31 The Village, SE7.
🍎 *Bulmers Traditional*

FIRE STATION (R)
150 Waterloo Rd, SE1
☎ 0171 620 2226
Open 12-11; closed Sun
🍎 **Weston's range**
Converted fire station now specialising in British and Mediterranean food.

FOX ON THE HILL (P)
149 Denmark Hill, SE5
☎ 0171 738 4756
Open all permitted hours
🍎 **Weston's**
Imposing Wetherspoon noted for its disabled facilities. Bar food lunchtime and evening; no-smoking area.

Golden Dragon (P)
48 St Norberts Rd, SE4.
☎ *0171 639 6934.*
 Bulmers Old Hazy

Hermit's Cave (P)
28 Camberwell Church Street,
SE5.
☎ *0171 703 3188.*
 Bulmers Old Hazy

Hogshead (P)
354 High Street, SE13.
☎ *0181 690 2054.*
 Bulmers Old Hazy

JT Davies (OL)
160 Jamaica Rd, SE16.
☎ *0171 237 1001.*
 Bulmers Traditional

Moon & Stars (P)
164 High Street, SE20.
 Weston's Old Rosie.

PHOENIX & FIRKIN (P)
5 Windsor Walk, SE5
Open 11-11
 Weston's Old Rosie
One of the earliest and most
characterful Firkin pubs,
rebuilt from the gutted remains
of Denmark Hill Station
booking office. Open plan with
gallery decorated with railway
memorabilia. Bar food
lunchtime and evening.

Streets (P)
121 Lower Marsh Rd, SE1.
☎ *0171 261 1782.*
 Bulmers Old Hazy

SOUTH-WEST

Adam & Eve (P)
81 Petty France, SW1.
☎ *0171 222 4575.*
 Bulmers Traditional

BEDFORD ARMS (P)
409 Clapham Rd, SW9
☎ 0171 274 2472
Open all permitted hours
 Bulmers Old Hazy
Whitbread bare-board alehouse
popular with students. Bar
food lunchtime. Bar billiards.

BRITANNIA (P)
353 Wandsworth Rd, SW8
☎ 0171 622 3507
Open all permitted hours
 Bulmers Old Hazy
High street pub popular with
local Portuguese community.
Disco weekends.

CHIMES (R)
26 Churton St SW1
☎ 0171 821 7456
Open 12-3, 5.30
 Weston's, Biddenden,
Dunkerton's
Wine bar and restaurant
specialising in cider and perry.
Menu and decor have an
English rustic accent. Bar food
lunchtime.

CROWN & SCEPTRE (P)
2 Streatham Hill, SW2
☎ 0181 671 0843
Open all permitted hours
 Weston's
Big Wetherspoon roadhouse,
home to local chess club. Bar
food lunchtime and evening;
no smoking area.

Euro Wines (OL)
32 Park Rd, Kingston
☎ *0181 546 9880*
Open 11-2, 4-9
 Weston's

FIGHTING COCKS (P)
56 London Rd, Kingston
☎ 0181 546 5174
Open all permitted hours
 Ciders vary
Popular town-centre alehouse
with Belgian bottled beers. Bar
food lunchtime.

FINANCIER & FIRKIN (P)
43 Market Place, Kingston
☎ 0181 974 8223
Open all permitted hours
 Weston's Old Rosie
Standard Firkin alehouse in old
bank, but no brewery on site.
Bar food lunchtime and
evening.

FLICKER & FIRKIN (P)
Duke's Yard, Duke Street,
Richmond
☎ 0181 332 7807
Open 11-11
🍎 **Weston's range**
Former indoor antiques
market, now a standard Firkin
brew pub. Food lunchtime and
evening; disabled access.

FLOWER & FIRKIN (P)
Station Parade, Kew
☎ 0181 332 1162
Open 11-11
🍎 **Weston's**
Extended former station tea-
rooms. Bar food lunchtime and
evening.

FREEDOM & FIRKIN (P)
196 Tooting High Street, SW17
☎ 0181 672 5794
Open 12-11
🍎 **Weston's**
Newly-opened Firkin named in
honour of Tooting Popular
Front. Bar food lunchtime and
evening. Disabled toilet, but
access to pub requires
negotiation of steps.

FRIESIAN & FIRKIN (P)
87 Rectory Grove, SW4
☎ 0171 622 4666
Open 12-11; 12-3, 7-10.30 Sun.
🍎 **Addlestone's on handpump**
Firkin pub with brewery on
site. Live music Fri, Sat, Sun.
Bar food lunchtime.

GRID INN (P)
22 Replingham Rd, SW18
☎ 0181 874 8460
Open all permitted hours
🍎 **Weston's GWR**
Wetherspoon alehouse with
local history theme. Bar food
lunchtime and evening.

HAND & RACKET (P)
25 Wimbledon Hill Rd, SW19
☎ 0181 947 9391
Open all permitted hours
🍎 **Bulmers Old Hazy**
Whitbread Hogshead alehouse
in former shop. Bar food till

8pm. Disabled access includes
low bar for wheelchair users.

KELLY ARMS (P)
2 Glenthorne Rd, Kingston
☎ 0181 546 8450
Open all permitted hours
🍎 **Weston's**
Victorian backstreet local. Bar
food lunchtime. Children
welcome.

MOON ON THE HILL (P)
9 Hill Rd, Sutton
☎ 0181 643 1202
Open all permitted hours
🍎 **Weston's**
Large Wetherspoon house in
former department store.
Terrace garden; bar food
lunchtime and evening; no
smoking area; disabled access.

MOON UNDER WATER (P)
194 Balham High Rd, SW12
☎ 0181 673 0535
Open all permitted hours.
🍎 **Weston's**
Wetherspoon shop conversion.
bar food lunchtime and
evening; separate restaurant
12-2.30 Mon-Sat. Disabled
access.

NEWT & FERRET (P)
46 Fairfield South, Kingston
☎ 0181 546 3804
Open all permitted hours
🍎 **Inch's**
Victorian Hall & Woodhouse
pub. Bar food lunchtime and
evening; barbecues at
weekends in summer.

PRINCE OF WALES (P)
2 Hartfield Rd, SW19
☎ 0181 946 5369
Open all permitted hours
🍎 **Bulmers Traditional**
Recently-refurbished pub with
magnificent tiled exterior. Bar
food lunchtime and evening.

PRIORY ARMS (P)
83 Lansdowne Way, SW8
☎ 0171 622 1884
Open 11-11; 12-3, 7-10.30 Sun.
🍎 **Thatcher's Scrumpy,**

Goverd's perry
Classic London pub. Grade II
listed and in conservation area.
Local pub of the year 1994. Bar
food lunchtime. Beers from
independent brewers. Jazz in
upstairs room at weekends.

RAILWAY (P)
202 Upper Richmond Rd,
SW15
☎ 0181 788 8190
Open all permitted hours
🍏 **Weston's**
Older Wetherspoon with
railway theme. Bar food
lunchtime and evening;
disabled access.

RAM (P)
34 High Street, Kingston
☎ 0181 546 4518
Open all permitted hours
🍏 **Bulmers Traditional**
Oldest pub in Kingston, now a
T&J Bernard alehouse. Beer
garden runs down to Thames.
Bar food lunchtime and
evening.

Ship (P)
47 High Street, Croydon.
☎ *0181 688 2878.*
🍏 *Bulmers Old Hazy*

SPOTTED DOG (P)
72 Garrett Lane, SW18
☎ 0181 875 9531
Open all permitted hours
🍏 **Weston's Old Rosie**
Typical Wetherspoon pub. Bar
food lunchtime and evening.

Stage Door (P)
3 Allington Street, SW1.
☎ *0171 834 7055.*
🍏 *Bulmers Traditional*

Stargazeys (P)
236 Fulham Rd, SW10.
☎ *0171 376 5827.*
🍏 *Bulmers Old Hazy*

SULTAN (P)
78 Norman Rd, SW19
☎ 0181 542 4532
Open all permitted hours
🍏 **Broadoak**

Two-bar 1950s pub; Hop Back
Brewery's first in London. Bar
food lunchtime.

SWAN (P)
89 Ridgway, SW19
☎ 0181 946 1652
Open all permitted hours
🍏 **Bulmers Traditional**
Big Victorian pub attracting
younger clientele. Bar food
lunchtime.

Tut'n'Shive (P)
16 Gillingham Street, SW1.
☎ *0171 834 2777.*
🍏 *Bulmers Old Hazy*

UNITY (P)
228 York Rd, SW11
☎ 0171 738 0924
Open all permitted hours
🍏 **Thatcher's**
Bareboard but elegant alehouse
with private booths. Excellent
bar food lunchtime and
evening.

Waldegrave Arms (P)
209 Waldegrave Rd, Teddington.
☎ *0181 977 1288.*
🍏 *Bulmers Traditional*

WETHERSPOONS (P)
Aberconway Rd, Morden
Open all permitted hours
🍏 **Weston's GWR**
Brand-new pub in shopping
mall attempts to reflect history
of the area. Bar food lunchtime
and evening; disabled access.

WETHERSPOONS (P)
Victoria Station, SW1
☎ 0171 931 0445
Open all permitted hours
🍏 **Weston's**
A must for thirsty travellers:
watch the departure board as
you drink! Bar food lunchtime
and evening; disabled access.

WHITE LION OF MORTIMER
(P)
223 London Rd, Mitcham
☎ 0181 646 7332
Open all permitted hours
🍏 **Weston's**

Big town-centre Wetherspoon. Bar food lunchtime and evening.

WIBBA'S DOWN INN (P)
6-12 Gladstone Rd, SW19
☎ 0181 540 6788
Open all permitted hours
🍏 Weston's
New two-bar Wetherspoon. Bar food lunchtime and evening; disabled access.

Willoughby Arms (P)
41 Willoughby Rd, Kingston.
☎ *0181 546 4236.*
🍏 *Bulmers Old Hazy*

WEST

Chariot (P)
34 High Street, Hounslow.
☎ *0181 572 8044.*
🍏 *Bulmers Old Hazy*

Fountains Abbey (P)
109 Praed Street, W2.
☎ *0171 723 2364.*
🍏 *Bulmers Traditional*

Gilray's (P)
26 Maddox Street, W1.
☎ *0171 409 2976.*
🍏 *Bulmers Traditional*

GRAFTON ARMS (P)
22 Grafton way, W1
☎ 0171 387 7923
Open 11-11
🍏 **Bulmers Old Hazy**
One-bar Hogshead alehouse. Bar food to 9pm.

Grapes (P)
16 Shepherd Market, W1.
☎ *0171 629 4989.*
🍏 *Bulmers Old Hazy*

Hogshead (P)
14 Blenheim Crescent, W11.
☎ *0171 727 8795.*
🍏 *Bulmers Old Hazy*

Hogshead (P)
11 Dering Street, W1.
☎ *0171 629 0531.*
🍏 *Bulmers Old Hazy*

JJ MOONS (P)
12 Victoria Rd, Ruislip Manor
☎ 01 895 622 373
Open all permitted hours
🍏 Weston's
Bustling Wetherspoon conversion of former Woolworths. Bar food lunchtime and evening; disabled access.

Kent Hotel (P)
2 Scotch Common, W13.
☎ *0181 997 5911.*
🍏 *Bulmers Old Hazy*

Kings Head (P)
33 Moscow Rd, W2.
☎ *0171 229 4233.*
🍏 *Bulmers Traditional*

LOAD OF HAY (P)
33 Villiers Street, Uxbridge
☎ 01 895 234 676
Open 11-3, 5.30-11.
🍏 **Cider range varies**
Cosy local with excellent restaurant. Bar food lunchtime and evening (not Sun or Mon evening). No smoking area.

LONDON WHOLEFOOD (OL)
24 Paddington Street, W1
☎ 0171 935 3924
Open 8.45am-6pm; 8.45-1 sat; Closed Sun
🍏 **Various organic bottled ciders**

MOON ON THE SQUARE (P)
30 The Centre, High Street, Feltham
☎ 0181 893 1293
Open 11-11
🍏 **Weston's GWR**
Wetherspoon conversion in pedestrian precinct. Bar food always available; no smoking area; disabled access.

MOON UNDER WATER (P)
86 Staines Rd, Hounslow
☎ 0181 572 7506
Open 11-11
🍏 **Weston's GWR**
Popular high street alehouse. Food always available; no smoking area; disabled access.

MOON UNDER WATER (P)
55 London Rd, Twickenham
☎ 0181 744 0080
Open 11-11
🍎 **Weston's GWR**
Early but recently-extended
Wetherspoon alehouse. Food
always available; no smoking
area; disabled access.

Plough (P)
297 Northfield Ave, W5.
☎ *0181 567 1416.*
🍎 *Bulmers Old Hazy*

Queens Arms (P)
233 Hanworth Rd, Hounslow.
☎ *0181 230 4775.*
🍎 *Bulmers Old Hazy*

Queens Head (P)
54 Windsor Street, Uxbridge.
☎ *01 895 258 750.*
🍎 *Bulmers Traditional*

Red Lion & Pineapple (P)
281 High Street, W3.
🍎 *Weston's Old Rosie.*

Rising Sun (P)
46 Tottenham Court Rd, W1.
☎ *0171 636 6530.*
🍎 *Bulmers Traditional*

ROYAL ALBION (P)
58 Hibernia Rd, Hounslow
☎ 0181 572 8461
Open 11-11
🍎 **Inch's**
Friendly side-street local.
Usher's ales. Bar food Mon-Sat
lunchtime.

Royal Oak (P)
58 Milson Rd, W14.
☎ *0171 602 2567.*
🍎 *Bulmers Old Hazy*

TAP & SPILE (P)
Terminal One, Heathrow
Airport
☎ 0181 897 8418
Open 9am-11pm (breakfast
only till 11am); 11-11 Sun.
🍎 **Crone's User Friendly,
Weston's Old Rosie, Bulmers
Old Hazy**
Now-famous real ale haven

with 11 beers on at a time,
attracts regular trade as well as
travellers. 1930s decor. Family
room, disabled access, bar
food, no-smoking area.

Greater Manchester

ALTRINCHAM

HOGSHEAD (P)
Old Market Place
☎ 0161 972 7062
Open all permitted hours
🍎 **Bulmers Old Hazy**
Former town hall, then a
coaching inn, now a Whitbread
alehouse. Family room, food
lunchtime and evenings, no
smoking area.

ASHTON-UNDER-LYNE

STATION (P)
2 Warrington Street
☎ 0161 330 6776
Open 11.30-11, 12-3, 7-11 Sun
🍎 **Thatcher's**
Five real ales in genuine free
house. Regular beer festivals.
Food lunchtime.

BOLTON

HOGSHEAD (P)
57 Bradshawgate
☎ 01 204 370 586
Open all permitted hours
🍎 **Bulmers Old Hazy**
Typical open-plan alehouse.
Bar food lunchtime. Disabled
access.

MAXIM'S (P)
26 Bradshawgate
☎ 01 204 526 048
Open 11.30-4, 7.30-11
🍎 **Bulmers Old Hazy**
Open plan brewer's Victorian
town-centre pub. Bar food
lunchtime; separate restaurant.
Children's certificate; disabled
access.

OLD MAN & SCYTHE (P)
Churchgate
☎ 01 204 527 267
Open 11-11; 12-4, 7-10.30 Sun
🍎 **Bulmers Old Hazy &
Traditional, Thatchers**
Famous and atmospheric
seventeenth-century town-
centre pub. Bar food lunchtime;
separate restaurant.

Robin Hood (P)
70 Halliwell Rd.
☎ *01 204 494 439.*
🍎 *Bulmers Old Hazy*

SWAN HOTEL (P)
-4 Churchgate
☎ 01 204 522 909
Open 11-3, 7-11; 7-10.30 Sun
🍎 **Up to three ciders and
perries in Malt & Hops bar**
Grade II listed old-fashioned
town-centre pub. Beer and
cider festival in summer. Food
till 7pm.

BROMLEY CROSS

FLAG INN (P)
0 Hardmans Lane
☎ 01 204 302 236
Open 11-11
🍎 **Bulmers Old Hazy**
Whitbread real ale house with
guest ales. Local pub of the
year 1994. Bar food to 7pm.

BURY

TAP & SPILE (P)
6 Manchester Road
☎ 0161 763 7483
Open 11-3, 5-11, 11-11 Fri/Sat
🍎 **Crone's**
Small friendly end-of-terrace
alehouse with own house
beers. Good home-cooked food
the korma is recommended.
No smoking area. Disabled
access.

CHEETHAM

QUEEN'S ARMS (P)
Honey Street, off Red Bank
☎ 0161 834 4239

Open 12-11
🍎 **Weston's Old Rosie**
Comfortable two-room pub
with good selection of real ales,
beer garden, children's play
area. Bar food lunchtime and
evening. Bar billiards, table
skittles.

CHORLTON

LASS O'GOWRIE (P)
36 Charles Street
☎ 0161 273 6932
🍎 **Bulmers Old Hazy**
Well-known Whitbread
brewpub opened in 1983.
Brewery visible from bar -
tours available

CRUMPSALL

Lancashire Heroes (P)
18 Cleveland Rd.
☎ *0161 795 1406.*
🍎 *Bulmers Traditional*

DIDSBURY

OLD COCK (P)
848 Wilmslow Road
☎ 0161 445 4405
Open all permitted hours
🍎 **Old Hazy plus guest**
Local CAMRA favourite with
up to 11 real ales and free
tasters. Large and busy,
popular with students. Folk
night Tuesday. Bar food
lunchtime and evening.

FALLOWFIELD

BREWERS ARMS (P)
151 Ladybarn Road
☎ 0161 224 5576
Open all permitted hours
🍎 **Bulmers Old Hazy**
Thriving Hogshead-style
Whitbread ale house with
changing real ales. Specialises
in pies. Disabled access.

GOLBORNE

RAILWAY HOTEL (P)
131 High Street
☎ 01 942 728 202
Open 12-11
⚫ Cider range varies
Traditional town-centre pub
with guest ales. Letting rooms.

HASLINGDEN

White Horse Hotel (P)
Holcombe Rd, Helmshore.
☎ 01 706 213 873.
⚫ Bulmers Old Hazy

HAZEL GROVE

St Peters Social Club (C)
Green Lane.
☎ 01 594 510 658.
⚫ Bulmers Traditional

HEYWOOD

Talbot Hotel (P)
72 Bridge Street.
☎ 01 706 69089.
⚫ Bulmers Traditional

HORWICH

Old Original Bay Horse (P)
206 Lee Lane.
☎ 01 204 696 231.
⚫ Bulmers Old Hazy

MANCHESTER

BEER HOUSE (P)
Angel Street
☎ 0161 839 7019
Open 11.30-11
⚫ Thatcher's plus up to three guests
Busy and basic pub with large
real ale menu, tiny beer
garden, and upstairs meeting
room. Occasional cider
festivals. Bar food lunchtime
and 5-7. Five minutes' walk
from Victoria Station.

FLEA & FIRKIN (P)
137 Grosvenor Rd, Manchester
All Saints
☎ 0161 274 3682

Open all permitted hours in
University term, much
restricted in vacations.
⚫ Weston's Old Rosie
Familiar Firkin style pitched
squarely at students. Own
brewery, but ales served under
a gas blanket. Food at
lunchtime.

HOGSHEAD (P)
64 High Street
☎ 0161 832 4824
Open 11.30-11 Mon-Sat,
12-5.30 Sun
⚫ Old Hazy
Up to 10 real ales including
four on gravity. Food
lunchtime and evening.
Children welcome at
weekends. Metro station
outside pub.

MARBLE ARCH (P)
73 Rochdale Road
☎ 0161 832 5914
Open 12-11 Mon-Sat,
 7-10.30 Sun
⚫ Biddenden plus guest
Magnificent barrel-vaulted
ceiling, elaborate tilework and
frieze in main bar give this pub
its character. Separate function
room, food at lunchtime.

SMITHFIELD (P)
37 Swan Street
☎ 0161 839 4424
Open 11-11; 7-10.30 Sun
⚫ Weston's range
Small open plan pub with
letting rooms. Bar food 12-8;
separate restaurant.

WETHERSPOON (P)
49 Piccadilly
Open all permitted hours
⚫ Westons First Quality
Enormous centrally-located
alehouse, originally a cinema.
Food lunchtime and evening.

White Lion (P)
43 Liverpool Rd,
Deansgate.
☎ 0161 832 7373.
⚫ Bulmers Traditional

OLDHAM

HOGSHEAD (P)
Union Street
☎ 0161 773 8663
Open all permitted hours
◆ **Bulmers Old Hazy**
Ten handpumps. Good
lunchtime food on weekdays.
Function room.

RADCLIFFE

Rose & Crown (P)
2 Cockey Moor Rd, Starling.
☎ *0161 761 7523.*
◆ *Bulmers Old Hazy*

Swan Hotel (P)
Stand Lane.
☎ *0161 280 5444.*
◆ *Taunton Traditional*

SALFORD

CRESCENT (P)
20 The Crescent
Open 12-11 Mon Fri, 7-11 Sat,
1-4, 7.30-10.30 Sun
◆ **Ciders vary**
Eighteenth-century one-bar
pub popular with students.
Value for money bar food.

DOCK & PULPIT (P)
Encombe Place
☎ 0161 834 0121
Open 12-3, 5-11 Sun-Fri, 12-3,
5.30-11 sat, 12-3, 7.30-10.30 Sun
◆ **Old Hazy plus guests,**
occasional perry
Basic but popular one-bar pub
between the old County Court
and a church. Bar food
lunchtime and evening.

KINGS ARMS (P)
Bloom Street
☎ 0161 839 4338
Open 12-11 Mon-Sat, 12-4.30, 7-
10.30 Sun.
◆ **Weston's Old Rosie plus**
occasional perry

Large Grade II listed two-room
Boddington Ale House. Good
range of real ales and foreign
bottled beers. Family room, bar
food at lunchtime.

SKELMERSDALE

White House (P)
1 Water Street.
☎ *0161 303 2582.*
◆ *Bulmers Old Hazy*

STOCKPORT

CROWN (P)
Heaton Lane
☎ 0161 429 0549
Open 12-11
◆ **Ciders vary**
Boddington Ale House in
shadow of railway viaduct.
Four rooms include well-used
vault. Up to nine real ales,
good bar food lunchtime, no
smoking area.

WITHINGTON

Iffy's (OL)
534 Wilmslow Rd.
◆ *Inch's*

RED LION (P)
532 Wilmslow Road
Open all permitted hours
◆ **Bulmers Old Hazy**
Busy main road two-bar pub
with bowling green. Children
allowed to 8pm; meals to 8pm.

Merseyside

BIRKENHEAD

CLAUGHTON CASK (P)
50 Upton Road
☎ 0151 652 2056
Open all permitted hours
◆ **Bulmers Old Hazy**
Whitbread pub where most
guest ales come from small
independent brewers. Sports
oriented – big TV screen in
lounge although nooks and

crannies offer escape.
Food till 8.

ROCK VILLA HOTEL (P)
329 Old Chester Rd, Rock Ferry
☎ 0151 645 3346
Open all permitted hours
🍎 **Bulmers Old Hazy**
Large Whitbread house with
family atmosphere. Children
welcome to 7pm. No food.

**TRANMERE HOMEBREW
CENTRE** (OL)
75 Greenway Rd, Higher
Tranmere
☎ 0151 653 3442
Open 10-5; closed Wed, Sun
🍎 **Cider range always includes
one draught**
Good value home-brew
supplier - cider customers
bring their own containers and
pay only 79p a pint.

CROSBY

Crosby Hotel (P)
Liverpool Rd.
☎ *0151 924 2574.*
🍎 *Bulmers Old Hazy*

CROWN (P)
128 Conway Street
☎ 0151 650 1095
Open 11.30-11; 12-3, 7-10.30
Sun
🍎 **Cider range varies**
Busy ale-house with live folk
music, bikers' nights, quizzes
etc. Separate public bar, family
room, Bar food lunchtime and
evening.

LIVERPOOL

Derby Arms (P)
1 Russell Street, Garston.
☎ *0151 427 7938.*
🍎 *Bulmers Old Hazy*

EVERYMAN BISTRO (P)
6 Hope Street
☎ 0151 708 9545
Open 12-12 Mon-Sat,
closed Sun.
🍎 **Bulmer's Traditional**
Below Everyman Theatre, near

RC Cathedral. Food from
midday-10pm. No-smoking
area for non-diners.

Hogshead (P)
195 County Rd, Walton.
☎ *0151 525 8523.*
🍎 *Bulmers Old Hazy*

SHIP & MITRE (P)
133 Dale Street
☎ 0151 236 0859
Open 11.30-11 Mon-Fri, 12.30-
11 Sat, closed Sun
🍎 **Cider range varies**
Large open-plan pub, gas-lit.
Up to 10 real ales always
available – four CAMRA
awards in four years. Bar food
lunchtime.

SWAN INN (P)
88 Wood Street
☎ 0151 709 5281
Open all permitted hours
🍎 **Thatcher's**
Lively pub on two floors,
frequented by bikers and
students. Food lunchtime.

WETHERSPOONS (P)
1-3 Gt Charlotte Street
☎ 0151 709 4802
Open all permitted hours
🍎 **Westons**
Big modern open-plan pub.
Food 11-10. No-smoking area
disabled access.

ST HELENS

New Inn (P)
90 Peasley Cross Lane.
☎ *01 744 454 153.*
🍎 *Bulmers Old Hazy*

WALLASEY

STANLEY'S CASK (P)
212 Rake Lane
☎ 0151 691 1093
Open all permitted hours
🍎 **Ciders vary**
Small olde-worlde multi-room
local. Quiz nights, live music
Food lunchtime and evening
disabled access.

Norfolk

EESTON

OUGHSHARE (P)
e Street
01 328 701 845
en 12-2.30, 6-11; 12-11 Sat
Kingfisher
venteenth-century
placement of fifteenth-
ntury pub. Families
elcome; occasional live folk
usic; bar food lunchtime and
ening.

URNHAM MARKET

OSTE ARMS (P)
e Green
01 328 738 257
en all permitted hours
Kingfisher
ulti-room seventeenth-
ntury inn with live jazz and
ues. Family room, letting
oms, bar food lunchtime and
ening, no-smoking area,
sabled access.

ANTLEY

ck (P)
or Rd.
01 493 700 340.
Kingfisher

d House (P)
tion Rd.
01 493 700 801.
Kingfisher

OLTISHALL

ilway (P)
tion Rd.
01 673 738 316.
Kingfisher

OWNHAM MARKET

ck Tavern (P)
Lym Rd.
01 366 385 047.
Kingfisher

EAST RUNTON

Fishing Boat (P)
High Street.
☎ *01 263 515 323.*
 Kingfisher

ERPINGHAM

APPLE SHOP (OL, R)
Alby Craft Centre, Cromer
Road
☎ 01 263 761 702
Open 10-5 Tues-Sun & Bank
Holidays
 Kingfisher
Multi-attraction craft centre
which is also nerve centre of
Norfolk Cider Company.
Families welcome, disabled
access, food lunchtime.

GELDESTON

GELDESTON LOCKS INN (P)
Station Road
☎ 01 508 518 414
Open 11.30-3, 7-11.
 James White
Atmospheric old real ale pub.
Bar food lunchtime and
evening; family room; campsite
with room for 70 tents.

GORLESTON

DOCK TAVERN (P)
Dock Tavern Lane
☎ 01 493 442 255
Open 11-11
 Kingfisher
Welcoming local near river
with collection of maritime
artefacts and outdoor
menagerie including pot-
bellied pig. Families welcome;
bar food lunchtime.

Old Commodore (P)
217 High Street.
☎ *01 493 441 721.*
 Kingfisher

GREAT YARMOUTH

Gallon Pot (P)
Market Place.
☎ 01 493 842 230.
🍎 *Bulmers Old Hazy*

HILBOROUGH

SWAN (P)
☎ 01 760 756 380
Open 11-3, 6-11
🍎 **Kingfisher**
Superb keg-free roadhouse.
Good food lunchtime and
evening.

HUNSTANTON

Lifeboat (P)
Ship Lane, Thornham.
☎ 01 485 512 236.
🍎 *Taunton Traditional*

LODDON

Swan (P)
Church Plain.
☎ 01 508 520 239.
🍎 *Bulmers Old Hazy*

MARKET DEEPING

Vine (P)
19 Church Street.
☎ 01 778 342 387.
🍎 *Bulmers Old Hazy*

NORWICH

ALEXANDRA TAVERN (P)
16 Stafford Street
☎ 01 603 627 772
Open all permitted hours
🍎 **Banham**
Friendly Victorian corner pub
which stocks ale from local
Chalk Hill Brewery. Disabled
access.

COACH & HORSES (P)
82 Thorpe Road
☎ 01 603 620 704
Open all permitted hours
🍎 **Banham, Kingfisher**
Busy alehouse, home of Chalk
Hill Brewery. Bar food
lunchtime and evening.

FAT CAT (P)
49 West End Street
☎ 01 603 624 364
Open 12-11.
🍎 **Banham Rum Cask,
Kingfisher**
Victorian alehouse with wide
range of ales from small
breweries. Disabled access.

Hotel Norwich (P)
Boundary Rd.
☎ 01 603 787 260.
🍎 *Bulmers Old Hazy*

Jubilee (P)
26 St Leonards Rd.
☎ 01 603 618 734.
🍎 *Kingfisher*

Merchants of Colegate (P)
30 Colegate.
☎ 01 603 664 175.
🍎 *Bulmers Old Hazy*

RIBS OF BEEF (P)
24 Wensum Street
☎ 01 603 619 517
Open all permitted hours
🍎 **Banham**
Comfortable riverside pub
with wide range of locally-
brewed ales. No-smoking
family room; bar food
lunchtime.

ST ANDREWS TAVERN (P)
4 St Andrews Street
☎ 01 603 614 858.
Open 11-11; closed Sun.
🍎 **Kingfisher**
Popular city centre venue,
especially busy at lunchtimes.
Food lunchtime.

Tap & Spile (P)
73 Oak Street.
☎ 01 603 620 630.
🍎 *Bulmers Old Hazy*

TRAFFORD ARMS
61 Grove Road
☎ 01 603 628 466
Open 11-11
🍎 **Kingfisher**

traditional city-centre local offering nine real ales. Bar food lunchtime and evening; no-smoking area lunchtime.

ORMESBY ST MARGARET

First & Last (P)
Yarmouth Rd.
☎ 01 493 731 413.
& *Bulmers Old Hazy*

REEDHAM

RAILWAY (P)
17 The Havaker
☎ 01 493 700 340
Open 12-3.30, 6.30-11; 12-11 Fri/Sat
& **Kingfisher**
Friendly local pub with letting rooms and camping, food lunchtime and evening, no-smoking area.

STIFFKEY

RED LION (P)
44 Wells Road
☎ 01 328 830 552
Open 11-2.30, 6-11
& **Kingfisher**
Old-fashioned local with separate restaurant in unspoilt village. Families welcome; home-cooked food lunchtime and evening.

SWAFFHAM

Norfolk Hero (P)
3 Station St.
☎ 01 760 723 923.
& *Kingfisher*

SWANTON ABBOTT

Weavers Arms (P)
Aylesham Rd.
☎ 01 692 538 655.
& *Bulmers Old Hazy*

THOMPSON

CHEQUERS (P)
Griston Road
☎ 01 953 483 360

Open 11-3, 6-11
& **Kingfisher**
Thatched Tudor village inn with low oak-beamed ceilings and quarry-tiled floors. Wide choice of ales; families welcome; bar food lunchtime and evening; disabled access.

UPTON

White Horse (P).
☎ 01 493 750 696.
& *Kingfisher*

WARHAM

THREE HORSESHOES (P)
69 The Street
☎ 01 328 710 547
Open 11-2.30, 6-11
& **Kingfisher, Whin Hill**
Basic village local with interesting 1921 electric pianola. Ales from local independent brewers; good home-cooked food. Families welcome. Letting rooms; bar food lunchtime and evening; no smoking area.

WATTON

Crown Hotel (P)
High Street.
☎ 01 953 882 375.
& *Bulmers Old Hazy*

WEST BECKHAM

Wheatsheaf (P)
Church Rd.
☎ 01 263 822 110.
& *Kingfisher*

WIGHTON

SANDPIPER (P)
High Street
☎ 01 328 820 752
Open 11-2.30, 6-11.
& **Kingfisher**
Nice old country pub with family room, accommodation, bar food lunchtime and evening.

WOODBASTWICK

FUR & FEATHERS (P)
☎ 01603 780 353
Open 11-3, 6-11; 12-3,
7-10.30 Sun
🍎 **Reedcutter**
Olde worlde pub serving
Woodforde ale range. Bar food
lunchtime and evening;
separate 45-seat restaurant; no
smoking area; disabled access.

WYMONDHAM

FEATHERS (P)
Town Green
☎ 01 953 605 675
Open 11-2.30, 7-11
🍎 **Occasional local farm
scrumpy**
Large popular one-room local;
bar food lunchtime and
evening.

Northamptonshire

ASHBY ST LEDGERS

OLD COACH HOUSE INN (P)
Main Street
☎ 01 788 890 349
Open 12-2.30, 6-11; 12-11 sat;
12-2.30, 7-10.30 Sun
🍎 **James White**
Classic country pub with
roaring fires and wood-
panelled walls. House beer
heads wide range of real ales.
Food lunchtime and evenings;
letting rooms; disabled access.

BRACKLEY

GREYHOUND INN (P)
101 High Street
☎ 01 280 703 331
Open 12-2.30, 7-11
🍎 **Cider range varies**
Two-room pub with 40 malt
whiskies. Families welcome.
Food lunchtime and evening;
separate restaurant specialises
in Mexican food.

BRIXWORTH

George (P)
Hardborough Rd.
☎ *01 604 881 439.*
🍎 *Bulmers Old Hazy*

CASTLE ASHBY

Castle Ashby Fine Foods (OL)
The Old Farmyard.
☎ *01 604 696 742.*
🍎 *Sheppy's*

CHIPPING WARDEN

GRIFFIN (P)
Culworth Road
☎ 01 295 660 230
Open 11-2.30, 6-11; all
permitted hours Sat/Sun
🍎 **Bulmers Traditional**
Delightful stone-built local in
pretty village. Family room;
accommodation; bar food
lunchtime and evening.

KETTERING

SHIRE HORSE (P)
18 Newland Street
☎ 01 536 519 078
Open 11-2.30, 6-11 Mon-Fri; 11-
11 sat; 12-3, 7-10.30 Sun
🍎 **Bulmers Traditional**
Popular town-centre local with
collection of ashtrays mounted
on the walls. Only real cider
outlet left in the area out of six
five years ago.

KING'S SUTTON

WHITE HORSE (P)
The Square
☎ 01 295 810 843
Open 12-4, 7-11
🍎 **Weston's perry**
Traditional village local.

MARSTON ST
LAWRENCE

MARSTON INN (P)
☎ 01 295 711 906
Open 12-2 (not Mon), 7-11
🍎 **Weston's Old Rosie**

One-bar village beerhouse with ale and cider both straight from the cask. Aunt sally played. Known for excellent home cooking, but no food Mon/Sun evenings. No smoking area. Hard to find: a mile off B4525.

NEWNHAM

Romer Arms (P)
The Green.
☎ 01 327 702 221.
🍎 *Bulmers Traditional, Taunton Traditional*

NORTHAMPTON

FISH INN (P)
1 Fish Street
☎ 01 604 234 040
Open 11-11
🍎 **Bulmers Traditional**
Popular town-centre pub with reputation for traditional games. Letting rooms; bar food lunchtime and evening.

Old Black Lion (P)
Black Lion Hill.
☎ 01 604 39472.
🍎 *Bulmers Traditional*

Race Horse (P)
5 Abington Square.
☎ 01 604 31997.
🍎 *Bulmers Traditional*

RUSHDEN

RUSHDEN HISTORICAL TRANSPORT SOCIETY (C)
Station Approach
☎ 01 933 318 988
Open 7.30-11; 12-2.30, 7.30-10.30 Sun.
Weston's GWR
Former railway station on line axed in 1962. More space in railway carriage on platform. Membership 50p a day.

UDBOROUGH

LANE ARMS (P)
Main Street
☎ 01 832 733 223

Open 11.30-3 (not Mon); 6-11
🍎 **Weston's range**
Outstanding free house in picturesque village. Nine real ales, 21 country wines, draught Belgian fruit beers, separate restaurant, letting rooms. No food Sun/Mon evenings. Disabled access.

THRAPSTON

Red Lion (P)
Clopton.
☎ 01 832 720 611.
🍎 *Bulmers Old Hazy*

TITCHMARSH

DOG & PARTRIDGE (P)
High Street
☎ 01 832 735 546
Open 12-2, 6-11
🍎 **Bulmers Old Hazy**
Welcoming one-room eighteenth-century local in quiet village.

WEEDON

Maltsters Arms (P)
West Street.
☎ 01 327 340 175.
🍎 *Bulmers Traditional*

WOODFORD HALSE

Fleur de Lys (P)
14 Smith Street.
☎ 01 327 61526.
🍎 *Bulmers Old Hazy*

YARDLEY

Gobion Sports & Social (C)
School Lane.
☎ 01 908 542 734.
🍎 *Bulmers Old Hazy*

Northumberland

BERWICK

BREWERS ARMS (P)
119 Marygate
☎ 01 289 302 641

Open 11-11
☘ Inch's
Pleasant olde-worlde pub with original bar fittings. Bar food lunchtime

CARTERWAY HEADS

MANOR HOUSE INN (P)
Shotley Bridge
☎ 01 207 255 268
Open 12-3, 6-11
☘ Cider range varies
Country inn with splendid views over Derwent Valley, good food, locally-brewed ales. On A68 six miles south of Corbridge.

CORBRIDGE

DYVELLS (P)
Station Road
☎ 01 434 633 566
Open 7-11
☘ Biddenden
Excellent base for exploring Hadrian's Wall. Accommodation.

FALSTONE

BLACKCOCK INN (P)
☎ 01 434 240 200
Open 11-3, 6-11; 11-11 Fri/Sat
☘ Bulmers Old Hazy
Historic pub on Kielder Water, popular with water-sports crowd and ramblers. Locally-brewed ales, excellent food. Family room, disabled access.

HALTWISTLE

Black Bull (P)
Market Square.
☎ 01 434 320 463.
☘ Bulmers Traditional

HEXHAM

TAP & SPILE (P)
Battle Hill
☎ 01 434 602 039
Open all permitted hours
☘ Weston's Old Rosie
Popular market town pub with ever-changing range of real ales. Bar food lunchtime; live music Monday evening.

MORPETH

TAP & SPILE (P)
Manchester Street
☎ 01 670 513 894
Open 12-2.30, 4.30-11
Mon/Tue, Thurs; 12-11 Wed, Fri, Sat,
12-10.30 Sun
☘ Weston's Old Rosie
Nine real ales in two-bar pub. Bar food lunch and early evening; children allowed in lounge until 8pm. Local pub of the year 1994.

WYLAM

BOAT HOUSE (P)
Station Road
☎ 01 661 853 431
Open 12-3, 6-11; 12-11 Fri/Sat
☘ Biddenden
Two-room pub next to station with great range of ales.

Nottinghamshire

BEESTON

VICTORIA HOTEL (P)
Dovecote Lane
☎ 0115 925 4049
Open 11-3, 5-11 Mon Thurs; 11-11 Fri/Sat; 12-5, 7-10.30 Sun
☘ Range varies
Victorian railway hotel on Platform 1 of Beeston Station. Popular Tynemill Inns alehouse also serves 100 whiskies. Bar food lunchtime and evening; no smoking area.

DAYBROOK

Grove Hotel (P)
35 Mansfield Rd.
☎ 0115 926 3867.
☘ Bulmers Traditional

GEDLING

Westdale Tavern (P)
Westdale Lane.
☎ *0115 987 8689.*
🍎 *Bulmers Old Hazy*

LENTON

Grove Hotel (P)
273 Castle Boulevard.
☎ *0115 941 0637.*
🍎 *Bulmers Traditional*

MANSFIELD

Plough (P)
180 Nottingham Rd.
☎ *01 623 23031.*
🍎 *Bulmers Old Hazy*

TAP & SPILE (P)
29 Leeming Street
☎ *01 623 21327*
Open 11.30-3, 5.30-11
🍎 **Crone's**
Children welcome in snug of traditional two-bar alehouse. Disabled access.

Widecombe Fair (P)
Southwell Rd West.
☎ *01 623 27144.*
🍎 *Bulmers Old Hazy*

NEWARK

Crown & Mitre (P)
53 Castlegate.
☎ *01 636 703 131.*
🍎 *Bulmers Old Hazy*

NOTTINGHAM

Canal Tavern (P)
2-4 Canal Street.
☎ *0115 941 2281.*
🍎 *Bulmers Old Hazy*

City Bar (P)
19 King Street.
☎ *0115 952 0064.*
🍎 *Bulmers Old Hazy*

Fellows Morton & Clayton (P)
Canal Street.
☎ *0115 950 6795.*
🍎 *Bulmers Traditional*

Hole in the Wall (P)
63 Sherwood Street.
☎ *0115 947 3162.*
🍎 *Bulmers Old Hazy*

Langtry's (P)
4 South Sherwood Street.
☎ *0115 947 2124.*
🍎 *Bulmers Old Hazy*

LIMELIGHT (P)
Wellington Circus
☎ *0115 941 8467*
Open 11-11
🍎 **Range varies**
City centre pub in 1960s shopping complex. Good range of ales; food until 8pm (not Sun); no-smoking area.

LINCOLNSHIRE POACHER (P)
161 Mansfield Road
☎ *0115 941 1584*
Open 11-3, 6-11.
🍎 **Biddenden, Thatchers, Inch's, Weston's on rotation. Occasional perry**
Ground-breaking real ale pub. Bar food lunchtime and evening; over 80 whiskies.

Old Colonial (P)
Compton Acres.
☎ *0115 945 5573.*
🍎 *Bulmers Old Hazy*

Royal Children (P)
50 Castle Gate.
☎ *0115 958 0207.*
🍎 *Bulmers Traditional*

RADCLIFFE

Royal Oak (P)
Main Rd.
☎ *0115 933 3798.*
🍎 *Bulmers Traditional*

RETFORD

CLINTON ARMS (P)
24 Albert Road
☎ *01 777 702 703*
Open 11-11
🍎 **Bulmers Old Hazy**
Two-bar pub with live music, bar food lunchtime and evening, and disabled access.

Old Sun (P)
Chapel Gate.
☎ 01 777 702 151.
🍎 *Bulmers Old Hazy*

RUDDINGTON

Red Lion (P)
1 Easthorpe Street.
☎ 0115 984 4654.
🍎 *Bulmers Traditional*

WEST BRIDGFORD

BRIDGFORD WINES (OL)
116 Melton Road
☎ 0115 981 6181
Open evenings and 12-2,
7-10 Sun
🍎 **Norbury's range inc perry,
plus guests**
Specialist off-licence for the
connoisseur. Disabled access.

WORKSOP

Old Ship Inn (P)
Bridge Street.
☎ 01 909 476 354.
🍎 *Bulmers Traditional*

Oxfordshire

ABINGDON

Lamb & Flag (P)
Farringdon Rd, Longworth.
☎ 01 865 820 208.
🍎 *Bulmers Old Hazy*

Red Lion (P)
63 The Vineyard.
☎ 01 235 521 128.
🍎 *Bulmers Old Hazy*

ASTON

Red Lion (P)
The Square.
☎ 01 993 850 491.
🍎 *Bulmers Old Hazy*

BANBURY

Elephant & Castle (P)
Bloxham.
☎ 01 295 720 383.
🍎 *Bulmers Traditional*

REINDEER INN (P)
47 Parsons Street, off North Bar
Street
☎ 01 295 264 031
Open 11-2.30, 5 (7 Sat)-11,
closed Sun
🍎 **Bulmers Traditional**
Superbly restored fifteenth-
century coaching inn with
Jacobean panelling in back
room. Smart dress, no under-
21s. Hook Norton ales.

Wheatsheaf (P)
68 George Street.
☎ 01 295 266 525.
🍎 *Bulmers Old Hazy*

CHURCHILL

Chequers (P)
Church Rd.
☎ 01 608 658 309.
🍎 *Bulmers Traditional*

CLAYDON

Rising Sun Inn (P)
☎ 01 295 89393.
🍎 *Bulmers Traditional*

GREAT TEW

FALKLAND ARMS (P)
☎ 01 608 683 653
Open 11.30-2.30, 6-11 Mon-Sat,
12-2, 6-10.30 Sun (closed Mon
lunch)
🍎 **Weston's Old Rosie &
Vintage**
Classic thatched sixteenth-
century inn with oak panelling,
oil lamps, flagstone floors, old
settles. In conserved village.
Traditional games include
shove ha'penny and table
skittles. Four letting rooms and
camping. Off B4022 five miles
east of Chipping Norton.

HAMPTON PYLE

Gonefish Inn (P)
Oxford Rd.
☎ *01 865 373 926.*
🍎 *Bulmers Old Hazy*

KINGHAM

Plough Inn (P)
☎ *01 608 658 327.*
🍎 *Bulmers Traditional*

NETHER WESTCOTE

New Inn (P)
☎ *01 993 830 827.*
🍎 *Bulmers Traditional*

OXFORD

FIR TREE TAVERN (P)
163 Iffley Road
☎ 01 865 247 373
Open 12-3, 5.30-11 Sun-Fri,
2-11 Sat
🍎 **Cider range varies**
Friendly local knocked into one
room. Live jazz and blues.

Grog Shop (OL)
Kinston Rd.
🍎 *Dunkerton's*

WT Palmer & Son (OL)
47 West Way, Botley
☎ *01 865 247 123*
Open 9-1, 2-7. Closed Wed pm.
🍎 *Weston's range*

Plasterers Arms (P)
9 Marston Rd,
St Clements.
☎ *01 865 247 114.*
🍎 *Bulmers Old Hazy*

Turf Tavern (P)
Bath Place.
☎ *01 865 243 235.*
🍎 *Bulmers Old Hazy*

Wheatsheaf (P)
129 High Street.
☎ *01 865 243 276.*
🍎 *Bulmers Old Hazy*

White Horse (P)
1 London Rd,
Headington.
☎ *01 865 62447.*
🍎 *Bulmers Old Hazy*

SONNING EYE

FLOWING SPRING (P)
☎ 01 734 693 207
Open all permitted hours
summer, 11.30-3, 5-11 winter
🍎 **Bulmers Old Hazy**
Fuller's pub. Traditional local
with piano, huge garden, all
home-cooked food.

SWINBROOK

SWAN (P)
☎ 01 993 822 165
Open 11.45-2.30, 6-11.
🍎 **Weston's Vintage**
Sixteenth-century country pub
on River Windrush. Flagstone
floor, wood-burning stove, real
ales, meals lunchtime and
evening. Hard to find: 1 mile
north of A40, 2 miles east of
Burford.

THAME

Hogshead (P)
Cornmarket.
☎ *01 844 212 933.*
🍎 *Bulmers Old Hazy*

Shropshire

ALVELEY

Three Horseshoes (P)
☎ *01 746 780 642.*
🍎 *Bulmers Traditional*

BISHOP'S CASTLE

THREE TUNS (P)
Salop Street
☎ 01 588 638 797
Open 11.30-2.30, 6.30-11 Mon-
Sat, 12-3, 7-10.30 Sun.
🍎 **Weston's Old Rosie**
Perhaps Britain's most famous

and oldest-established pub-brewery, with purpose-built late Victorian tower brewery dominating the small yard.

BRIDGNORTH

RAILWAYMAN'S ARMS (P)
Hollybush Road
☎ 01 746 764 361
Open 11-4 (12-2 winter), 7-11 Sun-Fri, 11-11 Sat
🍎 **Bulmers Traditional**
Bar on platform of Severn Valley Railway station – steam trains throughout summer. Collection of railway memorabilia. Good range of ales, hot snacks. Disabled access.

CLEE HILL

Craven Arms (P)
☎ *01 584 890 590.*
🍎 *Bulmers Traditional*

Golden Cross (P)
☎ *01 584 890 741.*
🍎 *Bulmers Traditional*

CLEOBURY MORTIMER

Blount Arms (P)
Cleobury Rd.
☎ *01 299 270 423.*
🍎 *Bulmers Traditional*

Three Horseshoes (P)
53 High Street.
☎ *01 299 270 494.*
🍎 *Bulmers Traditional*

CLUNTON

CROWN (P)
☎ 01 588 660 265
Open 12-11; 12-3, 7-10.30 Sun.
🍎 **Weston's Bounds Brand**
Two-bar village pub bought by locals when facing permanent closure. Good Tetley and Wood's ales, excellent bar food, separate dining room. One mile east of Clun.

CORFTON

SUN INN (P)
☎ 01 584 861 239
Open 11-2.30, 6-11 Mon-Sat, 12-3, 7-10.30 Sun
🍎 **Westons range**
Highly regarded seventeenth-century country alehouse with six regular real ales and three changing guests. Separate public bar. Bar meals and no-smoking restaurant. Home-made food using local ingredients. Disabled access. Children welcome. Hard to find: on B4368 north of Ludlow.

ELLERDINE HEATH

ROYAL OAK (P)
☎ 01 939 250 300
Open 11-3, 5-11 Mon-Fri, 11-11 Sat, 12-3, 7-10.30 Sun
🍎 **Weston's and guests**
Traditional two-bar country pub serving ales from independent brewers. Bar food except Tues lunchtime and Mon evening. Children welcome. Hard to find: 2 miles east of A53 north of Shrewsbury.

HENGOED

LAST INN (P)
☎ 01 691 659 747
Open 7-11 Mon-Sat, 12.30-2, 7-11 Sun
🍎 **Weston's range**
Large country inn with good food and ale. A long-standing CAMRA favourite. Families welcome. Disabled access.

HIGHLEY

Castle Inn (P)
Woodhill Rd.
☎ *01 746 862 843.*
🍎 *Bulmers Traditional*

LUDLOW

BULL HOTEL (P)
14 The Bull Ring
☎ 01 584 873 611
Open all permitted hours
❦ **Weston's First Quality**
Georgian front conceals Tudor
or late medieval rear, making
this Ludlow's oldest pub.
Marston's ales. Lively
atmosphere with youngish
clientele Fri-Sat. Food
lunchtimes only. Four letting
rooms.

Horse & Jockey (P)
Old Street.
☎ *01 584 873 482.*
❦ *Bulmers Traditional*

Lloyd's (OL)
Weeping Cross Lane
☎ *01 584 872 431*
Open 8.30-5 Mon-Sat.
❦ *Full Weston's range*

Unicorn (P)
Lower Corve Street.
☎ *01 584 873 555.*
❦ *Bulmers Traditional*

MUNSLOW

CROWN (P)
☎ 01 584 841 205
Open 12-2.30, 7-11 Mon-Sat, 12-
3, 7-10.30 Sun
❦ **Franklin's**
In glorious South Shropshire
countryside. Pub now brews its
own beer but also stocks M&B
Mild and Wadworth 6X. Bar
food lunchtime and evening
plus separate restaurant.
Children welcome. Hard to
find: 7 miles from Craven
Arms on B4378 Much Wenlock
road.

ORETON

New Inn (P)
Oreton Rd.
☎ *01 299 270 423.*
❦ *Bulmers Traditional*

ORLETON

Boot Inn (P)
☎ *01 568 780 228.*
❦ *Franklin's*

QUATT

CIDER HOUSE (P)
☎ 01 746 780 285
❦ **Bulmers Traditional**
Two-room country pub with
garden in deepest South
Shropshire.

RATLINGHOPE

HORSESHOE INN (P)
Bridges
☎ 01 588 650 260
Open 12-3, 6-11, but closed
Mon lunchtime and in winter
Tues-Wed lunchtime.
❦ **Westons range**
Local pub of the year in
spectacular setting. Real ales
include Adnams. Families
welcome. Hard to find in maze
of lanes between Stiperstones
and Long Mynd: OS ref SO 394
964.

RODINGTON

Bulls Head (P).
☎ *01 952 770 219.*
❦ *Bulmers Old Hazy*

SHIFNAL

Plough Inn (P)
26 Broadway.
☎ *01 952 460 678.*
❦ *Bulmers Traditional*

SHREWSBURY

Boathouse Inn (P)
New Street.
☎ *01 743 362 965.*
❦ *Bulmers Old Hazy*

CASTLE VAULTS (P)
16 Castle Gates
☎ 01 743 358 807
Open 11.30-3, 6-11 Mon-Sat, 12-
3, 7-10.30 Sun
❦ **Westons**

Town alehouse with eight real ales. Bar food lunchtime, no smoking area for diners. Separate Mexican restaurant. Seven letting rooms. Near BR.

Coracle (P)
Sundorne Rd.
☎ *01 743 367 072.*
🍺 *Bulmers Traditional*

TANNERS (OL)
26 Wyle Cop
☎ 01 743 232 400
🍺 **Westons, Dunkerton's, Pulling's**
Old-established and very highly regarded wine merchant. Branches in Welshpool, Hereford, Bridgnorth.

TELFORD

Anchor Inn (P)
Court Street, Madeley.
☎ *01 952 585 790.*
🍺 *Taunton Traditional*

COALBROOKDALE INN (P)
12 Wellington Rd, Coalbrookdale
☎ 01 952 433 953
Open 12-3, 6-11
🍺 **Bulmers Traditional**
Friendly two-bar eighteenth-century inn near Museum of Iron. Five guest beers. National Pub of the Year 1995.

OLD VAULTS WINE BAR (P)
29 High Street, Ironbridge
☎ 01 952 432 716
Open 11-11 summer, 12-3, 6.30-11 winter
🍺 **Weston's range**
Food-oriented and not cheap, but good choice of cask ales and bottled beers, and breathtaking setting with terrace overlooking the Iron Bridge itself.

Royal Oak (P)
High Street, Madeley.
☎ *01 952 585 598.*
🍺 *Bulmers Traditional*

WENLOCK EDGE

WENLOCK EDGE INN (P)
Hill Top (B4371)
☎ 01 746 785 403
Open 12-2.30 (not Mon), 7-11.
🍺 **Weston's**
Locally-brewed Hobson's ales in family-run pub in beautiful setting. Letting rooms; bar food lunchtime and evening.

WISTANSTOW

PLOUGH INN (P)
☎ 01 588 673 251
Open 12-3, 7-11.
🍺 **Westons range**
Home of the Wood Brewery. Large two-bar pub well-known for food. 1 mile north of Craven Arms: turn right at signpost off A489.

Somerset

ALLERFORD CROSSING

VICTORY INN (P)
☎ 01 823 461 282
Open 11-3, 6-11
🍺 **Sheppy's**
Large pub which welcomes families. Full-size train and bouncy castle in garden. Bar food lunchtime and evening; no smoking area; disabled facilities. Off B3227; OS 182 249.
Appley

GLOBE INN (P)
☎ 01 823 672 327
Open 11-3 (not Mon), 6.30-11
🍺 **Lane's**
Ancient village inn deep in the country. Several cosy rooms lead off stone-floored corridor. Families welcome; food always available; Cotleigh beers.

AXBRIDGE

LAMB (P)
The Square

☎ 01 934 732 253
Open 11.30-2.30, 6.30-11
🍎 Thatchers
Rambling old pub owned by
Butcombe Brewery. Large
garden; letting rooms; bar food
lunchtime and evening;
disabled access.

BAWDRIP

Fairways Caravan Park Shop
(OL)
Woolavington Corner, Bath Rd.
☎ *01 278 685 569.*
🍎 *Rich's*

BECKINGTON

Forester's Arms *(P)*
Goose Street.
☎ *01 373 830 864.*
🍎 *Cheddar Valley*

BERROW

Triangle Stores *(OL)*
240 Berrow Rd.
☎ *01 278 782 208.*
🍎 *Rich's*

BISHOPS HULL

Cavalier *(P)*
☎ *01 823 286 539.*
🍎 *Bulmers Traditional*

BREAN

ALLEN'S (OL)
South Road
☎ 01 278 751 247
8am-9pm summer; 8am-5pm
winter
**🍎 Weston's range; Rich's;
Thatcher's range; Sheppy's;
Inch's**
Off-licence in big general store
specialising in local produce in
very touristy area. Ramp and
wide doors for disabled.

Brean Down Inn *(P)*
Brean Down.
☎ *01 278 75142.*
🍎 *Taunton Traditional*

Central Stores *(OL)*
Coast Rd.
☎ *01 278 751 309.*
🍎 *Rich's*

Cove Shop *(OL)*
Brean Down.
☎ *01 278 751 613.*
🍎 *Rich's*

Milkmaid Stores *(OL)*
Unity Farm Caravan Park.
☎ *01 278 751 480.*
🍎 *Rich's*

BRIDGWATER

Bristol Rd News *(OL)*
105 Bristol Rd.
☎ *01 278 423 346.*
Open 5.30am-8pm.
🍎 *Rich's*

British Rail Staff Association
(C)
Wellington Rd.
☎ *01 278 421 599.*
🍎 *Rich's*

Bunch of Grapes *(P)*
St John Street.
☎ *01 278 451 106.*
🍎 *Rich's*

Crowpill Inn *(P)*
91 Chiltern Street.
☎ *01 278 422 129.*
🍎 *Bulmers Traditional*

Crowpill Stores *(OL)*
93 Chilton Street.
☎ *01 278 422 735.*
🍎 *Rich's*

Horse & Jockey *(P)*
☎ *01 278 424 283.*
🍎 *Taunton Traditional*

K&C Stores *(OL)*
15 North Street.
☎ *01 278 423 124.*
🍎 *Rich's*

Lion's Men's Social Club *(C)*
17 West Quay.
☎ *01 278 423 453.*
🍎 *Rich's*

North Pole Inn *(P)*
23 North Street.
☎ *01 278 451 930.*
🍎 *Bulmers Traditional*

Pig & Whistle *(P)*
Parkway.
☎ *01 278 423 804.*
🍎 *Bulmers Traditional*

Pitman's Stores *(OL)*
3 King George Ave.
☎ *01 278 423 371.*
🍎 *Rich's*

Rebels Retreat *(P)*
20 St Johns Street.
☎ *01 278 444 951.*
🍎 *Bulmers Traditional*

Royal Marines Association *(C)*
6 West Quay.
☎ *01 278 459 019.*
🍎 *Rich's*

Unity Club *(C)*
Dampier Street.
☎ *01 278 452 907.*
🍎 *Rich's*

Burnham-on-Sea
Ritz Club (C)
Victoria Street.
☎ *01 278 785 365.*
🍎 *Rich's*

ROYAL CLARENCE HOTEL (P)
The Esplanade
☎ 01 278 783 138
Open 11-11
🍎 **Rich's, Crossman's, Wilkin's**
Home of RCH Brewery: large
seafront hotel with letting
rooms, no-smoking area,
family room. Food lunchtime
and evening; disabled access.

BURTLE

BURTLE INN (P)
Catcott Road
☎ 01 278 722 269
Open 12-2.30, 6-11; 12-10.30
Sun
🍎 **Own-label cider**
Cider made from apples grown
in pub's own orchard,
fermented by a local farmer

and served from oak barrels.
Popular old inn; children's
certificate; bar food lunchtime
and evening; separate
restaurant.

CANNINGTON

KINGS HEAD (P)
☎ 01 278 652 293
🍎 **Rich's**
Bar food lunchtime and
evening and separate
restaurant; letting rooms; no-
smoking area. Skittle alley.

MALT SHOVEL INN (P)
Blackmore Lane
☎ 01 278 653 432
Open 11.30-2.30, 7-11
🍎 **Rich's, Lane's**
Bar food lunchtime and
evening in quiet pub. No
smoking area; skittle alley;
letting rooms; family room;
disabled access.

Rose & Crown *(P)*
High Street.
☎ *01 278 653 190.*
🍎 *Bulmers Traditional*

CARHAMPTON

BUTCHERS ARMS (P)
Main Road
☎ 01 643 821 333
Open 11-3, 6-11; 11-11 Sat
🍎 **Rich's**
Village local on West Somerset
Railway. Family room; letting
rooms; bar food lunchtime and
evening.

CASTLE CARY

Heart & Compass *(P)*
☎ *01 963 350 375.*
🍎 *Taunton Traditional*

Horse Pond Inn *(P)*
The Triangle.
☎ *01 963 350 318.*
🍎 *Taunton Traditional*

CATCOTT
King William Inn (P)
☎ 01 278 722 374

Open 11.30-3, 6-11
🍎 **Taunton Traditional**
Old village pub with modern restaurant. Glass-covered well in lounge found during extension work. Family room, skittle alley, bar food lunchtime and evening, disabled access.

CHEDDAR

Butchers Arms (P)
Cliff Street.
☎ 01 934 742 452.
🍎 *Taunton Traditional*

CHEDDAR VALLEY CHEESE DEPOT (OL)
The Gorge
☎ 01 934 743 113
Open 9-5.30
🍎 **Derrick's, Burrow Hill**
A must-visit for all serious students of cider, and proof that not everything sold to tourists is cheap tat, Tony Derrick's shop sells fine ciders, excellent cheese, and other top-quality local produce. Parking is difficult, but don't let the swarms of visitors deceive you or put you off: other shops in Cheddar also sell real ciders – Perry's, for instance – so persevere!

Kings Head (P)
Silver Street.
☎ 01 934 742 153.
🍎 *Bulmers Traditional*

White Hart (P)
The Cliffs.
☎ 01 934 742 672.
🍎 *Bulmers Traditional*

CHELYNCH

POACHERS POCKET (P)
☎ 01 749 880 220
Open 11.30-2.30, 6-11
🍎 **Wilkins**
Part-medieval village pub off A361. Local beers; good food lunchtime and evening.

CORTON DENHAM

QUEENS ARMS INN (P)
☎ 01 963 220 317
Open 11.30-3, 6.30-11
🍎 **Inch's**
Country pub popular with walkers. Ales from local micros. Letting rooms; bar food lunchtime and evening; disabled access.

CREECH ST MICHAEL

Riverside Inn (P)
☎ 01 823 442 257.
🍎 *Bulmers Traditional*

CREWKERNE

King William (P)
21 Barn Street.
☎ 01 460 74492.
🍎 *Bulmers Traditional*

Nags Head (P)
Market Sq.
☎ 01 460 72627.
🍎 *Taunton Traditional*

Printers Bar (P)
South Street.
☎ 01 460 72385.
🍎 *Taunton Traditional*

Royal Oak (P)
Hermitage Street.
☎ 01 460 72534.
🍎 *Taunton Traditional*

Swan Hotel (P)
4 Church Street.
☎ 01 460 74198.
🍎 *Bulmers Traditional*

CROWCOMBE

Carew Arms (P)
☎ 01 984 618 631.
🍎 *Lane's*

DITCHEAT

Alhampton Inn (P)
Alhampton.
☎ *01 749 860 210.*
🍎 *Bulmers Traditional*

DOWLISH WAKE

NEW INN (P)
☎ 01 460 52413
Open 11-3, 6-11
🍎 **Perry's**
Popular village pub with
letting rooms and good food
lunchtime and evening.

DULVERTON

Bridge Inn (P)
Bridge Street.
☎ *01 398 23694.*
🍎 *Taunton Traditional*

Lion Hotel (P)
Banks Sq.
☎ *01 398 23444.*
🍎 *Taunton Traditional*

Rock House (P)
Jury Rd.
☎ *01 398 23131.*
🍎 *Taunton Traditional*

DUNBALL

HENRY FIELDING INN (P)
☎ 01 278 683 308
🍎 **Rich's**
Bar food lunchtime and
evening; family room; skittle
alley. Pub is just off J23 of M5.

DUNSTER

Forresters (P)
West Street.
☎ *01 643 821 313.*
🍎 *Bulmers Traditional*

Luttrell Arms (P)
☎ *01 643 821 555.*
🍎 *Taunton Traditional*

Stags Head (P)
West Street.
☎ *01 643 821 229.*
🍎 *Rich's*

EAST CHINNOCK

Post Office (OL)
Fordhay
☎ *01 935 862 157*
Closed Sun
🍎 *Bridge Farm medium*

EAST COKER

Helyar Arms (P)
☎ *01 935 862 332.*
East Frome
🍎 *Taunton Traditional*

Lamb (P)
Christchurch Street.
☎ *01 373 463 349.*
🍎 *Taunton Traditional*

EAST LAMBROOK

ROSE & CROWN (P)
Silver Street
☎ 01 460 240 433
Open 11.30-2.30, 7-11
🍎 **Burrow Hill**
Cosy oak-beamed two-bar
village pub. Food lunchtime
and evening; children's
certificate; no-smoking area;
disabled access.

EVERCREECH

Brewers Arms (P)
☎ *01 749 830 303.*
🍎 *Taunton Traditional*

Shapway Inn (P)
☎ *01 749 830 273.*
🍎 *Taunton Traditional*

FAULKLAND

TUCKER'S GRAVE INN (P)
☎ 01 373 834 230
Open 11-3, 6-11
🍎 **Cheddar Valley**
Ancient three-room pub
without bar-counter but with a
spooky story. No food. On
A366 a mile E of village.

FITZHEAD

FITZHEAD INN (P)
☎ 01 823 400 667

Open 12-3, 7-11
👌 Bollhayes
Cosy village pub rated for its food – booking recommended. Disabled access.

FROME

Ring of Bells *(P)*
75 Broadway.
☎ *01 373 463 092.*
👌 *Bulmers Traditional*

Sun Inn *(P)*
Whatley.
☎ *01 373 836 219.*
👌 *Taunton Traditional*

Wheatsheaf *(P)*
Bath Street.
☎ *01 373 465 796.*
👌 *Taunton Traditional*

GLASTONBURY

Queens Head *(P)*
High Street.
☎ *01 458 832 745.*
👌 *Bulmers Traditional*

Rifleman's Arms *(P)*
Chilkwell Street.
☎ *01 458 831 023.*
👌 *Wilkin's*

HAMBRIDGE

Lamb & Lion *(P)*
The Green.
☎ *01 460 281 355.*
👌 *Taunton Traditional, Bulmers
Traditional*

HARDINGTON MANDEVILLE

MANDEVILLE ARMS (P)
☎ 01 935 862 418
👌 **Bridge Farm Cider**
Children and dogs welcome in friendly but smart country pub complete with oak beams and open fires. Bar food lunchtime and evening; separate restaurant. Skittle alley.

HARDINGTON MOOR

ROYAL OAK (P)
Moor Lane
☎ 01 935 862 354
Open 12-3 (not Mon), 7-11
👌 **Taunton Traditional**
Friendly former farmhouse with locally-brewed real ales and good food. Skittle alley for hire.

HATCH BEAUCHAMP

Hatch Inn *(P)*
☎ *01 823 480 245.*
👌 *Taunton Traditional*

HENSTRIDGE

BIRD IN HAND (P)
Ash Walk
☎ 01 963 362 255
Open 11-2.30, 5.30-11; 11-11 Sat
👌 **Taunton Traditional**
Classic oak-beamed village pub. Bar food lunchtime; disabled access.

HIGHBRIDGE

Burnham Rd Stores *(OL)*
Burnham Road
☎ *01 278 783 256*
Open 9am-10pm
👌 *Rich's*

Globe Inn *(P)*
17 Newtown Rd, Newtown.
☎ *01 278 783 440.*
👌 *Bulmers Traditional*

Happy Shopper *(OL)*
Moorland Road
☎ *01 278 795 540*
Open 9am-10pm
👌 *Rich's*

ILMINSTER

Bull Inn *(P)*
The Square.
☎ *01 935 840 318.*
👌 *Taunton Traditional*

Royal Oak (P)
Ditton Street.
☎ 01 460 54884.
🍎 *Bulmers Traditional*

KINGSBURY EPISCOPI

Wyndham Arms (P)
☎ 01 935 823 239.
🍎 *Burrow Hill.*

KNAPP

RISING SUN (P)
☎ 01 823 490 436
Open 11-2.30, 6.30-11
🍎 **Local farmhouse cider**
Late medieval pub with many
original features. Food
lunchtime and evening with
fish a speciality. Letting rooms.

LANGLEY MARSH

Three Horseshoes (P)
☎ 01 984 23763.
🍎 *Perry's from the wood*

LANGPORT

Crown (P)
Long Load.
☎ 01 458 241 333.
🍎 *Taunton Traditional*

White Lion (P)
North Street.
☎ 01 458 250 919.
🍎 *Taunton Traditional*

LIMINGTON

Lamb & Lark (P)
☎ 01 935 840 368.
🍎 *Taunton Traditional*

LUXBOROUGH

ROYAL OAK (P)
☎ 01 984 640 319
Open 11-2.30, 6-11
🍎 **Rich's, Derrick's**
Unspoilt village free house in
heart of Brendon Hills. Bar
food lunchtime and evening;
letting rooms; no smoking area.

MARK

PACKHORSE INN (P)
Church Street
☎ 01 278 641 209
Open 11-2.30, 6-11; 12-3,
7-10.30 Sun
🍎 **Wilkin's**
Characterful country pub
stocking ales from local micros.
Bar food lunchtime only.
Letting rooms; large functions
room; skittle alley.

White Horse Inn (P)
☎ 01 278 641 234.
🍎 *Bulmers Traditional*

MILBOURNE PORT

QUEENS HEAD (P)
High Street
☎ 01 963 250 314
Open 11-11
🍎 **Taunton Traditional, Bridge
Farm**
Busy village pub with good
real ale range. Bar food
lunchtime and evening;
separate restaurant. Skittle
alley; disabled access.

MILVERTON

White Hart (P)
☎ 01 823 400 218.
🍎 *Bulmers Traditional*

MINEHEAD

BUTLIN'S (C)
Somerwest World
☎ 01 643 703 331
🍎 **Bulmers Old Hazy**
Cask cider available in two
bars, Molly Malone's and
Highwayman, in updated
holiday camp.

Minehead FC (C)
☎ 01 643 705 573.
🍎 *Rich's*

Minimarket (OL)
45 The Avenue
☎ 01 634 703 979
Open 7.45am-6pm
🍎 *Rich's*

PLUME OF FEATHERS (P)
Blenheim Road
☎ 01 643 702 121.
🍎 **Rich's**
Family room and separate
public bar. Bar food lunchtime
and evening.

RED LION (P)
Quay Street
☎ 01 643 706 507
🍎 **Rich's**
Seafront hotel. Bar food
lunchtime and evening.

Royal British Legion (C)
Banks Street.
☎ *01 643 702 271.*
🍎 *Taunton Traditional*

Valiant Soldier (P)
Roadwater.
☎ *01 984 640 223.*
🍎 *Rich's*

MONTACUTE

Working Mens Club (C)
Mason Lane.
☎ *01 935 823 376.*
🍎 *Taunton Traditional*

MOORLAND

THATCHERS ARMS (P)
☎ 01 278 691 270
Open 12-2.30, 7-11
🍎 **Westcroft**
Olde worlde village inn. Bar
food available lunchtime and
evening; families and pets
welcome. Skittle alley.
Signposted from Moorland
village.

NETHER STOWEY

Cricket Malherbie Farm Shop
(OL)
☎ *01 278 732 084.*
🍎 *Rich's*

George Hotel (P)
☎ *01 278 732 248.*
🍎 *Taunton Traditional*

NORTH BREWHAM

OLD RED LION (P)
☎ 01 749 850 287
Open 12-3, 6-11
🍎 **Thatchers**
Isolated stone pub, once a
farm. Bar food lunchtime and
evening. Hard to find: on
Maiden Bradley-Bruton road,
OS 722 368.

NORTH CURRY

BIRD IN HAND (P)
Queen Square
☎ 01 823 490 248
Open 12-2.30, 7-11
🍎 **Rich's**
Olde worlde candlelit pub with
stone floors and inglenook
fireplaces. Four real ales; beer
festival May bank holiday. Bar
food lunchtime and evening;
separate restaurant; no-
smoking area. Shove ha'penny
and table skittles played.

NORTH PETHERTON

Lamb (P)
☎ *01 278 662 336.*
🍎 *Taunton Traditional*

West End Bakery (OL)
☎ *01 278 662 253.*
🍎 *Rich's*

PITMINSTER

QUEENS ARMS (P)
☎ 01 823 421 529
Open 11-3, 5-11
🍎 **Cider range varies**
Popular village pub with good
food and wide range of real
ales set in picturesque
Blackdown Hills. Bar food
lunchtime and evening; letting
rooms. Hard to find: off B3170
at Corfe.

PORLOCK

SHIP INN (P)
High Street
☎ 01 643 862 507

Open 10.30-3, 5.30-11
🍎 **Perry's**
Village inn mentioned in Lorna
Doone. Bar food evening and
lunchtime and separate
restaurant specialising in Aga
cookery. Families welcome;
letting rooms; disabled access.

PORLOCK WEIR

Culbone Stables Inn (P)
☎ 01 643 862 259.
🍎 *Rich's*

PRIDDY

NEW INN (P)
☎ 01 749 676 465
11.30-2.30, 7-11; 12-2.30, 7-10.30
Sun
🍎 **Wilkin's**
Fifteenth-century inn on village
green with good food
lunchtime and evenings.
Letting rooms; disabled access.

PURITON

PURITON SPORTS & SOCIAL
(C)
Churchfield Lane
☎ 01 278 684 457
Open 7-11 weekdays; 12-3
Sat/Sun
🍎 **Rich's**
Games include skittles, bowls,
archery, shooting.

RUDGE

FULL MOON (P)
☎ 01 373 830 936
Open 12-3, 6-11
🍎 **Thatchers**
Splendid 300-year-old pub
retaining many original
features including the stone
floors. Emphasis on food, but
there is also a good range of
real ales. Letting rooms; skittle
alley. Hard to find: 1 mile N of
A36 at Standerwick; OS 829
518.

SEVEN ASH

QUANTOCK COTTAGE INN (P)
☎ 01 823 432 467
Open 12-2.30, 6-11
🍎 **Lane's**
Comfortable family pub on
A38. Bar food lunchtime and
evening (not Mon or Tues).
Letting room; disabled
facilities.

SHEPTON MALLET

Bell Hotel (P)
High Street.
☎ 01 749 345 393.
🍎 *Taunton Traditional*

Clarke's Social Club (C)
Townsend Rd.
☎ 01 749 342 414.
🍎 *Taunton Traditional*

KING WILLIAM (P)
West Shepton Mallet
☎ 01 749 342 102
Open 12-3, 6-11 Mon-Fri; 11-11
sat; 12-10.30 Sun
🍎 **Taunton Traditional;
Bulmers West Country**
Snacks available in cider house
five minutes from town centre.

Victoria Inn (P)
Board Cross.
☎ 01 749 342 043.
🍎 *Taunton Traditional*

SHEPTON MONTAGUE

MONTAGUE INN (P)
☎ 01 749 813 213
Open 5.30-11 Mon-Fri; 12-3,
5.30-11 Sat/Sun.
🍎 **Thatcher's**
Remote country local. Hard to
find: off A359 south of Bruton;
OS 675 316.

SHIPHAM

ART'S SOMERSET SCRUMPY
(OL, R)
Lillypool Farm.
☎ 01 934 743 994.
Open seven days, 9-5 (winter);
9-7 (Summer).

🍎 Art's, Broadoak, Burrow Hill

Cider is no longer made at Lillypool Farm: its own-label is made by sister company Broadoak. Nevertheless, Art's is still well worth a visit while exploring the glorious Mendips, as a less congested alternative to Cheddar. Local cheese is on sale alongside the cider, and the cafe is fully licensed.

SHURTON

SHURTON INN (P)
☎ 01 278 732 695
Open 11-2.30, 6-11
🍎 **Lane's**
Village pub with Sunday flea markets held in skittle alley. Bar food lunchtime and evening; disabled access. Hard to find: follow signs for Hinkley Point nuclear power station.

SOMERTON

Elms Inn (P)
Somerton Rd.
☎ 01 458 42772.
🍎 *Bulmers Traditional*

SPARKFORD

SPARKFORD INN (P)
☎ 01 963 440 218
Open 11-2.30, 6.30-11
🍎 **Rosie's, Inch's**
Fifteenth-century coaching inn on A303, retaining many original features. Families welcome. Letting rooms; bar food lunchtime,e and evening; disabled access.

STOGUMBER

WHITE HORSE (P)
The Square
☎ 01 984 656 277
Open 11-2.30, 6-11
🍎 **Sheppy's**
Traditional pub in historic village. Bar food lunchtime and evening; separate restaurant; letting rooms.

STOKE-SUB-HAMPDEN

Cats Head (P)
☎ 01 935 881 231.
🍎 *Taunton Traditional*

HALF MOON INN (P)
☎ 01 935 824 890
Open 11-2.30; 6.30-11; 12-3, 7-10.30 Sun
🍎 **Bridge Farm Cider**
Olde-worlde stone-floored alehouse. Live blues and folk. No food.

TAUNTON

Foresters Arms (P)
East Reach.
☎ 01 823 277 698.
🍎 *Taunton Traditional*

Great Western Railway Staff Association (C)
Station Approach Rd.
☎ 01 823 275 048.
🍎 *Rich's, Taunton Traditional*

Monkton Inn (P)
West Monkton.
☎ 01 823 412 414.
🍎 *Taunton Traditional*

Oxford Inn (P)
Roman Rd.
☎ 01 823 337 424.
🍎 *Bulmers Traditional*

Priory Social Club (C)
Priory Bridge Rd.
☎ 01 823 284 656.
🍎 *Rich's*

ROSE INN (P)
Hamilton Road
☎ 01 823 275 571
🍎 **Rich's**
Bar food lunchtime and evening; separate public bar; no-smoking area.

ROYAL CROWN (P)
8 Wellington New Road
☎ 01 823 286 016
Open 11-11; 12-3, 7-10.30 Sun

Rich's
Meals 12-2.30, 6.30-10

Staplegrove Inn (P)
Staplegrove Rd.
☎ 01 823 271 037.
Bulmers Traditional

TEMPLECOMBE

Bird in Hand (P)
☎ 01 963 370 140.
Taunton Traditional

TINTINHULL

Lamb Inn (P)
Vicarage Street.
☎ 01 935 82251.
Taunton Traditional

TRUDOXHILL

WHITE HART (P)
☎ 01 373 836 324
Open 12-3, 7-11
Thatcher's
Comfortable village pub, home to Ash Vine brewery. Bar food lunchtime and evening.

WATCHET

Anchor Inn (P)
Anchor Street.
☎ 01 984 631 387.
Taunton Traditional

Liddymore Store (OL)
53 Liddymore Rd.
☎ 01 984 634 416.
Rich's

WATERROW

ROCK INN (P)
☎ 01 984 623 293
Open 11-2.30, 6-11
Sheppy's
Interesting old inn built into a rock face. Bar food lunchtime and evening; letting rooms; disabled facilities.

WELLINGTON

Green Dragon (P)
South Street.
☎ 01 823 662 281.
Taunton Traditional

Holywell Inn (P)
Holywell Lake.
☎ 01 823 672 770.
Bulmers Traditional

Victoria Inn (P)
North Street.
☎ 01 823 662 670.
Taunton Traditional

Weavers Arms (P)
Rockwell Green.
☎ 01 823 662 466.
Bulmers Traditional

WELLS

Cheddar Valley Inn (P)
22 Tucker Street.
☎ 01 749 670 698.
Bulmers Traditional

City Arms (P)
69 High Street.
☎ 01 749 73916.
Bulmers Traditional

Fountain Inn (P)
1 St Thomas Street.
☎ 01 749 672 317.
Bulmers Traditional

Globe Inn (P)
Priest Row.
☎ 01 749 672 093.
Bulmers Traditional

Mermaid Hotel (P)
1 Tucker Street.
☎ 01 749 672 343.
Bulmers Traditional

Rose & Crown (P)
St John Street.
☎ 01 749 677 556.
Bulmers Traditional

WEST COKER

Castle (P)
High Street.
☎ *01 935 86233.*
🍎 *Taunton Traditional*

West Coker Club (C)
High Street.
☎ *01 935 862 955.*
🍎 *Taunton Traditional*

WEST HUNTSPILL

CROSSWAYS INN (P)
Main Road
🍎 **Rich's**
Bar food lunchtime and
evening; real ales and good
wine-list. Letting rooms;
skittles.

WEST SHEPTON

King William (P)
☎ *01 749 342 102.*
🍎 *Bulmers Traditional*

WILLITON

FORESTERS ARMS (P)
55 Long Street
☎ 01 984 632 508
🍎 **Rich's, Taunton Traditional**
Seventeenth-century coaching
inn, then station hotel on West
Somerset line until Beeching
axe. Still used by passengers on
revived steam railway. Five-six
real ales, bar food lunchtime
and evening, family room,
letting rooms, disabled access.

Wyndham Arms (P)
10 High Street.
☎ *01 984 632 381.*
🍎 *Bulmers Traditional*

WINCANTON

Half Moon (P)
Horsington.
☎ *01 963 370 140.*
🍎 *Taunton Traditional*

ROSIE'S (OL)
Earl Cottage, Lawrence Hill,
Holton
☎ 01 963 32457
Open 9-5.30 Mon-Sat
🍎 **Rosie's cider; cider brandy**
Traditional cider served from
the wood in an antique shop?
Well, this is Somerset! Last real
cider (in fact it's Burrow Hill,
relabelled and none the worse
for it) before London: returning
holidaymakers should stock up
here.

WITHAM FRIARY

SEYMOUR ARMS (P)
☎ 01 749 850 742
Open 11-3, 7-11
🍎 **Rich's**
Unspoilt traditional local on
edge of village. Shove
ha'penny and bar billiards
played. Family room, but no
food.

WIVELISCOMBE

COURTYARD HOTEL (P)
10 High Street
☎ 01 984 623 737
Open 11.30-3, 7-11
🍎 **Thatchers**
Real ale pub with beers served
by gravity in cellar bar. Bar
food lunchtime; letting rooms.

WOOKEY HOLE

Wookey Hole Inn (P)
☎ *01 749 672 236.*
🍎 *Bulmers Traditional*

WOOLAVINGTON

Prince of Wales (P)
42 Woolavington Hill.
☎ *01 278 683 288.*
🍎 *Bulmers Traditional*

WRANTAGE

CANAL INN (P)
☎ 01 823 480 210
Open 12-3, 7-11
🍎 **Lane's**

137

Friendly local with skittle alley. Bar food lunchtime and evening.

YEOVIL

Alexandra's (P)
South West Terr.
☎ 01 935 23723.
🍎 *Taunton Traditional*

ARMOURY INN (P)
1 The Park
☎ 01 935 71047
Open 12-2.30, 6.30-11; 11-11 Fri/Sat
🍎 **Taunton Traditional**
Simple town beerhouse with good range of real ales. Bar snacks lunchtime; disabled access.

Beehive (P)
Huish.
☎ 01 935 76458.
🍎 *Taunton Traditional*

Black Horse (P)
Reckleford.
☎ 01 935 23878.
🍎 *Taunton Traditional*

Hole in the Wall (P)
Wine Street.
☎ 01 935 410 549.
🍎 *Taunton Traditional*

Labour Club (C)
Vicarage Street.
☎ 01 935 23450.
🍎 *Taunton Traditional*

Liberal Club (C)
Middle Street.
☎ 01 935 23037.
🍎 *Taunton Traditional*

MASON'S ARMS (P)
41 Lower Odcombe
☎ 01 935 862 591
Open 12-3 (not Tues), 7-11; 12-11 Sat
🍎 **Bridge Farm; Taunton Traditional**
Thatched seventeenth-century village inn two miles W of Yeovil with three real ales. Food lunchtime. Two skittle alleys. Disabled WC.

Nelson Inn (P)
Eastland Rd.
☎ 01 935 411 060.
🍎 *Taunton Traditional*

Picketty Witch (P)
Ilchester Rd.
☎ 01 935 23770.
🍎 *Taunton Traditional*

Railway Inn (P)
Hendford Hill.
☎ 01 935 75835.
🍎 *Taunton Traditional*

Royal Marine Inn (P)
☎ 01 935 74350.
🍎 *Taunton Traditional*

Staffordshire

BURSLEM

BULL'S HEAD (P)
14 St John's Square
☎ 01 782 834 153
Open 12-2.30, 5-11 Sun-Thurs, 12-11 Fri, 12-3, 6.30-11 Sat.
🍎 **Biddenden**
Titanic's first pub. Full Titanic range plus guests. Separate public bar.

HIGH OFFLEY

ANCHOR (P)
Old Lea
☎ 01 785 284 569
Open 12-3, 7-11.
🍎 **Weston's**
Two-bar canalside pub with gift shop. Not easily found: by Bridge 42 of the Shropshire Union Canal, OS 775 256.

KEELE

Lindsay Cafe Bar (P)
Keele University.
☎ 01 782 548 020.
🍎 *Bulmers Old Hazy*

LICHFIELD

Queens Head (P)
Queen Street.
☎ *01 543 410 932.*
🍺 *Bulmers Old Hazy*

PENN COMMON

BARLEY MOW (P)
Pennwood Lane, Wakeley Hill
☎ 01 902 333 510
Open 12-2.30, 6.30-11; 11-11 Sat
🍺 **Inch's Harvest**
Hidden seventeenth-century
gem with five local real ales.
Garden popular in summer.
Hard to find: OS 949 902.

NEWCASTLE

Cross Ways (P)
Nelson Place.
☎ *01 782 616 953.*
🍺 *Bulmers Traditional*

STAFFORD

STAFFORD ARMS (P)
Railway Street
☎ 01 785 253 313
Open 12-11
🍺 **Biddenden**
Owned by Burslem's Titanic
Brewery. Two annual beer
festivals. Food lunchtime and
evening (Not Sat and Sun
evening)

TAP & SPILE (P)
59 Peel Terrace
☎ 01 785 223 563
Open 11.30-11
🍺 **Crone's**
Excellent choice of real ales in
good alehouse conversion.
Families welcome, food
lunchtime, no smoking area.

STOKE-ON-TRENT

RISING SUN (P)
Knowle Bank Rd, Shraley
Brook, Audley
☎ 01 782 720 600
🍺 **Thatcher's, Weston's**
Well-known brew pub offering

something for cider lovers as
well.

TAMWORTH

Hamlet's Wine Bar (P)
13 Lower Gungate.
☎ *01 827 52277.*
🍺 *Bulmers Old Hazy*

UTTOXETER

Limes House (P)
Cheadle Rd.
☎ *01 889 564 768.*
🍺 *Bulmers Old Hazy*

Suffolk

BILDESTON

CROWN HOTEL (P)
104 High Street
☎ 01 449 740 510
Open 11-11; 12-2.30, 7-10.30
Sun
🍺 **James White**
Fifteenth-century coaching inn
retaining many original
features. Bar food lunchtime
and evening; separate
restaurant. 15 letting rooms.

KING'S HEAD (P)
132 High Street
☎ 01 449 741 434
Open 12-2.30, 5-11; 11-11 sat.
🍺 **Range varies**
Busy timber-framed pub on
market square, with interior
knocked into one rambling bar.
Regular live music. Bar food
lunchtime and evening;
separate restaurant.

BOXFORD

WHITE HART (P)
Broad Street
☎ 01 787 211 071
Open 12-2, 6-11
🍺 **Theobold**
Timber-framed riverside pub in
village centre with Adnams
beers and ever-changing guest

ales. Bar food lunchtime and
evening.

BRANDESTON

QUEENS HEAD (P)
The Street
☎ 01 728 685 307
Open 11.30-2.30, 5.30-11
🍺 **James White**
Good-value home-cooked food
lunchtime and evening in two-
bar country pub. Best-kept
garden in Adnams estate.
Brandon

White Horse (P)
Whitehorse Street.
☎ *01 842 811 557.*
🍺 *Kingfisher*

BRENT ELEIGH

COCK INN (P)
Lavenham Road
☎ 01 787 247 371
Open 12-3, 6-11
🍺 **Castlings Heath Cottage
Cider**
Outstanding and much-
photographed two-bar country
alehouse with classic unspoilt
interior. No food, no machines.

CRATFIELD

CRATFIELD POACHER (P)
Bell Green
☎ 01 986 798 206
Open all permitted hours
🍺 **James White**
Renowned food pub in tourist
country – even takes phone
bookings for bar meals! Real
ales and log fires are part of the
package.

DUNWICH

SHIP (P)
St James's Street
☎ 01 72 873 219
Open 11-3, 6-11; 11-11 summer
🍺 **James White**
Old smugglers' inn of great
character, with Tudor cellars
under an early nineteenth-

century building. Ancient fig
tree in garden. Adnams ales;
food lunchtime and evening;
letting rooms.

EARL SOHAM

VICTORIA (P)
☎ 01 728 685 758
Open 11-2.30, 5.30-11
🍺 **Shawsgate, Castlings Heath**
Well-known pub brewery with
good reputation for food.
Edwardstone

WHITE HORSE (P)
Mill Green
☎ 01 787 211 211
Open 12-3, 6-11
🍺 **Castlings Heath**
Excellent two-bar Greene King
village local with collection of
enamel signs and unusual pub
games. Food lunchtime and
evenings; book Sunday lunch.

IPSWICH

BREWERY TAP (P)
Tolly Cobbold Brewery, Cliff
Quay
☎ 01 473 281 508
Open 11-11
🍺 **Weston's**
Public bar in former brewer's
house, now Tolly Cobbold
visitors centre. Fine views from
large bay windows and
pleasant gardens. Bar food
lunchtime and evening.

MANNINGS (P)
Cornhill
☎ 01 473 254 170
Open 11-3, 5-11; closed Sun
🍺 **Bulmers Traditional**
Tiny town-centre gem saved
from conversion into building
society branch. Fine Jacobean
panelling upstairs. Bar food
lunchtime and evening.

PLOUGH (P)
2 Dogs Head Street
☎ 01 473 288 005
Open 11-3, 5-11; 11-11 Fri/Sat
🍎 **Bulmers Old Hazy**
Friendly town-centre alehouse
with up to 10 real ales. Bar
food Mon-Fri lunchtime only.

TAP & SPILE (P)
76 St Helens Street
☎ 01 473 211 270
Open 11-3, 5-11; 11-11 Thu-Sat
🍎 **Crone's**
Formerly the Dove, with many
original features surviving the
conversion. Families welcome;
bar food lunchtime; disabled
access.

KERSEY

WHITE HORSE (P)
The Street
☎ 01 473 823 353
Open 11-3, 7.30-11
🍎 **Castlings Heath**
Traditional two-bar local in
much-visited village. Adnams
and Greene King dispensed by
gravity. Bar food lunchtime
and evening.

LAVENHAM

COCK (P)
Church Street
☎ 01 787 247 407
Open 11-11
🍎 **Castlings Heath Cottage
Cider**
Popular two-bar real ale pub in
picturesque wool town. Bar
food lunchtime and evening;
family room; no-smoking area;
disabled access.

LAXFIELD

KINGS HEAD (P)
Gorams Mill Lane
☎ 01 986 798 395
🍎 **Castlings Heath Cottage
Cider; James White**
Traditional beer house but with
something of a name for its
food too. Families welcome.

Better known by its nickname,
the Low House.

LEISTON

WHITE HORSE HOTEL (P)
Station Road
☎ 01 728 830 694
Open all permitted hours
🍎 **James White**
Eighteenth-century edge of
town hotel with Greene King
ales and at least one guest. Bar
food lunchtime and evening;
separate restaurant; 13 letting
rooms.

LOWESTOFT

FACTORY ARMS (P)
214 Raglan Street
☎ 01 502 574 523
Open all permitted hours
🍎 **Kingfisher**
Lively one-bar back-street
boozer near town centre. No
food. Disabled access.

TRIANGLE (P)
29 St Peters Street
☎ 01 502 582 711
Open 11-11
🍎 **Bulmers Old Hazy,
Kingfisher, Old Cove**
Pub owned by Green Jack
Brewery and overlooking old
market place. Great range of
ales.

NEWMARKET

WAGGON & HORSES (P)
High Street
☎ 01 638 662 479
Open all permitted hours
🍎 **Biddenden, Bulmers Old
Hazy**
Busy sixteenth-century
coaching inn with wide range
of real ales. Bar food lunchtime
and evening.

OULTON BROAD

BREWERY TAP (P)
Harbour Road
☎ 01 502 587 905

Open 5.30-11 Mon-Fri; 11-11 Sat; 7-10.30 Sun
♠ Kingfisher, Old Cove
Green Jack Brewery's tap, actually and unromantically on an industrial estate near Lowestoft, but seven real ales brewed on site and live music Saturdays make it a popular venue. Disabled access.

THELNETHAM

WHITE HORSE (P)
Hopton Road
☎ 01 379 898 298
Open 12-3, 5-11
♠ Kingfisher
Tudor pub with original beams and fireplaces. Guest ales; bar food lunchtime and evening; separate restaurant.

UFFORD

UFFORD PARK HOTEL (P)
Yarmouth Road
☎ 01 394 383 555
Open all permitted hours
♠ James White
Bar and lounge in hotel which is also golf course and leisure centre. Bar food lunchtime and evening; separate restaurant; children welcome; no-smoking area; disabled access.

WALTON

Tap & Spile (P)
303 High Street.
☎ *01 394 282 130.*
♠ *Bulmers Old Hazy*

Surrey

BRAMLEY

JOLLY FARMER (P)
High Street
☎ 01 483 893 355
Open all permitted hours
♠ Weston's Old Rosie
Eight real ales in Egon Ronay-listed country free house. Bar

food lunchtime & evening; separate 65-cover restaurant in medieval barn. Letting rooms.

CATERHAM

CLIFTON ARMS (P)
110 Chaldon Road
☎ 01 883 343 525
Open 11.30-2.30, 6-11; 12-3, 7-10.30 Sun.
♠ Inch's Stonehouse
Four real ales and garden with menagerie including pot-bellied pigs, ponies, goat. Bric-a-brac includes local historical photographs, musical instruments, old cameras. Bar food at lunchtime.

COLDHARBOUR

PLOUGH (P)
Coldharbour Lane
☎ 01 306 711 793
Open 11.30-3, 6.30-11; 12-10.30 Sun.
♠ Biddenden
Free house in excellent walking country on slope of Leith Hill. Nine real ales. Family room, bar food lunchtime and evening, letting rooms.

ENGLEFIELD GREEN

BEEHIVE (P)
34 Middle Hill
☎ 01 784 431 621
Open 12-2.30 (4 Sat); 6-11
♠ Cider range varies
Small free house with up to five real ales. Beer festivals in garden on May and Aug bank holidays; cider festival Hallowe'en. Bar food lunchtime and evening.

ESHER

Wheatsheaf (P)
The Green.
☎ *01 372 464 014.*
♠ *Bulmer's Old Hazy*

GODALMING

RAM CIDER HOUSE (P)
Catteshall Lane
☎ 01 483 421 093
Open 11-3, 6-11 Mon-Thurs; all
permitted hours Fri-Sun.
🍎 **Bulmers, Weston's, guests**
Anything up to 30 ciders and
perries stocked in genuine
sixteenth-century cider house
popular with walkers, riders,
folkies, morris dancers etc.
Large garden with stream; bar
food lunchtime and evening;
no smoking area.

Red Lion (P)
Mill Rd.
☎ 01 483 415 207.
🍎 *Bulmers Traditional*

HALE

BALL & WICKET (P)
104 Upper Hale Road
☎ 01 252 735 278
Open 4-11; 11-11 Sat
🍎 **Weston's Bound's Brand**
Tile-hung pub overlooking
village green (and cricket-
pitch) Changing range of guest
ales.

PUTTENHAM

GOOD INTENT (P)
62 The Street
☎ 01 483 810 387
Open 11-2.30, 6-11; 11-11 Sat
🍎 **Inch's**
Good range of guest ales in
sixteenth-century coaching inn.
Bar meals lunchtime and Tue-
Sat evenings.

REIGATE

NUTLEY HALL (P)
8 Nutley Lane
☎ 01 737 241 741
Open all permitted hours
🍎 **Weston's Old Rosie**
Busy two-bar King & Barnes
local; bar food lunchtime.

TAP & SPILE (P)
96 High Street
☎ 01 737 243 955
Open all permitted hours
🍎 **Crone's, Bulmer's, Weston's,
Taunton**
Many original features
including two recently
uncovered inglenook fireplaces
in 350-year-old traditional
alehouse. Eight real ales; bar
food lunchtime.

STAINES

BEEHIVE (P)
35 Edgell Road
☎ 01 784 452 663
Open all permitted hours
🍎 **Biddenden**
Busy three-bar pub near the
Thames; good range of ales;
bar food lunchtime and
evening; letting rooms.

THAMES DITTON

Greyhound (P)
Western Green.
☎ 0181 398 1155.
🍎 *Bulmer's Old Hazy*

TONGHAM

HOG'S BACK BREWERY SHOP
(OL)
Manor Farm, The Street
☎ 01 252 783 000
Open 9-6 Mon-Sat (to 8.30
Wed); 10.30-4 Sun
🍎 **Weston's, Inch's, Gospel
Green, Gibbon Strangler,
others**
Wide range of bottled beers
from UK and abroad as well as
local produce, Hog's Back
products and merchandise in
eighteenth-century barn.
Viewing gallery overlooks
brewery.

WALTON-ON-THAMES

REGENT (P)
19 Church Street
☎ 01 932 243 980
Open all permitted hours

♣ Weston's
Typical Wetherspoon conversion of former cinema, popular with students. Bar food lunchtime & evening; no smoking area; disabled access.

Sussex

BECKLEY

Royal Oak (P)
Main Street.
☎ *01 797 260 312.*
♣ *Bulmers Traditional*

BILLINGHURST

Limeburners (P)
Newbridge.
☎ *01 403 782 311.*
♣ *Bulmers Traditional*

Railway Inn (P)
Station Rd.
☎ *01 403 789 298.*
♣ *Bulmers Old Hazy*

BOGNOR REGIS

Hogshead (P)
13 High Street.
☎ *01 243 863 883.*
♣ *Bulmers Old Hazy*

LAMB (P)
Steyne Street
☎ 01 243 868 215
Open 11-11
♣ **Bulmers Old Hazy**
Popular two-bar town centre pub serving ale from local independent brewer Arundel. Bar food lunchtime and evening (not Sun/Mon evening).

BRIGHTON

BLACK CHAPATI (R)
12 Circus Parade, New England Road
☎ 01 273 699 011
Open 7-10.30 Tue-Sat
♣ **Weston's, Thatcher's, local ciders, guests**

Egon Ronay, Michelin-listed restaurant proves that good cider goes with anything – even Asian cuisines!

EVENING STAR (P)
56 Surrey Street
☎ 01 273 328 931
Open 12-11
♣ **Thatchers, Gibbon Strangle**
Pub opened in 1992 has now sold approx 1,500 real ales – started brewing for itself last year.

HAND IN HAND (P)
33 Upper St James's Street
☎ 01 273 602 521
Open all permitted hours
♣ **Biddenden**
Busy one-bar pub which is also home to Kemptown Brewery. Bar food lunchtime and evening.

Quadrant (P)
12-13 North Street.
☎ *01 273 203 085.*
♣ *Bulmers Old Hazy*

WALMER CASTLE (P)
45 Queens Park Road
☎ 01 273 682 466
Open 5.30-11; 12-3, 5.30-11 Sat
♣ **Weston's Old Rosie**
Pizzas, baltis and live poetry are specialities in this wood-panelled corner local. Harvey's ales.

BURGESS HILL

Watermill Inn (P)
Leylands Rd.
☎ *01 444 235 517.*
♣ *Bulmers Old Hazy*

CHICHESTER

CHEQUERS (P)
203 Oving Road
☎ 01 243 786 427
Open 11-11
♣ **Inch's**
Popular two-bar local on edge of town. Bar food lunchtime.

HOGSHEAD (P)
50 South Street
☎ 01 243 785 753
Open 11-11
🍏 **Bulmers Old Hazy &
Traditional**
An inn since 1740, now a
Whitbread alehouse with a
wide range of real ales. Bar
food lunchtime and evening
(not Sun evening).

CRAWLEY

Hogshead (P)
85 High Street.
☎ 01 293 514 105.
🍏 *Bulmers Old Hazy*

CROWBOROUGH

White Hart (P)
1 Chapel Green.
☎ 01 892 652 367.
🍏 *Bulmers Old Hazy*

DITCHLING

WHITE HORSE (P)
16 West Street
☎ 01 273 842 006
Open 11-11
🍏 **Biddenden**
Real ales from Harvey's and
Timothy Taylor in welcoming
one-bar pub with haunted
cellar. Bar food lunchtime and
evening.

EASTBOURNE

HOGSHEAD (P)
57 South Street
☎ 01 323 723 107/722 640
Open all permitted hours
🍏 **Bulmers Old Hazy**
Wide range of real ales in
raucous themed alehouse. Bar
food lunchtime.

EXCEAT BRIDGE

GOLDEN GALLEON (P)
☎ 01 323 892 247
Open 11-2.30, 6-11
🍏 **Theobolds**
Large riverside brewpub,

formerly a tearoom. Well-
known for its gardens. Bar
food lunchtime and evening.
Felpham

OLD BARN (P)
Felpham Road
☎ 01 243 821 564
Open 11-11
🍏 **Bulmers Old Hazy**
One-bar pub popular with
locals and tourists alike. Real
ales from independent brewers.
Bar food lunchtime and
evenings; disabled access.

FIRLE

**ENGLISH FARM CIDER
CENTRE** (OL,R)
Middle Farm
☎ 01 323 811 411
Open 9.30-6 Mon-Fri; 9.30-5
Sat, Bank Hol; 10-5 Sun.
The essential place of
pilgrimage for cider lovers.
Over 180 draught and bottled
ciders and perries in 200-year-
old flint barn. Tasting
welcomed and accompanied by
informed and friendly advice.
Separate restaurant; disabled
access.

FISHBOURNE

BULL'S HEAD (P)
99 Fishbourne Road
☎ 01 243 785 707
Open 11-3, 5.30-11; 11-11 Sat
🍏 **Appledram, Thatchers**
Large comfortable Gale's pub
with skittle alley. Bar food
lunchtime and evening;
separate restaurant specialises
in fish in summer and game in
winter. No smoking area.

HARTFIELD

**PERRYHILL ORCHARD FARM
SHOP** (OL)
Edenbridge Road
☎ 01 892 770 595
Open 12-6 Mon-Fri, 10-6
Sat/Sun
🍏 **Weston's range, local ciders**

Old-established farm shop on commercial orchard which supplies many local cider makers.

HASTINGS

Smugglers (P)
43 White Rock.
☎ *01 424 424 295.*
🍎 *Bulmers Old Hazy*

HAYWARD'S HEATH

STAR (P)
1 The Broadway
☎ 01 444 413 267
Open 11-11
🍎 **Bulmers Old Hazy**
Whitbread Hogshead alehouse with up to 13 real ales and large selection of bottled beers. Bar food lunchtime and evening.

HENFIELD

Gardeners Arms (P)
Newtown Rd.
☎ *01 273 492 411.*
🍎 *Bulmers Traditional*

HORSHAM

Hogshead & Malt Shovel (P)
15 Springfield Rd.
☎ *01 403 254 543.*
🍎 *Bulmers Old Hazy*

Tut 'n' Shive (P)
38 East Street.
☎ *01 403 253 924.*
🍎 *Bulmers Traditional*

ICKLESHAM

QUEEN'S HEAD (P)
Parsonage Lane
☎ 01 424 814 552
Open 11-3, 6-11; 11-11 Sat
🍎 **Biddenden**
Tile-hung country pub with magnificent mahogany bar. Bar food lunchtime and evening; no smoking area.

LAVANT

EARL OF MARCH (P)
Lavant Road
☎ 01 243 774 751
Open 10.30-3, 6-11
🍎 **Weston's Old Rosie, Inch's**
Spacious pub with superb view of the Downs. Good range of real ales. Bar food lunchtime and evenings; game a speciality. Disabled access.

Royal Oak (P)
East Lavant.
☎ *01 243 527 434.*
🍎 *Bulmers Traditional*

LEWES

BREWERS ARMS (P)
91 High Street
☎ 01 273 479 475
Open all permitted hours
🍎 **Thatchers**
Quiet locals' pub; bar food lunchtime.

GARDENERS ARMS (P)
Cliffe High Street
☎ 01 273 474 808
Open 11-3, 5.30-11; 11-11 Thurs-Sat
🍎 **Thatchers**
Free house with up to eight real ales. Bar food lunchtime (not Sun).

Lansdown Arms (P)
Lansdown Place.
☎ *01 273 472 807.*
🍎 *Bulmers Old Hazy*

Kings Head (P)
9 Southover High Street.
☎ *01 273 474 628.*
🍎 *Bulmers Old Hazy*

MAPLEHURST

WHITE HORSE (P)
Park Lane
☎ 01 403 891 208
Open 12-2.30, 6-11
🍎 **Draught range varies; Bulmers No 7**

Three to five real ales always available in comfortable two-bar pub. Bar food evening and lunchtime.

OVING

GRIBBLE INN (P)
☎ 01 243 786 893
Open 11-2.30, 6-11
🍏 **Cider range varies**
Picturesque thatched sixteenth-century brewpub owned by Hall & Woodhouse. Brewery can be seen at work. Skittle alley. Bar food lunchtime and evening. Disabled access.

ROBERTSBRIDGE

OSTRICH (P)
Station Road
☎ 01 580 881 737
Open 11-11
🍏 **Bulmers Old Hazy, Gaymers Fat Boy**
Tastefully-restored former station hotel with many original features. Good range of real ales from independent brewers. Bar food lunchtime and evening; letting rooms; disabled access.

RUDGWICK

CATCHPOLE'S (OL)
Church Street
☎ 01 403 82239
Open 8-6 (7 Fri); 9-3.30 Sun
🍏 **Weston's Old Rosie**
Village store that sells just about everything.

MUCKY DUCK (P)
Tisman's Common, Loxwood Road
☎ 01 403 822 300
Open all permitted hours
🍏 **Weston's range**
Country pub in large gardens amid fields. Children's certificate; bar food lunchtime and evening and separate restaurant; letting rooms; disabled access.

SELHAM

THREE MOLES (P)
☎ 01 798 861 206
Open 11.30-2.30, 5-11; 11-11 Sat
🍏 **Weston's Old Rosie**
Isolated King & Barnes pub, a station inn before Beeching and a big favourite with local CAMRA. No food. Hard to find: off A272 at Halfway Bridge, OS 935 206.

SHOREHAM

Crabtree (P)
6 Buckingham Rd.
☎ *01 273 463 508.*
🍏 *Bulmers Traditional*

ROYAL SOVEREIGN (P)
6 Middle Street
☎ 01 273 453 518
Open 11-11
🍏 **Bulmers Old Hazy**
Small but busy Whitbread pub with good range of guest ales. Bar food lunchtime and evening – book Sunday lunch.

SLINFOLD

King's Head (P)
The Street.
☎ *01 403 790 339.*
🍏 *Bulmers Old Hazy*

STEYNING

CHEQUERS INN (P)
41 High Street
☎ 01 903 814 437
Open 10-2.30, 5-11; 10-11 Wed-Sat
🍏 **Bulmers Old Hazy**
Multi-room fifteenth-century gem in pretty town. Good choice of real ales; bar food lunchtime and evening.

WEST ASHLING

RICHMOND ARMS (P)
Mill Lane
☎ 01 243 575 730
Open 11-2.30, 5.30-11
🍏 **Thatchers**

Village alehouse near duckpond. Big ale range; good bar food lunchtime and evening.

WEST CHILTINGTON

ELEPHANT & CASTLE (P)
Church Street
☎ 01 798 813 307
Open 11-4, 6-11; 11-11 Fri/Sat
🍎 **Weston's Old Rosie**
Friendly two-bar low-beamed King & Barnes pub. Bar food lunchtime and evening.

FIVE BELLS (P)
Smock Alley
☎ 01 798 812 143
Open 11-3, 6-11
🍎 **Weston's Old Rosie, Biddenden**
Country beerhouse with constantly changing range of real ales. Bar food lunchtime and evening.

WORTHING

Hogshead Cask Ale Emporium (P)
25 Warwick Street.
☎ *01 903 206 088.*
🍎 *Bulmers Traditional*

Tyne & Wear

BYKER

TAP & SPILE (P)
33 Shields Road
☎ 0191 276 1440
Open all permitted hours
🍎 **Weston's Old Rosie, Crone's, guests**
Characteristic Tap & Spile bare-boards-and-bric-a-brac look. Five minutes' walk from Byker Metro station.

GOSFORTH

COUNTY HOTEL (P)
High Street
☎ 0191 285 6919

Open all permitted hours
🍎 **Bulmers Traditional**
One of Scottish Courage's T&J Bernard alehouse chain. Good range of guest ales; bar food at lunchtime.

VICTORY (P)
Killingworth Rd, South Gosforth
☎ 0191 285 1254
Open all permitted hours
🍎 **Bulmers Traditional**
Civil servants from nearby DoSS headquarters pack this T&J Bernard alehouse at lunchtime. Good range of ales.

JARROW

Allison Arms (P)
31 Straker Street.
☎ *0191 489 7342.*
🍎 *Bulmers Traditional*

LOW FELL

ALETASTER (P)
706 Durham Road
☎ 0191 487 0770
Open all permitted hours
🍎 **Bulmers Traditional**
Scottish & Newcastle T&J Bernard alehouse with 16 handpumps.

NEWCASTLE-UPON-TYNE

BALTIC TAVERN (P)
Baltic Chambers, Broad Chare
☎ 0191 261 7385
Open all permitted hours
🍎 **Addlestone's on genuine handpump**
Bare brick and boards give quayside alehouse opposite law-courts a basic feel. Don't lean on the rope bar-rail!

COOPERAGE (P)
33 The Close, Quayside
☎ 0191 232 8286
Open all permitted hours.
🍎 **Addlestone on genuine handpump; Bulmers Traditional**
Fourteenth-century building,

housing pub in former cooperage. Good range of beers, especially from local Hadrian Brewery; bar-food lunchtime and evening; separate restaurant upstairs 12-3. Disabled access.

Collingwood Arms (P)
Brandling Village.
☎ *0191 281 1271.*
🍎 *Bulmers Traditional*

Corner House Hotel (P)
Heaton Rd, Heaton.
☎ *0191 265 9602.*
🍎 *Bulmers Traditional*

CROFTER'S LODGE (P)
Kenton Lane.
☎ 0191 286 1235
Open all permitted hours
🍎 **Addlestone's, Bulmers Old Hazy, Biddenden**
Big estate pub with surprising range of ales and ciders. Bar food lunchtime.

FOG & FIRKIN (P)
City Road
☎ 0191 261 8272
Open all permitted hours
🍎 **Addlestone's on genuine handpump**
Split-level recently rebuilt Firkin pub with beers brewed at Fly & Firkin in Middlesbrough. Bar food lunchtime. Disabled access.

FORTH HOTEL (P)
Pink Lane
☎ 0191 232 6487
Open all permitted hours
🍎 **Addlestone's on genuine handpump**
Handy for Central Station.

HOTSPUR HOTEL (P)
Percy Street
☎ 0191 261 1900
Open all permitted hours
🍎 **Bulmers Traditional**
T&J Bernard alehouse. popular with staff of nearby hospital, university students. Good value bar food lunchtime.

NORTH TERRACE (P)
Claremont Rd, Spital Tongues.
☎ 0191 263 0011
Open all permitted hours
🍎 **Bulmers Traditional**
T&J Bernard alehouse popular with students. Bar food lunchtime.

STRAWBERRY (P)
Strawberry Place
☎ 0191 232 6865
Open all permitted hours
🍎 **Bulmers Traditional**
First in Scottish & Newcastle's T&J Bernard alehouse chain. Nearest pub to Newcastle United ground, fills up with football fans on match days, when it may close in the afternoon.

TAP & SPILE (P)
Nun Street
☎ 0191 232 0026
Opens all permitted hours
🍎 **Westons Old Rosie**
Tap & Spile on two floors. Bar food not always of the best. Cheap beer and wine on Mondays in term-time to attract the students.

Whitley Tavern (P)
Front Street.
☎ *0191 270 2421.*
🍎 *Bulmers Traditional*

NORTH SHIELDS

TAP & SPILE (P)
184 Tynemouth Road
☎ 0191 257 2523
Open all permitted hours.
🍎 **Westons Old Rosie**
Up to 11 real ales; bar food lunchtime and evening.

SHIELDFIELD

FLETCHERS (P)
89 Shield Street
☎ 0191 233 1391

Opens all permitted hours
🍎 Thatcher's, Biddenden
Mock-Tudor monstrosity
outside, friendly local inside.
Jennings beers

QUEENS ARMS (P)
1 Simpson Terrace
☎ 0191 232 4101
Open all permitted hours
🍎 Bulmers Traditional
T&J Bernard alehouse

SOUTH SHIELDS

Britannia (P)
Westoe Lane.
☎ *0191 455 2781.*
🍎 *Bulmers Traditional*

SUNDERLAND

BOROUGH (P)
Vine Place
☎ 0191 567 7909
Open all permitted hours
🍎 Bulmers Old Hazy
Vaux-owned city centre bar
with guest ale. Regular live
music.

Chesters (P)
Chester Rd.
☎ *0191 565 9952.*
🍎 *Bulmers Old Hazy*

TAP & SPILE (P)
Salem Street, Hendon
☎ 0191 514 2810
Open 11-3, 6-11 (7-10.30 Sun)
**🍎 Three real ciders from
Weston's, Bulmers, Inch's,
Taunton stables plus perry.
Keg-looking taps are electric
dispense**
Twelve real ales. Local pub of
the year three years running.
Bar food lunchtime and
evening. Bar billiards.

Three Horseshoes (P)
Washington Rd, North Hylton.
☎ *0191 519 1803.*
🍎 *Bulmers Old Hazy*

TYNEMOUTH

TURK'S HEAD (P)
41 Front Street
☎ 0191 257 6547
Open all permitted hours
🍎 Bulmers Traditional
T&J Bernard alehouse beside
the sea.

TYNEMOUTH LODGE (P)
Tynemouth Road
☎ 0191 257 7565
Open all permitted hours
🍎 Thatcher's
Unspoilt eighteenth-century
free house where Bass is still
excellent and landlord is an
authority on most things.

WHITLEY BAY

TAP & SPILE (P)
278 Whitley Road
☎ 0191 251 3852
Open all permitted hours
🍎 Westons Old Rosie
Good beer quality in typical
Tap & Spile.

Warwickshire

ALCESTER

Bulls Head (P)
☎ *01 789 772 242.*
🍎 *Taunton Traditional*

Dog & Partridge (P)
Bleachfield Street.
☎ *01 789 763 401.*
🍎 *Bulmers Traditional*

Lord Nelson Inn (P)
69 Priory Rd.
☎ *01 789 762 632.*
🍎 *Bulmers Traditional*

White Lion (P)
32 Evesham Rd.
☎ *01 789 400 391.*
🍎 *Bulmers Traditional*

ATHERSTONE

Hat & Beaver *(P)*
130 Long Street.
☎ *01 827 720 300.*
🍎 *Bulmers Old Hazy*

BIDFORD-ON-AVON

Anglo-Saxon *(P)*
High Street.
☎ *01 789 773 405.*
🍎 *Bulmers Traditional*

British Legion *(C)*
High Street.
☎ *01 386 446 339.*
🍎 *Bulmers Traditional*

ETTINGDON

White Horse *(P)*
Banbury Rd.
☎ *01 789 740 641.*
🍎 *Bulmers Traditional*

HARBURY

Crown Inn *(P)*
Crown Street.
☎ *01 926 612 283.*
🍎 *Bulmers Traditional*

LAPWORTH

NAVIGATION (P)
Old Warwick Road
☎ 01 564 783 337
Open 11-3, 5.30-11 Mon-Fri; 11-11 sat; 12-10.30 sun
🍎 **Cider range varies**
Characterful multi-room canalside pub with exposed beams, stuffed fish that didn't get away, oak settles, stone floors, traditional games, you name it. Five real ales include mild and two guests. Local pub of the year 1994 and '95. Excellent bar meals lunchtime and evening including vegetarian menu.

LEAMINGTON SPA

Bedford Inn *(P)*
Bedford Street.
☎ *01 926 339 551.*
🍎 *Bulmers Old Hazy*

Black Horse *(P)*
Princes Street.
☎ *01 926 425 169.*
🍎 *Bulmers Traditional*

GREEN MAN (P)
Lower Tachbrook Street
☎ 01 926 316 298
Open all permitted hours.
🍎 **Bulmers Old Hazy**
Newly refurbished community pub; bar food all day includes breakfasts.

Kelly's *(P)*
7 Court Rd.
☎ *01 926 428 655.*
🍎 *Bulmers Old Hazy*

Newbold Comyn Arms *(P)*
Newbold Terr East.
☎ *01 926 338 810.*
🍎 *Bulmers Old Hazy*

RAILWAY INN (P)
31 Clemens Street
☎ 01 926 888 958
Open 10.30-11
🍎 **Bulmers Traditional**
Traditional two-room Banks's pub. No food.

LONG COMPTON

Red Lion *(P)*
Main Street.
☎ *01 608 684 221.*
🍎 *Bulmers Old Hazy*

PAILTON

FOX INN (P)
Lutterworth Road
☎ 01 788 832 353
Open 11.30-3, 5.30-11
🍎 **Weston's range**
Two-bar village pub with letting rooms. Bar food lunchtime and evening; no smoking area.

RUGBY

ALEXANDRA ARMS (P)
72 James Street
☎ 01 788 578 660
Open 12-3, 5.30-11; 12-3,
7-10 Sun
● **Bulmers Traditional**
Small two-bar local handy for
theatre and town centre. Bar
food lunchtime and evening.
Northampton table skittles
played.

FITCHEW & FIRKIN (P)
28 Sheep Street
☎ 01 788 543 023
Open 11-11
● **Addlestone's**
Typical Firkin, although
without brewery. Bar food
lunchtime and evening;
disabled access.

IMPERIAL (P)
165 Oxford st
☎ 01 788 543 627
Open 11-11
● **Addlestone's**
Big two-bar back-street local.
Northampton table skittles
played. No food.

MADISON'S (P)
46 Chapel Street
☎ 01 788 574 008
Open 10-11; 12-3, 7-10.30 Sun
● **Bulmers Traditional**
Town-centre over-20s' pub
with dance-floor. Everard's
ales; no food.

RYTON-ON-DUNSMORE

RYTON GARDENS (OL, R)
Wolston Lane
☎ 01 203 303 517
Open 9-5.30 seven days
● **Dunkerton's range**
Shop and restaurant attached
to garden centre.

SHIPSTON-ON-STOUR

Royal Oak (P)
Whatcote.
☎ *01 295 680 319.*
● *Bulmers Traditional*

STOCKTON

CROWN (P)
High Street
☎ 01 926 812 255
Open 12-3, 7-11; 11-11 Fri/Sat
in summer
● **Hartland's**
Village local with six guest ales
and wide selection of whiskies.
Function room in 300-year-old
barn. Bar food lunchtime and
evening; separate restaurant.

STRATFORD-UPON-AVON

College Arms (P)
Lower Quinton.
☎ *01 789 720 342.*
● *Bulmers Traditional*

Firkin (P)
1 Arden Street.
☎ *01 789 293 894.*
● *Bulmers Traditional*

QUEENS HEAD (P)
54 Ely Street
☎ 01 789 204 914
Open 11.30-11; 12-10.30 Sun
● **Weston's range**
Local Bass pub off the tourist
track. Guest ale. Bar snacks
12-2.30.

STRETTON-ON-DUNSMORE

SHOULDER OF MUTTON (P)
Village Green
☎ 01 203 542 601
● **Knight's**
Totally unspoilt village pub
with tiled snug, two bars and,
oddly enough, a rifle range.
Occasional live jazz.

STUDLEY

JUBILEE INN (P)
Bromsgrove Road
☎ 01 527 852 836
Open 12-11
🍎 **Biddenden**
1930s roadhouse with large
garden. Excellent Hobson's
ales. Children's certificate; bar
food lunchtime and evening
(not Tues).

TWYCROSS

Curzon Arms (P)
Main Rd.
☎ *01 827 880 334.*
🍎 *Bulmers Old Hazy*

WARWICK

Simple Simon (P)
Emscote Rd.
☎ *01 926 491 050.*
🍎 *Bulmers Traditional*

WELFORD-ON-AVON

Bell Inn (P)
Binton Rd.
☎ *01 789 750 353.*
🍎 *Bulmers Traditional*

West Midlands

BILSTON

Old Bush (P)
Skidmore Rd.
☎ *01 384 42776.*
🍎 *Bulmers Traditional*

BIRMINGHAM

Cardiff Arms (P)
7 Stephenson Street.
☎ *0121 643 1997.*
🍎 *Bulmers Traditional*

Coach & Horses (P)
Bordesley Green.
☎ *0121 772 1048.*
🍎 *Bulmers Traditional*

Guild Arms (P)
Witton Rd, Aston.
☎ *0121 327 1102.*
🍎 *Taunton Traditional*

Hen & Chickens (P)
Lower Dartmouth Street.
☎ *0121 552 1058.*
🍎 *Bulmers Traditional*

Hollywood Wines (OL)
Trumans Heath Rd, Hollywood.
☎ *0121 430 7692.*
🍎 *Bulmers Traditional*

LONDON TAVERN (P)
1 High Street, Saltley
☎ 0121 327 4609
Open 11-11
🍎 **Thatcher's, Bulmers
Traditional**
Boisterous Victorian cider-
house in shadow of listed
Saltley Viaduct. Bar food and
Indian snacks lunchtime and
evening.

LORD CLIFDEN (P)
34 Great Hampton Street,
Hockley
☎ 0121 523 7515
Open 11-11
🍎 **Franklin's cider and perry**
Two-room pub near Jewellery
Quarter. Ales are real but on
electric pump – not keg. Food
lunchtime only.

Swan Hotel (P)
Washwood Heath Rd, Ward End.
☎ *0121 327 1759.*
🍎 *Bulmers Traditional*

Tipsy Gent (P)
Cherrywood Rd.
☎ *0121 772 1858.*
🍎 *Bulmers Traditional*

United Services Club (C)
Gough Street.
☎ *0121 643 2093.*
🍎 *Bulmers Traditional*

BRIERLEY HILL

Tap & Spile (P)
High Street.
☎ *01 384 573 302.*
 Bulmers Old Hazy

Woodman (P)
31 Leys Rd, Brockmoor.
☎ *01 384 78744.*
 Bulmers Traditional

COVENTRY

NURSERY TAVERN (P)
38 Lord Street, Chapel Fields
☎ 01 203 674 530
Open 11-11
 Bulmers Old Hazy
Lively three-room pub with
good range of ales. Children
welcome until 7.30pm. Bar
food lunchtime Mon-Sat and
evening Fri/Sat.

OLD WINDMILL (P)
Spon Street
☎ 01 203 252 183
Open 11.30-2.30, 6-11; 12-2, 7-
10.30 Sun
 Bulmers Traditional
Multi-room sixteenth-century
pub with good range of ales
and bar lunches. Disabled
access.

SPITTLEMOORE INN (P)
Lower Ford Street
☎ 01 203 221 939
Open 10-11
 Bulmers Traditional
Basic city-centre pub serving
independent brewers' ales. Bar
food lunchtime.

CRADLEY HEATH

Smiths Arms (P)
Fatherless Barn Housing Estate.
 Bulmers Traditional

DARLASTON

ROSE PARK OFF-LICENCE (OL)
144 Wolverhampton Street
☎ 0121 526 2571
Open 9.30-10.30 seven days
 Weston's range; Thatcher's

draught; seasonal guests
Well-known local specialist off-
licence.

DUDLEY

Barley Mow (P)
Constitution Hill.
☎ *01 384 258 768.*
 Bulmers Traditional

BRITISH OAK (P)
Salop Street, Eve Hill
☎ 01 384 236 297
 Bulmers Traditional
Brew pub which occasionally
makes its own cider.

FELLOWS (P)
The Broadway, Castle Hill
☎ 01 384 237 303
Open 11-11
 Bulmers Traditional
Once the gatehouse of Dudley
Zoo, now a Beefeater pub and
restaurant. Food lunchtime and
evening; disabled access.

Hearty Good Fellow (P)
3 Maughan Street.
☎ *01 384 237 887.*
 Bulmers Traditional

LAMP TAVERN (P)
116 High Street
☎ 01 384 254 129
Open 11-11
 Bulmers Traditional
Lively two-bar Batham's pub,
once a brewery. Food until 7.30;
disabled access.

HALESOWEN

Lyttleton Arms (P)
High Street.
☎ *0121 501 3657.*
 Bulmers Traditional

Swan Inn (P)
Long Lane.
☎ *0121 559 2484.*
 Bulmers Traditional

WAGGON & HORSES (P)
21 Stourbridge Road
☎ 0121 550 4989
Open 12-11

🍎 **Weston's Old Rosie**
Ever-changing range of real
ales including Batham and
Enville in drinker's pub – no
food.

HOCKLEY HEATH

Blue Bell (P)
Warings Green Rd.
☎ *01 564 702 328.*
🍎 *Bulmers Traditional*

KNOWLE

VAULTS BAR (P)
St John's Close
☎ 01 564 773 656
Open 12-2.30, 5-11
🍎 **Weston's range**
Cosy three-room pub attached
to nightclub. Five real ales; bar
food lunchtime. Turned from
keg to real cider after hearing
of CAMRA policy on
misleading dispense.
Traditional games include bar
billiards.

LOWER GORNAL

FOUNTAIN (P)
8 Temple Street
☎ 01 384 834 888
Open 12-3 (not Mon-Wed), 7-
11; 12-2.30, 7-10.30 Sun
🍎 **Bulmers Traditional**
Good range of ales in former
brewery.

LYE

Noahs Ark (P)
Grange Lane, Sheppard Brook.
☎ *01 384 422 061.*
🍎 *Bulmers Traditional*

Windmill Inn (P)
90 Dudley Rd.
☎ *01 384 423 313.*
🍎 *Bulmers Traditional*

ROWLEY REGIS

Manchester House (P)
15 High Street.
☎ *0121 559 2149.*
🍎 *Bulmers Traditional*

SEDGLEY

BULL'S HEAD (P)
27 Bilston Street
☎ 01 902 679 606
Open 1-3, 6-11 Mon-Wed; 1-11
Thur/Fri; 1-4, 6-11 Sat; 12-3,
7-10.30 Sun
🍎 **Rich's, Bulmers Traditional**
End-of-terrace two-bar local
run by ex-photographer,
decorated with local scenes (all
her own work). Holden's ales;
bar food lunchtime.

SHIRLEY

BERNIE'S (OL)
266 Cranmore Boulevard
☎ 0121 744 2827
Open 12-2 (not Mon), 5.30-10;
12-2, 7-9.45 Sun
🍎 **Rich's**
Usually three draught ciders
along with seven cask ales.
Area's longest continuous
Good Beer Guide entry.

STOURBRIDGE

Chequers (P)
High Street.
☎ *01 384 395 562.*
🍎 *Taunton Traditional*

Gate Hangs Well (P)
☎ *01 384 396 594.*
🍎 *Taunton Traditional*

Waggon & Horses (P)
31 Worcester Street.
☎ *01 384 393 602.*
🍎 *Bulmers Traditional*

SUTTON COLDFIELD

LAUREL WINES (OL)
63 Westwood Road
☎ 0121 353 0399
Open 12-2, 5.30-10.30
🍎 **Weston's, Inch's**
Specialist off-licence with wide
range of real ales.

TIPTON

PORT'N'ALE HOUSE (P)
178 Horseley Heath, Great
Bridge

☎ 0121 557 7249
Open 12-3, 6-11
🍎 **Bulmers Traditional**
Batham's plus unusual guest
ales. Bar food lunchtime and
evening; disabled access.

Rose & Crown (P)
Queens Rd.
☎ *0121 557 2406.*
🍎 *Bulmers Traditional*

Royal (P)
Bloomfield Rd, Princes End.
☎ *0121 557 8974.*
🍎 *Bulmers Traditional*

UPPER GORNAL

Cottage of Content (P)
☎ *01 902 676 024.*
🍎 *Taunton Traditional*

CROWN (P)
16 Holloway Street
☎ 01 902 665 177
Open 12-4, 7-11 Mon-Sat; 12-3,
7-10.30 Sun.
🍎 **Bulmers Traditional & Old
Hazy**
Two-bar Banks's local; bar food
lunchtime.

OLD MILL (P)
Windmill Street
☎ 01 902 887 707
Open 12-3, 6-11 Mon-Fri; 12-11
Sat; 12-4, 6.30-10.30 Sun.
🍎 **Bulmers Traditional; Inch's**
Two-bar local with separate
restaurant; family room; bar
food lunchtime and evening.

SHAKESPEARE (P)
105 Kent Street
☎ 01 902 880 820
Open 11-11
🍎 **Bulmers Traditional**
Basic one-room Banks's local.

WARLEY

Wharf (P)
135 Station Rd, Oldhill Heath.
☎ *0121 559 2323.*
🍎 *Bulmers Traditional*

WEDNESBURY

Bush Inn (P)
Leabrook Rd.
☎ *0121 556 1483.*
🍎 *Taunton Traditional*

WEDNESFIELD

VINE (P)
Lichfield Road
☎ 01 902 733 529
Open 11-3, 6-11
🍎 **Inch's plus guests**
Friendly local with guest ales
and usually a cask mild.
Family room; bar food
lunchtime and evening.

WEST BROMWICH

Hawthorn (P)
Dial Lane, Hill Top.
☎ *0121 557 2074.*
🍎 *Bulmers Traditional*

Queen's Head (P)
Church Lane.
☎ *0121 525 9234.*
🍎 *Taunton Traditional*

WHEATSHEAF (P)
379 High Street
☎ 0121 553 4221
Open 11-3, 5-11; 12-2.30,
7-10.30 Sun
🍎 **Inch's**
Lively, friendly two-bar
Holden's pub. Bar food
lunchtime.

WILLENHALL

FALCON (P)
77 Gomer St West
☎ 01 902 633 378
Open 12-11
🍎 **Bulmers Traditional**
Real ale house which has
served over 500 guest ales in
recent years.

WOLLASTON

Waterloo (P)
58 Bridgnorth Rd.
☎ *01 384 394 330.*
🍎 *Bulmers Traditional*

WOLVERHAMPTON

Barley Mow (P)
Stafford Street.
☎ *01 902 27029.*
🍎 *Taunton Traditional*

GREAT WESTERN (P)
Sun Street
☎ 01 902 351 090
Open 11-11 (closes Sat/Sun afternoon)
🍎 **Bulmers Traditional**
Former national Pub of the Year. Railway memorabilia; Batham's and Holden's ales; bar food lunchtime.

NEWHAMPTON INN (P)
Riches Street
☎ 01 902 745 773
Open all permitted hours
🍎 **Cider range varies**
Big three-room street-corner local with large garden and bowling green. Bar food lunchtime; no-smoking area.

WOOTTON WAWEN

Bulls Head (P)
Stratford Rd.
☎ *01 564 792 511.*
🍎 *Bulmers Old Hazy*

Wiltshire

BLUNSDON

Heart in Hand (P)
43 High Street.
☎ *01 793 721 314.*
🍎 *Bulmers Old Hazy*

BOX

QUARRYMAN'S ARMS (P)
Box Hill
☎ 01 225 743 569
Open 11-3, 7-11; 11-11 Thurs-Sat
🍎 **Thatchers**
Real ales from local independent brewers in country pub apparently hidden in maze of lanes but actually only 300 yards from A4. Superb views. Bar food lunchtime and evening. Hard to find: OS 834 693.

BRADFORD-ON-AVON

DOG & FOX (P)
33 Ashley Road
☎ 01 225 863 257
Open 11-2.30, 6-11; 11-11 Sat; 12-3, 7-10.30 Sun
🍎 **Thatchers, Bulmers Traditional**
Friendly two-bar edge-of-town pub with large garden. Bar food lunchtime and evening; family room.

BROKERSWOOD

KICKING DONKEY (P)
☎ 01 373 823 250
Open 11.30-2.30, 6.30-11
🍎 **Thatchers**
Seventeenth-century country pub with low beams, horse-brasses etc. Excellent range of real ales. Bar food lunchtime and evening; separate restaurant.
Hard to find: OS 833 520.

BULKINGTON

Well Inn (P)
☎ *01 380 828 741.*
🍎 *Bulmers Traditional*

CORSHAM

Cross Keys (P)
Pickwick.
☎ *01 249 712 323.*
🍎 *Taunton Traditional*

PACKHORSE (P)
High Street
☎ 01 249 701 929
Open 11.30-3, 6-11; 12-2, 7-10.30 Sun
🍎 **Thatchers**
Small friendly town-centre pub. Bar food lunchtime.

CORSLEY

CROSS KEYS INN (P)
Lyes Green
☎ 01 373 832 406
Open 12-3, 7-11; closed
Mon/Tue, Thu/Fri lunchtime.
🍎 **Bulmers Traditional**
Welcoming and characterful
free house serving Mole's and
Butcombe ales. Bar food
lunchtime and evening.

DEVIZES

BRITISH LION (P)
Estcourt Street
☎ 01 380 720 665
Open all permitted hours
🍎 **Inch's, guests**
Basic local which was keg-only
until a couple of years ago.
Now has own ale brewed by
Coach House. No food.

Southgate Inn (P)
Potterne Rd.
☎ *01 380 722 872.*
🍎 *Bulmers Traditional*

TOWN HALL WINE VAULTS
(OL)
St John's Street
☎ 01 380 724 423
Open 12-9
🍎 **Thatchers, Inch's**

DILTON MARSH

Kings Arms (P)
44 High Street.
☎ *01 373 822 829.*
🍎 *Bulmers Traditional*

DOWNTON

Wooden Spoon (P)
17 High Street.
☎ *01 725 510 223.*
🍎 *Bulmers Traditional*

EBBESBOURNE WAKE

HORSESHOE INN (P)
☎ 01 722 780 474
Open 11.30-3, 6.30-11
🍎 **Thatchers**
Rare outpost for Adnams ales

in remote seventeenth-century
former drovers' inn. Families
welcome; letting rooms; bar
food lunchtime and evening.
Hard to find: OS 242 993.

FORD

WHITE HART (P)
☎ 01 249 782 213
Open 11-2.30, 5.30-11
🍎 **Two changing real ciders**
Wide range of real ales in
picturesque inn. Families
welcome; bar food lunchtime
and evening and award-
winning separate restaurant.
Landlord does not advertise
his real ciders, so help him
overcome his embarrassment
and ask! Letting rooms;
disabled access.

HIGHWORTH

Fishes Inn (P)
High Street.
☎ *01 793 763 098.*
🍎 *Bulmers Old Hazy*

HILPERTON

Village Hall (C)
Whaddon Lane.
☎ *01 225 765 046.*
🍎 *Bulmers Traditional*

KILMINGTON

RED LION (P)
☎ 01 985 844 263
Open 11-3, 6.30-11
🍎 **Thatcher's Cheddar Valley**
Unspoilt National Trust-owned
pub near Stourhead gardens.
Letting rooms; bar food
lunchtime and evening.

KINGTON ST MICHAEL

JOLLY HUNTSMAN (P)
☎ 01 249 750 305
Open 11.30-3, 6.30-11 (11.30-11
in summer)
🍎 **Mole's Black Rat**
Popular village local offering at
least six real ales. Letting

rooms; bar food lunchtime and evening; disabled access.

LACOCK

RISING SUN (P)
32 Bowden Hill
☎ 01 249 704 363
Open 11.30-3, 6-11
🍎 **Mole's Black Rat**
Wide choice of real ales in seventeenth-century stone inn in famously unspoilt village. Bar food lunchtime; disabled access.

LANGLEY BURRELL

Brewery Arms (P)
☎ 01 249 692 707.
🍎 *Bulmers Traditional*

MALMESBURY

Borough Arms (P)
7 Oxford Street.
☎ 01 666 822 806.
🍎 *Bulmers West Country*

KNOLL HOUSE HOTEL (P)
Swindon Road
☎ 01 666 823 114
Open 11-11
🍎 **Weston's Old Rosie**
Country house hotel with beautiful views, 22 en suite rooms, heated outdoor pool – and real ale and cider. Food lunchtime and evening in public bar; also a separate, formal, restaurant.

MANTON

ODDFELLOWS ARMS (P)
High Street
☎ 01 672 512 352
Open 12-2.30, 6-11
🍎 **Weston's Old Rosie**
Cosy village pub with secluded garden. Bar food lunchtime and evening (not Sun evening)

MELKSHAM

Bear Hotel (P)
Bath Rd.
☎ *01 225 702 901.*
🍎 *Taunton Traditional*

New Inn (P)
Semington Rd.
☎ *01 225 703 179.*
🍎 *Taunton Traditional*

MERE

Butt of Sherry (P)
Castle Street.
☎ *01 747 860 352.*
🍎 *Bulmers Traditional*

ODSTOCK

Yew Tree Inn (P)
☎ *01 722 329 786.*
🍎 *Taunton Traditional*

OGBOURNE ST GEORGE

OLD CROWN (P)
Marlborough Road
☎ 01 672 841 445
Open 11.30-3, 6-11
🍎 **Inch's**
Cosy one-bar pub with separate restaurant. Letting rooms; bar food lunchtime and evening.

PINKNEY

EAGLE INN (P)
☎ 01 666 840 528
Open 11-2.30, 6-11
🍎 **Weston's range**
Two-bar village inn; food limited to filled rolls at lunchtime and evening.

POTTERNE

Bell (P)
☎ *01 380 723 067.*
🍎 *Taunton Traditional*

QUEMERFORD

Talbot (P)
London Rd.
☎ *01 249 812 198.*
🍎 *Taunton Traditional*

SEEND

Social Club (C)
☎ *01 380 828 796.*
🍎 *Taunton Traditional*

SEEND CLEEVE

BREWERY INN (P)
☎ 01 380 828 463
🍎 **Taunton Traditional, Thatcher's**
Popular local boozer five minutes' walk from Kennet & Avon canal. Family room; bar food lunchtime.

SHERSTON

RATTLEBONE INN (P)
Church Street
☎ 01 666 840 871
Open 11.30-3, 5.30-11; 11.30-11 Sat; 12-10.30 Sun
🍎 **Weston's, Inch's**
Many original features survive in 17th century two-bar stone inn in pretty village. Five real ales; traditional pub games. Bar food lunchtime and evening; no-smoking area; disabled access.

SWINDON

Hobgoblin (P)
8 Devizes Rd.
☎ *01 793 523 308.*
🍎 *Bulmers Traditional*

Princess Hotel (P)
45 Beatrice Street.
☎ *01 793 535 476.*
🍎 *Bulmers Traditional*

RISING SUN (P)
Albert Street, Old Town
☎ 01 793 529 916
Open 11-11

🍎 **Bulmers Traditional**
Busy back-street Usher's pub. Bar food lunchtime and evening.

Working Men's Club (C)
Chapel Street, Gorse Hill.
☎ *01 793 522 755.*
🍎 *Taunton Traditional*

TISBURY

CROWN INN (P)
Church Street
☎ 01 747 870 221
Open 11-2.30, 7-11
🍎 **Taunton Traditional**
Friendly old coaching inn with skittle alley and family room. Bar food lunchtime and evening; disabled access.

TROWBRIDGE

Anchor & Hope (P)
Frome Rd.
☎ *01 225 75279.*
🍎 *Taunton Traditional*

Black Swan (P)
1 Aldcroft Street.
☎ *01 225 752 600.*
🍎 *Taunton Traditional, Bulmers Traditional*

Pickled Newt (P)
2 Seymour Rd.
☎ *01 225 752 905.*
🍎 *Bulmers Traditional*

Stallards Inn (P)
Stallard Street.
☎ *01 225 774 942.*
🍎 *Taunton Traditional*

WARMINSTER

Anchor Hotel (P)
Market Place.
☎ *01 985 21286.*
🍎 *Taunton Traditional*

Cock Inn (P)
West Street.
☎ *01 985 21330.*
🍎 *Taunton Traditional*

Copheap Stores (OL)
Copheap Lane.
 Rich's

Fox & Hounds (P)
6 Deverill Rd.
☎ 01 985 216 711.
 Rich's

WESTBURY

CROWN INN (P)
Market Place
☎ 01 373 822 828
Open 11-2.30, 6-11
 Taunton Traditional
Welcoming local with skittle
alley. Bar food lunchtime (not
Sun) and Fri/Sat evening.

White Lion (P)
Market Place.
☎ 01 373 822 700.
 Taunton Traditional

WEST OVERTON

Bell Inn (P)
Bath Rd.
☎ 01 672 861 663.
 Bulmers Old Hazy

WORTON

Rose & Crown (P)
High Street.
☎ 01 380 724 202.
 Bulmers Traditional

WROUGHTON

CARTER'S REST (P)
High Street
☎ 01 793 812 288
Open 11.30-2.30, 5.30-11;
11-11 Sat
 Inch's
Archer's pub with lively public
bar. Bar food lunchtime.

Worcestershire

ARLEY

NEW INN (P)
Pound Green

☎ 01 299 401 271
Open 7-11 weekdays; 12-3, 7-11
weekends
 Westons range
Folksy pub specialising,
bizarrely enough, in
accordionists. Games include
boules, skittles, quoits. Bar
food, separate restaurant. Hard
to find: off B4194 at Buttonoak.
One mile from Arley station on
Severn Valley steam line.

BABOURNE

New Pope Iron (P)
Pope Iron Rd.
☎ 01 905 21178.
 Bulmers Traditional

BADSEY

Wheatsheaf (P)
Main Street.
☎ 01 386 830 380.
 Bulmers Traditional

BENGEWORTH

Swan Inn (P)
Port Street.
☎ 01 386 49587.
 Bulmers Traditional

BERROW GREEN

ADMIRAL RODNEY (P)
☎ 01 886 821 375
Open 12-2.30, 7-11 Mon-Sat, 12-
5, 7-10.30 Sun.
 Cider range varies
Large rambling country pub
with suitable nautical theme.
Bar food lunchtime and
evenings except Mon, skittle
alley.

BEWDLEY

TIPPLERS (OL)
70 Load Street
☎ 01 299 402 254
Open 10-10 Mon-Sat, 12-3,
7-10 Sun
 **Weston's, Dunkerton's and
others**

Real ale off-licence with unusual British and foreign bottled beers.

BISHOPS FROME

Majors Arms (P)
Halmonds Frome.
☎ *01 531 640 371.*
🍎 *Bulmers Old Hazy*

BREDON

ROYAL OAK (P)
☎ 01 684 772 393
Open 11-3, 5.30-11; 11-11 sat; 12-3, 7-10.30 Sun
🍎 **Bulmers Traditional**
Old coaching inn with garden. Bar food lunchtime and evening; separate restaurant; no smoking area.

BRETFORTON

FLEECE (P)
The Cross
☎ 01 386 831 173
Open 11-2.30, 6-11; 12-2.30, 7-10.30 Sun
🍎 **Bulmers Traditional, Weston's Old Rosie**
Perhaps Britain's most famous country pub in heart of Vale of Evesham. Ancient and unspoilt, with no bar-counter. Smoke-free family room, fine choice of ales, food lunchtime and evening.

BROADWAY

CROWN & TRUMPET (P)
Church Street
☎ 01 386 853 202
Open 11-3, 5-11; 11-11 Sat.
🍎 **Bulmers Traditional**
Fine 17th century stone inn in Cotswold's most-visited town. Oak beams, log fires, real ales, food lunchtime and evening, no smoking area and disabled access too.

BROMSGROVE

GOLDEN CROSS (P)
20 High Street
☎ 01 527 870 005
Open 11-11
🍎 **Weston's**
Smart Wetherspoon pub. Long bar with 21 handpumps (although not 21 ales!). Bar food lunchtime and evenings, no-smoking area; disabled access.

BURLINGHAM

Swan Inn (P).
☎ *01 386 750 485.*
🍎 *Bulmers Traditional*

CAUNSALL

ANCHOR (P)
Cookley Road
☎ 01 562 850 254
Open 12-4, 7-11
🍎 **Bulmers Traditional**
Pleasant two-room village pub near canal. Bar food lunchtime and evening; disabled access.

ROCK TAVERN (P)
☎ 01 562 850 416
Open 11-11; 12-3, 7-10.30 Sun
🍎 **Bulmers Traditional, Weston's Old Rosie**
Homely one-bar pub cut into the rock. Banks's ales plus guest. Bar food lunchtime and evening.

Childswickham Inn (P).
Childswickham.
☎ *01 386 852 461.*
🍎 *Bulmers Traditional*

COLWALL

CROWN INN (P)
Walwyn Road
☎ 01 684 541 047
Open 11-11 Mon-Sat, 12-3, 7-10.30 Sun
🍎 **Weston's range**
Two-bar village pub opposite railway station. Splendid garden with spectacular view

of Malvern Hills. Carlsberg-Tetley ales, food lunchtime and evening

CONDERTON

YEW TREE (P)
☎ 01 386 725 364
Open 12-3, 6-11; 12-10.30 Sun
🍎 **Minchew's, Weston's Old Rosie**
16th century village inn under Bredon Hill. Garden with play area; bar food lunchtime and evening.

COOKLEY

BULL'S HEAD (P)
10 Bridge Road
☎ 01 384 850 242
Open 11.30-3, 6-11; 12-3, 7-10.30 Sun
🍎 *Inch's*
Large canalside village pub with family room and garden. Bar food lunchtime and evening; separate restaurant; no smoking area; disabled access.

Cookley Sports & Social Club (C)
Lea Lane.
☎ 01 562 850 055.
🍎 *Taunton Traditional*

DROITWICH

Gardeners' Arms (P)
Vines Lane.
☎ 01 905 772 936.
🍎 *Bulmers Traditional*

RING O' BELLS (P)
7 The Holloway
☎ 01 905 770 083/556 911
🍎 **Bulmers Traditional, Weston's range**
Locals' two-bar back-street pub; no food.

Westcroft Inn (P)
Ombersley Rd.
☎ 01 905 772 816.
🍎 *Bulmers Traditional*

ECKINGTON

Anchor Inn (P)
Cotheridge Lane.
☎ 01 386 750 356.
🍎 *Bulmers Traditional*

Bell Inn (P)
Main Rd.
☎ 01 386 750 205.
🍎 *Bulmers Traditional*

ELDERSFIELD

GREYHOUND (P)
Lime Street
☎ 01 452 840 381
Open 11.30-3.30, 6-11; 11.30-11 Mon/Tues.
🍎 **Weston's Old Rosie**
Gravity-dispensed beers and quoits in most traditional of pubs. Camping in grounds; garden full of animals. Family room. Hard to find: north at junction of B4211 and B4212, signed Lime Street, OS 814 305.

ELMLEY CASTLE

Old Mill (P)
☎ 01 386 710 407.
🍎 *Taunton Traditional, Bulmers Traditional*

EVESHAM

Angel Vaults (P)
Port Street.
☎ 01 386 47188.
🍎 *Bulmers Traditional*

Beewell Health Food Store & Deli (OL)
3 Vine Street.
☎ 01 386 443 757.
🍎 *Dunkerton's*

Bear (P)
43 Port Street.
☎ 01 386 45428.
🍎 *Bulmers Traditional*

Golden Hart (P)
Cowl Street.
☎ 01 386 446 024.
🍎 *Bulmers Traditional*

Green Dragon (P)
17 Oat Street.
☎ 01 386 446 337.
🍎 *Bulmers Old Hazy*

King Edward VII (P)
South Littleton.
☎ 01 386 830 225.
🍎 *Bulmers Old Hazy &*
Traditional

Oddfellows Arms (P)
Briar Close, Queens Street.
☎ 01 386 442 179.
🍎 *Bulmers Traditional*

Old Red Horse (P)
Vine Street.
☎ 01 386 442 784.
🍎 *Bulmers Traditional*

FAIRFIELD

Fairfield Inn (P)
Battleton Rd.
☎ 01 386 41292.
🍎 *Bulmers Traditional*

FECKENHAM

Lygon Arms (P)
1 Droitwich Rd.
☎ 01 527 893 495.
🍎 *Bulmers Old Hazy &*
Traditional

Rose & Crown (P)
High Street.
☎ 01 527 892 188.
🍎 *Bulmers Traditional*

GREAT MALVERN

CHASE INN (P)
Chase Rd, Upper Colwall
☎ 01 684 540 276
Open 12-2.30, 6-11
🍎 **Westons range**
Small two-bar country pub
near crest of Malvern Hills.
Home-cooked food lunchtime
(not Tues and Sun).
Donnington & Wye Valley ales.

CROSS KEYS (P)
79 Belmont Road
☎ 01 684 572 945
Open 12-3, 7-11; 12-11 Fri/Sat

🍎 **Weston's plus local guests**
Sporting pub with pets
including pigs and goats in
garden.

Star (P)
Cowleigh Rd.
☎ 01 684 574 280.
🍎 *Bulmers Traditional*

Unicorn Inn (P)
Belle Vue Terr.
☎ 01 684 574 152.
🍎 *Bulmers Old Hazy*

Vaults (P)
102 Worcester Rd.
☎ 01 684 575 774.
🍎 *Bulmers Traditional*

GRIMLEY

Camp House Hotel (P)
Camp Lane.
☎ 01 905 772 816.
🍎 *Bulmers Traditional*

HANLEY CASTLE

THREE KINGS (P)
☎ 01 684 592 686
Open 12-3, 7-11.
🍎 **Weston's Old Rosie and Top**
Line
Unspoilt fifteenth-century
village inn, run by same family
for 80 years. Real ales from
independent brewers. Food
lunchtime and evening, family
room, separate public bar. No
smoking room.

HARVINGTON

Coach & Horses (P)
Church Street.
☎ 01 386 870 249.
🍎 *Bulmers Traditional*

KIDDERMINSTER

GRAND TURK (P)
207 Sutton Road
☎ 01 562 66254
Open all permitted hours
🍎 **Bulmers Traditional,**
Richard's

Small, friendly Banks's local. Bar food lunchtime and evening.

PRINCE ALBERT (P)
21 Bewdley Road
☎ 01 562 753 705
Open all permitted hours
🍎 Bulmers Traditional
Down-to-earth Banks's pub with family room but no food.

LOWER BROADHEATH

Bell Inn (P)
Martley Rd.
☎ 01 905 640 220.
🍎 Bulmers Traditional

MAMBLE

Sun & Slipper (P)
☎ 01 299 832 018.
🍎 Bulmers Traditional

MARTLEY

Crown (P)
☎ 01 886 888 265.
🍎 Bulmers Traditional

PENSAX

BELL (P)
☎ 01 299 896 677
Open 12-3, 6.30-11
🍎 Bulmers Traditional
Real ale pub in lovely corner of Worcestershire. Family room, food lunchtime and evening, disabled access.

PERSHORE

BRANDY CASK (P)
25 Bridge Street
☎ 01 386 552 602
Open 11.30-2.30, 7-11
🍎 Bulmers Old Hazy
Riverside free house with guest beers and live music. Bar food lunchtime and evening; separate restaurant.

MILLERS ARMS (P)
Bridge Street
☎ 01 386 553 864
Open 11-3.30, 7-11

🍎 Taunton Traditional
Characterful town-centre pub; northern outpost of Wadworth's. Guest ales, occasional live folk. Food lunchtimes; evenings in summer.

Plum Tree (P)
St Andrews Rd.
☎ 01 386 5525 567.
🍎 Bulmers Traditional

Talbot Hotel (P)
Newlands.
☎ 01 386 553 575.
🍎 Bulmers Traditional

Victoria Hotel (P)
Newlands.
☎ 01 386 553 662.
🍎 Bulmers Traditional

White Horse Hotel (P)
Church Street.
☎ 01 386 552 689.
🍎 Taunton Traditional, Bulmers Traditional

REDDITCH

Brodies (P)
Headless Cross.
☎ 01 527 550 448.
🍎 Bulmers Traditional

Oddfellows Arms (P)
Foregate Street, Astwood Bank.
☎ 01 527 892 806.
🍎 Bulmers Traditional

Wine Rack (OL)
81 Mason Rd, Headless Cross.
☎ 01 527 41854.
🍎 Bulmers Traditional

RUSHWICK

Whitehall Inn (P)
Bransford Rd.
☎ 01 905 422 660.
🍎 Bulmers Traditional

SALFORD PRIORS

Bell Inn (P)
☎ 01 789 773 200.
🍎 Bulmers Traditional

Queens Head (P)
Irons Cross.
☎ *01 386 871 012.*
🍎 *Taunton Traditional, Bulmers Traditional*

SEDGEBERROW

Queens Head (P)
Main Street.
☎ *01 386 881 447.*
🍎 *Bulmers Traditional*

STOKE PRIORS

Bowling Green (P)
Shaw Lane.
☎ *01 527 861 291.*
🍎 *Bulmers Old Hazy*

STOURPORT

ANGEL HOTEL (P)
Severnside
☎ 01 299 822 661
Open 11-11
🍎 **Bulmers Traditional**
Two-room riverside Banks's pub. Family room, accommodation. Food lunchtime and, in summer, evenings.

Kings Arms (P)
Astley Cross.
☎ *01 299 827 132.*
🍎 *Bulmers Traditional*

Squirrel Inn (P)
Areley Kings.
☎ *01 299 826 872.*
🍎 *Bulmers Traditional*

TENBURY WELLS

THE VAULTS (P)
Teme Street
☎ 01 584 811 883
Open 11-11.30; 12-3, 7-10.30 Sun
🍎 **Franklin's**
Bass ales with guest. Quoits played. Occasional live music.

UPHAMPTON

FRUITERERS ARMS (P)
Uphampton Lane
☎ 01 905 620 305

Open 12-2.30, 7-11.
🍎 **Weston's Old Rosie**
Rural two-bar pub incorporating Canon Royall Brewery. Food lunchtimes. May produce own cider this year. Hard to find: off A449, OS 839 649.

UPTON SNODSBURY

Red Lion Inn (P).
☎ *01 905 381 480.*
🍎 *Bulmers Traditional*

UPTON-UPON-SEVERN

SWAN (P)
☎ 01 684 592 299
Open all permitted hours
🍎 **Cider range varies**
Riverside Banks's pub with separate restaurant and letting rooms. Families welcome.

Talbot Head Hotel (P)
High Street.
☎ *01 684 592 194.*
🍎 *Bulmers Traditional*

WEST MALVERN

BREWERS ARMS (P)
Lower Dingle
☎ 01 684 568 147
Open 12-3, 7-11
🍎 **Bulmers Old Hazy**
Small two-bar pub strategically sited half-way along Malvern walk.

Lamb Inn (P)
West Malvern Rd.
☎ *01 684 72994.*
🍎 *Bulmers Traditional*

WICKHAMFORD

Sandys Arms (P)
Pitchers Hill.
☎ *01 386 830 535.*
🍎 *Bulmers Traditional*

WORCESTER

Berwick Arms (P)
250 Bath Rd.
☎ *01 905 351 335.*
🍎 *Bulmers Traditional*

Brunswick Arms (P)
Malvern Rd.
☎ *01 905 421 579.*
🍎 *Bulmers Traditional*

Crown & Anchor (P)
Hylton Rd.
☎ *01 905 421 481.*
🍎 *Bulmers Traditional*

DRAGON INN (P)
51 The Tything
☎ 01 905 25845
Open 11-11; 7-10.30 only Sun
🍎 **Bulmers Old Hazy**
Folk pub with good real ale
range

DRAKES DRUM (P)
Tudor Way, Dines Green
☎ 01 905 420 842
Open 4-11 Mon-Fri; all day
sat/Sun
🍎 **Bulmers Traditional**
Estate pub with comfortable
lounge. Bar food. Banks's ales.

Old Bush Inn (P)
Callow End.
☎ *01 905 830 792.*
🍎 *Bulmers Old Hazy*

Red Lion (P)
45 The Village,
Powick.
☎ *01 905 830 203.*
🍎 *Bulmers Old Hazy*

Red Lion (P)
Sidbury.
☎ *01 905 767 178.*
🍎 *Bulmers Old Hazy*

STAR (P)
38 Bransford Road
☎ 01 905 421 173
Open 11-3, 7-11
🍎 **Bulmers Traditional**
Two-room local in St John's
district.

Toad & Tulip (P)
53 Lowesmoor Rd.
☎ *01 905 26876.*
🍎 *Bulmers Traditional*

Washington Inn (P)
42 Washington Street.
☎ *01 905 24876.*
🍎 *Bulmers Traditional*

Yorkshire

APPLETREEWICK

NEW INN (P)
Main Street
☎ 01 756 720 252
Open 12-3, 7-11; closed Mon
lunch except Bank Holiday
🍎 **Wilkins**
Premier country pub with large
range of bottled beers. Family
room, letting rooms, food
lunchtime. Stunning views.

BARNSLEY

Beggar & Gentleman (P)
Market Street.
☎ *01 226 742 364.*
🍎 *Bulmers Old Hazy*

BATLEY

Butchers Arms (P)
57 Halifax Rd, Staincliffe.
☎ *01 924 402 956.*
🍎 *Bulmers Old Hazy*

BAWTRY

Station Hotel (P)
93 Station Rd.
☎ *01 302 710 445.*
🍎 *Bulmers Old Hazy*

BIRSTALL

Horse & Jockey (P)
97 Low Lane.
☎ *01 924 472 259.*
🍎 *Bulmers Traditional*

BRADFORD

FIGHTING COCK (P)
Preston Street
☎ 01 274 726 907
Open 11.30-11
🍎 **Thatcher's, Biddenden**
Down-to-earth bareboards
alehouse with live music.
Famous sandwiches lunchtime
(not Sun).

NEW BEEHIVE (P)
171 Westgate
☎ 01 274 721 784
Open 11-11
🍎 **Bulmers Traditional**
Multi-room Edwardian pub
still lit by gas with skittle alley
and concert-room. Letting
rooms, bar food lunchtime.

STEVE BIKO BAR (C)
Floor D, Richmond Building,
Bradford University, Great
Horton Road
☎ 01 274 733 466
Open 11-11; 7-11 Sat/Sun
🍎 **Bulmers Old Hazy**
Noisy student bar with big real
ale range. Live music; no
smoking area; disabled access.

BREARTON

MALT SHOVEL (P)
☎ 01 423 862 929
Open 12-3, 6.45-11 (closed
Mon)
🍎 **Pipkin**
Unspoilt sixteenth-century
village inn with much stone
and exposed beams. Excellent
bar food lunchtime and
evening (not Sun evening). Off
B6165 between Knaresborough
and Ripley.

BRIGHOUSE

RED ROOSTER (P)
123 Elland Rd, Brookfoot
☎ 01 484 713 737
Open 12-2, 5-11
🍎 **Cider range varies**
Popular and genuine free

house with wide range of ales
from small independent
brewers.

BURNLEE

Farmers Arms (P)
2 Liphill Bank Rd.
☎ *01 484 683 713.*
🍎 *Weston's Old Rosie*

DANBY

DUKE OF WELLINGTON (P)
West Lane
☎ 01 287 660 351
Open 11-3, 7-11; 11-11 summer
🍎 **Bulmers Traditional**
Early eighteenth-century
coaching inn now the village
local with everything: family
room, letting rooms, beer
garden. food lunchtime and
evening, camping, no-smoking
area, disabled access.

DEWSBURY

SIR GEOFFREY BOYCOTT OBE
(P)
125 High Street, West Town
☎ 01 924 457 610
Open 11-11, closed Tue/Wed
🍎 **Cider range varies**
Traditional Yorkshire pub with
open fire and stone floors.
Food lunchtime and evening.
Disabled access.

**WEST RIDING LICENSED
REFRESHMENT ROOMS** (P)
Wellington Road
☎ 01 924 459 193
Open 11-11
🍎 **Inch's**
Three-room conversion of
former railway station waiting
room, now a legendary real ale
pub. Families welcome, food to
7pm (earlier Sun), no-smoking
area, disabled access. Owner
has just acquired second pub,
Beer Street.

DONCASTER

HALL CROSS (P)
33 Hallgate
☎ 01 302 328 213
Open 11-11; closes 4-6 Sat
🍎 **Bulmers Traditional**
Outlet for local independent
brewer Stocks. Brewery can be
seen from beer garden. Food
lunchtime.

LEOPARD (P)
1 West Street
☎ 01 302 363 054
Open 11-11
🍎 **Taunton Traditional**
Lively street corner pub with
superb tiled frontage. Guest
ales from all over the country.
Food lunchtime.

RED LION (P)
Market Place
☎ 01 302 368 908
Open 11-11; closes 4-7 Sat.
🍎 **Bulmers Old Hazy**
Market-place pub with food
lunchtime and evening and no-
smoking area. Disabled access.

ELLAND

Church Tavern (P)
Northgate.
☎ 01 422 310 610.
🍎 *Bulmers Traditional*

FULFORD

Gimcrack Hotel (P)
294 Fulford Rd.
☎ 01 904 658 485.
🍎 *Bulmers Old Hazy*

HALIFAX

Griffs (P)
21 George Street.
☎ 01 422 353 610.
🍎 *Bulmers Old Hazy*

Pump Room (P)
New Rd.
☎ 01 422 381 465.
🍎 *Bulmers Old Hazy*

TAP & SPILE (P)
1 Clare Road
☎ 01 422 353 661
Open 11-11; 12-10.30 Sun
🍎 **Westons range inc perry,
Bulmers Old Hazy, Crone's**
1930s Tudor town-centre pub,
originally Ramsden's brewery
tap. Timbers from one of the
last wooden battleships, HMS
Newcastle. Bar food and
separate restaurant lunchtime.
Shove ha'penny and bar
skittles. No-smoking area.

WOODCOCK (P)
213 Gibbett Street
☎ 01 442 359 906
Open 11-11
🍎 **Thatchers, Biddenden**
Long-standing real ale bastion.
Food all day.

HARROGATE

TAP & SPILE (P)
Tower Street
☎ 01 423 526 785
Open all permitted hours
🍎 **Weston's Old Rosie,
Bulmers Old Hazy**
Traditional two-bar real ale
house with up to 10 ales.
sandwiches and toasties only.

HEBDEN BRIDGE

Shoulder of Mutton (P)
New Rd.
☎ 01 422 883 165.
🍎 *Bulmers Old Hazy*

HOLMFIRTH

Shoulder of Mutton (P)
Dunford.
☎ 01 484 684 414.
🍎 *Westons Old Rosie, Bulmers
Old Hazy & Traditional*

HUDDERSFIELD

ELECTRICIANS ARMS (P)
159 Manchester Rd, Longroyd
Bridge
☎ 01 484 429 779
Open 12-1, 7.30-11; 11-11 Sat.

♣ Cider range varies
Stone-built local with unusual
pub games including Ring the
Bull.

Marsh House (P)
Westbourne Rd.
☎ *01 484 420 462.*
♣ *Taunton Traditional*

OLD COURT BREW HOUSE (P)
Queen Street
☎ 01 484 454 035
Open 10-11; 12-10.30 Sun
♣ Bulmers Old Hazy
Former County Court building,
built 1825, pub and brewery
since 1994. Food lunchtime and
evening. No-smoking area,
disabled access.

RAT & RATCHET (P)
40 Chapel Hill
☎ 01 484 516 734
Open 3-11 Mon/Tue; 12-11
Wed-sat; 12-4, 7-10.30 Sun
♣ Cider range varies
Up to 14 real ales at a time.
Brewery on premises. Bar food
lunchtime and evening.

Woodman (P)
862 Leeds Rd, Bradley.
☎ *01 484 531 993.*
♣ *Bulmers Old Hazy*

KEIGHLEY

GRINNING RAT (P)
2 Church Street
☎ 01 535 609 747
Open 11-11
**♣ Biddenden plus occasional
guests**
Popular pub and nightclub
with up to eight guest ales. Bar
food lunchtime; disabled
access.

KETTLEWELL

Kings Head Inn (P)
☎ *01 756 760 242.*
♣ *Bulmers Traditional*

KIRKBURTON

SPRING GROVE (P)
20 Penistone Road
☎ 01 484 605 826
Open 11-11, 4-11 Mon-Thurs
♣ Bulmers Old Hazy
True free house serving six real
ales, three of them guests.

KNARESBOROUGH

BLIND JACK'S (P)
19 Market Place
☎ 01 423 869 148
Open 11.30-11 (5.30 Mon);
12-10.30 Sun
♣ Pipkin
Best new pub of 1992; superb
conversion of Georgian
building. Bar food lunchtime
and evening; separate
restaurant.

LEEDS

ALE SHOP (OL)
79 Raglan Road
☎ 0113 242 7177
Open 2-10 seven days
♣ Thatcher's plus guests
Real ale offie near university.

BEER PARADISE (OL)
Riverside Place, Bridgwater
Rd, Cross Green
☎ 0113 235 9082
Open 10-6 8 Thu/Fri); 12-3 Sun
♣ Biddenden
Huge emporium specialising in
foreign bottled beers.
Membership required.

Brown Cow (P)
62 Town Street, Horsforth.
☎ *0113 258 1106.*
♣ *Bulmers Old Hazy*

DUCK & DRAKE (P)
48 Kirkgate
☎ 0113 246 5806
Open 11-11
♣ Biddenden, Thatchers
Popular and raucous two-bar
bareboards alehouse. Food
lunchtime.

EAGLE TAVERN (P)
North Street
☎ 0113 245 7146
Open 11-3, 5.30-11
🍎 **Biddenden**
Two-bar Georgian pub which
has served more than 1,000 real
ales in five years. Letting
rooms; food at lunchtime.

FEAST & FIRKIN (P)
Woodhouse Moor
☎ 0113 245 3669
Open 11-11
🍎 **Weston's Old Rosie**
Former public building
housing police station, fire
station and library, converted
1994. Brewing on site. No
smoking area, disabled access.

Gascoignes Arms (P)
6 Aberford Rd, Garforth.
☎ *0113 286 2451.*
🍎 *Bulmers Old Hazy*

New Inn (P)
68 Otley Rd, Headingley.
☎ *0113 275 5035.*
🍎 *Bulmers Traditional*

TAP & SPILE (P)
Merrion Centre
☎ 0113 244 5355
Open 11-3, 5-11; 11-11 Fri;
closed Sun.
🍎 **Bulmers Old Hazy,
Weston's, Crone's**
Raucous one-room shopping
centre alehouse with brilliant
ale range.

LINTHWAITE

SAIR INN (P)
Lane Top, Hoyle Ing
☎ 01 484 842 370
7-11 Mon-Fri; 12-3, 7-11
Sat/Sun
🍎 **Thatchers**
Established home-brew pub
with commanding views.

LONG PRESTON

MAYPOLE INN (P)
Main Street
☎ 01 729 840 219

Open 11-3, 6-11 Mon-Fri; 11-11
Sat; 12-3, 5-10.30 Sun
🍎 **Bulmers Traditional**
Two-bar pub on village green.
Bar food lunchtime and
evening, separate dining room.
Good range of real ales, six
letting rooms.

MALHAM

LISTER ARMS (P)
☎ 01 729 830 330
Open 12-3, 7-11
🍎 **Bulmers Traditional**
Fine pub dated 1702 with
sheltered beer-garden. Bar-food
lunchtime and evening, four
letting rooms. Rare opportunity
to play bagatelle, even rarer
opportunity to find draught
Kriek.

NORTHALLERTON

TANNER HOP (P)
2 Friargate
☎ 01 609 778 482
Open 11-11
🍎 **Bulmers Old Hazy**
Converted tithe barn used as a
dance hall in the war. Wide
range of ales, food lunchtime
and evening.

TAP & SPILE (P)
High Street
☎ 01 609 772 719
Open 11-11; closed 4-7 Sun.
🍎 **Weston's Old Rosie,
Bulmers Old Hazy**
Traditional two-bar pub on
edge of town with bar food
lunchtime and evening; no-
smoking area. Up to eight real
ales. Table skittles.

NORTH DUFFIELD

KING'S ARMS (P)
Main Street
☎ 01 757 288 492
Open 12-2, 4-11
🍎 **Biddenden**

Traditional eighteenth-century village inn. Children welcome. Bar food lunchtime and evening.

NOSTERFIELD

FREEMASONS ARMS (P)
☎ 01 677 470 548
Open 12-3 (not Mon, 6-11)
 Pipkin
Friendly stone-floored country pub with collection of wartime memorabilia. Good bar food lunchtime and evening; no smoking area.

OSSETT

BREWERS PRIDE (P)
Low Mill Road
☎ 01 924 273 865
Open 12-3, 5.30-11; 12-11 Fri/Sat.
 Biddenden plus occasional guests
Cosy popular free house with good selection of foreign bottled beers. Food lunchtime except Sun.

PONTEFRACT

TAP & SPILE (P)
28 Horsefair
☎ 01 977 793 468
Open 12-11; 12-3, 7-10.30 Sun
 Choice from Crone's, Weston's Old Rosie, Taunton Traditional, Bulmers Old Hazy & Traditional
Three-bar Victorian-style ale-house with 11 guest ales. Bar food Lunchtime (not Sun).

ROTHERHAM

Tut 'n' Shive (P)
Wellgate.
☎ *01 709 364 562.*
 Bulmers Old Hazy

Yorkshire Terrier (P)
Whitehill Rd, Brinsworth.
☎ *01 709 377 271.*
 Bulmers Old Hazy

SCARBOROUGH

HOLE IN THE WALL (P)
26-32 Vernon Street
☎ 01 723 373 746
Open 11-2.30, 7-11
 Inch's
Busy pub with many guest ales. Bar food lunchtime; disabled access.

TAP & SPILE (P)
94 Falsgrave Road
☎ 01 723 363 837
Open 11-11
 Weston's Old Rosie
Busy three-room pub with large garden. Bar food lunchtime and (in summer) evenings. No-smoking area; disabled access.

SHEFFIELD

Aunt Sally (P)
7 Clarkehouse Rd.
☎ *0114 267 9552.*
 Bulmers Old Hazy

Broadfield (P)
482 Abbeydale Rd.
☎ *0114 255 0200.*
 Bulmers Old Hazy

CASK & CUTLER (P)
Henry Street
☎ 0114 272 1487
Open 12-3. 5.30-11; 11-11 Fri/Sat
 Weston's Old Rosie
Traditional two-bar free house; food to 6.30.

Cross Scythes (P)
Baslow Rd, Totley.
☎ *0114 235 2631.*
 Bulmers Old Hazy

FAT CAT (P)
23 Alma Street
☎ 0114 272 8195
Open 11-3, 5-11
 Choice of Biddenden, Theobolds, Thatcher's
Tap for Kelham Island Brewery. Non-smoking room, family room, food at lunchtime.

FROG & PARROT (P)
64 Division Street
☎ 0114 272 1280
Open 11-11
🍎 **Bulmers Old Hazy**
Whitbread brewpub. Bar food lunchtime.

HOGSHEAD (P)
25 Orchard Street
☎ 0114 272 1980
Open 11-11
🍎 **Bulmers Old Hazy**
Typical Whitbread real ale house. Bar food lunchtime.

OLD GRINDSTONE (P)
Crookes
☎ 0114 266 0322
Open 11-11; 11-3, 7-10.30 Sun
🍎 **Bulmers Old Hazy**
Ward's Brewery flagship pub. Bar food lunchtime.

Old Queens Head (P)
40 Pond Hill.
☎ *0114 279 8383.*
🍎 *Bulmers Old Hazy*

Orchard (P)
Orchard Street.
☎ *0114 272 1980.*
🍎 *Bulmers Old Hazy*

TAP & SPILE (P)
42 Waingate
☎ 0114 272 6270
Open 11.30-3, 5.30-11 Mon-Fri; 11.30-3, 7-11 Sat; 7-10.30 Sun
🍎 **Westons range inc perry**
Cosy alehouse, businessmen lunchtime, students evening. Food 12-2.30. Family room and no-smoking area.

TUT'N'SHIVE (P)
Hartshead
☎ 0114 272 1594
Open 11-11
🍎 **Bulmers Old Hazy**
Typical Whitbread alehouse; bar food lunchtime.

Wordsworth Tavern (P)
Wordsworth Avenue, Parsons Cross.
☎ *0114 232 2349.*
🍎 *Bulmers Old Hazy*

Yorkshire Grey (P)
69 Charles Street.
☎ *0114 275 6675.*
🍎 *Bulmers Old Hazy*

SKIPTON

COCK & BOTTLE (P)
30 Swadford Street
☎ 01 756 794 734
Open 11-11
🍎 **Bulmers Old Hazy**
Characterful eighteenth-century coaching inn refurbished as a Hogshead alehouse. Bar food lunchtime.

SOWERBY BRIDGE

PUZZLE HALL (P)
21 Hollins Mill Lane
☎ 01 422 835 547
Open 12-11
🍎 **Biddenden**
Two-room pub with twice-weekly folk nights. Bar food 12-7.

STOKESLEY

WHITE SWAN (P)
West End
☎ 01 642 710 263
Open 11.30-3, 7-11
🍎 **Cider range varies**
Cosy two-room pub with oak-panelled lounge. Bar snacks to 10pm.

THORNTON-IN-LONSDALE

MARTON ARMS (P)
☎ 01 524 241 281
Open 12-3, 6-11 (closed weekday lunchtimes in winter)
🍎 **Weston's Old Rosie**
Two bar seventeenth-century coaching inn with up to 15 ales. Bar food lunchtime and evening; letting rooms.

WAKEFIELD

TAP & SPILE
77 Westgate End
☎ 01 924 375 887

Open 12-11
♣ Weston's Crone's
Stone-floored, gas-lit alehouse formerly the Beer Engine. Up to eight real ales. Bar food lunchtime.

Tut 'n' Shive (P)
38 Teale Street.
☎ *01 924 374 191.*
♣ *Bulmers Old Hazy*

WAKEFIELD LABOUR CLUB (C)
18 Vicarage Street
☎ 01 924 371 626
Open 7-11; 11-3, 7-11 Sat;
12-2 Sun
♣ Stott's, Ashwood (when available)
Club noted for Taylor's ales and guests. CAMRA membership card or current Good Beer Guide qualifies bearer for admission. Families welcome; disabled access.

WHITBY

TAP & SPILE (P)
New Quay Road
☎ 01 947 603 937
Open 11-11; 12-4.30,
7-10.30 Sun.
♣ Old Rosie, Crone's
Bareboard alehouse; folk night Tues. Families welcome. Bar food lunchtime. No-smoking area. Shove ha'penny, bar skittles.

YORK

Lendal Cellars (P)
26 Lendal.
☎ *01 904 623 121.*
♣ *Bulmers Traditional*

MALTINGS (P)
Tanners Bridge, Lendal Row
☎ 01 904 655 387
Open 11-11
♣ Crone's, Bulmers Old Hazy
Small but busy alehouse. Bar food lunchtime.

THE OTHER TAP & SPILE (P)
15 North Street
☎ 01 904 656 097

Open 11.30-11; 12-3,
7-10.30 Sun.
♣ Bulmers Old Hazy, Weston's range, Crone's
Three-room alehouse, families welcome, bar food lunchtime, no-smoking area.

Punch Bowl (P)
Blossom Street.
☎ *01 904 622 619.*
♣ *Bulmers Old Hazy*

TAP & SPILE (P)
Monkgate
☎ 01 904 656 168
Open 11-11
♣ Bulmers Old Hazy, Crone's, Weston's, Scatterbrain
Typical Tap & Spile alehouse. Bar food lunchtime.

Waggon & Horses (P)
Gillygate.
☎ *01 904 654 103.*
♣ *Bulmers Old Hazy*

YORK BEER SHOP (OL)
Sandringham Street, Fishergate
☎ 01 904 647 136
Open 11-11; 12-2. 7-10 Sun
♣ Thatchers plus Dunkerton's, Hartland, Burrow Hill, Naish, Franklin, Sheppy or Wilkin's
The ultimate off-licence – also artisanal cheeses, organic wines.

WALES

Clwyd

BRYNFORD

LLYN Y MAWN INN (P)
Brynford Hill
☎ 01 352 714 367
Open 12-3 (not Mon), 5.30-11
🍎 **Weston's**
Medieval inn, family run and a
finalist in 1995 Pub of the Year.
Bar food lunchtime (not Sun)
and evening; no smoking area;
disabled access.

GLAN YR AFON

WHITE LION (P)
Llanasa Road
☎ 01 745 570 280
Open 12-2.30 (not Mon), 6.30-
11; 12-4, 6-11 Sat.
🍎 **Wilkin's**
Old-fashioned country pub,
birthplace of playwright Emlyn
Williams. Bar food lunchtime
and evening; separate
restaurant.

LLANGEDWYN

GREEN INN (P)
☎ 01 691 828 234
Open 11-3, 6-11
🍎 **Cider range varies**
Isolated pub in picturesque
Tanat Valley. Popular with
walkers on the Berwyn Hills.
Four real ales, food in
restaurant.

LLANRHAEADR-YM-MOCHNANT

HAND INN (P)
Park Street
☎ 01 691 780 413.
🍎 **Bulmers Traditional**
Alehouse in picturesque
country town near Wales's
highest falls.

MOLD

DROVERS ARMS (P)
Denbigh Road
☎ 01 352 753 824
Open 12-11
🍎 **Bulmers Old Hazy plus guest**
Modern two-room town pub –
multiple satellite TV screens
and loud music.

RHES-Y-CAE

Miners Arms (P)
Rhes-y-Cae.
☎ *01 352 780 567.*
🍎 *Bulmers Old Hazy*

RHYL

WHITE HORSE INN (P)
Bedford Street
☎ 01 745 334 927
Open 11-11
🍎 **Bulmers Old Hazy**
Basic back-street boozer with
widest choice of real ales for
miles around.

Dyfed

CAPEL BANGOR

TYNLLIDIART ARMS (P)
☎ 01 970 880 248
Open 11-2.30, 6-11; closed Sun
in winter
🍎 **Weston's Old Rosie**
Small seventeenth-century two-
bar country pub on A44. Beers
from small independent
brewers. Bar food lunchtime
and evening.

CARDIGAN

Red Lion Inn (P)
Pwllhai.
☎ *01 239 612 482.*
🍎 *Bulmers Traditional*

CWMANN

Cwmann Tavern (P)
☎ *01 570 423 861.*
🍎 *Bulmers Traditional*

DALE

GRIFFIN (P)
01 646 636 227
Open 11-11
🍎 **Biddenden**
Seaside pub popular with
water-sports crowd. Beers from
Uley Brewery; bar food
lunchtime and evening.

DREENHILL

DENANT MILL INN (P)
Dale Road
☎ 01 437 766 569
Open 12-3, 6-11
🍎 **Sheppy's**
Gourmet's pub, with excellent
food and beers from all over
the UK and Belgium. Families
welcome; letting rooms; bar
food lunchtime and evening;
no smoking area.

LLANDOVERY

Greyhound Inn (P)
Stone Street.
☎ *01 550 20325.*
🍎 *Bulmers Traditional*

Station Hotel (P)
1 College View.
☎ *01 550 20441.*
🍎 *Bulmers Traditional*

LLANELLI

Barbican Hotel (P)
2 Stepney Street.
☎ *01 554 755 205.*
🍎 *Bulmers Traditional*

HALF MOON INN (P)
71 Wern Road
☎ 01 554 772 626
Open 11.30-3, 6-11; 11.30-11
Fri/Sat in summer
🍎 **Bulmers Traditional**
Lively local with folk nights.
Crown Buckley ales. Bar food

lunchtime and Wed-Sat
evenings; disabled access.

LLANSTEFFAN

Yr Hen Tafarn (P)
☎ *01 267 83656.*
🍎 *Bulmers Traditional*

MILFORD HAVEN

Neyland Athletic Club (C)
Frederick Street.
☎ *01 646 600 229.*
🍎 *Bulmers Traditional*

PEMBROKE

OLD CROSS SAWS (P)
109 Main Street
☎ 01 646 682 475
Open 11-11
🍎 **Bulmers Traditional**
Friendly rugby pub serving
Crown Buckley ales. Letting
rooms; bar food lunchtime and
evening; disabled access.

PEMBROKE DOCK

Royal (P)
95 Queen Street.
☎ *01 646 682 947.*
🍎 *Bulmers Traditional*

PISGAH

HALFWAY INN (P)
Devil's Bridge Road
☎ 01 970 880 631
Open 11.30-2.30, 6.30-11; 12-3,
7-10.30 Sun
🍎 **Weston's range**
Traditional pub with splendid
mountain views and extensive
grounds. Stone floors, log fires,
real ales. Bar food evening and
lunchtime; separate restaurant.
Two letting rooms.

Glamorgan

ABERBARGOED

*Arthur Balfour Conservative
Club* (C)

Commercial Street.
☎ 01 443 830 218.
🍎 Bulmers Traditional

ABERCYNON

Ynysboeth Hotel (P)
Main Rd, Ynysboeth.
☎ 01 443 740 832.
🍎 Bulmers Traditional

ABERDARE

Cambrian Hotel (P)
Seymore Street.
☎ 01 685 879 120.
🍎 Bulmers Old Hazy

Ivy Bush (P)
Kingsbury Place.
☎ 01 685 877 501.
🍎 Bulmers Traditional

ABERTRIDWR

Aber Hotel (P)
☎ 01 222 831 456.
🍎 Bulmers Traditional

BARGOED

Bargoed Ex-Servicemen's Club
(C)
99 Gilfach Street.
☎ 01 443 832 261.
🍎 Bulmers Traditional

Bargoed Social Club (C)
Church Place.
☎ 01 443 830 129.
🍎 Bulmers Traditional

BEDLINOG

Bedlinog Conservative Club
(C)
Pleasant View.
☎ 01 443 710 223.
🍎 Bulmers Traditional

BEDWAS

Bedwas WMC (C)
Bedwas Rd.
☎ 01 222 885 283.
🍎 Bulmers Traditional

BIRCHGROVE

BRIDGEND INN (P)
265 Birchgrove Road
☎ 01 792 321 878
Open 12-2, 6-11; 12-11 Fri/Sat
🍎 **Bulmers Traditional**
Comfortable two-room local
with up to six real ales. Bar
food lunchtime; evening meals
on request; disabled access.

BISHOPSTON

JOINER'S ARMS (P)
50 Bishopston Road
☎ 01 792 232 658
Open 12-11
🍎 **Weston's Old Rosie**
Popular free house on Gower
peninsula. Wide range of real
ales; bar food lunchtime and
evening.

BLAENCWM

Hendrewen Hotel (P)
Hendrewen Rd.
☎ 01 443 771 678.
🍎 Bulmers Traditional

BLAENCLYDACH

Liberal Club (C)
12 Maddox Street.
☎ 01 443 432 829.
🍎 Bulmers Traditional

BLAENLLECHAU

Blaenllechau Radical Club (C)
7 Commercial Street.
☎ 01 443 730 368.
🍎 Bulmers Traditional

BRIDGEND

King Alfred Hotel (P)
1 Commercial Street.
☎ 01 656 739 090.
🍎 Bulmers Traditional

Royal British Legion (C)
122 Commercial Street.
☎ 01 656 732 155.
🍎 Bulmers Traditional

CARDIFF

Earl Haig British Legion Club
(C)
23 Penlline Rd.
☎ *01 222 626 015.*
🍎 *Bulmers Traditional*

CYMMER

Croeserw WMC (C)
Brynheulog Rd.
☎ *01 639 850 333.*
🍎 *Bulmers Traditional*

CWMAMAN

Fforchneol Arms (P)
Brynmair Rd.
☎ *01 685 871 284.*
🍎 *Bulmers Old Hazy*

FERNDALE

Anchor (P)
The Strand.
☎ *01 443 756 261.*
🍎 *Bulmers Traditional*

Band Club (C)
53 Lake Street.
☎ *01 443 730 414.*
🍎 *Bulmers Traditional*

Conservative Club (C)
57 Lake Street.
☎ *01 443 730 596.*
🍎 *Bulmers Traditional*

Ex-Servicemen's Club (C)
Tylorstown.
☎ *01 443 730 486.*
🍎 *Taunton Traditional*

Imperial Conservative Club (C)
Rhondda Rd.
☎ *01 443 438 737.*
🍎 *Bulmers Traditional*

Maerdy Hotel (P)
Maerdy Rd.
☎ *01 443 755 505.*
🍎 *Bulmers Traditional*

Rhondda Hotel (P)
Dyffryn Street.
☎ *01 443 733 711.*
🍎 *Taunton Traditional*

Salisbury Hotel (P)
Station Rd.
☎ *01 443 687 792.*
🍎 *Bulmers Traditional*

GORSEINON

West End Hotel (P)
1 West Street.
☎ *01 792 894 217.*
🍎 *Bulmers Traditional*

HENGOED

Fox & Hounds (P)
Gelligaer.
☎ *01 443 816 424.*
🍎 *Bulmers Traditional*

Lindsay Constitutional Club
(C)
Cefn Hengoed.
☎ *01 443 862 599.*
🍎 *Bulmers Traditional*

**Ystrad Mynach Sports &
Social** (C)
38 Penalta Rd, Ystrad Mynach.
☎ *01 443 814 491.*
🍎 *Bulmers Traditional*

KILLAY

RAILWAY INN (P)
553 Gower Road
☎ 01 792 203 946
Open 12-11
🍎 **Bulmers Traditional**
Old-fashioned three-bar former
station in picturesque valley.
Crown Buckley ales. Food
lunchtime.

LLWYNPIA

Llwynpia WMC (C)
95 Partridge Rd.
☎ *01 443 776 865.*
🍎 *Bulmers Traditional*

MAUDLAM

Angel Inn (P)
Marlas Rd, Pyle.
☎ *01 656 740 456.*
🍎 *Bulmers Traditional*

MAESTEG

Athletic Club (C)
Humphries Terrace.
☎ 01 656 732 471.
🍎 *Bulmers Traditional*

Labour Club (C)
Caerau.
☎ 01 656 732 424.
🍎 *Taunton Traditional*

Navigation Hotel (P)
8 Navigation Terrace, Caerau.
☎ 01 656 732 275.
🍎 *Bulmers Traditional*

Oddfellows Rest (P)
200 Bridgend Rd, Garth.
☎ 01 656 732 073.
🍎 *Taunton Traditional, Bulmers Traditional*

Royal British Legion (C)
76 Hermon Rd, Caerau.
☎ 01 656 732 450.
🍎 *Bulmers Traditional*

Victoria (P)
Commercial Street.
☎ 01 656 736 842.
🍎 *Taunton Traditional*

White Hart Inn (P)
42 Bridgend Rd, Garth.
☎ 01 656 738 794.
🍎 *Bulmers Traditional*

MERTHYR TYDFIL

Court of Request (P)
Dynevor Street, Georgetown.
☎ 01 685 373 495.
🍎 *Bulmers Traditional*

Fox & Hounds (P)
Bridge st, Troedyrhiw.
☎ 01 443 693 071.
🍎 *Bulmers Traditional*

White Horse (P)
Twynrhodyn Rd.
☎ 01 685 723 323.
🍎 *Bulmers Traditional*

Windsor Hotel (P)
Old Cardiff Rd, Merthyr Vale.
☎ 01 443 690 360.
🍎 *Bulmers Old Hazy*

Wyndham Arms (P)
55 Glebeland Street.
☎ 01 685 723 917.
🍎 *Bulmers Traditional*

MONKNASH

PLOUGH & HARROW (P)
☎ 01 656 890 209
Open 12 (6 Mon)-11
🍎 **Cider range varies**
Lively local on site of medieval grange. Just off coastal walk; popular with trippers. Live folk and poetry. Bar food lunchtime in summer.

MOUNTAIN ASH

Cefn Pennar Inn (P)
Blackberry Terrace, Cefn Pennar.
☎ 01 443 472 160.
🍎 *Bulmers Traditional*

Osborne Hotel (P)
Rheola Street, Penrhiwceiber.
☎ 01 443 473 737.
🍎 *Bulmers Traditional*

Penrhiwceiber Constitutional Club (C)
129 Penrhiwceiber Rd.
☎ 01 443 473 217.
🍎 *Bulmers Traditional*

Tynte Hotel (P)
Main Rd, Mathewstown.
☎ 01 443 478 931.
🍎 *Bulmers Traditional*

NEATH

Cross Keys (P)
St Davids Street.
☎ 01 639 643 927.
🍎 *Bulmers Traditional*

OGMORE

PELICAN (P)
Ewenny Road
☎ 01 656 880 049
Open 11.30-3, 6.30-11; 11-11 Sat
🍎 **Bulmers Traditional**
Comfortable country pub. Bar food lunchtime and evening; separate restaurant.

PANT

Pant Cad Ifor Inn (P)
Pant Rd.
☎ *01 685 723 688.*
🍎 *Bulmers Old Hazy*

PENTRE

Comrades of the Great War (C)
55 Albert Street.
☎ *01 443 435 156.*
🍎 *Bulmers Traditional*

Kit Kat Club (C)
98 Llewellyn Street.
☎ *01 443 440 770.*
🍎 *Bulmers Traditional*

Penrhys RAOB (C)
Heol-Pendyrus, Penrhys.
☎ *01 443 755 942.*
🍎 *Bulmers Traditional*

Pentre Hotel (P)
Llewellyn Street.
☎ *01 443 441 316.*
🍎 *Taunton Traditional, Bulmers Traditional*

Pentre Labour Club (C)
57 Llewellyn Street.
☎ *01 443 432 753.*
🍎 *Bulmers Traditional*

Queens Hotel (P)
102 Llewellyn Street.
☎ *01 443 430 338.*
🍎 *Bulmers Traditional*

Star Hotel (P)
Tyntyla Rd.
☎ *01 443 441 744.*
🍎 *Bulmers Traditional*

PORTH

New York (P)
1 York Street.
☎ *01 443 682 767.*
🍎 *Bulmers Traditional*

Rhondda (P)
High Street.
☎ *01 443 682 388.*
🍎 *Bulmers Traditional*

Rickard Arms (P)
Trebanog Rd,
Trebanog.
☎ *01 443 687 626.*
🍎 *Bulmers Traditional*

Station Hotel (P)
Ynyshir Rd.
☎ *01 443 687 792.*
🍎 *Bulmers Traditional*

Union Jack Club (C)
Gynor Place, Ynyshir.
☎ *01 443 682 163.*
🍎 *Bulmers Traditional*

Ynyshir WMC (C)
Ynyshir Rd.
☎ *01 443 682 797.*
🍎 *Bulmers Traditional*

Vintage Wine Bar (P)
75 Hanna Street.
☎ *01 443 687 407.*
🍎 *Bulmers Traditional*

ST HILARY

BUSH INN (P)
☎ 01 446 772 745
Open 11-11
🍎 **Weston's Old Rosie, Bulmers Traditional**
Thatched village pub with two bars, family room, and high standard of ales. Bar food lunchtime and evening; separate restaurant.

SCURLAGE

Countryman Hotel (P)
☎ *01 792 390 597.*
🍎 *Bulmers Old Hazy*

SKEWEN

Travellers Well (P)
Dynevor Place.
☎ *01 792 812 002.*
🍎 *Bulmers Traditional*

SWANSEA

Queen's Arms (P)
Dillwyn Street.
☎ *01 792 641 777.*
🍎 *Taunton Traditional*

TONYPANDY

Clydach Vale (P)
Wern Street, Clydach Vale.
☎ 01 443 432 310.
🍎 *Bulmers Traditional*

Marxian WMC & Institute (C)
118 Court Street.
☎ 01 443 434 650.
🍎 *Bulmers Traditional*

Mid Rhondda WMC (C)
32 Court Street.
☎ 01 443 433 202.
🍎 *Bulmers Traditional*

Turberville Hotel (P)
Tylacelyn Rd, Penygraig.
☎ 01 443 432 843.
🍎 *Bulmers Traditional*

White Rock Hotel (P)
Swan Terrace, Penygraig.
☎ 01 443 434 697.
🍎 *Bulmers Traditional*

TREALAW

Paddy's Goose (P)
Trealaw Rd.
☎ 01 443 434 679.
🍎 *Bulmers Traditional*

Royal Hotel (P)
Brithweunydd Rd.
☎ 01 443 435 293.
🍎 *Bulmers Traditional*

TREFOREST

Crown Hotel (P)
17 Fothergill Street.
☎ 01 443 404 632.
🍎 *Bulmers Traditional*

TREHAFOD

Trehafod Hotel (P)
118 Trehafod Rd.
☎ 01 443 682 146.
🍎 *Bulmers Traditional*

TREHARRIS

Dan-y-Graig Labour Club (C)
27 Mary Street.
☎ 01 443 410 239.
🍎 *Bulmers Traditional*

Treharris WMC (C)
21 Bargoed Terrace.
☎ 01 443 410 324.
🍎 *Bulmers Traditional*

TREHERBERT

Castle Hotel (P)
Bute Street.
☎ 01 443 776 439.
🍎 *Bulmers Traditional*

Dunbar (P)
Dunraven Street.
☎ 01 443 777 079.
🍎 *Bulmers Traditional*

Dunraven Hotel (P)
Dunraven Street.
☎ 01 443 777 773.
🍎 *Bulmers Traditional*

Marquis of Bute (P)
Bute Street.
☎ 01 443 777 656.
🍎 *Bulmers Traditional*

New Inn (P)
Baglan Street.
☎ 01 443 772 376.
🍎 *Bulmers Traditional*

Ninian Stuart Constitutional WMC (C)
15 Station Street.
☎ 01 443 771 220.
🍎 *Bulmers Traditional*

TRELEWIS

Bontnewydd Hotel (P)
High Street.
☎ 01 443 411 728.
🍎 *Bulmers Traditional*

TREORCHY

Crown Hotel (P)
Ynyswen Rd.
☎ 01 443 772 805.
🍎 *Bulmers Traditional*

Royal Oak (P)
Treherbert Rd.
☎ *01 443 772 592.*
🍎 *Taunton Traditional*

Treorchy Health & Leisure Club (C)
Ynyswen Rd.
☎ *01 443 776 865.*
🍎 *Bulmers Traditional*

Treorchy Hotel (P)
Bute Street.
☎ *01 443 772 028.*
🍎 *Bulmers Traditional*

YSTRAD

Gelligaled Inn (P)
Gelligaled Rd.
☎ *01 443 438 737.*
🍎 *Bulmers Traditional*

Gwent

ABERCARN

OLD SWAN (P)
58 Commercial Rd, Cwmcarn
☎ 01 495 243 161
Open 12-11
🍎 **Bulmer's Traditional, Inch's**
Two-room local with mining memorabilia in former colliery village. Noted for its range of snuff, popular among ex-miners. Bar food lunchtime and evening.

ABERGAVENNY

STEPHAN'S CELLAR (OL)
Lewis's Lane
☎ 01 873 850 668
10-10; 12-10 Sun
🍎 **Weston's range**
Noted real ale off-licence.

ABERTILLERY

CLYNMAWR HOTEL (P)
Ty Bryn Road
☎ 01 495 212 323
Open 2-11

🍎 **Bulmers Traditional**
Traditional pub patronised by local RUFC. Skittle alley; family room. Crown Buckley ales.

Cwmtillery Private Members' Club (C)
Gwern Berthi Rd.
☎ *01 495 217 732.*
🍎 *Bulmers Traditional*

Six Bells (P)
Victoria Rd.
☎ *01 495 212 568.*
🍎 *Bulmers Traditional*

BASSALEG

TREDEGAR ARMS (P)
Caerphilly Road
☎ 01 633 893 247
Open 11-11
🍎 **Bulmers Old Hazy**
Two-bar Whitbread alehouse with spacious garden. Bar food lunchtime and evening.

BLACKWOOD

Twynyfold Constitutional Club (C)
Bedwellty Rd.
☎ *01 443 830 223.*
🍎 *Bulmers Traditional*

BLAENAVON

Castle Inn (P)
Broad Street.
☎ *01 495 792 477.*
🍎 *Bulmers Traditional*

FOUNTAIN INN (P)
18 King Street
☎ 01 495 792 532
Open 12-11
🍎 **Bulmers Traditional**
One-bar terraced local. No food.

BLAINA

Blaina WMC (C)
73 High Street.
☎ *01 495 290 215.*
🍎 *Bulmers Traditional*

BRITHDIR

Brithdir WMC (C)
30 Station Terrace.
☎ *01 443 830 026.*
🍎 *Bulmers Traditional*

BRYNMAWR

Croeso Inn (P)
103 King Street.
☎ *01 495 312 356.*
🍎 *Bulmers Traditional*

NEW GRIFFIN HOTEL (P)
Beaufort Street
☎ 01 495 311 725
Open 11-11
🍎 **Bulmers Traditional**
Large town-centre pub with disco.

Punch & Judy (P)
33 Bailey Street.
☎ *01 495 313 597.*
🍎 *Bulmers Traditional*

CAERLEON

GOLDCR2OFT INN (P)
Goldcroft Common
☎ 01 633 420 504
Open 11-11; 12-10.30 Sun
🍎 **Bulmers Traditional**
Popular pub on common, near Roman remains. Bar food lunchtime and evening.

CALDICOT

CROSS INN (P)
Newport Road
☎ 01 291 420 692
Open 11-4, 7-11; 11-11 Sat
🍎 **Bulmers Traditional**
Best range of ales in town in popular two-bar beerhouse.

CHEPSTOW

COACH & HORSES (P).
Welsh Street
☎ 01 291 622 626
Open 11-3, 6-11
🍎 **Ciders vary**
Popular traditional pub with good range of real ales. Bar food lunchtime; letting rooms.

THREE TUNS (P)
Bridge Street
☎ 01 291 623 497
Open 11-3, 5.30-11
🍎 **Bulmers Traditional**
Friendly two-bar pub in shadow of the castle. Bar food lunchtime and evening.

White Lion Inn (P)
Bank Square.
☎ *01 291 622 854.*
🍎 *Taunton Traditional*

CLYTHA

CLYTHA ARMS (P)
☎ 01 873 840 206
Open 11.30-3 (not Mon), 6-11;
11-11 Sat
🍎 **Weston's range**
Up to five real ales in converted dower house with spacious grounds. Bar food lunchtime and evening; excellent separate restaurant. Letting rooms.

CWMBRAN

ODDFELLOWS ARMS (P)
20 Commercial Street,
Pontnewydd
☎ 01 633 866 051
Open 11-11
🍎 **Bulmers Traditional**
Old-established two-room village local.

CWMTILLERY

New Bridgend Inn (P)
Penybont Rd.
☎ *01 495 213 519.*
🍎 *Bulmers Traditional*

EBBW VALE

Angel Inn (P)
Brewery Terrace.
☎ *01 495 304 320.*
🍎 *Bulmers Traditional*

Beaufort Arms (P)
105 The Rise, Beaufort.
☎ *01 495 303 074.*
🍎 *Bulmers Traditional*

Castle Inn (P)
Brierley Hill.
☎ *01 495 302 641.*
🍎 *Bulmers Traditional*

GILWERN

Forge & Hammer (P)
Heads of the Valleys Rd.
☎ *01 873 830 252.*
🍎 *Bulmers Traditional*

LLANELLY HILL

Jolly Colliers (P)
☎ *01 837 830 408.*
🍎 *Bulmers Traditional*

LLANGENNY

Dragons Head (P)
☎ *01 873 810 350.*
🍎 *Bulmers Traditional*

LLANHILLETH

Central Hotel (P)
Commercial Rd.
☎ *01 495 214 244.*
🍎 *Bulmers Traditional*

LLANISHEN

Carpenters Arms (P)
☎ *01 600 860 405.*
🍎 *Bulmers Traditional*

LLANTHONY

HALF MOON (P)
☎ 01 873 890 611
Open 11-3, 6-11 (in theory)
🍎 **Bulmers Traditional**
Stone-floored old country pub in good walking country. Bar food lunchtime and evening. Wise to check ahead as opening times can be erratic.

MARDY

Crown & Sceptre (P)
Hereford Rd.
☎ *01 873 852 295.*
🍎 *Bulmers Traditional*

MONMOUTH

IRMA FINGAL-ROCK (OL)
64 Monnow Street
Closed Tues
🍎 **Dunkerton's range**
Family-run delicatessen specialising in local produce.

NEWPORT

CHARTISTS ARMS (P)
Market Arcade, 11 High Street
☎ 01 633 257 870
Open 11-11
🍎 **Bulmers Traditional**
Lively one-bar local in former arcade opposite railway station.

Mariners Hotel (P)
82 Commercial Rd.
☎ *01 633 250 201.*
🍎 *Bulmers Traditional*

QUEENS HOTEL (P)
Bridge Street
☎ 01 633 262 992
🍎 **Taunton Traditional**
Two-bar town-centre residential hotel. Bar food lunchtime; separate restaurant.

RED LION (P)
47 Stow Hill
☎ 01 633 264 398
Open 12-11
🍎 **Inch's**
Genuine local with bags of character. Usher's ales. Bar food lunchtime.

Ridgway Inn (P)
Ridgway Avenue.
☎ *01 633 251 489.*
🍎 *Bulmers Old Hazy*

ST JULIAN INN (P)
Caerleon Road
☎ 01 633 258 663
Open 11.30-11
🍎 **Bulmers Traditional**
Well-established, popular riverside pub with guest ales and good food lunchtime and evening (not Sun). Gwent Pub of the Year 1995; finalist in Wales Pub of the Year 1995.

WETHERSPOON'S (P)
10-12 The Cambrian Centre,
Cambrian Road
☎ 01 633 251 752
Open all permitted hours
🍎 **Weston's Old Rosie**
Large busy pub with
photographic display of local
history. Bar food to 10pm. No-
smoking area; disabled access.

PENALLT

BOAT INN (P)
Lone Lane
☎ 01 600 712 615
Open 11-3, 6-11
🍎 **Cider range varies**
Popular two-bar pub beside
River Wye; car park is on the
other side and access is by
footbridge from Redbrook.
Real ales on gravity dispense.
Folk and jazz nights. Bar food
lunchtime and evening.

PONTLLANFRAITH

Plough Inn (P)
Newbridge Rd.
☎ *01 495 229 736.*
🍎 *Bulmers Traditional*

White Hart (P)
Newbridge Rd.
☎ *01 495 223 067.*
🍎 *Bulmers Traditional*

PONTNEWYDD

Cross Keys Inn (P)
55 Locks Rd.
☎ *01 633 861 545.*
🍎 *Bulmers Traditional*

PONTYPOOL

Sally's (P)
Tranch Rd.
☎ *01 495 753 477.*
🍎 *Bulmers Traditional*

RAGLAN

SHIP INN (P)
High Street
☎ 01 291 690 635
Open 11.30-11

🍎 **Hayward's**
Sixteenth-century coaching inn
with guest ales. Bar food
lunchtime and evening.

RHYMNEY

Royal Hotel (P)
High Street.
☎ *01 685 840 506.*
🍎 *Bulmers Traditional*

SHIRENEWTON

TAN HOUSE INN (P)
☎ 01 291 641 770
Open 12-3, 6-11 (12-11 in
summer)
🍎 **Bulmer's, Inch's**
Pleasantly-situated two-bar
village pub. Bar food
lunchtime and evening;
Usher's ales.

TALYWAIN

GLOBE INN (P)
Commercial Road
☎ 01 495 772 053
Open 6-11; 11-11 Sat
🍎 **Cider range varies**
Friendly two-bar local with
changing guest ales.

TINTERN

CHERRY TREE (P)
Devauden Road
☎ 01 291 689 292
Open 11-3, 6-11
🍎 **Bulmers Traditional**
Superb unspoilt one-room
country pub 10 minutes' stroll
from the abbey.

ROSE & CROWN (P)
1 Monmouth Road
☎ 01 291 689 254
Open 11-3, 6-11; 11-11 Sat
🍎 **Bulmers Traditional**
Two-bar riverside pub on main
road close to attractions. Bar
food lunchtime and evening;
separate restaurant.

TREDEGAR

Fernbank Club (C)
Mount Street.
☎ 01 495 722 485.
🍎 Bulmers Traditional

Mountain Air Inn (P)
Nantybwch.
☎ 01 495 253 116.
🍎 Bulmers Old Hazy

USK

Cross Keys (P)
Bridge Street.
☎ 01 291 672 535.
🍎 Bulmers Traditional

Gwynedd

BANGOR

TAP & SPILE (P)
Garth Road
Open 11-11
🍎 Weston's Old Rosie
Wales's first Tap & Spile,
opened January 1996 and
vowing to support Welsh-
brewed real ales.

LLANDUDNO

CROSS KEYS (P)
28 Madoc Street
☎ 01 492 876 132
🍎 Bulmers Old Hazy
Friendly and popular local. Bar
food to 9pm.

LLANDWROG

HARP HOTEL (P)
Tin Llan
☎ 01 286 831 071
12-3, 6-11; 11-11 in summer
🍎 Haywards
Lovely old country inn four
miles from Caernarfon. Bar
food lunchtime and evening;
separate restaurant; family
room; no smoking area. Letting
rooms.

Powys

ARDLEEN

HORSESHOE (P)
☎ 01 938 590 318
Open 12-3, 5.30-11
🍎 Weston's
Welcoming country pub with
family room. Bar food
lunchtime and evening.

BRECON

Wellington Hotel (P)
The Bulwark.
☎ 01 874 625 225.
🍎 Bulmers Old Hazy

CARNO

Aleppo Merchant (P)
☎ 01 686 420 296.
🍎 Bulmers Traditional

CRICKHOWELL

Britannia (P)
High Street.
☎ 01 873 810 553.
🍎 Bulmers Traditional

Grasshoppers (P)
Beaufort Street.
☎ 01 873 810 402.
🍎 Bulmers Traditional

HAY-ON-WYE

THREE TUNS (P)
Belmont Road
🍎 Weston's range inc perry
Extraordinary pub untouched
by time, used in the film of
Bruce Chatwin 's locally-set
novel On The Black Hill to
represent a pub at the time of
the Great War.

KNIGHTON

Red Lion (P)
☎ 01 547 528 231.
🍎 Bulmers Traditional

LLANGORSE

Boat House Bar (C)
Lakeside.
☎ *01 874 84226.*
🍎 *Bulmers Traditional*

NEW RADNOR

EAGLE HOTEL (P)
Broad Street
☎ 01 544 21208
Open 11-3, 7-11; 11-11 Sat
🍎 **Bulmers Traditional, Ralph Owen**
Coaching inn with fine range of ales including Hook Norton. Bar food lunchtime and evening includes vegan specialities. Disabled access; no smoking area; letting rooms.

TALGARTH

New Inn (P)
Bronllys Rd.
☎ *01 874 711 581.*
🍎 *Bulmers Traditional*

TALYBONT-ON-USK

STAR INN (P)
☎ 01 874 676 635
Open 11-11
🍎 **Weston's Old Rosie**
Riverside pub with up to 12 real ales. Experimented briefly with making own cider. Bar food lunchtime and evening. Just off A40 between Crickhowell and Brecon.

SCOTLAND

Borders

ALLANTON

ALLANTON INN (P)
☎ 01 890 818 260
Open 12-2.30, 6-11; 12-11.45 sat;
12.30-11 sun
🍎 **Inch's**
Old coaching inn with
Belhaven beers. Letting rooms;
bar food lunchtime and
evening; separate restaurant;
disabled access.

GALASHIELS

AULD MILL INN (P)
58 Bank Street
☎ 01 896 758 655
Open 11-11
🍎 **Addlestone's**
One-room local; Caledonian
ales.

PEEBLES

CROSS KEYS HOTEL (P)
Northgate
☎ 01 721 724 222
Open 11-midnight
🍎 **Addlestone's**
Rambling historic bar and
restaurant which hosts many
beer festivals. Bar food
lunchtime and evening;
separate restaurant; disabled
access.

Central

FALKIRK

Behind the Wall (P)
14 Melville Street.
☎ *01 324 33338.*
🍎 *Bulmers Traditional*

Dumfries & Galloway

CANONBIE

RIVERSIDE INN (P)
☎ 01 387 371 512
Open 12-3, 6.30-11
🍎 **Thatchers**
Comfortable country inn on the
banks of the Esk. Bar food
lunchtime and evening; letting
rooms.

Fife

LEUCHARS

Ye Olde Inn (P)
Main Street.
☎ *01 334 839 257.*
🍎 *Bulmers Traditional*

DUNFERMLINE

Commercial (P)
13 Douglas Street.
☎ *01 383 733 876.*
🍎 *Bulmers Traditional*

NEWBURGH

Abbey (P)
Tay Street.
☎ *01 337 840 761.*
🍎 *Bulmers Traditional*

ST ANDREWS

Central Bar (P)
77 Market Street.
☎ *01 334 78296.*
🍎 *Bulmers Traditional*

West Port Hotel (P)
170 South Street.
☎ *01 334 473 186.*
🍎 *Bulmers Traditional*

Grampian

ABERDEEN

BLUE LAMP (P)
121 Gallowgate
☎ 01 224 647 472
Open 11-midnight
🍏 **Biddenden**
Popular two-bar pub. Disabled access.

Booth's (P)
1 Back Wynd.
☎ 01 224 646 476.
🍏 *Bulmers Traditional*

BRENTWOOD HOTEL (P)
101 Crown Street
☎ 01 224 595 440
Open 11-2.30, 5-12; 6-11 Sun
🍏 **Bulmers Traditional**
Carriages Bar in basement sells up to nine real ales as well as cider. Food lunchtime and evening; letting rooms.

Howff (P)
363 Union Street.
☎ 01 224 580 092.
🍏 *Bulmers Traditional*

DUFFTOWN

Fife Arms Hotel (P)
The Square.
☎ 01 340 820 220.
🍏 *Bulmers Traditional*

INVERURIE

Old Meldrum (P)
Kirkbrae.
☎ 01 651 872 353.
🍏 *Bulmers Old Hazy*

Highland

INVERNESS

BLACK FRIARS (P)
93 Academy Street
☎ 01 463 233 881
Open 11-11

🍏 **Bulmers Traditional**
Alehouse under Scottish & Newcastle's T&J Bernard banner. Wide range of real ales and foreign beers; bar food lunchtime & evening.

Lothian

BALERNO

Currie RUFC (C)
Balvey Rd.
☎ 0131 337 1286.
🍏 *Bulmers Traditional*

JOHNSBURN HOUSE HOTEL (P)
Johnsburn Road
☎ 0131 449 3847
Open 12-2.30, 6.30-11;12-12 Sat; 12.30-10.45 Sun; closed Mon
🍏 **Bulmers Traditional**
Cosy bar and highly-regarded restaurant in listed eighteenth-century mansion. Six real ales. Disabled access.

EDINBURGH

BARON BAILLIE (P)
2 Lauriston Place
☎ 0131 229 3201
Open noon-1am
🍏 **Bulmers Traditional**
Old Town alehouse popular with students. No food; loud juke-box.

Caley Sample Room (P)
58 Angle Park Terrace, Tynecastle.
☎ 0131 337 1286.
🍏 *Bulmers Old Hazy &*
Traditional

CUMBERLAND BAR (P)
1-3 Cumberland Place
☎ 0131 558 3134
Open 12-11.30; closed Sun
🍏 **Bulmers Old Hazy**
Wood-panelled two-bar New Town pub. No food. Caledonian ales.

Doctor's (P)
32 Forrest Rd.
☎ 0131 225 1819.
🍏 Bulmers Traditional

Hamilton's (P)
18 Hamilton Place.
☎ 0131 226 4199.
🍏 Bulmers Traditional

Haymarket Station Restaurant (R)
1-3 Haymarket Terrace.
☎ 0131 337 1006.
🍏 Bulmers Traditional

K JACKSON'S (P)
40 Lady Lawson Street
☎ 0131 228 4284
Open 11am-midnight;
12.30-11 Sun
🍏 Inch's
Small busy local with up to 10
real ales. Can get smoky.

MALT & HOPS (P)
45 The Shore
☎ 0131 555 0083
Open 12-11 (1am Fri/Sat)
🍏 Addlestone's
Mid eighteenth-century one
bar pub opening on to Water of
Leith. Bar food lunchtime (not
Sun).

Maltings Bar (P)
St Leonards Street.
☎ 0131 667 5946.
🍏 Bulmers Traditional

Milne's Bar (P)
35 Hanover Street.
☎ 0131 225 6738.
🍏 Bulmers Traditional

Porkie's Cider House (P)
122 Rose Street Lane South.
☎ 0131 225 7210.
🍏 Bulmers Traditional

SOUTHSIDER (P)
5 West Richmond Street
☎ 0131 667 2003
Open 11.30-midnight;
12.30-11 Sun
🍏 Addlestone's
Popular Maclay's two-bar pub.
Families welcome, but no food.

Theatre Royal Bar (P)
26 Greenside Place.
☎ 0131 557 2142.
🍏 Bulmers Traditional

West End Oyster Bar (R)
28 West Maitland Street.
☎ 0131 225 3861.
🍏 Bulmers Traditional

LEITH

Nobles Bar (P)
44 Constitution Street.
☎ 0131 554 2024.
🍏 Bulmers Traditional

Strathclyde

GLASGOW

ARAGON BAR (P)
131 Byres Road
☎ 0141 339 3252
Open 11-11 (11.45 Fri/Sat)
🍏 Bulmers Traditional
Pub in T&J Bernard alehouse
chain

ATHENA TAVERN (R)
780 Pollockshaws Road
☎ 0141 424 0858
Open 11-2.30, 5-11; closed Sun
🍏 Bulmers Old Hazy
Belhaven ales and Belgian
bottled beers in public bar
attached to Greek restaurant.
Busy at weekends.

BABBITY BOWSTER (P)
16 Blackfriar Street
☎ 0141 552 5055
Open 11-midnight
🍏 Bulmers Traditional
Maclay's ale in airy Georgian-
style cafe-bar. Letting rooms;
food from 8am.

BLACKFRIARS (P)
36 Bell Street
☎ 0141 552 5924
Open 11-midnight
🍏 Addlestone's

Lively real ale bar with strong bias towards youth. Live bands three nights a week. Draught and bottled Belgian beers. Bar food lunchtime and evening.

BON ACCORD (P)
153 North Street
☎ 0141 248 4427
Open 11-11.45; 12.30-11 Sun
🍏 **Bulmers Traditional**
T&J Bernard alehouse. Bar food lunchtime and evening (not weekends). Disabled access.

Boswell Hotel (P)
27 Mansion House Rd,
Langside.
☎ *0141 632 9812.*
🍏 *Bulmers Traditional*

BREWERY TAP (P)
1055 Sauchiehall Street
☎ 0141 339 8866
Open 12-11
🍏 **Addlestone's**
Lively two-room pub with live music at weekends. Selected German and Belgian beers.

Cask & Still (P)
154 Hope Street.
☎ *0141 333 0989.*
🍏 *Bulmers Traditional*

Chambers Bar (P)
57 Cochrane Street.
☎ *0141 552 1740.*
🍏 *Bulmers Traditional*

Hubbards (P)
508 Great Western Rd.
☎ *0141 334 2995.*
🍏 *Bulmers Traditional*

THREE JUDGES (P)
141 Dumbarton Way
☎ 0141 337 3055
Open 11-11 (midnight Fri/Sat)
🍏 **Addlestone's**
Busy West End saloon which has served 1,000 ales in four years. Local CAMRA favourite.

UBIQUITOUS CHIP (P)
12 Ashton Lane
☎ 0141 334 7109
🍏 **Bulmers Traditional**

Busy bar above popular restaurant. Caledonian ales. Bar food lunchtime and evening.

PAISLEY

Waiting Room (P)
42 Old Sneddon Street.
☎ *0141 889 5163.*
🍏 *Bulmers Old Hazy*

RENFREW

FERRY INN (P)
1 Clyde Street
☎ 0141 886 2104
Open 11-11 (1am Fri)
🍏 **Bulmers Old Hazy**
Popular Clydeside local.

SALTCOATS

HIP FLASK (P)
13 Winton Street
☎ 01 294 465 222
Open 11-midnight (1am Thurs-Sat)
🍏 **Bulmers Old Hazy**
Friendly bar handy for town-centre and beach. Children welcome. Bar food lunchtime and evening.

STRATHAVEN

Bow Butts (P)
Gilmourton.
☎ *01 357 40333.*
🍏 *Bulmers Old Hazy*

Tayside

DUNBLANE

Tappit Hen (P)
Kirk Street.
☎ *01 786 825 226.*
🍏 *Bulmers Traditional*

CIDER PRODUCERS

The list below of nearly 150 cidermakers large and small is far from exhaustive. True, once you have listed HP Bulmer and Matthew Clark Taunton, you have accounted for 93 per cent of all cider made in Britain.

But there are 300, maybe 400, maybe 500 small makers at work, most of them producing under 1,500 gallons a year and so exempt from duty, most of them known only to a handful of regulars in the immediate locality. As there is no centrally-kept register of duty exemptions – or none that is publicly available, at any rate – there is no way of knowing just how many of these cottage producers there are.

What is for sure is that the number of traditional farm-based cider operations is dwindling as older farmers retire and older orchards stop bearing useful crops. There are still very many of them left – perhaps even one or two in East Anglia – but it does seem that the younger generation of farmers are less interested in, or in the age of monoculture have less time for, traditional cidermaking.

In their place, though, there is a legion of newcomers. Many of them are large-scale fruit-growers seeking a use for the smaller or superficially-blemished apples which Sainsbury's rejects. Others are winemakers looking for a better return on the capital invested in wine-presses and bottling lines. Others still are hobbyists for whom selling cider is merely a means of paying for the fun of making it.

The lifeline for all these operations, though, is the 1,500-gallon duty exemption.

There are rumours that Customs would like to reduce the number of small-scale cidermakers exploiting this loophole, left open when cider was first taxed 20 years ago in order to protect the traditional farm-based makers.

We at CAMRA would like to say to them: Don't! It may be argued that the exemption is no longer fulfilling its original function; but it is now playing the equally important roles of making marginally-profitable fruit farms and wineries viable and encouraging new enterprises in parts of the country which desperately need them. Companies like Cassel's sold just 50 gallons each in their first year of duty-exempt registration: would they have bothered to set up at all if they had had to pay duty on such tiny quantities?

If anything, we agree with the South-West Cidermakers Association that the duty-exempt level should be extended to cover all cidermakers, large and small, in the same way that everybody, rich or poor, has the same allowance before income tax.

The present tax-exempt limit is something of a glass ceiling for small makers because they have to sell 3,000 gallons duty-paid to get back to the same level of income that they earned from 1,500 gallons duty-free. A decision to extend it to all would encourage new businesses in deprived areas at no cost to the taxpayer.

VISITING CIDERMAKERS

Many enthusiasts don't really feel that they've drunk the cider until they've seen where and how it's made. Less zealous folk – holidaymakers planning day excursions, perhaps – also want to see cider being made or would at least like to buy otherwise unobtainable ciders at the farm gate. Trouble is, many cideries – most cideries, even – are hard to find, lost in labyrinths of uncharted lanes.

The predecessor to this guide offered detailed instructions on how to find the less accessible farms, even printing Ordnance Survey reference numbers on occasion. The trouble with detailed directions is that they don't help you if you do take a wrong turn; while the problem with OS numbers is that most people navigate by road atlas rather than walker's map. In this edition, therefore, we have copped out and are advising all who want to visit the more hidden cideries to ring ahead, both to ask directions and to make sure someone will be in.

ABBEYGATE

Abbeygate Cider, Abbeygate Farm, Musbury Road, Axminster, Devon.
☎ 01 297 33541
Roy Mear only makes 1,000 gallons or so a year using cider apples from neighbouring orchards, but cider lovers and tourists alike will find Abbeygate Farm a congenial base for Devonian explorations. Camping on the farm is less cluttered than it is on the coast, but Axmouth and Seaton are a only short drive away. Abbeygate is handy even if you don't drive: it's a few minutes' walk from Axminster Railway Station.
CIDERS: Medium, dry 6.5%.
OPEN: Any reasonable time, but phone ahead. Also sells farm produce.

APPLEDRAM

Appledram Farm Products, Pump Bottom Farm, Birdham Road, Chichester, W Sussex PO20 7EH.
☎ 01 243 773 828
Being in the mood to forgive bad puns helps you appreciate Appledram ciders: it's actually at Apuldram on Chichester Creek, but bearing in mind its main product, the misspelling is excusable. As well as the cider and apple juice Julian Moores has been producing for some 15 years, the farm raises and sells

free range Bronze and Norfolk Black turkeys. The Dram o'
Apples (honestly) Cider House is fully licensed, serving
around 40 ciders, bottled and draught, as well as traditional
English food and tapas.
CIDERS: Appledram (Dry, Medium, Sweet) 7.5%; Centurion 5
Year Old Vintage 8.5%; Appledram Honey Gold 7%
OPEN: (Easter-Nov) 9.30am-7pm; (Nov-Easter) 10am-6.30pm.

ASHILL

Ashill Cider, Ashtons Farm, Ashill, near Ilminster, Somerset
TA19 9NE.
☎ 01 823 480 513
Business hasn't been so good at Ashill Cider since the village
was bypassed and in a locally famous planning row, the
council limited the firm to two virtually invisible signs off the
A358 Taunton-Chard road. Worth seeking out, though, for the
natural cider made only from local apples – but go early in the
season, as the farm only makes a limited quantity and it soon
runs out!
CIDERS: Scrumpy (Dry, Medium, Sweet) 6%

ASHWOOD

Ashwood Farm, Shipham Hill, Cheddar, Somerset.
☎ 01 934 742 393
Phil and Carole Ford have been making natural cider here for
fifteen years, and only when each barrel has stopped working
do they decide whether it's dry, medium or sweet. Their mill
dates back to 1868, and they use an old two-screw wooden
press. The apples are from orchards at Wookey and Street.
CIDERS: Scrumpy 7%
OPEN: 9-9 Mon-Sat; Sunday if they're in. Also cheese and eggs.

ASPALL

Aspall Cyder, Aspall Hall, Debenham, Stowmarket, Suffolk
IP14 6PD
☎ 01 728 860 510
Aspall was founded in 1728 by the Chevallier family, whose
descendants still own it. The original cyder house still stands,
complete with stone mill, imported from Normandy at a cost
of £6, and press. Little cyder is made today, as the firm
concentrates on high quality fresh-pressed juice and cyder
vinegar; but what cyder is produced is made, unusually for
East Anglia, from proper cider apples including Kingston
Black and Yarlington Mill.
BOTTLED CIDERS: Still Dry Cyder, Still Sweet Cyder, 6%
OPEN: No shop, tours by arrangement (and limited).

When visiting producers, please telephone ahead.

AVALON

Avalon Vineyard, East Pennard, Shepton Mallet, Somerset BA4 6UA.

☎ 01749 860393

Avalon is principally a vineyard, but with a vigorous sideline in organic cider. Originally owner Dr Hugh Tripp only made bottled sparkling natural cider, using the complicated and labour-intensive Methode Champenoise, which was widespread in the British cider industry in the nineteenth century but died out when artificial carbonation became easier. This has now been taken up by a number of other makers, notably Bollhayes, Burrow Hill, and Gospel Green; sadly, though, Dr Tripp has discontinued the experiment himself for lack of demand, but still makes a sought-after draught. Perhaps he can be prevailed upon to start again, seeing what a success Burrow Hill has made of its version.

CIDERS: Pennard Natural Draught (Dry, Medium, Sweet) 6-7%
OPEN: 2pm-6pm daily (other times by arrangement). Tours by arrangement.

B&T

The Brewery, Shefford, Beds.

☎ 01 462 815 080

Long-established micro-brewery which has been experimenting with making its own cider for some time. Success at last! Shefford Scrumpy is an excellent product which should show the way for other small brewers.

CIDER: Shefford Scrumpy, 7%
OPEN: Tours by arrangement.

BAGBOROUGH

Bagborough Vineyard, Bagborough Lane, Pylle, Shepton Mallet, Somerset.

☎ 01 749 831 146

Stephen Brooksbank has been making wine at Bagborough since 1989, and three years ago decided to add cider to his repertoire as well, mainly to attract the cider-seeking tourists pouring down the A37 nearby. Production has slowly crept up as the cider's reputation has grown, and a little is now released to the retail trade in the area.

CIDERS: Strong Cider, 8%
OPEN: Any reasonable time, but ring ahead out of season.

BALLARD'S

Colwall, Herefordshire.

☎ 01 684 540 142

A perfect example of a craft maker proving himself as good as the more commercial outfits, Mr Ballard's cider and perry are greatly appreciated when they appear in public. A businessman, Mr Ballard grows a few perry pears and cider apples at his home and, when the crop is good enough and/or when he has time, he makes cider and perry for sale to friends, a handful of regulars, and the odd lucky CAMRA Beer Festival buyer. In years when he doesn't make cider and perry, his crop goes to Much Marcle to be used by prize-winning Jean Nowell.

BANHAM CIDER

The Appleyard, Kenninghall Rd, Banham, Norfolk.
☎ 01 953 888 593

Former teacher Ryan Burnard started making cider in a unit in the craft centre opposite Banham Zoo in 1991. It proved a happy move for the Cornish expatriate, for his business has gone from strength to strength and now produces some 10,000 gallons a year. The location is a large part of the appeal, but the quality of the cider lives up to the promise. Ryan likes to experiment with different blends and styles – single varietals, blends, oak-aged, rum-cask aged, even a perry made of the local miniature pear variety, Robins – and he believes his customers like to as well. At the cidery customers are encouraged to sample from the different casks on display behind the counter and make up their own customised blend to take home. As this book was going to press, Ryan was applying for a licence to turn part of his unit into a cider bar.
CIDERS: Farmhouse 5-6%; Strong Dry 8.4%; Strong Rough 7-8%; Oak Cask, Old Hardy 7-8.4%; Norfolk Croak 7.5%; single varietal ciders, Robin perry strength according to season.
OPEN: All day, every day.

BENNETT

V V Bennett, Chestnut Farm, Edithmead, near Burnham-on-Sea, Somerset.
☎ 01 278 785 376/783 429

"If you put rubbish in, you get rubbish out" is the motto of Tom Bennett, who hand-picks the apples that go into this family firm's cider. Tom has been cidermaking since boyhood, but the family only went into commercial production twelve years ago and now makes about 3,500 gallons a year. The Bennetts – the firm is now run by Tom's son Vyv – have won a string of competitions since going commercial: they were Royal Bath & West Show champions for five years running and it's said that larger companies refuse to enter any competition in which the Bennetts are represented. The farm does not attract attention to itself despite the existence of a large caravan park nearby; instead, the Bennetts prefer to deal mainly with regular and wholesale customers.

BIDDENDEN

Biddenden Vineyards Ltd, Little Whatmans, Biddenden, Ashford, Kent TN27 8DH.
☎ 01 580 291 726
Biddenden Vineyards were founded in 1969 and, as many English vineyards have started doing since, started producing ciders and apple juices to add to its range of English wines 15 years ago. It is now the largest producer of real cider in the South-East, making over 30,000 gallons a year, and its products are distributed nationally.
CIDERS: Strong Still Kentish Cider 8%; Sparkling Cider 6%; Monk's Delight Mulling Cider 7.5%; Special Reserve Cider 13%
OPEN: March-Oct: Mon-Fri 10am-5pm, Bank Holidays 11am-5pm, Sat 11am-5pm, Sun 12-5pm. Nov-Feb: Mon-Fri 10am-5pm, Sat 1am-3pm, Sun 12noon-3pm, closed Bank Holidays. Closed Sundays in Jan and Feb. Closed Dec 24 noon till Jan 2. Tours by arrangement.

BOLLHAYES

Bollhayes Cider, Clayhidon, Cullompton, Devon EX15 3PN.
☎ 01 823 680 230
Founded in 1988 by Alex Hill of Vigo Vineyard Supplies, whose principal business was (and is) supplying equipment to vineyards and cidermakers both commercial and home-based. Alex is also one of the leading revivalists of the bottle-fermented or Methode Champenoise ciders once common but long superseded by artificial carbonation.
CIDERS: Draught cider 7%; Draught perry 7%; Bollhayes Bottle-fermented 8%

BRAIN'S

Brain's Cider, The Orchards, Edge Hills, Littledean, Cinderford, Glos GL14 3LQ.
☎ 01 594 822 416
Cider has been made in the old-fashioned way at Edge Hills for over a century. Callers are still welcome today to sample the product – but come early in the summer, as only some 500 gallons are made.
CIDERS: Farmhouse Dry 4.5-7.5%

BRICKFIELD

Brickfields Horse Country, Newnham Rd, Binstead, Ryde, Isle of Wight PO33 3TH.
☎ 01 983 566 801/615 116
As its name suggests, this is a tourist attraction featuring Shires and other horses, where a small amount of cider has been made every year since 1983 for sale in the Horseshoe Bar. Cider apples are imported from Herefordshire, where proprietors

Philip and John Legge used to live, milled by horsepower, pressed on an 1860 mobile press, and fermented and conditioned in oak. The Legges produce about 300 gallons a year which is diluted, as much farm cider used to be, with about two parts water to three parts cider to produce a dry, light-bodied cider.
CIDERS: Dry cider, abv varies

BRIDGE FARM
Bridge Farm Cider, East Chinnock, Yeovil, Somerset BA22 9EA.
☎ 01 935 862 387
Founded by Nigel Stewart at the family farm in Sandford Orcas in 1988, Bridge Farm Cider moved to its present address shortly afterwards and has quickly established itself as a growing force in the region. Nigel is another apostle of bottle-fermented cider, and his Fordhay won its class at the Devon County Show last year. Nigel is also the custodian of the dwindling supply of Warwick Billing's bottle-fermented Scrumptious (5.5%). Warwick has just completed a degree in wine-making at the University of Adelaide and plans to press again this season: the results of importing Australian wine-making methods into a very traditional English cider industry could be revolutionary.
CIDERS: Bridge Farm (Dry, Medium, Sweet) 6.5-7.5%
BOTTLED CIDERS: Fordhay Sparkling Cider Dry Bottle Fermented Somerset Cider 8%
OPEN: Tours by arrangement.

BRIMBLECOMBE
Brimblecombe's Devon Cider, Farrants Farm, Dunsford, Exeter.
☎ 01 647 252 783
Farrant's Farm, and the Brimblecombe name, were bought last December by Ron and Beverley Barter when old favourite Cliff Brimblecombe finally called it a day. It ain't broke, so the Barters don't plan to fix it. Instead, they aim to plant 150 new cider-apple trees to ensure future supplies of varieties including Redstreak, Foxwhelp, Golden Pippin, Pearmain, Hang Me Down, Slap Me Girdle, Sweet Alford, Tom Putt and some newer varieties. They also hope to develop the 400-year-old barn and mill as a museum and visitors' centre.
CIDERS: Dry, Medium, Sweet; Vintage dry, medium, sweet 6%.
OPEN: Open 9.30-6pm seven days. Tours by arrangement.

BROADOAK
Broadoak Cider Co, Blackberry Hill, Clutton, Somerset.
☎ 01 761 453 119
Now one of the largest independent commercial cidermakers in the region, Broadoak has only been going for around 10 years. Its most popular brand is Moonshine, a traditional

equivalent of Diamond White which achieves its pallid colour through heavy filtration. Broadoak also produces the draught and bottled cider sold under the name Art's at Shipham, near Cheddar. The company once tried its hand at perry but discontinued the experiment because of the impossibility of guaranteeing supplies of suitable pears.

CIDERS: Farmhouse dry, medium, sweet 6%; Kingston Black, Moonshine 8.4%
BOTTLED CIDER: Moonshine 8.4%

BROMELL

E&P Bromell, Lower Uppercott, Whitestone Rd, Tedburn St Mary, Exeter, Devon EX6 6AZ.
☎ 01 647 61294
Lower Uppercott is a mixed farm on the edge of the Dartmoor National Park. The apples which go into the farm's 20,000 gallon annual output all come from local orchards, and Eric Bromell will willingly blend ciders from different barrels to suit your individual taste. Don't go for a picnic on the moor without calling at Bromell's first!

CIDERS: Sweet, medium sweet, medium dry, dry – strength varies by season; Devon Farm Scrumpy 6%
OPEN: 7am-7pm daily. Tours by arrangement.

BUDDEN

Higher Hacknell Farm, Burrington, Devon.
☎ 01 769 560 292
Mainly a beef and sheep farmer, Tim Budden started planting cider apple trees 10 years ago after inheriting an old mill in poor repair and a rather shaggy orchard in which he found a number of rare local varieties. Now makes around 500 gallons of Soil Association certificated organic ciders a year in the old fashioned and entirely natural way. His farm shop also sells organic meat from the farm.

CIDER: Dry 6.5%
OPEN: Reasonable times but ring ahead please.

HP BULMER

HP Bulmer, The Cider Mills, Plough Lane, Hereford HR4 0LE.
☎ 01 432 352 000
Still the undisputed giant despite the acquisition of Taunton Cider last year by Matthew Clarke, which already owned the Gaymer Group. Bulmers was founded in 1887 and took over the even-older Symonds of Stoke Lacey a few years ago. It was one of the first companies to turn its back on tradition in the 1950s and '60s, churning out vile fizz such as Strongbow and Woodpecker and, in the 1980s, joining the stampede towards heavily-branded and over-processed strong bottled brands

which did so much to bring cider into disrepute. It is also responsible for Scrumpy Jack, a keg cider widely served through a fake handpump which, ironically, is of a good blend and would be perfectly acceptable if served in its natural, still form. (As indeed, would Bulmers Original.) However Bulmers never completely turned its back on traditional cider; in fact it is still far and away the biggest producer of traditional cider, with a huge following in the Valleys of South Wales and elsewhere for its Traditional and West Country brands. More recently it has pioneered the introduction of cask-conditioned cider to the national stage with the launch of Old Hazy, which has spread like wildfire thanks in part to strong distribution through Whitbread, and has taken over Inch's of Winkleigh in Devon, which not only stretches its lead over Taunton-Gaymer but also gives its sales force another range of traditional ciders to take to the nation's publicans. Bulmers is also rapidly establishing Herefordshire as the headquarters of cider apple growing with a massive – and expensive – planting programme (Gaymers please note).

CIDERS: Bulmers Traditional Draught 4.25%; Bulmers West Country 5.5%; Symond's Old Hazy 5.5%; Inch's Stonehouse, Harvest dry, Harvest sweet 6%; Inch's Harvest Scrumpy medium dry, medium sweet 8%

BOTTLED CIDERS: No 7, 6%. Inch's Vintage, Harvest Scrumpy 8%

OPEN: Visitors' centre on site. Tours by arrangement.

BURROW HILL

Burrow Hill Cider, Pass Vale Farm, Burrow Hill, Kingsbury Episcopi, Martock, Somerset TA12 5BU.
☎ 01 460 240 782

Cider has been made at Burrow Hill for 150 years. Under its present owner Julian Temperley it has emerged as a major force in the region, owning more traditional orchards than anyone else in the South-West, boosting production to 80,000 gallons a year, and joining the revival of bottle-fermented methode champenoise cider. Not content with that, Julian has also revived the long-dead art of cider brandy distilling, producing up to 8,000 cases of Somerset Royal Cider Brandy (42%) a year and has been an influential and very vocal spokesman for the traditional cider-makers of the South-West.

CIDERS: Draught medium and dry 6.4%

BOTTLED CIDERS: Burrow Hill Bottle-Fermented 8%; Burrow Hill Farmhouse 6.5%

OPEN: 9am-5.30pm Mon-Sat; tours by arrangement.

When visiting producers, please telephone ahead.

BURSCOMBE FARM CIDER

Burscombe Farm, Sidford, Sidmouth, Devon.
☎ 01 395 597 648
Spiller's Cider was taken over by Mr and Mrs Pearse and family after Gordon Spiller's retirement. It's still running, though, and still using the small orchard of mixed cider varieties, and still housed in the ancient stone barn lined with 80-year-old barrels (the secret, apparently, is not to let them dry out).
CIDERS: Medium, dry, 3-year-old Vintage
OPEN: Ring ahead – and ask for directions! Burscombe Farm is only a couple of miles from Sidford, but they could be the longest couple of miles of your life if you don't know the way.

CASSELS

Cassels Cider, 72 High Street, Great Shelford, Cambridge CB2 5EH.
☎ 01 223 842 373
Probably Cambridgeshire's only commercial cidermaker, book conservator James Cassels was actually brought up amid cider-apple orchards in Devon. He and his wife decided to start growing their own apples after inheriting a little land, but it was a long time before their first five-gallon barrel found its way onto a pub bar. Encouraged by the reception their naturally-fermented dry cider had, the Cassels went into full-scale production in October 1995, producing 1,000 gallons in their first year.
CIDERS: Dry, medium, 6.4%

CASTLE

Castle Cider Company, Larkins Farm, Hampkins Hill Road, Chiddingstone, Kent.
☎ 01 732 455 977
Firm started by brothers Tim and Richard Davies in 1986 to make the best of the abundant local apples. As well as ciders in four styles – medium sweet, medium dry, dry and bone dry – the company also makes hot cider mustard. Castle Cider now has retail customers all along the south coast and into Essex, and can be found at many county shows.
CIDERS: Chiddingstone Cider 8%; Higlers Cider 5.5%
BOTTLED CIDERS: Chiddingstone (75cl corked bottles) 8%

CASTLINGS HEATH

Castlings Heath Cottage Cider, Groton, Sudbury, Suffolk.
☎ 01 787 210 899
Certified as organic by the Soil Association, Castlings Heath cider and perry – which is a rarity in East Anglia – are matured

in oak vats until they are dry yet smooth. John Norton started making cider in 1987 but only makes 500-1,000 gallons each year and is choosy about which pubs he sells it to. A small amount is also to be found at beer and music festivals.
CIDERS: Dry Cider 7.5%, Medium Perry 6.5%, Vintage

CHAFFORD
Chafford Cider, Chafford Rise, Fordcombe, Kent TN3 0SH.
☎ 01 892 740 437
Christopher Ballenden started cidermaking using a small wine press in 1980 and went into full-scale production in 1987, although he still only produces some 1,200 gallons a year. He uses a blend of about two-thirds Bramley and a third mixed Coxes and Worcester Pearmain grown in his own (unsprayed) orchards, and ages the cider for up to two years before packaging it in three-gallon shrinkpacks and four-pint jars. Christopher is also a familiar sight in Kent's orchards at harvest time with his mobile hydraulic press, crushing freshly-picked apples for other makers.
CIDER: Traditional Kent Dry Cider 6.5%

CHURCHWARD
Churchward Cider, Yalberton Farm, Yalberton Road, Paignton, Devon TQ4 7PE.
☎ 01 803 558 157
The family of the late Vic Churchward have continued the tradition of cidermaking since his death two years ago, and although other makers have encroached on Churchward's pub trade, its location just a mile inland from Paignton, near the zoo, guarantees it a busy farm-gate business.
CIDERS: Sweet, medium, dry, Devon Mix
OPEN: Winter Mon-Sat 9am-5.30pm; Summer 9am-8pm; Sun 12-3pm and 7-8pm. Tours by arrangement.

CLARKS
Clarks Farm Cider, Shortridge Hill, Seven Crosses, Tiverton, Devon EX16 8HH.
☎ 01 884 252 632
Absolutely traditional Devon cidermaker, still using a century-old mill and a double-screw press and fermenting and maturing in oak.
CIDERS: Clarks Cider, Medium Dry or Medium Sweet
OPEN: Open all reasonable hours, but ring to check. Tours by arrangement.

CLAWFORD
Clawford Vineyard, Clawton, Holsworthy, Devon EX22 6PN.
☎ 01 409 254 177
When owner John Ray planted 25 acres of vines here in 1992

he also put in 22 acres of cider apples, so when both plantings come to maturity he will be able to make 135,000 bottles of wine and 20,000 gallons of cider. Production is not at that level yet, but the three ciders made from five apple varieties are already finding a healthy trade both at the farm gate – where there should soon be a proper shop and sampling-room – and in a number of local off-licences. Cidermaking and winemaking complement each other to a great extent, as many winemakers are discovering: cidermaking gets extra work out of the expensive wine-press, while winemaking brings technical advances, especially in fermentation techniques, to cidermaking. Here, as in most vineyard/cideries, the yeast used is a wine yeast: few winemakers would risk having all those wild, uncontrollable cider yeasts floating around in the presence of 100,000 litres of unfermented grape must!

CIDERS: Harvest Moon, Black Knight 8%, Vintage 7%
OPEN: Easter to end-Oct Mon-Fri 11-6; July-Sept Sun 12-3pm. Tours by arrangement.

COCKS

Gully's Farm, Sunday Hill Lane, Rockhampton, Avon.
☎ 01 454 260 313
David Cocks only makes 1,500 gallons a year at the farm where he has lived for 12 years, but before he moved in Gully's Farm was the home of Woodward's, a substantial business which not only made cider on quite a scale but also imported apples for processing from the Continent via nearby Avonmouth. Today the main business of the farm is sheep, which graze in the shade of the old-fashioned standard trees in the farm's many orchards. And it's not only the orchards which are old-fashioned: most of the equipment is mid-Victorian, and there is even older equipment no longer in use.

CIDERS: Dry 8%
OPEN: Ring ahead for farm gate sales.

COKESPUTT

Cokesputt Cyder, Cokesputt Farm, Payhembury, Honiton, Devon EX14 0HD.
☎ 01 404 841 289
Established in 1993, Cokesputt has few ambitions other than to produce cider as traditionally and as naturally as possible from an orchard planted only a few years ago. Output was 600 gallons last year. All production is bottled but is unpasteurised, unfiltered and, in the words of the proprietor, "unmessed about".

CIDERS: Cokesputt Cyder 7.5%; Kingston Black single varietal 8%
OPEN: Tours by arrangement.

COLDHARBOUR

Coldharbour Cider, Leith Hill Place Lodge, Coldharbour, Dorking, Surrey.

☎ 01 306 712 140

Established in 1990 to produce a bottle-conditioned cider with Norman/Breton cidre bouche as a model, although a naturally sparkling draught version is promised. Produced only very limited qualities in the past: going commercial this year. However the cider is available only by the case, and visits are by appointment only.

BOTTLED CIDER: Dry 7.6%

OPEN: Visits strictly by arrangement.

COOMBES

Coombes Somerset Cider, Japonica Farm, Mark, near Highbridge, Somerset TA9 4QD.

☎ 01 278 641 265

Chris and Rita Coombes welcome all comers to a farm which has been producing cider since 1919 (at least). Chris is the third-generation Coombes to make cider at Japonica Farm and sees no reason to change the methods his grandfather used. The farm's facilities include a tea-room for the faint-hearted.

CIDERS: Cider medium, dry, extra dry 6%; Kingston Black 8.4%; Perry 7%

OPEN: 1 May-30 Sept: 9-6.30 Mon-Sat; 12-3 Sun. 1 Oct-30 April: 9-6 Mon Sat. Tea room open daily in tourist season.

CORNISH

Cornish Cider Co, Trevean Farm, Coombe Lea, Truro, Cornwall.

☎ 01 872 573 356

The ciders made here under the name Apple Blossom are interesting in that they are mainly a mixture of juices from the king of cider apples, Kingston Black, and the king of cooking apples, Bramley. Since the last Cider Guide was published Cornish has dramatically changed its policy of not selling from the farm gate: now it has a farm shop selling not only its ciders in 500ml to five-litre bottles and jars, it also sells country wines, juices, jams, and fudge, and the bottling room has a viewing area.

CIDERS: Dry, sweet 7%

OPEN: Mon-Fri 9-6. Sat 9-6 Easter-end Oct; Sun 10-6 July & August. Closed Jan.

When visiting producers, please telephone ahead.

CORNISH SCRUMPY

Cornish Scrumpy Co Ltd, Callestock Cider Farm, Penhallow, Truro, Cornwall TR4 9LW.

☎ 01 872 573 356

David and Kay Healey have been making traditional still cider since 1980 and are now producing some 60,000 gallons a year. The most recent development at this energetic firm is a 3,000 square foot pressing and bottling barn complete with viewing gallery. Callestock Farm has its own shop which sells juices, jams and country wines as well as cider, and the cider itself is widely distributed throughout the region in supermarkets and off-licences.

CIDERS: Cornish Scrumpy 8%

OPEN: Mon-Fri 10am-5pm. Tours by arrangement.

COTSWOLD

Bottle Green Drinks Co, Spring Mills Estate, Avening Road, Nailsworth, Glos.

☎ 01 453 872 882

Bottle Green founder Dr Kit Morris is a winemaker by trade, having worked for the Three Choirs Vineyard at Newent before setting up on his own. Cider is not Bottle Green's main business: Dr Morris makes only 1,500 gallons, which is sold in 75cl wine bottles alongside the elderflower products which are the firm's staple. But get some while you can: connoisseurs rate it highly at table.

CIDERS: Cotswold Cider 6.5%

OPEN: 9-5 weekdays, but ring ahead.

COUNTRYMAN

Countryman Cider, Felldown Head, Milton Abbot, Tavistock, Devon PL19 0QR.

☎ 01 822 870 226

Some 20,000 gallons are produced in the fifteenth-century barn of a former coaching inn, the Kelly Arms. A cider press dating from 1858 was in use until 1979, when it was pensioned off and retired to the Cornwall Museum at Camelford along with other items of equipment. The hydraulic press which replaced it is no stripling – it's more than 40 years old. Until a few years ago the main business was pressing apples for local farmers, who then took away the juice to ferment for themselves. Now all the produce is packaged on site for public sale. The cider is fermented naturally and, unusually for the region, contains a proportion of dessert apples to sharpen the flavour. The whole process is open to public inspection, with a sample room at the end of the tour.

CIDERS: Still cider, dry, medium, sweet 6%; Gold Label Strong still cider, medium 8%

OPEN: Mon-Fri 9am-6pm, Sat (May-Sept) 9am-6.30pm. Tours by arrangement.

COWHILL
Cowhill Cider, Fishermans Cottage, Cowhill, near Thornbury, Bristol BS12 1QJ.
☎ 01 454 412 152
Surely one of the most basic and traditional of the operations listed in the Guide, Cowhill was taken on by John Tymko when his father-in-law Tommy Jones died. But little was changed: John produces 100% traditional farmhouse cider using English cider apples and nothing else but also applies the cidermaker's knowledge to make oddities like a light single-varietal Christmas cider, made from the early-cropping Morgan Sweet in September and ready to drink by Christmas.
CIDERS: Dry 6%; Medium 6%
OPEN: During daylight hours.

CRIPPLEDICK
Crippledick Cider Co, Roxeth Cottage, Highview Close, Boughton-under-Blean, Faversham, Kent ME13 9AY.
☎ 01 227 750 817
Commercial production started in 1993 using a 200-year-old granite press made in Gloucestershire and an ancient scratter-mill salvaged from Shropshire. However the operation expanded and soon had to buy more modern kit and move to its present home, Mt Ephraim Fruit Farm in Boughton, where up to 7,000 litres a year are produced for sale to local pubs. It can also be found at local functions and festivals and is for sale at the farm gate. The owners are also trying for a perry.
CIDERS: Dry 7%; Medium 7%

CRONE'S
Crone's Cider, Fairview, Fersfield Road, Dam Green, Kenninghall, Norfolk NR16 2DP.
☎ 01 379 687 687
Cabinetmaker Robbie Crone started making cider in the traditional Norfolk way, using only culinary and dessert apples, as a hobby in 1984 but found it impossible to keep a good thing to himself. Soon after going into commercial production in 1988, he was making 10,000 gallons a year and is now supplying the Tap & Spile chain of alehouses. He also makes perry and a Special Reserve cider made with locally-grown cider apples as well as the more common cookers and eaters. His ciders are all organic, and he also makes a range of award-winning organic juices.
CIDERS: User Friendly 6.2-6.5%; Original 7.8-8.2%; Special Reserve 7.8-8.2%; Cider Mead 7.8-8.2%; Vintage 8.5%

BOTTLED CIDERS: User Friendly 6.2-8.5%; Original 7.8-8.2%; Special Reserve 7.8-8.2%
OPEN: Phone to check if open. Tours by arrangement.

CROSSMAN

Ben Crossman's Prime Farmhouse Cider, Mayfield Farm, Hewish, Weston-super-Mare, Avon BS24 6RQ.
☎ 01 934 833 174
The cider business is one aspect of a mixed farm in the heart of North Somerset's holiday district. The cider is absolutely traditional, and Mayfield Farm also sells fresh eggs and other farm produce, so if the tat of Weston-super-Mare fills you with horror, here is a nearby haven of authenticity and quality.
CIDERS: Dry, Medium, Sweet, 6%.
OPEN: Mon-Sat 8.30am-7pm, Sun 12-1pm. Tours by arrangement.

CULLIMORE

The Cullimore Partnership, Berkeley Heath Farm, Berkeley, Glos GL13 9EW.
☎ 01 453 810 220
Tony Cullimore has been making traditional cider for over 20 years on a farm which could truly be called mixed. In fact the cider is something of a sideline: the farm specialises in cattle of different breeds, even including buffalo and bison! During the week the cider is for sale at the agricultural equipment shop which is another string in the farm's bow, while at weekends the farm, complete with adventure playground, is open to the public and the cider is sold in the Cattle Country gift shop.
CIDERS: Tony Cullimore's Genuine Farmhouse Cider
OPEN: 8-5 Mon-Fri; 8.30-1 Sat (winter); 10.30-5 Sat/Sun (summer). Farm tours by arrangement.

DERRICK'S

A J Derrick, Cheddar Valley Cheese Depot, The Gorge, Cheddar, Somerset BS27 3QE.
☎ 01 934 743 113
The Derricks established their thriving retail business at the Cheddar Valley Cheese Depot in 1974 but had been producing cider in the area for 200 years before that. Today, a visit to the Cheese Depot makes all the hassle of trying to park in the Gorge well worth it. As well as Derrick's own products, the shop sells other makers' ciders, notably Burrow Hill, and all sorts of other regional specialities – especially, as the name suggests, genuine local Cheddar cheese. You could source an entirely local picnic here and then head for the hills to consume it in glorious peace and quiet. Or you could load your car with many other makes of cider by plundering not only Derrick's

but also the other shops in the Gorge. Unmissable.
CIDERS: Country Bumpkin Dry 6.5%; Country Bumpkin
Sweet 6.5%; Tanglefoot Medium Dry 6.5%
BOTTLED CIDERS: Country Bumpkin Dry 6.5%; Country
Bumpkin Sweet 6.5%; Tanglefoot Medium Dry 6.5%
OPEN: Every day March-November; weekends only in winter.

DEWCHURCH

Haig Partners, Hill Farm, Much Dewchurch, Hereford HR2
8EG.
☎ 01 981 540 286
The Haig family has been making cider and perry on its fruit
farm only since 1990, and like many revivalists are great
enthusiasts and experimenters. Robin Haig has even
completed a cider-making course at the Worcestershire College
of Agriculture. Most of the Haigs' cider is made from the
Kingston Blacks they grow themselves, but they are
experimenting with other varieties including Stoke Red and
now make a perry too. Being apple growers with a long eye to
the future, they are planting the varieties they think they will
need in future, so that although they only make 1,000 gallons a
year at present, their cider and perry should be much more
widely available in due course.
CIDERS: Dewchurch Cider and Perry, 6-7%
OPEN: Daily 9am-5pm.

DOUBLE VISION

Double Vision Cider Company, Gunthorpe, Clapper Lane,
Staplehurst, Kent TN12 0JT.
☎ 01 580 891 387
The Cramp family have been making traditional cider for their
own use for more than a century but only went into
commercial production when Ken Cramp retired as an
electrical engineer and was joined by partner Simon Boarer.
The reputation of their ciders, made only from locally grown
culinary and dessert apples, soon spread and the Double
Vision Cider Company was formed a couple of years later.
Most of the cider is sold at the gate but the partners are hoping
for wider distribution for a clear, clean and crisp product they
describe as a pleasing alternative to table-wine.
CIDERS: Double Vision 8.4%; Kenny's Dry 8.4%
OPEN: Every day. Tours by arrangement.

When visiting producers, please telephone ahead.

DUNKERTONS

Dunkertons Cider Co, Hays Head, Luntley, Pembridge, Leominster, Herefordshire HR6 9ED.
☎ 01 544 388 653 (01 544 388 654 restaurant)
The revivalists par excellence, former TV producer Ivor and theatre administrator Suzie started making cider at Hay's Head in 1982. Or re-started, for cider had been made on the site for generations, and was only stopped by the last owners before the Dunkertons, who were fervent chapel. In the early years the Dunkertons had to buy what apples they could from established growers, but as time has gone by the orchards they have planted themselves came into maturity and they are now making single varietal and blended cider and perry from their own, organically grown, trees. Their bottled products have won national distribution through delicatessens and wholefood shops, but have made little headway in the local, Bulmers-dominated, pub trade. As a consequence Ivor and Suzie have established a truly gourmet restaurant at Hays Head where their ciders can be enjoyed straight from the wood.
CIDERS: Dunkertons Fine (Medium Dry, Medium Sweet) 5.5%; Traditional (Dry, Medium Dry, Medium Sweet, Sweet) 7-8%; Kingston Black, Princess Pippin, Court Royal, Breakwells Seedling 7-8%; Perry (Dry or Medium Sweet) 7-8%
BOTTLED CIDERS: Traditional Dry, Princess Pippin, Court Royal, Kingston Black, Dry Perry 7-8%
OPEN: (shop) 10am-6pm Mon-Sat all year, but please check at Christmas time; (restaurant) 10-6 Mon-Thurs; 10-7.30 Fri & Sat. Please book. Tours by arrangement, but mill open to casual visitors most days.

FRANKLIN'S

Franklin's Cider, The Cliffs Cider Farm, Little Hereford, near Ludlow, Shropshire SY8 4LW.
☎ 01 584 810 488
Jim and Lincoln Franklin planted their first orchard in 1974 and 10 years later went into full-scale commercial cider and perry production. Now they produce up to 7,000 gallons a year of cider and 5,000 gallons of perry and have won too many prizes to list. Both cider and perry are produced entirely naturally and matured in oak barrels. The vast majority of the produce is sold through the farm's own shop, but three local pubs and another farm shop also stock it.
CIDERS: Dry, Medium, Sweet 6.5%; Perry, Dry or Sweet 6%
OPEN: 8am-6.30pm. Tours by arrangement.

When visiting producers, please telephone ahead.

FRIAR'S

Friars Cider, Woolvens Farm, Billingshurst Lane, Ashington, W Sussex RH20 3BB.
☎ 01 903 892 273
John Friar has been making cider at Woolvens Farm for 40 years. Since 1986 he has also been spreading his experience about a bit, pressing other growers' apples both for plain juice and for fermenting and giving advice to the increasing number of revivalist cidermakers in the region.
CIDERS: Farm Draught 8%
OPEN: No shop as such, but cider is usually available for sale at the gate.

GAYMER'S

See Matthew Clark Taunton

GIBBON STRANGLER

Gibbon Strangler Cider, Ridgeway, Peasmarsh, Rye, E Sussex TN31 6XH.
☎ 01 797 230 094
The partners in Gibbon Strangler, enthusiasts all and including leading cider writer David Kitton, started making traditional Eastern-style cider for their own pleasure several years ago, but in 1993 decided that the rest of us deserved a share too. They now produce 800 gallons a year of pure natural cider, made in the Eastern tradition with culinary and dessert apples, and sold to a handful of pubs and specialist off-licences in the region. There are no retail sales.
CIDERS: Gibbon Strangler (Medium, Dry) 7%

GODSHILL

Godshill Cider Company, The Cider Barn, High Street, Godshill, Isle of Wight PO38 3HZ.
☎ 01 983 840 680
Founded in 1979 in a cider orchard of 200 Yarlington Mill, Dabinette, Taylors Seedling, Chisel Jersey and Nehu trees planted a few years earlier. One caveat about proprietor Peter Cramp might be that he's not the most politically correct kind of bloke: his main product, Rumpy Pumpy Scrumpy, is also described as "passion juice" and "the fruity one from Godshill". Sadly, it's carbonated; but Peter produces the real unadulterated stuff too. His dry farmhouse cider is a deceptively gentle but very pleasant tipple. Peter started off using an old wooden twin-screw press, which after nine years had to be retired because of its size and inefficiency and which is now on display as a museum piece. Godshill's main outlets on the Island are supermarkets, but the Cider Barn is popular with overners (the Island term for out-of-Island folk), too.
CIDERS: Rumpy Pumpy Scrumpy 6%

BOTTLED CIDERS: Rumpy Pumpy Scrumpy (Dry, Medium) 6%; Farmhouse Cider (Medium or Sweet) 6%; Dry Farmhouse Cider 6%
OPEN: Gift Shop open daily March-Christmas 10am-5pm (9.30 in Summer).

GOSPEL GREEN

Gospel Green Cider, near Haslemere, Surrey GU27 3BH.
☎ 01 428 654 120
James and Cathy Lane are the acknowledged pioneers of the revival of Méthode Champenoise cidermaking. The Lanes ferment their blend of 70% dessert to 30% culinary apples in 180-gallon stainless steel fermenters for six months. Then they rack it into clean casks to clear and add champagne yeast and cane sugar before bottling in proper champagne bottles. The cider now undergoes a secondary fermentation in bottle lasting a further ten months, after which the bottles are inverted slightly and given a quarter-turn every day for three weeks. When all the sediment has settled in the neck it is frozen and uncorked. The pressure in the bottle blows the cap of frozen sediment, and the bottle is topped up with more cider and sugar before being recorked and firmly wired. Production started in 1990 and is now up to 8,500 bottles a year, and the Lanes supplement their income by making cheese as well.
CIDERS: Gospel Green "Champagne Method" Cyder 8%
OPEN: Tours by arrangement. No retail sales.

GOVERD, Keith

The Bailiff's Cottage, The Green, Compton Dando, Avon.
☎ 01 761 490 624
Formerly the head of the technical department at the now-defunct Long Ashton Cider Research Centre near Bristol, Keith is now principally a consultant who set up, among other operations, the cidermaking at the Mason's Arms in Cumbria. He presses juice from a number of rare apple and pear varieties and also makes small quantities of a perry to die for.

GRAYS

Grays Farm Cider, Halstow, Tedbury St Mary, Exeter, Devon EX6 6AN.
☎ 01 647 61236
The Grays claim to be the oldest-established cidermaker in Devon, having been farming at Halstow for 300 years. They are also one of the largest, producing 17,000 gallons a year by completely natural means from locally-grown cider apples. Gray's is widely distributed throughout Devon in pubs and off-licences as well as at the farm gate.
CIDERS: Devon Cider (Dry, Medium, Sweet) 7%; Farm Cider

(Dry, Medium, Sweet) 7%
OPEN: Cider available from farm Mon-Sat 8-5pm.

GREAT OAK

Great Oak Cider & Apple Co, Roughmoor, Eardisley, Hereford
HR3 6PR.
☎ 01 544 327 400
Brian Jones has been producing cider at Roughmoor for over
15 years. He also presses fruit for other local makers using a
Norman travelling press. He doesn't sell his cider at the farm
gate, but it is available in a number of local outlets, and cider
from the house vat may be sampled by prior appointment.
CIDER: Great Oak Cider, abv varies

GREEN VALLEY

Green Valley Cyder, Marsh Barton Farm, Clyst St George,
Exeter, Devon EX3 0QH.
☎ 01 392 876 658
The founders of Green Valley were refugees from the long-
established Whiteway's of Whimple, closed down 10 years ago
by parent company Allied Breweries. As can be expected of
such experts, they produce a wide range of ciders in a wide
range of styles including premium table ciders in corked 75cl
bottles which invite comparison with wine. They also make the
occasional perry, bottle-conditioned cider, and country wine as
the mood takes them.
CIDERS: Devonshire Farmhouse Scrumpy Traditional (cloudy),
Dry, Medium, Sweet (filtered) 7%; Stillwood Vintage, Table
Cyder 8.3%
OPEN: 9-5.30 Mon-Fri; 10-5.30 Sat. Tours by arrangement.

GWATKIN

Moorhampton Farm, Abbey Dore, Herefordshire.
☎ 01 981 550 258
Previous generations of the Gwatkin family had made cider at
Moorhampton for many years, as had previous owners of the
farm before them, but the practice died out somewhere around
World War II and all the apples grown on the farm were sold
to Bulmers. Dennis decided to revive the tradition eight years
ago, keeping back some of the older apple varieties such as
Cherry Norman and, in particular, Kingston Black, for his own
efforts. He also makes perry using fruit from some of his own
old trees, some from his uncle Brian Browning of
Minsterworth, Gloucestershire, and a few capfuls from the 20
new trees he planted three years ago. Although Dennis stays
below the 1,500-gallon duty-exempt level, he has won prize
after prize and is CAMRA's current (1995-96) National
Champion Cidermaker of the Year – in fact, CAMRA beer

festivals are the best place to find his products. (His uncle Brian, incidentally, is also no mean cider and perry maker, producing some 500 gallons a year, mainly of perry.)
CIDERS: Cider, Perry 8%
OPEN: Farm gate sales at reasonable times.

HAMSTEAD CIDER

Hamstead Vineyard, Homemead, Hamstead Rd, Cranmore, Yarmouth, Isle of Wight PO41 0YB.
☎ 01 983 760 463
Proprietor Terry Munt has been making cider since 1984 and now produces about 1,000 gallons a year from an acre of cider apple trees, including Kingston Black, and some Bramleys. Sells in local shops and in the Buddle Inn, Niton.
CIDER: Strong Yarmouth, 6.5%

HANCOCK'S

Hancock's Devon Cider, Mill House, Clapworthy Mill, South Molton, Devon EX36 4HU.
☎ 01 769 572 678
Hancock's has developed considerably in recent years, extending its craft centre and starting unguided tours of the factory complete with video show. Underlying the new developments, though, are five generations of quality cidermaking. Ciders available on site are all bottled; draught is available for the pub trade.
CIDERS: Extra dry, dry, medium, sweet 6%; dry, medium 8%
OPEN: 9-5 Mon-Sat. Tours Easter-Sept.

HARTLAND

Hartland's Farmhouse Cider & Perry, Tirley Villa, Tirley, Glos GL19 4HA.
☎ 01 452 780 480
The Hartlands previously farmed at Flat Farm nearby, where the family had made cider and perry for generations. Commercial production, however, only started in 1980. Demand for their fine natural products – the perry is especially admired – gradually increased until output reached 5,000 gallons. Sadly the family's elder statesman, Ray Hartland, known as much for his irrepressible if morbid sense of humour as for his cider, died in 1996, but the family is carrying on with son Dereck at the helm. There is no formal shop or visitors' centre, but there is a "cider room" where customers can try before they buy in comparative comfort.
CIDERS: Sweet, Medium or Dry 6%; Perry 6%

When visiting producers, please telephone ahead.

HAYE FARM

Haye Farm Cider, Haye Farm, St Veep, Lostwithiel, Cornwall
☎ 01 208 872 250
Haye Farm is one of the largest of a cluster of small makers in
the area south of Lostwithiel, producing several thousand
gallons a year from a wide range of cider and culinary apples
including Russetts, James Grieve, Redstreak and many others
far less well known. Owner Colin Vincent supplies a number
of pubs in the area, but your best bet is the back door of the
farmhouse, whence Mrs Vincent dispenses two-litre flagons
stored in a handy fridge. The farm is signposted off the St Veep
road.
CIDER: Medium sweet, medium 7.4%
OPEN: There should be someone around during daylight
hours seven days a week. If in doubt, ring ahead.

HAYWARDS

Haywards Cider & Perry Co, Fferm Bryn Cul, Tregarth,
Gwynedd LL57 4AE.
☎ 01 286 880 195
The business was started by Patrick Hayward in Raglan,
Gwent, producing 450 gallons in 1993, winning the Best Cider
at the Cardiff Beer Festival in 1994, and moving to the opposite
end of the country in 1995. Now produces 1,200 gallons a year,
of which 150 gallons is perry.
CIDERS: Seidr Y Berllan 6%
OPEN: Callers welcome by appointment.

HECKS

W E Hecks & Son, 9-11 Middle Leigh, Street, Somerset BA16
0LB
☎ 01 458 442 367
The family has been making traditional cider since 1896 and
shows no sign of stopping, now producing 10,000 gallons a
year from traditional varieties. An occasional Kingston Black
single varietal is rich, deep, complex and very slightly sweet.
Heck's also produces the Torside range of fresh-pressed juices
and runs a general produce shop near the town centre.
CIDERS: Hecks Farmhouse Cider, Sweet, Medium or Dry 6%
OPEN: Mon-Sat 9am-6pm; Sun 10am-12.30pm. Tours by
arrangement.

HENRY'S

Henry's Farmhouse Scrumpy, Tanpits Cider Farm, Dyers Lane
Bathpool, Taunton, Somerset TA2 8BZ.
☎ 01 823 270 663
Small husband-and-wife business making cider by traditional
methods, started by the current Henry's grandfather in 1912.

The farm is rather cut off by new dual carriageways, and it's worth phoning ahead of a buying expedition in case Mr and Mrs Pring, the proprietors, are out.

CIDERS: Henry's Rocket Fuel 6.5%; Henry's Scrumpy 6.5%; Ploughman's Tipple 6.5%

OPEN: Tours by arrangement, Sep-Dec only.

HINDLIP

Hindlip Cider, Worcestershire College of Agriculture, Hindlip, Worcester WR3 8SS.

☎ 01 905 451 310/451 002

Hindlip has been producing cider for over 10 years in conjunction with cidermaking courses which are now internationally known and cover every aspect of the process from growing the fruit to marketing the cider. However commercial production only started three years ago, combining the most up-to-date techniques with the most time-honoured of traditions, as a useful means of subsidising the course and introducing the students to the hard-nosed end of the business. As is only to be expected, the ensuing ciders and perries have proved an award-winning hit. Hindlip also offers consultancy to commercial cidermakers. The college is now planning to plant a cider orchard of its own.

CIDERS: Hindlip Cider, Sweet, Medium or Dry 6-7%; Hindlip Sparking Cider 6-7%; Hindlip Premium Cider 8%; Hindlip Perry 6-7%; Hindlip Sparkling Perry 5-6%

OPEN: Mon-Fri 9am-5pm. Tours by arrangement.

HOGSHEAD

Hogshead Cyder, Park Fruit Farm, Great Holland, Frinton-on-Sea, Essex CO13 0ES.

☎ 01 255 674 621

Louise Elsworth decided to make her hobby into a business only last year, partly as a way of finding a valuable use for the "seconds" grown by her parents but rejected by the supermarket buyers for minor imperfections, partly because she is passionate about English apples. She ferments her cyder to complete dryness and recommends dilution with fresh-pressed apple juice as a sweetener for those who need it. The farm shop in which her 1,000-gallon output is sold also stocks 30 varieties of apples, plums, pears, raspberries and other produce.

CIDERS: Hogshead Cyder 7%

BOTTLED CIDERS: Hogshead Cyder 7%

OPEN: Aug-March, Mon-Sat 9am-5pm; Sun 10am-4pm (closed Sundays after Christmas). Tours by arrangement.

When visiting producers, please telephone ahead.

HOME HOUSE

Home House Cider, Home House, Combeinteignhead,
Newton Abbot, Devon TQ12 4RE

☎ 01 626 872 591

Orthopaedic surgeon David Halpin has been making cider,
using apples from his own orchards, since he brought a press
in the early 1980s. He and his wife now make about 500
gallons a year, and although summer visitors may enjoy calling
in to buy a few bottles, they're not there when the wassailing
takes place – and that really is something to see, involving the
whole village and an awful lot of cider.

CIDERS: Medium, dry strength according to the vintage
OPEN: all reasonable hours, ring ahead if in doubt.

HUNT

Sharewood Farm, Sedlescombe, East Sussex.

☎ 01 424 870 567

Fruit farmer Chris Hunt doesn't actually make his own cider,
but he does grow and select the apples and pears which he
sends to neighbouring Biddenden to be fermented, which is
the next best thing. He enjoys experimenting with different
blends: as well as "cookers and eaters". He grows cider apples
for Taunton, and some of them generally find their way into
the blend. He also grows Conference pears from which he
often has perry made: last year he made over 1,500 gallons of a
hybrid cider-perry using 50:50 bittersweet apples and
Conference pears, which made up half of his total output. Why
has he done it for over 20 years? Not, as many growers do, to
use up the "seconds", or fruit which is perfectly sound but is
not shapely enough for Safeway, but to create a product which
will add interest to his farm shop.

CIDERS: Various and interesting
OPEN: Tues-Sat 10-5.

HUNT'S

Hunt's Devon Cider, Higher Yalberton Farm, Collaton St Mary,
Paignton, Devon.

☎ 01 803 557 694

Not a stone's throw from Churchward's is Hunt's, established
in 1952 and now selling some 5,000 gallons a year. The cider is
completely natural and as traditional as it is possible to be: one
wonders whether those holidaymakers who regard cider like
this as rustic rocket-fuel deserve – given the limited supply – to
be allowed to buy any. Perhaps supplies should be limited to
alco-anthropologists who would treat it with the proper awe,
but then again, perhaps not.

CIDERS: Farm Cider 6%
OPEN: 9-6 winter, 9-8 summer.

INCH'S
See HP Bulmer

INDIAN HERBS (Europe Ltd)
Kingdown House, Priddy, Wells, Somerset BA5 3BR.
☎ 01 749 870 603

Local vet Graham Wheeler runs a bewildering variety of businesses from his former farm high on the Mendips: as well as his veterinary practice, he imports veterinary herbal remedies from India (hence the company's name), and makes cider from two endangered orchards in the valley below almost as a conservation measure, having promised to buy all the produce of the orchards concerned if the owners would go back on their decisions to grub them up. Output is variable: last year's dipped below 1,000 gallons because one of Graham's farmers was too ill to harvest his orchard. But the big Voran press at Kingsdown House could easily handle more than the 1,500 gallon duty-exempt limit, and as the house stands in an area of outstanding natural beauty where there is no shortage of thirsty walkers, Graham reckons he could sell all he could make.

CIDERS: Very dry, strength varies
OPEN: When you're passing.

JAMES WHITE
James White Apple Juice and Ciders, Whites Fruit Farm, Ashbocking, Ipswich, Suffolk IP6 9JS.
☎ 01 473 890 111

Founded in 1980, the company quickly gained a name for the quality of its strong draught ciders but could not find its financial feet and went through two changes of ownership before settling down under the proprietorship of Lawrence Mallinson – best-known as a co-founder of the New Covent Garden Soup Company – in 1989. Finding the pub trade hard to crack, Mallinson has concentrated on developing sales of bottled ciders and, in particular, single varietal apple juices. Nevertheless cider sales have continued to flourish, and the firm expanded into its present home in 1993. Since the closure of the long-established Gaymer's factory at Attleborough in Norfolk James White has become the largest producer in East Anglia, turning out over 25,000 gallons a year. Its delicate, aromatic, products are ideal table ciders.

CIDERS: Suffolk Cider (Strong Dry, Medium) 8.2%; Special Edition 6%; October Gold 6%
OPEN: Daily 9.30am-5.30pm (except some Bank Holidays). Tours by arrangement.

JOLLY DRY CIDER

Wilmington House, The Street, Wilmington, East Sussex.
☎ 01 323 871 054

An engineer who clearly takes his hobby seriously, John Marshall started making cider when he moved to Wilmington three years ago and sought a use for the crop from the orchards that came with the house. A keen home-brewer for many years, he realised that cider-making called for different skills and actually attended the cidermaking course at Hindlip College, Worcester. Now he makes around 300 gallons a year of a clear, dry cider he describes as a speciality product, made with a wine yeast, fermented in plastic, but aged in wood for a very strongly apple-y flavour. The cider is packed in bag-in-box to retain its freshness and is only available for retail sales at the English Farm Cider Centre at Firle near Lewes, although seekers of wholesale quantities may ring the number above.
CIDER: Dry 6%

KNIGHTS

Knights Cider Co Ltd, Crumpton Oaks Farm, Storridge, Malvern, Worcs WR13 5HP.
☎ 01 684 574 594

The Knights started planting cider orchards at their fruit farm in the shadow of the magnificent Malvern Hills in 1973 and have been unable to stop. Deeply concerned with the future of traditional cider fruit, they planted 52 acres in 1994 and '95 and plan another 75 acres next year. The ciders and a perry are traditionally made, then cold filtered. They have won a string of awards, and plans are in hand to bottle them. The farm also grows soft fruits for the PYO trade and makes an excellent base for many woodland walks.
CIDERS: Knights Dry, Medium or Sweet 6%
OPEN: Wed-Sat 10.30am-5pm.

LAKELAND

Lakeland Brewing Co, Masons Arms, Strawberry Bank, Cartmel Fell, Grange-over-Sands, Cumbria LA11 6NW.
☎ 01 539 568 686

Enterprising pub brewery which in 1992 decided to augment its own apples with cider apples brought in from the South-West to make its own cider. It now produces 1,000 gallons a year, sold only through the pub and occasionally at beer festivals. Like the pub's beers, the cider takes its name from the works of Arthur Ransome, who lived nearby: the knickerbockerbreaker was a fearsome slide which ripped children's trousers.
CIDERS: Knickerbockerbreaker 6%

LAMBOURN VALLEY CIDER

The Malt House, Great Shefford, Hungerford, Berks RG17 7ED.
☎ 01 488 648 441

Cider enthusiast Roy Bailey decided to register his operation after 15 years of home brewing and cidermaking using the fruit of a couple of Dabinette trees of his own but also scouring the highways and byways of Berkshire for odd varieties, crab apples and so on to make truly fascinating hedgerow ciders. Welford Wonder cider is made from an otherwise unidentified variety Roy found growing wild on a railway cutting. The ciders are fermented out to dryness, without added sugar, so their strength depends on the season. Production at present is small but will grow. Sales are wholesale only.
CIDERS: Royal County Dry, Lambourn Valley Gold 5%

LANE'S

Lane's Cider, Overton, West Monkton, Taunton, Somerset TA2 8LS.
☎ 01 823 412 345

Gary Lane started cidermaking when he was only 14 but started a commercial operation in 1983. Since then he has planted 20 acres of cider apples including Kingston Black and Morgan Sweet. Gary has been unable to get planning permission for a farm shop and so sells in wholesale quantities only (minimum 20 litres) at the farm gate between 5pm and 7pm on Fridays and 10am and noon on Saturdays and Sundays. However his products are widely distributed in the licensed trade throughout Somerset, Devon and Cornwall, and should become even more widely available now that packaged distribution has been taken up by ex-Taunton Cider man Roger Clark's Kingston Vale Cider Company.
CIDERS: Lane's Dry, Medium 6%
BOTTLED CIDERS: Kingston Vale medium, Golden Rutter dry, 6%

LOWER WHIDDON FARM

Lower Whiddon farm, Ashburton, Devon.
☎ 01 364 652 840

Gerry Vallance makes just 100 gallons of cider every year, using local apples, pressed on an ancient single-screw press, fermented by naturally-occurring yeasts, then matured in oak barrels.
CIDERS: Medium
OPEN: Telephone ahead please.

LUSCOMBE

Luscombe Cider, Luscombe Farm, Buckfastleigh, Devon.
☎ 01 548 550 256

Luscombe chugged along making less than the duty-exempt

1,500 gallons for many years before partners Julian David and Stephen Bradley decided to go for growth in 1988, planting 300 trees and expanding capacity tenfold. Today it makes around 15,000 gallons of cider a year, which it delivers directly to 200 accounts and distributes further afield through The Beer Seller wholesaler's Paignton depot. Its main product is a straightforward traditional still cider, but two major changes in the market persuaded the company that it needed to innovate to survive: the gradual demise of the old-style pint-swigging rustic reduced the speed at which pubs could get through the usual five-gallon polycask, resulting in spoiled cider and reduced orders; while the sale of several hundred Courage pubs in the region to Usher's, which still has a cider tie, closed off an important avenue for local sales. Luscombe's solution is Flowne's Nectar, a quasi keg cider. It's made with fresh-pressed juice and naturally-occurring yeast, coarse-filtered and unpasteurised, but served (through a keg tap, not a fake handpump) under low-volume CO_2 or mixed gas so that little or no extraneous gas is dissolved into the cider. Its advantages are that it will keep longer than the old-style polycask, it will travel further without being damaged, and landlords who want an authentic cider but don't want their bars cluttered up with polycasks can stock it in their cellars. But is Flowne's Nectar an acceptable hybrid? Or is it keg pure and simple, and anathema to all purists? Luscombe contends that it's an acceptable hybrid, and far preferable to Olde English or Strongbow or Dry Blackthorn. Readers will have to make up their own minds.

CIDERS: Farmhouse, 6-6.5%

OPEN: Tours by arrangement.

LYME BAY

Lyme Bay Cider Co Ltd, Manor Farm, Seaton, Devon EX12 2TF.

☎ 01 297 22887

Founded only in 1993, this extraordinarily energetic company is already producing 25,000 gallons a year, has a very lively retail trade both in its local area and, increasingly, further afield, and has big plans to grow further still. The next steps are likely to be planting its own orchards and setting up a mail-order business. The ciders themselves range from traditionally cloudy to filtered bright and are named after a notorious Dorset smuggler, Jack Rattenbury.

CIDERS: Jack Ratt Traditional (Dry, Medium, Sweet) 6%; Jack Ratt Vintage (Dry, Medium) 8%

BOTTLED CIDERS: Jack Ratt Traditional Filtered (Dry, Medium Sweet) 6%; Jack Ratt Vintage Filtered (Dry, Medium Sweet) 8%; Lyme Bay Cider Filtered 6%; Lyme Light Filtered 4.5%

OPEN: Summer 10am-6pm (Sun 12-6pm); Winter 10am-4.30pm (closed Sun). Tours by arrangement.

LYNE DOWN

Lyne Down Cider, Lyne Down Farm, Much Marcle, Ledbury, Herefordshire, HR8 2NT.

☎ 01 531 660 691

Get to Jean Nowell's farm early in the season – she only makes 1,500 gallons of her award-winning cider and perry, and it tends to go fast! Jean and her late husband Terry revived the tradition of cidermaking at Lyne Down in 1984. Mrs Nowell has no immediate plans to expand beyond the duty-exempt limit and is beginning to weight her output more and towards perry, although an occasional Kingston Black single varietal dubbed Mother's Special is another favourite with her many fans.

CIDERS: Cider 7%; Perry 7%; Mother's Special 8.5%.

OPEN: Phone ahead to check please. Tours by arrangement.

MATCHING

The Old Barn, Hay Green, Matching, Essex.

☎ 01 378 520 363

Steve deLarre started making cider commercially in 1992 and now produces 800 gallons a year for sale through a handful of local pubs and the cider bars of CAMRA beer festivals. Old Moulder is a still, clear cider made, as local tradition dictates, from eating apples – in this case the time-honoured duo of Cox and Bramley aromatised with locally-grown Russets. Molly Dancer – the local name for a morris man – has a 10% admixture of cider apples imported from the West Country for their tannin content. The farm has no shop, and sadly visits and tours are impossible for Steve to fit in, so orders must remain wholesale only at least for the time being.

CIDERS: Old Moulder, Molly Dancer

MATTHEW CLARK TAUNTON

Matthew Clark Taunton Ltd, Whitchurch Lane, Bristol BS12 0JZ.

☎ 01 275 836 100

The very existence of Matthew Clark Taunton is evidence of much of what is wrong with the cider industry. In the late 1980s there were three cider companies that mattered, in terms of size. Bulmers, the largest, was and is independent. Taunton, founded in the 1920s, was the second largest and was owned by a consortium of brewers including Bass and Courage. Coates-Gaymer, the third largest, was wholly owned by Allied Breweries, having been created in the merger-mad 1950s and '60s by a series of takeovers involving Coates of Nailsea,

Showerings of Shepton Mallet (the Babycham company), Gaymer's of Attleborough in Norfolk, Whiteway's of Whimple, Devon, and other smaller firms such as Vine Products and Goldwell. When the Monopolies & Mergers Commission abolished the cider tie in national brewery tenanted estates, both Taunton and Coates-Gaymer were sold to their respective managements. But despite their size and prominence, neither could stand on its own two feet. Coates-Gaymer quickly lost its way and started losing market share, and was soon gobbled up by the highly-acquisitive Matthew Clark group. Worn out by the ceaseless high-intensity struggle to develop, market and advertise new brands, Taunton followed not long after – but even though the newly-formed supergroup had over 40 per cent of the market, there was no hint that the acquisition would be referred to the MMC, and the resulting duopoly was further reinforced when, earlier this year, Bulmers bought the next-largest contender, Inch's. Matthew Clark and Bulmers now control 93% of the total cider market between them; and 90 per cent of what they produce is, frankly, rubbish. What traditional ciders they do churn out are not a patch on the quality products of the better independent firms such as Franklin's, Gray's, Burrow Hill and others. In the case of the Gaymer Group the "real" ciders are Taunton Traditional, a still, slightly hazy, golden cider of medium strength, and Addlestone's, first of the new-generation real ciders, most of which is now sadly served under a heavy CO_2 blanket (although canny cellarmen, especially in Scotland, have found how to vent the sealed casks and serve the cider by unaided handpump).
CIDERS: Taunton Traditional 5.2%; Addlestone's 5%

MAYFIELD

Mayfield Cider, Pennybridge Farm, Mayfield, E Sussex TN20 6QB.
☎ 01 453 873 873
Martin Clarke has been turning out around 1,000 gallons a year for over 20 years, using an ancient stone mill and a double-screw press. Like an increasing number of Eastern makers, he is using a proportion of proper cider apples to give a tannic bite to the blend of culinary and dessert apples traditional in the region. Most of the output is sold in local pubs and farm shops, but it is available at the farm gate in quantities from five litres to five gallons.
CIDERS: Mayfield Draught Still Cider 6-8%

When visiting producers, please telephone ahead.

MEON VALLEY VINEYARDS

Meon Valley Vineyards, Swanmore, Southampton, Hants.
☎ 01 489 877 435

Christopher Hartley is one of many English winemakers who has started making small quantities of cider to get a little extra value out of the vineyard's equipment. In Christopher's case, though, there is a sentimental angle too: his parents were well-known cidermakers in the area many years ago, he grew up making cider, and after his parents retired long-standing customers asked when he was going to pick up the torch. He has actually planted a proper cider orchard on his 25-acre vineyard and makes a few hundred gallons each year for sale at the farm gate and at local agricultural shows.

CIDER: Medium, dry 8%
OPEN: 11-4 Mon-Sat.

MILLHOUSE

Millhouse Cider, Millhouse Nurseries, Owermoigne,
Dorchester, Dorset DT2 8HZ.
☎ 01 305 852 220

Given that it also houses a fine collection of long-case and other clocks, Millhouse is a literal time-capsule. Its collection of antique cidermaking equipment is surely unsurpassed, even though it was started less than 30 years ago. Thousands of gallons of absolutely authentic cider are now made at Millhouse from local apples milled and pressed on restored equipment of great age and matured in the traditional oak. Thomas Hardy's cottage is nearby, and Owermoigne figures in his Wessex landscape as Nethermoynton. And if Millhouse's cider and literary associations are not enough of an attraction, it is also still the nursery it was before owner Dennis Whatmoor started collecting all those years ago, with 300 varieties of fuschia alone.

CIDERS: Dry, medium, sweet 6%
OPEN: 9-5 year-round.

MINCHEW

Minchews Real Cyder & Perry, Rose Cottage, Aston Cross,
Bredon Rd, Tewkesbury, Glos.
☎ 01 684 773 427

Kevin Minchew started cidermaking after the nearest traditional ciderhouse, or pub which made its own cider, closed in 1984. He felt someone had to carry the torch, and was especially keen that the long tradition of perry making should not die out. As the years as have gone by, he has been increasingly concerned with saving near-extinct local varieties of cider apple and perry pear, touring the county at blossom time, grafting knife at the ready, and transplanting specimens from hedgerows, railway cuttings, back gardens, derelict orchards and wherever else he finds them to the safety of friends' and relatives' gardens. He has only been making cider and perry on a commercial scale since 1993, but his hard-won expertise and scholarly enthusiasm have won golden opinions. Sales, sadly, are wholesale only.

CIDERS: An ever-changing range of single varietal and blended ciders and perries ranging from 7.2% to 8.2%

NADDER VALLEY
Trafalgar Estate, Downton, Wiltshire.
☎ 01 722 503 504

Love of good cider and dissatisfaction with what was available persuaded 35-year-old single mother of three Philippa Sprott to launch her own micro cider-making operation last year.

"So much of the mass market cider tastes as if it hasn't seen a proper cider apple. I wanted to make cider noted for a real apple taste," she says. "And so much cider is so strong. I want to make cider at a strength that won't have people falling over after a few pints."

Philippa has always been a keen cider drinker. A job at Salisbury's Hop Back Brewery, where she saw at first hand how great oaks could indeed from little acorns grow, persuaded her to start making her own. Premises were found at an ex-dairy on Lord Radnor's Trafalgar Estate near Downton, while equipment was gathered from a variety of sources like an ex-winery in Wiltshire. Blackenadder is an unfiltered natural cider made from 60 per cent bittersweets and 40 per cent dessert apples. Fermentation starts with the natural yeast, takes at least three months, and includes a late pitching with wine yeast.

CIDERS: Blackenadder 6%

NAISH
Naish's Cider, Piltown Farm, West Pennard, Glastonbury, Somerset.
☎ 01 749 890 260

Not much has changed at Naish's over the years, except that the Naish brothers are a few years older and now only own seven orchards instead of nine. Naish's is an excellent surviving example of the kind of cidermaking operation once common in the Glastonbury area, and although they make less cider than they did, a visit is still recommended.

CIDER: Absolutely dry, strength varies according to season
OPEN: Ring ahead.

NEW FOREST
New Forest Cider, Littlemead, Pound Lane, Burley, Ringwood, Hants BH24 4ED.
☎ 01 425 403 589

The Töpp family started cidermaking on their smallholding seven years ago, and have built up the business to production of 20,000 gallons a year. You can arrange to visit the farm during pressing time in the autumn, and even lend a hand if so inclined. There may be farm animals around for the children to see. The next venture for New Forest Cider is to start making cider brandy on a Normandy Calvados still.
CIDERS: New Forest Traditional Farmhouse Cider 6%
BOTTLED CIDERS: Snakecatcher Scrumpy 7%; Kingston Black Vintage Dry 8%
OPEN: Daily, Winter 10am-6pm, Summer 10am-8pm.

NORBURY

Norbury's Black Bull Cider Co, The Farm Buildings, Holywell, Storridge, Malvern, Worcs WR13 5HD.
☎ 01 886 832 206
Tom Norbury started his cidermaking in 1979 to use up surplus fruit, but the business is now flourishing to the extent that new premises will be needed by the year 2000. The award-winning cider and perry are made on the farm by hand, with no artificial additives.
CIDERS: Black Bull, Medium dry, Sweet 7%; Black Bull Scrumpy 7%; Black Bull Medium Dry Perry 8%
OPEN: Wed-Fri 2-5pm; Sat-Sun 10am-5.30pm during PYO season; also available all year from Montandon's Farm Shop, Crowcroft.

NORFOLK CIDER

Norfolk Cider Company, 2 St Andrews Close, Old Buckenham, Norfolk NR17 1RZ.
☎ 01 953 860 533
Established in 1986, Norfolk Cider is the oldest maker in Norfolk since the Gaymer's factory was closed last year. It has won Best Cider at the Norfolk CAMRA Festival for three years, and has been runner up at the Great British Beer Festival. The product is sold in around 70 pubs in Norfolk and North Suffolk. Proprietor Stephen Fisher also travels East Anglia giving demonstrations of traditional apple milling and pressing on genuine nineteenth-century Norfolk machinery. Lectures on traditional cider making can be arranged on request.
CIDERS: Kingfisher Farm Cider (Medium, Dry) 7.5%
BOTTLED CIDERS: Kingfisher Farm Cider (Medium, Dry) 7.5%
OPEN: Tue-Sun 10am-5pm and Bank Holiday Mondays at The Apple Shop, Alby Craft Centre, Cromer Road, Erpingham. ☎ 01 263 761 702. Tours by arrangement.

When visiting producers, please telephone ahead.

OLD COVE

Wrentham, Suffolk.

☎ 01 502 675 692

If you've had any of Dick Ashton's Old Cove cider lately, you're luckier than most: the 250 gallons made in 1994 acetified in last year's heatwave, and Dick was unable to make any last year because of illness – all rather unfortunate, as the last good batch had been named Cider of the Festival at CAMRA's Ipswich Beer Festival not long before. But Dick, a teacher by trade, regards it as only a temporary setback and is making another batch this year in his own peculiar way: he lets culinary apple juice ferment up to 12.5% alcohol, maturing it for a year in oak before transferring it to stainless steel and cutting it down to legal strength with fresh-pressed apple-juice as it is sold. Old Cove is not open to the public: the cider is occasionally available at a couple of local pubs and at CAMRA beer festivals.

CIDER: Old Cove 8.2%

OWEN, Ralph

Old Badland Farm, Kinnerton, Powys.

☎ 01 544 350 304

For 10 years, Ralph was Anglesey's only cider producer when, as farm manager on the late Bertram Bulmer's estate, he supplemented his pay by brewing up a few hundred gallons for local consumption, importing cider apples from Herefordshire. Ten years ago he moved to Powys to farm on his own account, and promptly discovered that there were quite a few old cider orchards whose crops were rotting where they fell. Adding their harvests to the fruit from his own small orchards, he started up again and now makes up to 700 gallons of all-natural, all-organic cider a year. The produce is mainly available in a couple of local pubs, but Ralph has plans to buy a more modern press, expand production, and develop a proper traditional cider-cellar where customers will be able to sample sociably from the various barrels before deciding what to buy.

CIDERS: Farm cider 8.5%

OPEN: No farm gate retail sales at present.

OWLET

Owlet Cider, Owl House Fruit Farm, Mount Pleasant, Lamberhurst, Kent TN3 8LY.

☎ 01 892 890 553

Former Bulmers and Burrow Hill cidermaker Colin Corfield has scaled down his cider operation of late to concentrate on his fresh-pressed juice business, but he is still making several hundred gallons of eastern cider, having discontinued his previous habit of buying in West Country bittersweets to add to the blend. His clear, pale, clean cider is only available on draught, so prospective buyers should bring their own containers with them.

CIDERS: Dry, medium 7%
OPEN: Telephone ahead.

PALMERSHAYES

Palmershayes Cider, Palmershayes, Calverleigh, Tiverton, Devon EX16 8BA.
☎ 01 884 254 579/252 900

Cider has been made on the farm, which has four acres of its own orchards, since 1905 and in recent years its reputation has spread as satisfied holidaymakers have told their friends and neighbours of its strong and full-bodied product.

OPEN: Reasonable times, but ring ahead.

PARADISE

Paradise Cider, Cherry Tree Farm, Ilketshall St Lawrence, Beccles, Suffolk NR34 8LB.
☎ 01 986 781 353

This is a small family firm which has been producing single varietal apple juices and traditional cider since 1980. The local Suffolk apples are pressed on antique presses and grinding mills, and are fermented and matured in seasoned oak barrels. Visitors can see the presses in action between September and December, and the proprietors will be happy to give explanations of the procedure. On A144 between Bungay and Halesworth.

CIDERS: Extra Dry, Dry, Medium, Sweet, 5.5%
BOTTLED CIDERS: Extra Dry, Dry, Medium, Sweet, 5.5%
OPEN: 9-1, 2-6, 7 days a week, all year. Tours are available by arrangement for up to 20 people.

PARSONS CHOICE

P J Dolding, Parsonage Farm, West Lyng, Taunton, Somerset TA3 5AP.
☎ 01 823 490 978

Parsons Choice has been trading for six years. The cider is made without additives from a blend of cider apples including Bulmers Norman, Crimson King, Hangmedown and Kingston Black grown in orchards on the edges of the Somerset Levels, and the Doldings will supply a honey-based syrup to sweeten it if it is too dry for the untrained palate. The farm is also a centre of falconry and the Doldings even keep owls.

CIDERS: Parsons Choice 7-8%
OPEN: Mon-Sat 8am-8pm; Sun 12-3pm. Tours by arrangement.

PAWLEY

Pawley Farm Cider, Pawley Farm, Painters Forstal, Faversham, Kent ME13 0EN.

☎ 01 795 532 043

Pawley Farm cider is made to a 250-year-old family recipe using mainly Bramleys, with a few Coxes added for sweetness, all grown on the 50-acre farm. The apples are harvested twice a year, and the cider is brewed in the traditional oak casks. The cider is often used as a table wine, and they also produce a new naturally effervescent variety. The farm is situated in the picturesque village of Painters Forstal, two miles from Faversham in the North Downs.

CIDERS: Pawley Farm Cider (Dry, Medium, Sweet) 7.5%
OPEN: Daily dawn till dusk. Tours by arrangement.

PENPOL

Penpol Cider, Middle Penpol Farm, St Veep, Lostwithiel, Cornwall.

☎ 01 208 872 017

Cider is made here, as it has been for generations, as a sideline to the main business of running the farm. It's not far from Hayes Farm, another very traditional cidermaker, so you might take advantage of a fine summer's day and visit both.

CIDERS: Farm cider 7.5%
OPEN: 9-9 in summer, but closed Sunday afternoons.

PERRY'S

Perry's Cider Mills, Dowlish Wake, Ilminster, Somerset TA19 0NY.

☎ 01 460 52681

Perry Brothers has been established in picturesque Dowlish wake for almost a century and boasts a fine collection of antique cidermaking equipment and farm waggons and implements as well as its shop and, of course, its cidery. Marguerite Perry is a widow now, but has put into action her late husband's dream of creating a single varietal cider from the Somerset Redstreak apple – and a fine cider it is too, spicy and pungent. The output is all entirely natural.

CIDERS: Farmhouse, Vintage, Somerset Redstreak 6.5%
OPEN: 9-1, 1.30-5.30 weekdays; 9.30-1, 1.30-4.30 sat; 12-1 Sun.

PIPKIN

Pipkin Cider, 1 Swinton Terrace, Masham, North Yorkshire HG4 4HS.

☎ 01 423 866 876 (answerphone) or 01 765 689 102

A very small 'cottage industry' set up by two local CAMRA members, Pipkin started selling cider in December 1995. Its aim is to encourage people to appreciate a new taste in a non

cider-producing area, and they now have six local outlets, and supply to local beer festivals. The partners have so far been using Kentish apples, but hope to try fermenting Yorkshire apples from an organic orchard in the near future.
CIDERS: Medium dry 6-6.5%, Hardcore 7%

PIPPIN

Pippin Cider, Badgers Hill Farm, Newcut Road, Chilham, near Canterbury, Kent CT4 8BW.
☎ 01 227 730 573
Claire Raraty-Squires and Bruce de Courcy have been making and selling natural ciders on this fruit farm since 1985. They are also oak-barrel merchants, and the bar of their cidery is made of old examples of their stock-in-trade. Badgers Hill Farm aims at a "Darling Buds of May" version of the good life with antiques and bygones liberally scattered about and home-made pickles, mustards, cakes etc very much in evidence. Free tastings are available of the juices and ciders – Pippin is mainly Cox and Pilgrim mainly Bramley – while during the four weeks of cider-making, juice is available in bulk for home cider-makers to take away.
Chilham railway station is five minutes' walk away.
CIDERS: Pippin 8.5%; Pilgrims (Kneebender) 8%
BOTTLED CIDERS: Pippin 8.5%; Pilgrims (Kneebender) 8%
OPEN: (shop & cidery) 10am-5pm daily; closed Christmas Eve to end Feb.

PIPPINFIELD

Pippinfield Cider, Pippinfield, Harepath Hill, Seaton, Devon, EX12 2TA.
☎ 01 297 20597
Long-standing owner Dennis Hunt had been making cider and country wine since before the War until he finally retired, using an old twin-screw press he found in a hedge-bottom. The business has now been sold to East Anglian expatriate Barrie Spanton. Mr Spanton, who has run hotels in the area for over 10 years, says he plans to make no changes but is running it below the duty-exempt level of 1,500 gallons a year.

PIPPINS

Pippins Cider, Pippins Farm, Stonecourt Lane, Pembury, Tunbridge Wells, Kent TN2 4AB.
☎ 01 892 824 544/624
Established in 1984, Pippins currently produces 1500 gallons a year from a former oast-house. As is the tradition in the region, the cider is made mainly from Coxes and Bramleys to produce a crisp, clean, wine-like cider. The cider is sold on the farm from June to December, and through local outlets.

CIDERS: Vintage Kent Cider
OPEN: 9-6 daily.

POOK HILL

Pook Hill Cider Company, Lower Tilton Farm, West Firle,
Lewes, East Sussex BN8 6LJ.
☎ 01 323 811 208.
The company was founded in 1992 by Ian and Helen Marsh,
who are also managers of the English Farm Cider Centre at
Middle Farm, just up the road. They set out with the intention
of bettering some of the ciders in the EFCC's range – initially,
they candidly admit, they were proved wrong, but they're
improving with experience!
CIDERS: Goodfellow (made with cider apples), True Leveller
(made with cookers and eaters), perry (based on Conference
pears with some Bramley juice), and strong cider. Alcohol will
vary from vintage to vintage.

PORTHALLOW VINEYARDS

Porthallow, Cornwall
☎ 01 326 280 050
Hertfordshire mining engineer Ted Jeffries arrived in
Porthallow nine years ago planning to make wine but just in
time to stop the local tradition of cidermaking from dying out
completely. Most local farms had small orchards, but none
were still using the fruit – so Ted did. Now he makes wine and
cider in equal volumes, both of them available in his shop.
CIDERS: Dry, medium dry, medium sweet, Vintage 7%
OPEN: 11-1, 2-6 Mon-Sat Easter-October.

REDDAWAY

Reddaway's Farm Cider, Lower Rixdale, Luton, Ideford,
Newton Abbot, Devon.
☎ 01 626 775 218
Cidermaking here is part of the traditional agricultural mix –
very traditional, in fact, as one of the barrels on the farm is
reckoned to be two centuries old. However the practice had
died out in John Reddaway's father's time, and was only
revived in the 1970s. By this time some of the old cider apple
trees were well past their prime, and a fair amount of grubbing
up and replanting was necessary. Perhaps that is one reason
why Reddaway's, uncharacteristically for the region, uses a
proportion of eating-apples in its cider; but this departure from
custom seems to have done no harm as the cider has won
many awards.
CIDERS: Medium, dry
OPEN: All day Mon-Sat.

REEDCUTTER

Ranworth Farms Ltd, The Old House, Ranworth Broad,
Norwich NR13 6HS.
☎ 01 603 270 722
Cidermaking is, as tradition dictates in this region, mainly a
by-product of commercial fruit growing. The apples used are
Spartans, Coxes, Crispins and James Grieve which combine to
produce a dry cider distributed only locally.
CIDERS: Reedcutter 6%
BOTTLED CIDERS: Reedcutter 6%

REED'S

Reed's Cider, Broadhayes Sawmills, Stockland, Honiton,
Devon.
☎ 01 404 831 456
Timber-merchant Bill Reed has been making cider the natural
way for nigh on 40 years, fermenting his mix of cider apples
with their natural yeasts and maturing the resulting brew – as
was traditional in the West Country until Harold Wilson
stopped the navy's rum ration – in surplus rum casks. These
days Bill is buying in a lot of apples from friends of his who
have stopped making cider but have not been succeeded by
the next generation. One tradition which has not died out is his
custom of holding court at the sawmill every Sunday morning,
when those who wish to buy are welcome to do so (but bring
your own container).
CIDERS: As Nature intends
OPEN: Sunday morning.

RICH'S

Rich's Farmhouse Cider, Mill Farm, Watchfield, Highbridge,
Somerset TA98 4RD.
☎ 01 278 783 651
Gordon Rich has been a leading cidermaker in the area for
more than 40 years, producing up to 200,000 gallons a year of
entirely organic cider without additives. The 10,000-gallon oak
maturing vats are a sight to see, but you don't have to go all
the way to Watchfield to taste the drink they produce: Rich's is
one of the country's most widely-distributed natural ciders.
CIDERS: Rich's Farmhouse (Dry, Medium, Sweet) 6%
OPEN: Daily 9am-7pm. Tours by arrangement.

RICHARD'S

Office: Richards Cider, 6 Park Road, Congresbury, Bristol.
Shop: The Corner Cottage, Smallway, Congresbury, Bristol
BS19 5HN.
☎ 01 934 833 158
Richards is a small family business which has been going for

three generations. As well as running its own off-licence, the firm supplies pubs, off-licences and tourist attractions over a wide area.

CIDERS: Richard's Traditional Draught (Dry, Medium, Sweet) 6%; Richard's Draught Perry (Medium, Dry) 7%

BOTTLED CIDERS: Richard's Somerset Gold (Dry, Medium) 6%; Richard's Somerset Sunset (Medium, Sweet) 6%; Richard's Apple Wine 8.4%

OPEN: Mon-Sat 9am-6pm; Sun 10am-1.30pm.

RIDDLE

M J Riddle, Oak Farm, Oldbury Lane, Thornbury, Bristol BS12 1RD.

☎ 01 454 413 263

Cider has been made here time out of mind as a normal part of mixed farming in the Severn Valley, and has only recently been discovered by wholesalers with more than a local distribution. The cider is entirely natural and is matured in oak barrels to be served into customers' own (clean) containers. It's slightly unusual for the region in that a proportion of Bramley apples go into the blend, as does a small quantity of perry pear juice. The result is golden, hazy, and very dry. The proprietor usually has time to talk cider with fellow-enthusiasts – but then, cider has that effect.

CIDERS: Traditional Farmhouse 6%

OPEN: Daylight hours – but ring ahead if unsure.

ROSEMARY CIDER

Rosemary Vineyard, Rosemary Lane, Ashey, Ryde, Isle of Wight PO33 2UX.

☎ 01 983 811 084

Conrad Gauntlet has just over an acre of cider apples and four acres of various cookers and eaters, from which he produces a blended cider and fresh-pressed juice. He started cidermaking in 1991 and now turns out around 1,300 gallons, some of it coarse-filtered and sulphited before bottling, some it naturally carbonated by the Méthode Champenoise. A draught version is being considered.

BOTTLED CIDERS: Rosemary 6.5%; Méthode Champenoise 8.5%

ROYAL OAK

Royal Oak Hotel, The Southend, Ledbury, Herefordshire HR8 2EY.

☎ 01 531 632 110

Pub owner Andrew Riga is a true revivalist. Shortly after taking over this venerable fifteenth-century pub in one of Herefordshire's most picturesque towns, he found that there had been brewing on the premises until the 1920s. Now there is brewing on the premises again, and cidermaking is due to start this year too. However, committed to choice as he is, Andrew says he will still stock traditional ciders and perries from Weston's and Hartlands alongside his own.

SAUL'S

Saul's Farmhouse Cider, Saul's Farm, Wembworthy, near Chulmleigh, Devon EX18 7RW.

☎ 01 769 580 750

Research scientist Nigel Kemp never planned to make cider when he arrived from London nearly a decade ago, but when he found that his two acres of vines were sitting in a frost-hollow which made bumper harvests something of a rarity, he took a closer look at the 60 cider apple trees that came with the property – and promptly planted another 60. This happy decision came just as Inch's announced that it would no longer buy in small lots of cider apples, which meant that Dr Kemp had the pick of the crop from around 20 little old orchards on surrounding farms to choose from. He does have some wine made from his grapes, and he runs a few sheep too, but his main business today is fresh-pressed apple juice and natural farm cider, which won the O'Hagan cup at the Devon County Show in 1993.

CIDERS: Dry, medium dry, medium sweet, bottle-conditioned 6.5%

OPEN: Mon-Sat 10am-5pm, Sun 12-3pm.

SEDLESCOMBE VINEYARD CIDER

Robertsbridge, E Sussex TN32 5SA.

☎ 01 580 830 715

As is traditional in the region, Roy Cook makes his cider from a blend of culinary and dessert apples, fermented slowly with its natural yeast and usually not bottled until July, having started working the previous September. What is unusual is that most of his apples come from orchards on Southern Water land, which are strictly organic to prevent run-off from polluting the neighbouring reservoirs. He has first refusal on all seconds from the orchards, and Southern water has promised that if it ever sells the land, it will be with a covenant giving him continued first refusal. Roy has been at Sedlescombe since 1979 and went into cidermaking because for the first few years while the vines were being established he could not make enough wine to get by. As well as cider, he makes an apple wine using a higher proportion of the more acidic culinary varieties and a wine yeast. The site boasts 15 acres of vineyards and a nature trail with picnic areas.

CIDERS: Medium dry, apple wine 8%

OPEN: 10-6 seven days Easter-Christmas.

SEPHAM FARM

Sepham Farm, Tilston Lane, Shoreham, Sevenoaks, Kent TN14 5JT.

☎ 01 959 522 774/523 626

One of many fruit-growers who have branched out into cider-making is Nick Chard of Sepham Farm at Sevenoaks, Kent, whose products are natural right down to the yeast. "Our main business is apples, pears and soft fruit," he says. "We were pressing juices when some started to ferment, and rather than chuck it we decided to see if it was potable. It was, so we had the yeast checked and it's a good, clean yeast. It adds to our income and uses the lower-grade fruit, and most of the work is in autumn and winter when things are quiet."

CIDER: Medium Dry Clear Still Cider 7.5%

BOTTLED CIDER: Medium Dry Clear Still Cider 7.5%

OPEN: Tues-Sun Sept-May; ring ahead.

SHAWSGATE CIDER

Shawsgate Vineyard, Bodingham Rd, Framlingham, Suffolk

☎ 01 728 724 060

Rob Hemphill takes his cidermaking seriously, having studied oenology in Germany. Shawsgate is, at 25 years old, one of the country's better-established vineyards. Rob has been running it for 12 of those years, and the idea of branching out into apples came from his German mentor, who pointed out that apple-based dessert wines were gaining in popularity in Germany. The year that Rob lost an entire vintage of grapes, he decided to take up the suggestion. That was nine years ago, and Rob has never looked back. He uses wine technology, milling his Coxes and Bramleys with the wine augur and berry-mill, pressing the pomace on a wine-press, and using two modified champagne yeasts. He gets less juice out of his fruit than cidermakers using more brutal equipment, but reckons he gains in quality. He also gets more use out of his bottling-line this way, as all his apple products – 6,000 bottles of cider a year and the same amount of dessert wine every two or three years – are bottled and corked.

BOTTLED CIDERS: Cider 7.5%; Dessert wine 12%

OPEN: 10.30-5 seven days.

SHEPPY'S

R J Sheppy & Son, Three Bridges, Bradford-on-Tone, Taunton, Somerset TA4 1ER.

☎ 01 823 461 233

Well-established and well-distributed traditional maker with its own orchards. Museum of cidermaking and rural life is an up-to-date and very well-patronised tourist stop-off on the outskirts of Taunton. Sheppy's ciders, like Weston's in Herefordshire, are the ideal crossover for inquisitive drinkers who have tried the keg product and want to sample the real thing.

CIDERS: Draught Cider 6%; Bullfinch (Medium) 7%; Goldfinch (Dry) 7%; Gold Medal (Sweet, Medium, Dry) 8%; Oakwood Draught (Medium, Dry) 6.5%; Oakwood Special (Medium Dry) 6.5%

OPEN: (shop & museum) Mon-Sat 8.30am-6pm. Tours by arrangement.

SNELL'S

Snell's Farm Cider, Styles Barton Farm, Whitestone, Exeter, Devon.

☎ 01 392 81280

The Snell family have made cider for over 40 years, but as was once almost universal in the region cidermaking is only one aspect of a mixed farm which also runs beef cattle and sheep and grows cereals. What is remarkable is that this traditional farm is a mere three miles from Exeter city centre.

CIDER: Sweet, Medium or Dry 5%

OPEN: Usually – but ring ahead, as this is a working farm.

STANCOMBE

Stancombe Cider, Stancombe Farm, Sherford, Kingsbridge, Devon TQ7 2BE.

☎ 01 548 531 634

This is as traditional as it gets. The cider is produced in a genuine seventeenth-century cider barn on a twin-screw press of uncertain age and is fermented and conditioned in oak. The alcoholic strength is determined by the season's growing conditions: it has been known to hit 12 per cent alcohol by volume. The proprietors conduct this journey into the past with modern presentational skills including a specially-commissioned video.

CIDERS: Traditional varieties, different each year, 7-12%

OPEN: Daily 9am-5pm. Tours by arrangement.

STEAMING BILLY CIDER

Fleckley, Leicestershire.

At time of going to press this project of Derbyshire brewer Bill Allingham's was well-advanced, and the first batch of juice should start bubbling any day now. Bill, who owns the Leatherbritches Brewery at Ashbourne, decided to start cidermaking in the cold storage unit he owns at Fleckney to provide house cider for his two pubs and extra product to sell into the free trade. He has built his own press and is buying in cider apples from Herefordshire, but plans to stay below the 1,500-gallon duty-exempt limit.

STOTT'S

Stott's Superb Cider, Shotts Farm, Wookey, Wells, Somerset.
☎ 01 749 674 731/673 323

Shott's Farm – no, it's not a misprint – is mainly in the dairy business, but like many others in the strange and enchanted Somerset Levels it has not forgotten the tradition of cidermaking. Mr Stott uses both his own apples and crops from farms where the custom of cidermaking has died out but where the apple trees are still bearing to make around 1,500 gallons of strong, full-bodied, orange-coloured cider a year.

CIDERS; Sweet, medium, dry

OPEN: Ring ahead (and don't forget to ask for directions).

SUMMER'S

Summers Perry and Cider, Slimbridge Lane, Halmore, Berkeley, Glos GL13 9HH.
☎ 01 453 811 218

Established in 1982, Summer's has lately started specialising in the production of single-varietal perries. Rodney Summers also does a mix – a "pider" – which you can watch being drawn from the oak barrels and blended. However only small amounts are produced, so take an Easter break to be sure of supplies. The product is entirely organic, the orchards being manured from above by the many migrant birds passing overhead to and fro the nearby Slimbridge Wildfowl Trust.

CIDERS: (Medium, Dry) 5-6.5%; Perry (Medium, Dry) 5-7.5%

OPEN: Mon-Sat 9am-1pm, 2pm-6pm.

SYMONS

Symons Farm Cider, Borough Farm, Holbeton, Plymouth, Devon PL8 1JJ
☎ 01 752 830 247

Tenant farmer John Walters-Symonds uses apples from his own and other farms on the Fleet estate to make his 1,500 gallons of cider a year, and has also joined the growing number of cidermakers involved in the lucrative fresh-pressed juice market. He has been making cider for 10 years and is now well-established in the area, but your best bet for finding his cider is to try either of Holbeton's pubs, the Mildmay Colours and the Dartmoor Union, as he sells very little from the farm gate.

CIDERS: Medium, dry 6%

OPEN: Real enthusiasts find the place, but if you must visit do ring ahead.

TAUNTON

See Matthew Clark Taunton

TEIGNHEAD

Teignhead Farm Cider, Higher Farm, Stokeinteignhead, Newton Abbot, Devon.
☎ 01 626 873 394

The present Mr French's father and grandfather made cider on the farm up until 1939, but it wasn't for another 45 years that the tradition was revived. Production is still small, only around 1,000 gallons, but new trees have been planted, and the stone barn now used for cidermaking is the ideal environment.
CIDERS: Dry or Medium 6.5%
OPEN: No shop or tours; ring ahead.

THATCHER'S

Thatcher's Cider, Myrtle Farm, Sandford, Bristol BS19 5RA.
☎ 01 934 822 862

Thatcher's was founded in 1904 and is now one of the largest independent makers in the country, right up there with Weston's and Inch's. In recent years it has expanded considerably, buying Cheddar Valley Cider in 1984 and producing own-brand ciders for many companies including Mole's Brewery. Although it possesses 100 acres of orchards of its own and continues to grow more, it still has to buy in from growers as far afield as Herefordshire to produce its current output of a million gallons a year. Its ciders are still traditionally produced and although CAMRA disapproves heavily of artificially carbonated ciders, Thatcher's bottled single varietal Katy is a distinctive product as good as any Moscato d'Asti, and a good deal cheaper. Try it at your wedding (or your daughter's).
CIDERS: Thatcher's Farmhouse Draught 6%; Cheddar Valley Farmhouse Draught 6%; Mendip Magic 5%; Old Rascal 6%; Katy 8.4%; White Magic 8.4%
BOTTLED CIDERS: Mendip Traditional 6%, Katy 8%
OPEN: Mon-Sat 8am-6pm. Tours by arrangement.

THAMES VALLEY VINEYARD

Stanlake Park Estate, Twyford, Berkshire.
☎ 01 734 340 176

Another vineyard where cider is made as a sideline, Thames Valley Vineyard is based in the outbuildings of Stanlake Park's Home Farm, and the cider is made from the Victorian culinary and dessert orchards which were planted to serve the Big House. Cider is not made every year – none was made in 1995-96, for example – and what is made is all bottled using the winery's bottles and filling-line and sold in the vineyard shop. The shop now has an on-licence, enabling the Vineyard to host outdoor and marquee functions in the estate's splendid parkland in summer.
BOTTLED CIDER: Still dry 7%
OPEN: 9-5 Mon-Fri; 12-5 Sat-Sun Mar-Dec.

THEOBOLDS

Theobolds Cider, A Riccini & Sons, Heronsgate Farm,
Stourmouth, Canterbury, Kent CT3 1HZ.
☎ 01 227 722 275
The present generation of the Riccini family is the third to
grow fruit here, but cidermaking only started in 1984. Since
then Theobolds has won CAMRA's national cider
championship twice and has become one of the best-
distributed independent brands in Kent, with limited
distribution in London, Essex, and even Suffolk.
CIDERS: Dry, Medium & Sweet, Still or Sparkling, 6% and 8%
BOTTLED CIDERS: Dry, Medium & Sweet, Still or Sparkling,
6% and 8%
OPEN: Tue-Sun 10am-5pm; Mon 10am-2pm (10am-5pm Bank
Holidays). Tours by arrangement.

THREE COUNTIES CIDER

Three Counties Cider, 16 Broadwater Gardens, Harefield,
Middx UB9 6AL
☎ 01 895 824 268/822 058
Amateur cidermakers for 20 years, Michael Jones and Richard
Ives harvest apples from old – and therefore largely organic –
orchards all over Middlesex, Hertfordshire, and
Buckinghamshire to make their prize-winning cider.
CIDER: St Mary's Dry 8%

TILLEY'S

Tilley's Cider and Perry, Moat Farm, Malleson Road,
Gotherington, Cheltenham, Glos.
☎ 01 242 676 807
Tilley's represents the perfect balance between old and new.
The moated farmhouse dates back to 1700, but the cattle went
eight years ago to be replaced by horses, for Peter Tilley is an
expert at exploiting his 30-acre property. Moat Farm is now a
guest house complete with swimming pool, riding school, and
3,000-gallon cider factory. The cider too blends ancient and
modern: Tilley's has been making cider the traditional way for
years, but Peter has recently completed a cidermaker's course
which has taught him the most up-to-date methods of
sterilisation and racking procedures, to keep his ciders fresher
for longer and endow them with a clarity to rival that of wine.
Tilley's once made perry, but gave up for lack of pears.
CIDERS: Sweet, medium, dry 5.4%
OPEN: 6am-8pm, but ring ahead.

TORRE

Torre Cider, Washford, Watchet, Somerset TA23 0LA.
☎ 01 984 640 004
This 120-year-old family business makes cider from local apples and plans to develop a visitor attraction in the near future.
CIDERS: Torre Traditional Farmhouse (Extra Dry, Medium Dry, Medium Sweet) 6.5%; Tornado 8.4%
BOTTLED CIDERS: Torre Traditional Farmhouse (Extra Dry, Medium Dry, Medium Sweet) 6.5%; Tornado 8.4%
OPEN: Mon-Sat 9am-6.30pm; Sun 12-6.30pm.

TOWY VALLEY

Towy Valley Cyder Company, Llwynhaf Farm, Llanddarog Road, Carmarthen, Dyfed SA32 8AR.
☎ 01 267 275 509
One of the leaders of the Welsh revival – cidermaking is an ancient Celtic art and only died out in Wales earlier this century – Towy Valley has grown to supply a number of outlets around West Wales but is also available at the farm gate. As well as its medium and sweet farmhouse ciders, it produces a three-year-old oak-matured vintage cider as fine as any wine.

UPTON CIDER

Upton Fruit Farm, Upton, Didcot, Berks.
A far-eastern outpost for cider apples in what is a fast-growing centre of the cider revival. Owner oddly coy, and is in fact ex-directory.
CIDERS: Dry, Medium, or Sweet
OPEN: Fri-Sat May-Dec 12-5.

VERYAN

Veryan Vineyard, Tregenna, Portloe, Truro, Cornwall TR2 5PS.
☎ 01 872 501 404
A family business, Veryan started making wine in 1981 and planted its first cider apple orchards in 1986. Given the climate and the nature of the local market, cidermaking soon eclipsed winemaking and Veryan ciders now have an enviable local distribution. However, the Kington family has never forgotten that wine was its first love and aims to produce ciders which can challenge wine at the best of tables. Wines and ciders now coexist at the inventive and innovative Veryan with fresh-pressed juices and even preserves; the common theme that links the company's products is authenticity, with no bought-in concentrates or artificial methods.
CIDERS: Traditional Still Cornish Cyder (Dry, Medium Dry) 7.5%; Selected Medium Dry 7.5%; Sparkling Cornish Cyder

(Medium Dry) 7.5%; Sparkling Cornish Apple Wine 10%
OPEN: Easter to Harvest Mon-Sat 2-6pm. Tours by
arrangement.

VICKERY

Vickery's Cider, Hisbeers Farm, Hare Lane, Buckland St Mary,
Chard, Somerset.
☎ 01 460 234 378
Tim and Dave Vickery have kept the business going since their
father Jack died five years ago, and Hisbeers Farm sees just as
constant a stream of cider-seeking visitors as ever it did. The
cider is also available in a few local pubs.
CIDERS: Medium, dry
OPEN: Reasonable times, but do ring ahead.

WESTBURY

Westbury Wines, Lower Henwick Farm, Turnpike Road,
Thatcham, Newbury, Berks.
☎ 01 734 844 366
Helen Tarry has been making superior table wines for some
years at the Westbury Vineyard at Purley near Reading. Now
she has only turned her attention to the possibilities of the
apple in recent years, and has actually planted her own cider-
apple orchard. Her Saxon cider is entirely naturally made from
local apples and is oak-matured, whereas Cyser is a hydromel,
made with added honey.
BOTTLED CIDERS: Westbury Saxon Cider, 7%; Cyser 8.5%

WEST CROFT

West Croft Cider, West Croft Farm, Brent Knoll, Highbridge,
Somerset TA9 4BE.
☎ 01 278 760 259
John Harris had long planned to revive the tradition of cider
making on the family farm when 10 years ago he planted a
cider apple orchard. Production, though, had to wait until just
three years ago when the orchard started bearing, and John
now turns out 4,000 gallons a year, all made on an elderly
twin-screw manual press. As well as his regular sweet and dry
ciders, John produces a number of specials including a single
varietal Kingston Black, which is matured in old oak
hogsheads, and a light blend of early-cropping Tom Putt and
Morgan Sweets.
CIDERS: Traditional 6%, various specials
OPEN: All hours, but ring ahead.

When visiting producers, please telephone ahead.

WESTONS

H Weston & Sons Ltd, The Bounds, Much Marcle, Ledbury,
Herefordshire HR8 2NQ.
☎ 01531 660 233

Weston's prides itself on its antiquity – cidermaking has been
carried on at Bounds since the early eighteenth century – and
its authenticity, but in many ways it is in a precarious position.
It exists in an uneasy territory between the Big Two (Bulmers
and the Gaymer-Taunton combine) and the pushier companies
in cider's Division Two: Inch's, Thatcher's, Biddenden, James
White, Broadoak. Weston's bosses have the dread example of
Merrydown eternally before them: a promising company
which compromised its quality without cutting its costs,
Merrydown eventually squandered its fine reputation in
exchange for the chimera of wide third-party distribution.
Cider-lovers should constantly remind Weston's that the road
to hell for a smallish company competing with giants is the
road of compromise. Top-quality products made by top
companies should command top prices: if cider's larger
independents start scrabbling for volume based on price
instead of profitability based on premium values, they will be
wiped out.

CIDERS: Old Rose Scrumpy 7.3%; Vintage Sweet or Dry 7.3%;
GWR Bounds Brand Scrumpy 4.8%; GWR 1st Quality
Traditional 5%; Draught Perry 4.5%; Extra Strong Scrumpy and
Extra Strong Traditional (in 3 pint jugs) 8%

OPEN: Mon-Fri 9.30am-4.30pm; Sat 10am-1pm. Tours by
arrangement; phone Tours Organiser on 01531 660233 9am-
5pm weekdays to book. Small charge for tour, which takes
approx 2.5 hours.

WHIN HILL

Whin Hill Cider, Fountain House, Wells-next-the-Sea, Norfolk.
☎ 01 328 711 033

Anglia Water engineer Peter Lynn originally produced only
small quantities of cider from the cooking and eating apple
trees in his own garden, and using traditional methods.
Recently he has bought 12 acres of farmland to plant with
proper cider apple trees unusual in the Eastern region,
fermenting pure juice from a blend of cider apples including
Dabinette, Harry Masters Jerseys, Ellis Bitters and others.

CIDERS: Whin Hill Special Dry 5%; Medium 5%

OPEN: No shop – phone for sales.

WHITEHEAD

Whitehead's Cider, Tootle Bridge Farm, Barton St David,
Somerton, Somerset.
☎ 01 458 50220

The Whitehead family now concentrate on their dairy business and make less cider then before: where once they used to buy in other farmers' apples to make their full 1,500-gallon duty-exempt allowance, today they only use the apples from their own six acres of orchard. Output changes according to season: last year it was about 300 gallons, all made absolutely traditionally.

CIDER: Dry 7-8%

OPEN: Ring ahead, ask for directions, and bring your own container.

WHITE MONK CIDER

121 Gillscliff Rd, Ventnor, Isle of Wight PO38 1AD.

☎ 01 983 855 672

Surely one of Britain's most bizarre cideries. For a start, the founder was an ex-monk; secondly, the cider is made with whatever apples come to hand and boosted up to around 12 per cent alcohol with sugar; thirdly, the cidery itself is in a cave in a hillside above Ventnor, where the cider is matured for years in huge oak casks.

CIDER: White Monk, 12%

WHITESTONE

Whitestone Cider Company, Riverside Farm, East Cornworthy, Totnes, Devon TQ9 7NF.

☎ 01 803 722 532

Tom Bertelson started as cidermaker for AK Wilson-Gough at Beenleigh Manor in 1987 and moved with him to the present location a couple of years later. In 1993, though, the farm was bought by present owner Ted Tuppen of Enterprise Inns, and Tom set up in his own right, renting his cidery from the farm. He has now won wide distribution and produces more than 8,000 gallons a year of its still, clear ciders. Old Pig Squeal is rapidly establishing itself as a favourite – will Mr Tuppen adopt it as Enterprise's house brand? Hundreds of thousands of pubgoers in the Midlands would be in for a happy education if he did!

CIDERS: Old Pig Squeal 8.4%; Whitestone Black Label 8%; Whitestone Red Label 6%

WILKINS

Roger Wilkins, Lands End Farm, Mudgley, Wedmore, Somerset BS28 4TU.

☎ 01 934 712 385

One of the great characters of the traditional cider scene, Roger Wilkins' family have been producing cider at Mudgley since 1918. Roger decided to expand in the 1970s after the 1,500-gallon duty-exempt level was introduced, and now makes around 50,000 gallons a year. He no longer makes perry, alas, because of the shortage of perry pears, but sells Richard's from the farm shop which has become something of a social centre for locals and tourists alike.

CIDERS: Wilkins Cider (Dry, Medium, Sweet) 6%

OPEN: Mon-Sat 10am-8pm; Sun 10am-1pm. Tours by prior arrangement.

WOLFETON

Wolfeton House, near Dorchester, Dorset.

☎ 01 305 263 500

Fine cider is made absolutely traditionally in the original cider barn at this magnificent medieval and Elizabethan country house, using cider apples bought in from local farms and continuing the custom of near self-sufficiency once common in the stately homes of England.

CIDERS: Vary with the seasons

OPEN: May to Sept Tue-Thur 2-6. Otherwise by prior appointment only.

APPENDIX 1:
Cider Wholesale Distributors

Traditional ciders can be as hard to get for retailers as for consumers. None of the major wholesale distributors carry a traditional cider, although with Inch's coming into the Bulmer's stable this may start changing.

However there is a network of small wholesalers dealing in real ciders – some specialising in real ale and carrying the odd real cider as a sideline, some few actually specialising in traditional cider – which can deliver to the licensed trade across most of the country.

The biggest of the specialists is undoubtedly John Hallam of Bedminster, Bristol (0117 966 0221), who can deliver almost any make of cider to pubs across the South of England, the South-west, London, the Midlands, Wales and the North-west. He will even deliver to private houses if he's passing – and a polycask or two of rare West Country cider will certainly be a talking point at a party.

Westray's of Stoke-on-Trent (01 782 822 150) delivers a narrower range of 12 or 13 traditional ciders and perries including Biddenden, Dunkerton's, Thatcher's, Sheppy's, Crossman's, and Richard's in the West Midlands, Yorkshire and Lancashire – although the firm can source most brands and deliver over a wider area if the order is large enough.

Further east, Small Beer of Lincoln (01 522 540 431) is a real ale wholesaler which carries Weston's, Biddenden, Inch's and Broadoak but can also deliver Ashwood, Bollhayes, Bridge Farm and others, while Big Ears of Stow Maries, Essex, (01 245 322 000) will deliver Theobolds, Weston's, and Thatcher's.

In the South-East, the English Farm Cider Centre of Firle, Sussex (01 323 811 411) stocks nearly 200 real ciders, bottled and draught, and although it doesn't actually deliver it is reasonably central and is well worth the trip.

Finally, East-west Ales (01 892 834 040) is the most important wholesaler of independent brewers' ales and also delivers Thatcher's and Biddenden traditional ciders nationwide, year-round.

So accept no excuses! Wherever you live, your local landlord can get hold of real cider if you want him to badly enough. If he doesn't believe you, show him the above phone numbers and make a fuss!

APPENDIX 2:
Organisations and Associations Involved with Cider

The South West of England Cidermakers' Association

The Association is the voice of the small cidermaker in the South West.

Its origins date back to the founding of the Somerset Cidermakers' Association in 1937. There are currently about 60 members, over half of them working cidermakers.

Membership is mostly within the counties of Avon, Somerset, Devon, Cornwall and Dorset, with full membership open to any bona fide cidermaker making for sale not less than 1,000 gallons of cider a year. There are also a number of honorary and associate members closely connected with the industry in different ways.

The Association exists to represent and promote the interests of its members and to keep them informed of legislative and other changes. It holds robust and lively meetings twice a year, the winter meeting normally in seminar format, the summer one a more formal business meeting.

SWECMA is affiliated to the National Association of Cidermakers (NACM), which represents chiefly the larger UK cidermaking businesses.

The contact is mutually beneficial. NACM, with its much greater resources, undertakes a great deal in the form of research, technical reference information, technical and marketing codes of practice and of course political lobbying. SWECMA adds an element of realism, keeping NACM in touch with the origins of the industry in English cider apples.

Common Ground

Common Ground aims to inspire and inform community involvement in the conservation of everyday places – buildings, nature, history in city and in country.

Through model projects, publications, exhibitions and events, the organisation encourages debate and practical action in both professionals and local people.

Common Ground's interest in orchards began in 1987 when working to raise interest in our cultural as well as ecological relationship with trees, through a project called Trees, Woods and the Green Man.

Common Ground discovered that few of its colleagues in the

environment movement were interested in orchards as woods, wild life habitats or cultural landscapes. It found that Devon had lost 90 per cent of its orchards since 1965, and that this was not unusual.

The more it delved, the more Common Ground realised what rich places orchards are. It saw that, as they disappeared, the loss was not only for the landscape, the economy and for wild life, but that the cultural associations had nothing to sustain them – the knowledge of pruning, grafting and planting, of local varieties and the particular songs, wassailing, recipes, for cider all began to slip away.

It amazed Common Ground that 6,000 varieties of apples have been grown in this country and that cider varieties added hundreds more to the list.

Members were excited to find the wonderful names, histories and strong associations with place. They began to use the power of the apple to capture the popular imagination about varieties, orchards and local distinctiveness.

People are entranced by names: Slack Ma Girdle, Yarlington Mill, Norfolk Beefing, Keswick Codlin, Hoary Morning and also links with place and produce.

As places and food are becoming more bland and uniform, people are searching for authentic, good quality food and drink. Demanding real cider from local orchards is one way we can keep the drink, culture and landscapes alive.

CAMRA helped to draw in thousands of people to the very first Apple Day (October 21st) in 1990 in Covent Garden. The task since then has been to encourage others to take on the idea for themselves: by 1995 events were being organised in over 160 places countrywide.

'The Apple Source Book, particular recipes for diverse apples. 'Apples, Games and Customs', The Apple Map (poster), The Apple Broadcast (16 page newsletter), Community Orchards and Apple Day pamphlets are all available from Common Ground, Seven Dials Warehouse, 44 Earlham Street, London WC2H 9LA.

Three Counties Cider and Perry Association

The Three Counties Cider and Perry Association was formed in July 1993 by a group of cider and perry makers in Herefordshire, Worcestershire, and Gloucestershire seeking to improve their image.

The founders had originally come together while taking part in the Big Apple cider and perry making competition held at Putley near Ledbury, Herefordshire, at the beginning of May every year.

The association organises meetings of a technical and/or practical nature, arranges visits to each other's cider and perry making facilities, and exchanges views and information.

It also informs and supports members in dealing with legal, health and all other regulatory burdens.

Most importantly, it provides an opportunity for the small makers, who often work on their own in isolated places, to get together to discuss any relevant matters concerning the industry, especially where these relate to the Three Counties.

Anyone who is a cider or perry maker is welcome to join, although the association chiefly represents those who live and work in the Three Counties. There is also an associate grade of membership for those who are not makers but interested in cider and perry and the aims of the association.

Meetings are held quarterly in January, April, July and September, moving around the area with the July meeting normally being a visit to someone's works and the September meeting being a clinic. The Annual General Meeting is held in January.

If you are interested in joining, please apply to the secretary at Glebe Farm, Aylton, Ledbury, Herefordshire HR8 2RQ.

CAMRA BOOKS

The CAMRA Books range of guides helps you search out the best in beer (and cider) and brew it at home too!

BUYING IN THE UK

All our books are available through bookshops in the UK. If you can't find a book, simply order it from your bookshop using the ISBN number, title and author details given below. CAMRA members should refer to their regular monthly newspaper *What's Brewing* for the latest details and member special offers. CAMRA books are also available by mail-order (postage free) from: CAMRA Books, 230 Hatfield Road, St Albans, Herts, AL1 4LW. Cheques made payable to CAMRA Ltd. Telephone your credit card order on 01727 867201.

BUYING OUTSIDE THE UK

CAMRA books are also sold in many book and beer outlets in the USA and other English-speaking countries. If you have trouble locating a particular book, use the details below to order by mail or fax (+44 1727 867670).

Carriage of £3.00 per book (Europe) and £6.00 per book (US, Australia, New Zealand and other overseas) is charged.

UK BOOKSELLERS

Call CAMRA Books for distribution details and book list. CAMRA Books are listed on all major CD-ROM book lists and on our Internet site:
http://www.cityscape.co.uk/users/al96/beer/html

OVERSEAS BOOKSELLERS

Call or fax CAMRA Books for details of local distributors.

Distributors are required for some English language territories. Rights enquiries (for non-English language editions) should be addressed to the managing editor.

GOOD BEER GUIDES

These are comprehensive guides researched by professional beer writers and CAMRA enthusiasts. Use these guides to find the best beer on your travels or to plan your itinerary for the finest drinking. Travel and accommodation information, plus maps, help you on your way and there's plenty to read about the history of brewing, the beer styles and the local cuisine to back up the entries for bars and beverages.

GOOD BEER GUIDE TO MUNICH AND BAVARIA
by Graham Lees
206 pages   **Price: £8.99**

A fifth of the world's breweries – some 750 – are located in the region covered by this guide. The beers have rich, deep flavours and aromas and are generously hopped. You will find dark lagers, wheat beers, members of the ale family, wonderfully quenching and refreshing beers that have become cult drinks. The guide tells you where to find the best beers and the many splendid bars, beer halls and gardens, and the food to match. You'll also find all the background information for the world's most famous beer extravaganza, the Munich Oktoberfest.

Author Graham Lees, a founder member of CAMRA, has lived and worked in Munich for several years and has endlessly toured Bavaria in search of the perfect pint.

Use the following code to order this book from your bookshop:
ISBN 1-85249-114-0

GOOD BEER GUIDE TO BELGIUM AND HOLLAND
by Tim Webb
286 pages   **Price: £9.99**

Discover the stunning range and variety of beers available in the Low Countries, our even nearer neighbours via Le Tunnel. There are such revered styles as Trappist Ales, fruit beers, wheat beers and the lambic and gueuze specialities made by the centuries-old method of spontaneous fermentation.

Channel-hopping Tim Webb's latest edition of the guide offers even more bars in which an incredible array of beers can be enjoyed. If you are going on holiday to this region then you'll find details of travel, accommodation, food, beer museums, brewery visits and festivals, as well as guides to the cafés, beer shops and warehouses you can visit. There are maps, tasting notes, beer style guide and a beers index to complete the most comprehensive companion to drinking with your Belgian and Dutch hosts.

Use the following code to order this book from your bookshop:
ISBN 1-85249-115-9

GOOD BEER GUIDE
edited by Jeff Evans
546 pages   **Price: £10.99**

Fancy a pint? Let CAMRA's *Good Beer Guide* lead the way. Revised each year to include around 5,000 great pubs serving excellent ale – country pubs, town pubs and pubs by the sea.

The guide includes information about meals, accommodation, family rooms, no-smoking areas and much more.

Fully and freshly researched by members of the Campaign for Real Ale, real enthusiasts who use the pubs week in, week out. No payment is ever taken for inclusion. The guide has location maps for each county and you can read full details of all Britain's breweries (big and small) and the ales they produce, including tasting notes.

CAMRA's Good Beer Guide is still Britain's best value pub guide – a must for anyone who loves beer and pubs.

KNOWN TREASURES & HIDDEN GEMS
– A POCKET GUIDE TO THE PUBS OF LONDON
by Peter Haydon
224 pages   **Price: £7.99**

If you live in or visit London, then you need this guide in your top pocket! It will take you to the well-known and historic pubs you must not miss, but also to the pubs which are tucked away and which locals keep to themselves.

The grass roots organisation of CAMRA and beer journalist Peter Haydon have brought London's pubs alive through their descriptions of ale, food, entertainment, history and architecture. These pubs have a story to tell.

The pubs in this pocket, portable, guide are listed by locality with a street address and London postal code districts heading pages so that you can easily match your location with the nearest pub. The guide covers pubs which are near tube and railway stations and gives relevant bus route numbers. It covers central London out to the commuter belts of Bushey and Surbiton.

Use the following code to order this book from your bookshop:
ISBN 1-85249-118-3

CAMRA GUIDES

Painstakingly researched and checked, these guides are the leaders in their field, bringing you to the door of pubs which serve real ale and more…

GOOD PUB FOOD
by Susan Nowak
448 pages   **Price: £9.99**

The pubs in these pages serve food as original and exciting as anything available in far more expensive restaurants. And, as well as the exotic and unusual, you will find landlords and landladies serving simple, nourishing pub fare such as a genuine ploughman's lunch or a steak and kidney pudding.

You'll discover cooking from a new wave of young chefs who would prefer to run a pub than a restaurant. Many pubs are producing the traditional dishes of their regions, building smokeries, keeping cattle and goats, growing vegetables and herbs, creating vibrant, modern cuisine from fresh ingredients. Recipes from some of them are dotted about this guide so you can try them at home.

Award-winning food and beer writer Susan Nowak, who has travelled the country to complete this fourth edition of the guide, says that 'eating out' started in British inns and taverns and this guide is a contribution to an appreciation of all that is best in British food…and real cask conditioned ale.

Use the following code to order this book from your bookshop:
ISBN 1-85249-116-7

ROOM AT THE INN
by Jill Adam
242 pages   **Price: £8.99**

From the first pub claiming to have sold Stilton cheese to travellers in 1720 to old smugglers haunts in Dorset, *Room at the Inn* gives details of pubs up and down the country offering generous hospitality. Travellers and tourists looking for a traditional British alternative to bland impersonal hotels need look no further than this guide.

The guide contains almost 350 inns – plus some hotels and motels – which provide overnight accommodation and a wholesome English breakfast. Some have been welcoming visitors for centuries. You'll also find a good pint of real ale on your arrival. To help you further there are maps, information on pub meals, family facilities, local tourist attractions and much more. Room at the Inn is a must for the glove compartment of the family car and vital reading for anyone planning a bed and breakfast break, sports tour or business trip.

Use the following code to order this book from your bookshop:
ISBN 1-85249-119-1

BREW YOUR OWN

Learn the basics of brewing real ales at home from the experts. And then move on to more ambitious recipes which imitate well-loved ales from the UK and Europe.

GUIDE TO HOME BREWING
by Graham Wheeler
240 pages   **Price: £6.99**

The best way to learn successful home-brewing basics is over the shoulder of expert Graham Wheeler, in this second edition of his popular guide. Find out how to brew ales, stouts, lagers and wheat beers from kits, malt extract and full mash. If some of this jargon is new to you then read on… Equipment, ingredients, yeast, water, boiling and cooling, fermenting, finishing, bottling, kits, measurements and calculations. These are just some of the subjects fully covered in this definitive beginner's guide to home brewing. There are also many classic recipes with which to try out your new-found skills. The perfect gift for the home-brewer in your life!

Use the following code to order this book from your bookshop:
ISBN 1-85249-112-4

BREW YOUR OWN REAL ALE AT HOME
by Graham Wheeler and Roger Protz
196 pages   **Price: £6.99**

This book is a treasure chest for all real ale fans and home brew enthusiasts. It contains recipes which allow you to replicate some famous cask-conditioned beers at home or to customise brews to your own particular taste. The authors have examined the ingredients and brewing styles of well-known ales and have gleaned important information from brewers, with and without their co-operation. Computer-aided guesswork and an expert palate have filled in the gaps where the brewers would reveal no more.

As well as the recipes, the brewing process is explained along with the equipment required, all of which allows you to brew beer using wholly natural ingredients. Detailed recipes and instructions are given along with tasting notes for each ale. Conversion details are given so that the measurements can be used world-wide.

Use the following code to order this book from your bookshop:
ISBN 1-85249-113-2

Brew Classic European Beers at Home
by Graham Wheeler and Roger Protz
196 pages   **Price: £8.99**

Keen home brewers can now recreate some of the world's classic beers. In your own home you can brew superb pale ales, milds, porters, stouts, Pilsners, Alt, Kolsch, Trappist, wheat beers, sour beers, even the astonishing fruit lambics of Belgium... and many more.

Graham Wheeler and his computer have teamed up with Roger Protz and his unrivalled knowledge of brewing and beer styles. Use the detailed recipes and information about ingredients to imitate the cream of international beers. Discover the role played by ingredients, yeasts and brewing equipment and procedure in these well-known drinks. Measurements are given in UK, US and European units, emphasising the truly international scope of the beer styles within.

Use the following code to order this book from your bookshop:
ISBN 1-85249-117-5

JOIN CAMRA

If you like good beer and good pubs you could be helping to fight to preserve, protect and promote them. CAMRA was set up in the early seventies to fight against the mass destruction of a part of Britain's heritage.

The giant brewers are still pushing through takeovers, mergers and closures of their smaller regional rivals. They are still trying to impose national brands of beer and lager on their customers whether they like it or not, and they are still closing down town and village pubs or converting them into grotesque 'theme' pubs.

CAMRA wants to see genuine free competition in the brewing industry, fair prices, and, above all, a top quality product brewed by local breweries in accordance with local tastes, and served in pubs that maintain the best features of a tradition that goes back centuries.

As a CAMRA member you will be able to enjoy generous discounts on CAMRA products and receive the highly rated monthly newspaper *What's Brewing*. You will be given the CAMRA members' handbook and be able to join in local social events and brewery trips.

To join, complete the form below and, if you wish, arrange for direct debit payments by filling in the form overleaf and returning it to CAMRA. To pay by credit card, contact the membership secretary on (01727) 867201.

Full membership £12; Joint (living partners') membership £14; Life membership £120/£140

Please delete as appropriate:

I/We wish to become members of CAMRA.

I/We agree to abide by the memorandum and articles of association of the company.

I/We enclose a cheque/p.o. for £   (payable to CAMRA Ltd.)

Name(s)
Address
Signature(s)

CAMRA Ltd., 230 Hatfield Road, St Albans, Herts AL1 4LW

GUIDE TO REAL CIDER

If you come across a new cider producer or outlet then please let us know by sending in this form (or copy). Thanks.

County _____

Town or village _____

Name of pub _____

Address _____

Location (A or B road) _____

Tel no. _____ Name of licensee _____

Description of pub (including bars, food, family room and any special facilities)

_____
_____
_____
_____
_____
_____

Ciders _____
_____
_____
_____

Reasons for inclusion in/deletion from the guide

_____
_____
_____
_____

Your name and address_____
_____
_____
Postcode_____